PSYCHE

Psyche and Soma

Physicians and metaphysicians on the mind–body problem from Antiquity to Enlightenment

Edited by

JOHN P. WRIGHT

and

PAUL POTTER

CLARENDON PRESS · OXFORD

2000

OXFORD

UNIVERSITY PRESS

Great Clarendon Street, Oxford OX2 6DP

Oxford University Press is a department of the University of Oxford.
It furthers the University's objective of excellence in research, scholarship,
and education by publishing worldwide in

Oxford New York

Auckland Bangkok Buenos Aires Cape Town Chennai
Dar es Salaam Delhi Hong Kong Istanbul Karachi Kolkata
Kuala Lumpur Madrid Melbourne Mexico City Mumbai Nairobi
São Paulo Shanghai Taipei Tokyo Toronto

Oxford is a registered trade mark of Oxford University Press
in the UK and in certain other countries

Published in the United States
by Oxford University Press Inc., New York

First published 2000
Published new as paperback 2002

British Library Cataloguing in Publication Data

Data available

Library of Congress Cataloging in Publication Data

Data available

ISBN 0-19-823840-1 (hbk.)
ISBN 0-19-925674-8 (pbk.)

1 3 5 7 9 10 8 6 4 2

Typeset by SNP Best-set Typesetter Ltd., Hong Kong
Printed in Great Britain
on acid-free paper by

A la mémoire de

ROSELYNE REY

(1951–1995)

ACKNOWLEDGEMENTS

Our first debt is, without question, to our contributors, who have donated of their knowledge and their time with unstinting generosity: to them we express our heartfelt thanks.

We are also grateful to Professor John Thorp of the Department of Philosophy at the University of Western Ontario, for his inspiration and active participation in the early phases of the project, to Mrs Nancy Patrick for preparing the typescripts and computer disks for the Press, and to Associated Medical Services, whose generous help made available through the Hannah Institute for the History of Medicine allowed the contributors to meet under ideal conditions to discuss their draft chapters. We owe further debts of thanks to Professor M. A. Stewart and the Press's two anonymous reviewers for their helpful comments.

All chapters are published for the first time in this volume. Paul Potter translated Chapter 5 from its original German version, and Chapters 10, 12, and 13 from the French.

J. P. W.
P. P.

January 1999

CONTENTS

CONTRIBUTORS

FRANÇOIS AZOUVI is a researcher at the CNRS in Boulogne. He is author of *Maine de Biran: La Science de l'homme* (Paris, 1995) and, together with Dominique Bourel, of *De Königsberg à Paris: Histoire de la réception du Kantisme en France* (Paris, 1991).

FRANÇOIS DUCHESNEAU is Professor of Philosophy at the University of Montreal. Among his monographs are *La Physiologie des Lumières: Empirisme, modèles et théories* (The Hague, 1982), *La Genèse de la théorie cellulaire* (Montreal, 1987), *Leibniz et la méthode de la science* (Paris, 1993), *La Dynamique de Leibniz* (Paris, 1994), *Philosophie de la biologie* (Paris, 1997), and *Les Modèles du vivant de Descartes à Leibniz* (Paris, 1998).

BEATE GUNDERT teaches at the University of Western Ontario. She has published on topics in ancient medicine, and is currently preparing an edition of Galen's *De symptomatum differentiis* for the Corpus Medicorum Graecorum (Berlin).

THEO K. HECKEL is a Protestant clergyman in the city of Fürth, Bavaria. He holds his *Habilitation* in New Testament Theology from the University of Erlangen, and is author of *Der Innere Mensch* (Tübingen, 1993).

THOMAS M. LENNON is Professor of Philosophy at the University of Western Ontario. He has published, together with Paul J. Olscamp, a translation of Nicolas Malebranche's *The Search after Truth* (Columbus, Ohio, 1980), and is author of *The Battle of the Gods and Giants: the Legacies of Descartes and Gassendi, 1655–1715* (Princeton, 1993).

GARETH MATTHEWS is Professor of Philosophy at the University of Massachusetts, Amherst. He has written *Thought's Ego in Augustine and Descartes* (Ithaca, NY, 1992) and *The Philosophy of Childhood* (Cambridge, Mass., 1994).

EMILY MICHAEL is Professor of Philosophy at Brooklyn College. She has published widely on philosophical topics ranging from the medieval period to the eighteenth century.

PAUL POTTER is Hannah Professor of the History of Medicine at the University of Western Ontario. He has edited and translated Hippocratic texts for the Corpus Medicorum Graecorum (1980) and the Loeb Classical Library (Cambridge, Mass., 1988–95).

ROSELYNE REY[†] was a researcher at the Centre A. Koyré of the CNRS in Paris. Her publications include *Histoire de la douleur* (Paris, 1993), which appeared the same year in English translation, and *Naissance et développement du vitalisme en France, de la deuxième moitié du XVIIIe siècle à la fin du Premier Empire* (Oxford, 1999).

T. M. ROBINSON is Professor of Philosophy at the University of Toronto. He is author of *Heraclitus: Fragments* (Toronto, 1987) and *Plato's Psychology* (2nd edn., Toronto, 1995).

PHILIP J. VAN DER EIJK is Professor of Greek at the University of Newcastle upon Tyne. He is author of *Aristoteles: De insomniis, De divinatione per somnum* (Berlin, 1994), editor of *Ancient Histories of Medicine: Essays in Medical Doxography and Historiography in Classical Antiquity* (Leiden, 1999), and co-editor of the 2 volumes *Ancient Medicine in its Socio-Cultural Context* (Amsterdam and Atlanta, 1995).

HEINRICH VON STADEN holds a research position at the Institute for Advanced Studies in Princeton. He is author of *Herophilus: The Art of Medicine in Early Alexandria* (Cambridge, 1989).

STEPHEN VOSS is Professor of Philosophy at the University of the Bosporus in Istanbul. He has published an annotated translation of Descartes' *The Passions of the Soul* (Indianapolis, 1989), and is editor of *Essays on the Philosophy and Science of René Descartes* (New York, 1993).

JOHN P. WRIGHT is Professor of Philosophy in the Department of Philosophy and Religion at Central Michigan University. He is author of *The Sceptical Realism of David Hume* (Manchester and Minneapolis, 1983) and co-editor, with M. A. Stewart, of *Hume and Hume's Connexions* (Edinburgh, 1994). He has also published a number of articles on seventeenth- and eighteenth-century philosophy and medicine.

Introduction

Her pure and eloquent blood
Spoke in her cheeks, and so distinctly wrought,
That one might almost say, her body thought.

John Donne

Few subjects have stimulated a more intensive intellectual interchange among physicians and philosophers than the nature of the human soul and its relationship to the body. Each of the thirteen chapters in this volume, which together span over 2,000 years of Western thought, records and analyses the realms of psyche and soma[1] in one or more important authors writing in a particular historical context. Our study begins with reflections on the use of the terms in the earliest extant literature of the ancient Greeks, the Homeric poems (c.750 BC), and traces their evolution in the Hippocratic Collection of medical writings (c.400 BC) and the philosophical works of Plato (428–349 BC) and Aristotle (384–322 BC). It ends with two chapters devoted to medical and philosophical writings in France at the end of the eighteenth century, a time from which we can date the birth of psychology as a separate and distinct science of mind.

At first glance, the resulting accounts seem—in spite of the frequent recurrence of common themes—so divergent in basic assumptions and goals that the question arises whether any central core of shared meaning is represented by the pair of terms at all. On closer examination, however, we find a series of basic problems which recur in different contexts, and a series of core meanings which change through time under the pressure of specific influences.

---

[1] The English terms 'psyche' and 'soma' without italics are used in this book interchangeably with 'soul'/'mind' and 'body' respectively. *Psychē* and *sōma* are transliterations of the Greek terms ψυχή and σῶμα.

I. DUALISM AND THE IMMATERIALITY OF
THE SOUL

The following studies reveal that the soul is distinguished from the body for a variety of purposes, and that the nature of their subsequent relationship varies accordingly. These purposes, as different chapters illustrate, include the medical, the philosophical, the scientific, and the religious. Often a single thinker will combine these purposes in developing an overall theory of the soul–body relationship.

Different interests result in different perspectives on the relationship in the writings of each of the two most influential soul–body dualists in the history of Western philosophy, Plato and René Descartes (1596–1650). While the distinctness of the soul and the body as separate substances is stressed in works such as the *Phaedo* and the *Meditations* in which the central issue is the survival of the soul after the death of the body, a very different conception of the relationship appears when issues of health and disease come to the fore. In Chapter 2, T. M. Robinson argues that a monistic conception of soul and body emerges in the Platonic dialogue *Charmides*, where the views of a Thracian physician on the importance of a holistic approach to the person (i.e. the soul) in curing disease are under discussion. Here, far from being separate substances, soul and body are related as whole to part. In Chapter 8, Stephen Voss notes that Descartes stressed what he called a 'close and intimate union of our mind with the body' in discussing the importance of psychological factors in the cure of bodily diseases—an opinion which he adopted when he recognized the limited applicability of current knowledge of the body itself in medical practice.

Of course, this does not mean that history has been wrong to regard Plato and Descartes as paradigmatic proponents of soul–body dualism. But it does raise the question of the nature of their dualisms, and whether, as is so commonly said, such dualisms absolutely preclude the influence of one of the soul–body pair on the other. For Plato, it is misleading in any case to speak in general terms about his position on the relationship between the soul and the body, since, as Robinson shows, he experimented over his lifetime with different conceptions. In the dialogue *Gorgias*, the body is seen as a kind of possession of the soul, which in this case constitutes the entire person: at death the body is merely sloughed off. On this conception, the power of the soul over the body is absolute. In the *Phaedo*, on the other hand, which was probably written shortly after the *Gorgias*, the body is at one point seen as a kind of counter-person with its own set of desires, resulting in a constant combat, the body seeking to override the soul's desires with its own, and the soul struggling to assert itself against the body. But again there are other Platonic accounts of the soul and the body which put the possibility of the influence of the one on the other into doubt: in another passage in the *Phaedo*, the soul is described as invisible, unchanging, and indestructible, like the transcendental Forms which it apprehends; it is a unity, wholly without parts—entirely unlike the body. But while some of these properties may seem to make a mutual interaction between the soul and the body difficult, they are discussed by Plato together with other properties that clearly presuppose such interaction (Chapter 2).

In the case of Descartes, who attempted to develop a single systematic theory, the issue is more complex. His successors such as Nicolas Malebranche (1638–1715) and Gottfried Wilhelm Leibniz (1646–1716) contended that his conception of the soul as unextended thinking substance and of the body as extended unthinking substance precluded all real causal interaction. This, however, was clearly not something which troubled Descartes himself, who located soul–body interaction in the brain, specifically in the pineal gland.

Joseph Priestley (1733–1804), a materialist writer of the second half of the eighteenth century, maintained that, prior to Descartes, the idea of the soul as a non-extended substance was virtually unknown.[2] The discussions about the ancients in this book give some support to Priestley's claim. Aristotle characteristically considered the soul as one aspect of a single living embodied being, not as a separate entity (Chapter 3). In Chapter 4, Heinrich von Staden argues that Hellenistic philosophers and physicians held that the soul is distinct from the body only in the sense that it consists of a particular kind of matter (*pneuma*, or spirit), which, while different from the grosser parts of the body, is still corporeal. Even Plato, in the *Phaedo* and the *Laws*, writes of *psychē* as a kind of ectoplasm which pervades the universe (Chapter 2). Moreover, according to Priestley, many of the early Church Fathers, while asserting that the soul is distinct from the body, still maintained the ancient belief that it is 'properly corporeal' (*Disquisitions*, 268); this view, as we shall see in a moment, gains plausibility in the light of Theo K. Heckel's discussion of St Paul in Chapter 5.

Even so, there are good reasons to think that what Priestley calls 'the doctrine of pure spiritualism' (*Disquisitions*, 269) had gained a firm foothold long before Descartes; indeed, we find a far more complex history than that narrated by Priestley in his attempt to legitimate his own materialist position. Gareth Matthews shows that 1,200 years before Descartes, St Augustine (354–430) claimed on the basis of the reflective knowledge which the soul has of itself that it cannot be a material thing (Chapter 6). Moreover, in the very work in which he puts

[2] Joseph Priestley, *Disquisitions Relating to Matter and Spirit* (London, 1777).

forward this original argument, *De Trinitate*, Augustine explicitly distinguished the body from the soul as an extended thing. As Emily Michael demonstrates in Chapter 7, Augustine's 'internalist argument' was adopted by Renaissance philosophers such as Francesco Piccolomini (*fl.* 1600). At the very least, these discussions suggest that the most radical type of mind–body dualism had a well-established history long before Descartes.

It is true that none of this answers the philosophical question whether, by distinguishing soul and body in the way they did, these thinkers precluded the possibility of their interaction. A more fruitful question from a historical point of view is the question concerning the purpose served by the doctrine of a non-extended immaterial soul. Michael argues that Descartes takes his place at the end of a line of Latin pluralists who were attempting to solve a soul–body *separation* problem which arose out of late medieval and Renaissance disputes about the materialism implicit in the Aristotelian hylomorphic conception of the soul. Rather than making a single soul responsible for all functions of the body, as St Thomas (1225–74) had, these thinkers held that the rational soul is a distinct immaterial form which, unlike other substantial forms, does not require a material organ, and can therefore exist independently of the body. In supplying this context, she throws new light on the background of Cartesian dualism, and Descartes' reference to the Lateran Council in his letter of dedication to the Theological Faculty of the Sorbonne at the beginning of the *Meditations*.

At the same time, it must be recognized that philosophers have had reasons other than strictly religious ones for stressing the immateriality of the soul, or at least a part of it. Voss suggests a philosophical motive based in Descartes' denial that there could be any science of soul, since the soul, unlike the body, must be free of determinism (Chapter 8). If Voss is right, the Cartesian doctrine of the immaterial unextended soul served to open up a space for human freedom which would have been precluded if, as opponents claimed, the soul were material. Similarly, Aristotle may have been influenced by his desire to regard man as capable of free will and rational deliberation in arguing that the human intellect somehow transcends the soul–body unity which he otherwise endorses. (See Philip J. van der Eijk's discussion in Chapter 3.)

Be that as it may, religious motivations have clearly played an important role in the discussions of soul and body as two separate substances, for many medical men, as well as philosophers (Chapter 11). At the same time, this did not preclude their belief in the dependence of the states of the mind on those of the body. Hermann Boerhaave (1668–1738), a staunch eighteenth-century dualist, instructs his fellow physicians to treat only the body, even in diseases that involve a loss of mental function; for, with the correction of the state of the body, a correction of the thoughts of the mind will follow automatically.

However, Priestley was certainly correct in pointing out that there were Christian writers who have held that the immortality of the soul does *not* require its immateriality. In Chapter 5, Heckel argues that in his correspondence with the Corinthians, St Paul was puzzled by their Platonic conception of the soul as an entity separate and independent from the body; this went against his own Jewish conception of the person as a unity. Paul's response was to explain to his Corinthian correspondents that, as they are reborn into the new religion, they become part of a new body—the body of Christian believers—which acts in a quasi-teleological way as the instrument of the Word. Disputing medieval Christian interpretations of Aristotle, such as that of St Thomas, the Renaissance philosopher Pietro Pomponazzi (1462–1524) maintained that the soul was a material form, and that its immortality could be established only on the basis of Scripture (see Chapter 7). Similarly, writing in the context of the seventeenth-century revival of Epicureanism by Pierre Gassendi (1592–1655), Pierre Bayle (1647–1706) argued that Christians should accept the doctrine of life after death on the basis of faith, not reason. Bayle's view, as Thomas M. Lennon points out in Chapter 9, comes close to that of his contemporary John Locke, who held that the continuity of a person even after death does not require the existence of an immaterial soul.

II. IDENTIFYING THE SOUL IN THE BODY

It is important to recognize that just because a thinker associates the soul with a material substance, this does not mean that he is unconcerned to distinguish it from the body. Many physicians who seek to uncover the links between the body and its functions, nevertheless speak of the soul or mind as the origin of these functions. In the early Greek medical writings attributed to Hippocrates, terms like *psyche*, *nous* (mind), and *gnōmē* (thought), which signify various aspects of mental activity, frequently stand for functions rather than specific entities *per se*; yet still these functions are often associated with particular bodily locations, such as the brain, the breath, or the blood, or with the elements fire and water. Furthermore, just as mental activity can be explained in terms of the body's structures and fluids, so, inversely, observable clinical effects of the psyche on the soma are often recorded (see Beate Gundert's account of Hippocratic medicine in Chapter 1).

It is not always recognized that Aristotle also was concerned to identify physical correlates for the vast array of psychic functions which he discusses in his biological treatises, including even the higher cognitive functions of the human being. While he describes the material aspect of these functions in humoural terms familiar from the medical tradition, he is less concerned than the medical writers, and even than Plato, to locate psychic functions in particular parts of the body. It is true that Aristotle describes the heart as the seat of the soul, and even sometimes refers to the soul as a separate entity. But, as van der Eijk stresses in Chapter 3, the Aristotelian soul is, strictly speaking, 'the dynamic structure and the organizational pattern according to which, and for the purpose of which, the physical body is shaped, constituted, and internally arranged' (see p. 63 below).

Certainly there have been writers who, on the basis of their materialist principles, have denied the actual existence of the soul: von Staden mentions the third-century physician Andreas. A similar sentiment is expressed by the militant eighteenth-century atheist Baron d'Holbach (1723–89) discussed by François Azouvi in Chapter 13: D'Holbach wrote that 'moral man is nothing but this physical being considered from a particular point of view' (see p. 272 below). At the same time he went on to identify the 'moral' as the sum of various cognitive characteristics of the individual, and allowed that the moral influences the physical, as well as the physical influencing the moral. For his successor Pierre Cabanis (1757–1808), such an influence is described as the influence of the brain on the other organs of the body.

Von Staden shows in Chapter 4 that the attempt to identify the physical ground for mental functions has played a key role in medical and philosophical discussions of soul and mind at least since the third century BC, when human dissection and possibly vivisection were first performed in Hellenistic Alexandria. Herophilus (*fl.* 300) brought newly acquired knowledge of the structure and function of the nervous system to bear, locating the *psychē* in the fourth ventricle of the brain, and assigning many of its functions to the peripheral nervous system, which he differentiated into 'sensory' and 'voluntary' components. By distinguishing between different kinds of *pneuma*, a fine material drawn in as breath, the Stoic philosophers and later Galen (129–199) provided a material basis for the separation of natural functions (i.e. functions of the body) performed by the *pneuma physikon* and the *pneuma zōtikon* from the psychic functions (mental and nervous) performed by the *pneuma psychikon*.

This interest in the physical basis of mental functions was not limited to materialists, however. In the early modern period the precise site of functions associated with consciousness became a matter of general contemplation after Descartes postulated the pineal gland as the principle locus of the soul's activities. Following the investigations of Thomas

Willis (1622–75) and others, Hermann Boerhaave located thought functions in the cerebral hemispheres, and the source of autonomic nervous stimulation in the cerebellum (Chapter 11). His student Albrecht von Haller explored more precisely the relationship between nervous stimulation and muscular contraction, coming to the conclusion that muscular activity is ultimately due to a force resident in the muscle itself (*vis insita*), which in the case of autonomic functions, such as the heartbeat, accounts by itself for contraction, but in volitional acts requires the actions of specific nerves. He used his experimental work to support a sharp distinction between conscious functions and the purely autonomic motions of the body—a distinction which was challenged by Scottish and French physicians in the latter part of the eighteenth century.

III. THE FUNCTIONS OF PSYCHE AND SOMA

Among the meanings of psyche we discover the following: the life principle of the body, the principle of sensation and purposeful movement, the morally significant part of the human being, the principle of a being which has self-movement, the intellectual part of the self, the 'form' of a natural body possessing the potentiality of life, the inner person who can reflect on himself, an intellectual being constantly required for the maintenance of the body, a force that represents the teleological and integrative processes of the living organism. The soma, which is contrasted with psyche, is seen variously as the shell of a real living person, a kind of counter-self with desires and goals of its own, the sensible and affective part of ourselves, the unactualized potentiality of a living being, the 'nature' of the organism which carries out the operations of life, the community of Christian believers, a mechanical automaton, a mechanism which is in a constant state of corruption.

To tell the history of psyche and soma is to trace the way these ideas get associated, how they get separated, how they are transferred from one realm to the other. It is to explain the concerns which are involved in such associations, separations, and transfers. The present study can claim to be no more than a modest beginning of such a history. Yet, already, we find some surprising results.

An exploration of the different functions ascribed to psyche and soma and their cognates reveals a fascinating story of the complex motivations which lie behind the different accounts discussed in these pages. In the earliest writings we have from ancient Greece—the Homeric epics—the psyche is regarded as a kind of life principle which leaves the body at death and carries on a kind of shadowy existence apart from the body. It was perhaps only with the advent of Orphic religion in the sixth century BC that psyche began to be seen as the real person, an idea taken up by Socrates (469–399) among others. And while the original idea of the psyche as the principle of life never disappears completely from Greek thought and language, among medical writers the functions of psyche and *nous* (mind) are from the beginning limited more strictly to cognitive processes and the emotions, as one of the two major groups of life functions—the other group being the functions of the soma—which together constitute the individual's *physis* (nature) (Chapters 1 and 4).

Central in all Plato's writings is the idea that the soul represents the most important part of the person, the moral self. Two further important features ascribed to psyche in later Platonic dialogues are self-movement and perception of the transcendental Forms—functions that in some later writers come to play an important role in defining what psyche is. Self-movement is invoked to distinguish the souls of animals in general, perception of the Forms to distinguish the human soul. However, as Plato explores these and other features of the soul, he never totally surrenders the older Homeric idea of the soul as the principle of life (Chapter 2).

It was Aristotle who made this idea *central* to his conception of the soul and made the soul the principle of all powers of a living being, from nutrition to theoretical thinking. Even plants have a soul, according to Aristotle. 'To have a soul means to be alive and to have the capacity to exercise the vital functions appropriate to the category of living beings to which an individual belongs' (see p. 64 below). In defining the soul as 'the first *entelecheia* of a natural body that has the potential to live', he implies that there are no functions of a living being that take place without the soul, and that cognition is no more than one manifestation of the life principle in the beings which possess it—albeit the highest. At the same time, as mentioned earlier, there are puzzling remarks in Aristotle's biological writings suggesting that the functions of the intellectual soul or mind of the human being are somehow immaterial and, unlike the functions of the senses and the imagination, require no bodily organ (Chapter 3). These remarks gained a new significance in the discussions of the soul among Christian philosophers of the late Middle Ages and Renaissance who adopted the Aristotelian philosophy (Chapter 7).

Later Hellenistic thinkers came to narrow the powers of the soul to cognition. Following the discovery of the nerves and the central nervous system by Herophilus around 300 BC, Stoics such as Chrysippus distinguished between *psychē* and *physis* (nature), ascribing the functions of the nervous system to the former, and the functions of the rest of the body to the latter, thereby bisecting the general Hippocratic 'nature'.

This division was taken up by Galen, for whom the soul's powers consisted in cognition and voluntary movement (Chapter 4).

In the philosophical discussions of the Middle Ages the conceptions of the soul attributed to Plato and Aristotle were predominant. Even though St Augustine identifies the essential function of the soul as self-knowledge, he still regards the soul as the source of life in the body, as Matthews notes in Chapter 6. It is only with the Christian pluralists (discussed by Michael in Chapter 7), who ascribe cognition and nutrition to *distinct* souls, that a substantial basis for distinguishing between cognition and other functions is again available. It was these thinkers who cleared the way for René Descartes' clear expression of the distinct functions of soul and body.

In one sense, Descartes' revolution was merely terminological. He simply identified the soul with the mind—which for other thinkers had been only a part of the soul or a distinct soul: 'I consider the mind not as part of the soul but as the thinking soul itself.'[3] The most significant result of this narrowing of the soul's functions to one was to leave all the other functions of life soulless. They are left to be derived from a purely corporeal process in the heart: movement becomes the living principle of an animal, and the basic source of health and disease (Chapter 8). Should we say that, in separating *soul* and *body* in the way he did, Descartes was simply returning to the dualism between *psychē* and *physis* adopted by Galen and his Hellenistic precursors? In one sense, this must certainly be acknowledged. At the same time, however, drawing on his Christian predecessors, Descartes developed a radically new idea of body or nature, which was in strong contrast to that of the ancient thinkers. Descartes' physics is far removed from ancient *physis*: he writes that in his physics he considers 'nothing apart from the sizes, shapes, positions, and movements of the particles of which bodies are made up'.[4] Moreover, any similarity that this statement might seem to have with ancient atomist thought is erased by Descartes' further requirement that all such modes be conceived of and expressed *mathematically*. However crude Descartes' own mechanistic models of the living automaton may have been, it can be argued that his investigative programme has dominated medicine and biology ever since.

However, the Cartesian way of dividing psyche and soma has also had its vociferous opponents, both physicians and metaphysicians. One of

[3] *The Philosophical Writings of Descartes*, trans. John Cottingham, Robert Stoothoff, and Dugald Murdoch (2 vols., Cambridge, 1985–6), ii. 246; cf. *Oeuvres de Descartes*, ed. Charles Adam and Paul Tannery (11 vols., Paris, 1964–74), vii. 356.
[4] *The Philosophical Writings of Descartes: The Correspondence*, trans. John Cottingham, Robert Stoothoff, Dugald Murdoch, and Anthony Kenny (Cambridge, 1991), 224; cf. Voss's discussion on p. 177 below.

the most influential and immediate of these was the German doctor Georg Stahl (1660–1734), whose ideas are discussed by François Duchesneau in Chapter 10. Stahl rejected the Cartesian notion of the body as a mechanical automaton, regarding it instead as an inherently unstable instrument of life, constantly in need of regulation and repair by the soul. Once again, the soul becomes the fundamental principle of life, but with a difference: on Stahl's view, this soul (*logos*) acts as an intelligent and free agent in performing the vital functions of the body. In a certain sense, the Stahlian soul takes over the role of the *physis* of Galen; in another, it takes over the role of the Aristotelian psyche, in so far as it controls all the life functions of the body. But it is also fundamentally different from both, in so far as, in all its operations, it possesses the intellectual and decision-making powers of a mind or intellectual soul.

Duchesneau analyses the famous debate which took place between Leibniz and Stahl. Although Leibniz opposed Stahl on other fundamental issues, he also held that *soul* was the principle of the life processes of the body. Certainly, he rejected Stahl's view that the soul can causally affect bodily processes; but, the Leibnizian soul is not limited to conscious processes, and its appetites and perceptions are indispensable to understanding the animate body. Leibniz denied that it is possible to account for the harmony and integration of the organic processes of a living body on the basis of mechanical principles alone. His theory of pre-established harmony as applied to living beings requires two parallel but independent sets of laws governing these processes—the teleological laws of the soul and the mechanical laws of the body.

Following Descartes, many of the major medical theorists in the early part of the eighteenth century, including Boerhaave, Haller, Jerome Gaub (1703–77), Julien Offray de La Mettrie (1709–51), and William Cullen (1712–90) limited soul functions to those involving consciousness, and argued that the body itself generally operates as a self-regulating machine. It is within the context of this basic model that these mechanists discussed the question of the effect of the soul/brain complex on the vital functions of the body—those of the heart, lungs, digestive tract, etc. (See John P. Wright's discussion in Chapter 11.)

However, many other eighteenth-century medical theorists believed that the neat distinction between the conscious functions of the soul, on the one hand, and the life functions of the body, on the other, left out many important phenomena of life. Opposed both to the mechanistic medical writers and to the Stahlians were physicians such as Robert Whytt (1714–66), who regarded the soul as a sensible principle which operates unconsciously in human beings and other animals. But, as Roselyne Rey argues in Chapter 12, it was especially in France that a group of medical writers, who were later called 'vitalists', focused their attention on functions that seemed to belong clearly to neither the soul nor the body. The Montpellier physician Henri Fouquet (1727–1806), writing in the Diderot–D'Alembert *Encyclopédie* (1751–65), attributed both simple biological phenomena and aesthetic taste to the principle of 'sensibility', while Jean Jacques Ménuret de Chambaud (1733–1815) showed a particular interest in phenomena such as somnambulism, which became immediately distorted if they were forced into either of the Cartesian categories of a conscious soul or a mechanical body. Theories of morbid sensibility were employed by two other Montpellier physicians, Théophile Bordeu (1722–76) and Paul Barthez (1734–1806), to account for chronic diseases such as hysteria, which involve causes and symptoms that span both of the traditional mental and physical realms.

In our final chapter, François Azouvi argues that during the second half of the eighteenth century the distinction between body and soul came to be replaced in medicine by a new dualism expressed by the terms 'physical' and 'moral', a development culminating in the publication of Pierre Cabanis's *Rapports du physique et du moral de l'homme* in 1802. This moral–physical distinction served in a way that the mind–body distinction could not, to encompass both 'mental' phenomena irreducible simply to consciousness and 'physical' phenomena irreducible simply to mechanism. In essence, the region of the 'moral' covers those phenomena which later in the nineteenth century came to be grouped under the category of the 'psychological' within the boundaries of the new discipline of the same name.

I

Soma and Psyche in Hippocratic Medicine

BEATE GUNDERT

The intuitive feeling that man is something other than the strength of his limbs and the appearance of his physique, something that manifests itself as his thoughts and behaviour, is as old as Greek literature: in Homeric poetry (*c.*750 BC), thought (*phrenes*) and works, together with form and stature, make up the whole of the person.[1] In life, man's true self, his essence *qua* human being, is apparently his mind (*nous*), which remains constant, even though his outward appearance, his bodily frame, and his voice may change, as happens to Odysseus' companions when they are transformed into wild beasts by Circe's spell.[2] At death, on the other hand, what is identified as the 'person' (*autos*: he himself) is his corpse (*sōma*), while his soul (*psychē*), which is similar to breath or air, passes to the house of Hades, where, without its body, it continues a shadowy existence; this soul does seem to retain some of its identity, for it is recognizable, and through the consumption of blood it may regain some of the person's former mental powers.[3] For Homer, *psychē* is the life principle that leaves the body at death and persists as image in Hades. Intellectual activity (*nous*) in life is not linked to the *psychē*, but to the body, and is located in the chest (*phrenes, thymos, kēr*), which is also the centre of emotions.[4]

Between Homer and Plato, the term *psychē*, while keeping its original

---

[1] Homer, *Iliad* 1, 115; cf. ibid. 419–20: Hephaestus's golden handmaids have human qualities, viz. mind (*nous*), voice, and strength.

[2] Homer, *Odyssey* 10, 239–40. Cf. J. Eccles and K. Popper, *The Self and the Brain* (Berlin, 1977), 154.

[3] Homer, *Iliad* 1, 3–4; cf. ibid. 16, 856; *sōma* as the dead body after the departure of *psychē*: *Odyssey* 11, 51–4; the dead as shadows: ibid. 10, 495; consumption of blood: ibid. 11, 98–9, 152–4, 207–8, 222. Cf. Shirley Darcus Sullivan, *Psychological and Ethical Ideas: What Early Greeks Say* (Leiden, 1995), 77–90.

[4] Cf. E. Rohde, *Psyche: Seelencult und Unsterblichkeitsglaube der Griechen*, 7th and 8th edn. (2 vols., Tübingen, 1921), i, 2–8; trans. W. B. Hillis as *Psyche: The Cult of Souls and Belief in Immortality among the Greeks* (London, 1925), 4–8; R. B. Onians, *The Origins of European Thought about the Body, the Mind, the Soul, the World, Time, and Fate*, 2nd edn. (Cambridge, 1954), 116; Thomas Jahn, *Zum Wortfeld 'Seele-Geist' in der Sprache Homers* (Munich, 1987).

meaning 'life'—albeit now in the *living* person—comes through a fusion with the many specific expressions for perception, thought, and the emotions to denote in addition the mental correlate to *sōma*: the pair *psychē* and *sōma* stands for the living person in his totality. Individuals can still be referred to on occasion by one of the two words alone, however, depending upon which aspect of the 'self' is being emphasized: Sophocles in *King Oedipus*, for example, has the hero in one situation call himself 'my *psychē*' (63–4), in another 'my *sōma*' (643).[5]

In pre-Socratic thought the soul or mind is characterized in a number of different ways: by some it is held to be immortal and to return to its like, namely fiery air (*aithēr*), after death;[6] as the animating principle, it is closely linked to movement, sensation, and thought. According to Aristotle, *psychē* is endowed by the early philosophers with these faculties on the basis of its material constituents: a very fine and easily penetrating substance consisting of the same material substrate as the rest of existence. This *psychē* is associated with air by Anaximenes and Diogenes of Apollonia, and with fire by Heraclitus and Democritus. Others relate *psychē* to the blood, as agent of sensation (Critias), or to water, as the main ingredient in the seed, on account of its generative power (Hippon).[7] Because of its motility and its connection to the *archē*, or first principle, *psychē* may furthermore partake of the divine, and is said by some thinkers, notably the Pythagoreans, to be indestructible and immortal. According to Democritus, on the other hand, '*psychē* is *sōma*' and perishes together with the body at death. *Psychē* in Greek thought down to the time of the Hippocratic writings, the decades around 400 BC, signifies both life *qua* life, and in particular the living phenomena of sensation, motion, thought, emotions, and character.[8]

---

[5] Cf. E. R. Dodds, *The Greeks and the Irrational* (Berkeley, 1951), 135–9. *Psychē* as life: e.g. Pindar, *Isthmian Odes* 1, 68; Herodotus 9, 37; Sophocles, *Oedipus at Colonus* 1326; Euripides, *Orestes* 1171. As correlate to *sōma*: e.g. Pindar, *Pythian Odes* 1, 48; Sophocles, *Antigone* 176, 227. 'Body and soul': e.g. Xenophon, *Memorabilia* 1, 3, 5; *Anabasis* 3, 2, 20; cf. Pindar, *Nemean Odes* 9, 39; Xenophon, *Cyropaedia* 1, 3, 10. For an incongruity of body and soul see e.g. Lysias, *Against Theomnestus* 1, 29.

[6] Cf. W. K. C. Guthrie, *The Greeks and their Gods* (Boston, 1955), 262–4, and Dodds, *Greeks and the Irrational*, 139–56.   [7] *De anima* 403b20–405b10.

[8] On *psychē* in pre-Socratic thought see W. K. C. Guthrie, *A History of Greek Philosophy*, i and ii (Cambridge, 1967 and 1969). Darcus Sullivan, *Psychological and Ethical Ideas*, 18–122, in her discussion of the main psychological terms in epic and lyric poetry and in pre-Socratic thought, shows (1) how *psychē* gradually assimilates activities within the living person from other psychological entities, (2) how *psychē* from being the breath of life that departs at death comes to be part of the divine principle, and (3) how the fate of *psychē* after its separation from the body at death, from consisting in a lamentable state of insubstantiality in Hades, in Pythagorean and Orphic thought comes to be a desirable condition whose precise nature is determined by the person's moral behaviour during life. For the semantic evolution of the term *psychē* from Homer to Plato see David B. Claus, *Toward the Soul* (New Haven, 1981).

In the account that follows,[9] I shall first present a brief introduction to Hippocratic medical thought as a necessary background (I), and then discuss a series of questions: Does *psychē* play a role in Hippocratic accounts of how life begins and ends and of what constitutes the human being? How are particular characteristics of body and mind determined in the individual? (II) How are (a) sense perception, (b) cognition and thought processes, and (c) emotions explained? (III) Under what circumstances, and how, do sense perception, intelligence, and emotions become impaired? (IV) Is there a mutual influence between psychic and somatic processes? Finally, in my conclusion: (V) What do body and mind signify, and what is their relationship?

I

In general, Hippocratic physiology and pathology are based on the implicit belief that the human body consists of solid and fluid components, and that there exist certain interactions among these. The solid elements are the different parts of the body as they were known through human injuries and animal analogy. Each individual part is considered to have a certain shape and texture that makes it more or less apt to attract, receive, retain, and/or expel fluids. Fluids include all the bodily excretions and secretions—for example, urine, seed, milk, sputum, and also, most importantly, blood and air. In addition to these, there are two less evident fluids, bile and phlegm, which in health are so perfectly mixed with the blood as to be imperceptible, but in disease become noticeable through changes in the colour, smell, taste, and consistency

On the immortality of the soul cf. Walter Burkert, *Weisheit und Wissenschaft* (Nuremberg, 1962), 98–142.

[9] The core of the Hippocratic writings dates from *c.*450–350 BC. I exclude from my discussion treatises that with some certainty have been shown to be post-Aristotelian. I also do not consider *Sevens*, since the Orphic views expressed in this treatise are not representative of Hippocratic thought in general. In the treatises under consideration the Greek word *psychē* (ψυχή) occurs hardly ninety times, with more than two-thirds of the occurrences in *Regimen*; see G. Maloney and W. Frohn, *Concordance des oeuvres Hippocratiques* (5 vols., Quebec, 1984), s.v. ψυχή.

In order to avoid confusion, the following procedure in terminology has been adopted: the Greek word ψυχή is routinely transliterated as *psychē* or translated as 'soul', except where this makes for difficult or unnatural English, in which case an alternative rendering is given and '*psychē*' is put in brackets after the word: e.g. ghost (*psychē*).

On specific aspects of the mind–body relationship in the Hippocratic writings see B. Simon, *Mind and Madness in Ancient Greece: The Classical Roots of Modern Psychiatry* (Ithaca, NY, 1978), ch. 2; P. N. Singer, 'Some Hippocratic Mind–Body Problems', in J. A. López Férez (ed.), *Tratados Hipocráticos* (Madrid, 1992), 131–43; P. J. van der Eijk, 'Hart en hersenen, bloed en pneuma: Hippocrates, Aristoteles en Diocles over de lokalisering van cognitieve functies', *Gewina*, 18 (1995), 214–29.

of the patient's body and/or secretions. Disease occurs when various balances within the body are upset—that is, when a change occurs in the amount or temperature of blood, bile, or phlegm. In this case, bile and phlegm are set in motion, separate from the blood, and either disturb the normal flow of blood and air through the vessels, or flow to some part, settle there, and by distending or irritating the part cause symptoms. Health is restored when the harmful fluid has left the body, and the injured part is healed.[10]

Usually the Hippocratic writers are interested in the constituents of the body only in so far as these determine health and disease, but some general accounts of the human being do exist. The author of *Fleshes*, for example, promises 'to explain how man and the other animals are formed and come into being, what the soul is, what health and sickness are, what in man is evil and what good, and where death comes from'.[11] The following chapters, however, deal only with the first point—namely the formation of the human body (chs. 3–14)—unless the second part of the treatise (chs. 15–18), which explores the mechanisms of hearing, smell, sight, and speech, refers to 'what the soul is'. The author explains that the structures and textures of the different parts result from the effects of heat and cold on his 'elements', the 'fatty', 'gluey', and 'moist'.[12] The 'hot' (once called a divine principle)[13] resides mainly in the vessels and the heart, and gives movement to these, as well as providing breath by drawing in cold air as nourishment for itself[14]—that is, it is the origin of respiration and bodily movement.

In the embryology of *Nature of the Child* it is breath (*pneuma*) that causes growth and articulation.[15] The origin of this breath the author explains as follows: the seed, being in a warm place, acquires breath, just as anything else that is heated does, and then, on becoming full, sends this breath back out again, thereby forming a passage through which it can draw in cold air for nourishment. The analogies the author adduces to illustrate this process include a further principle: if moisture is heated, it evaporates: it is the evaporation of moisture due to heat, then, which initiates the breathing process that marks the beginning of life.[16]

[10] See Paul Potter, *Short Handbook of Hippocratic Medicine* (Quebec, 1988), 38–45, and Beate Gundert, 'Parts and their Roles in Hippocratic Medicine', *Isis*, 83 (1992), 453–65.

[11] *Fleshes* 1 (8. 584. 6–9). Hippocratic references in this paper are given in parentheses and refer to volume, page, and line number in É. Littré, *Oeuvres complètes d'Hippocrate* (10 vols., Paris, 1839–61). My discussion, however, is based on more recent editions as recorded in J. Jouanna, *Hippocrate* (Paris, 1992), 527–63. My English translations are based on those of the Loeb Classical Library *Hippocrates* where these exist.

[12] *Fleshes* 3–5 (8. 584. 19–590. 23).   [13] Ibid. 2 (8. 584. 10–11).

[14] Ibid. 6 (8. 592.1–594. 5).   [15] *Nature of the Child* 17 (7. 496. 17–498. 2, 15–17).

[16] Ibid. 12 (7. 486. 1–488. 13). Cf. Iain M. Lonie, *The Hippocratic Treatises 'On Generation', 'On the Nature of the Child', 'Diseases IV'* (Berlin, 1981), 147–50.

According to *Regimen*, life begins when secretions from the two parents, each consisting of a mixture of fire and water, unite in the uterus: the seed, being moist, is moved by the fire, flames up, and attracts nourishment from food and breath entering the mother; the fire, furthermore, structures the embryo's body, creating cavities and passages by using up moisture, and bones and cords by hardening what is dry; the moisture that is left behind congeals and becomes flesh.[17]

In all three accounts, although they differ in details, it is heat that ultimately engenders life by attracting breath. The beginning of life is seen as a natural process, and is explained in terms of contemporary thoughts about materials and forces.[18] Still, the hot, or the fire, is said to have something of the divine, and, according to *Regimen*, in its purest form contains soul (*psychē*), mind (*nous*), intelligence (*phronēsis*), movement, growth, decrease, change, sleep, and waking[19]—that is, the principles of life.

Death results from an injury in a vital part,[20] interception of the breath,[21] loss of heat and movement in the blood,[22] or desiccation of the body through the heat of fever.[23] What precisely happens at the moment of death is only rarely hinted at: according to *Diseases 4* the life-giving part of moisture, when no longer cooled by respiration, evaporates.[24] *Nature of Man* explains that at death the 'elements' that constitute the body return to their like.[25] These are the moist, the dry, the warm, and the cold, or, more concretely in the human body, the humours blood, phlegm, yellow, and black bile, to which the four qualities are attributed in pairs.[26] The author, in his attempt to refute those who claim that man consists of only one 'element', goes on to explain that this mistaken belief arose when its proponents deduced that man was what they saw coming out of his dying body: that is, phlegm, bile, or blood. 'This', he continues with reference to blood, 'they believed to be man's

[17] *Regimen* 1, 9 (6. 482. 14–484. 16); cf. ibid. 27 (6. 500. 8–17).

[18] Cf. Lonie, *Hippocratic Treatises*, 149–55.

[19] *Fleshes* 2 (8. 584. 10–11); *Regimen* 1, 10 (6. 486. 7–11).

[20] e.g. *Diseases 1* 3 (6. 144. 1–2): brain, spinal marrow, cavity, liver, diaphragm, blood vessel, heart; cf. *Aphorisms* 6,18 (4. 566. 18–568. 2): bladder, brain, heart, diaphragm, intestines, cavity, liver.

[21] e.g. *Breaths* 4 (6. 96. 6–8); *Diseases 1* 32 (6. 202. 13–20); cf. *Nature of Man* 5 (6. 42. 15–18).

[22] *Diseases 1* 34 (6. 204. 12–14); *Diseases 2* 6 (7. 14. 18–20), 8 (7. 16. 19–22); *Sacred Disease* 7 (6. 374. 15–17), 8 (6. 376. 1–2).

[23] e.g. *Diseases 1* 33 (6. 202. 21–204. 4): desiccation leads to coagulation and consequent cooling of the blood.

[24] *Diseases 4* 47 (7. 574. 13–22); cf. Lonie, *Hippocratic Treatises*, 326 ad 47, 1.

[25] *Nature of Man* 3 (6. 38. 10–18); cf. ibid. 5 (6. 42. 8–44. 2). For parallels in contemporary philosophical thought see J. Jouanna, *Hippocrate: La Nature de l'homme*, Corpus Medicorum Graecorum I, 1, 2 (Berlin, 1975), 254–5.

[26] *Nature of Man* 4 (6. 38. 19–40. 2).

soul.'[27] *Psychē*, then, is seen here as the life-giving principle that leaves the body at death, and is equated with blood. The author himself, however, never uses the term *psychē* in reference to the substances that he proposes as the constituents of the human being.[28]

The traditional idea that at death some life-giving principle disappears from the body is also preserved in the occasionally used circumscription of death: 'to give up the ghost (*psychē*)'.[29] Temporary loss of consciousness, too, is often expressed in terms indicating the loss of soul,[30] or of *thymos*,[31] the Homeric word standing for everything that life subjectively encompasses.

More often *psychē* is used as correlate to *sōma*. In conjunction, these terms denote the two aspects of man's nature: outward appearance and character, which includes intelligence and disposition. How specific sex-related characteristics of an individual's body and soul are determined is laid out in *Regimen* in some detail. Each parent contributes to the formation of the child a secretion that is either male or female, and the sex of the child's body is determined by the coincidence of these secretions, or, if they are of different sexes, by the secretion that predominates, the other secretion losing its specificity and adapting. The characteristics of the soul, on the other hand, depend on the combination of male and/or female components.[32] There are three possibilities for each sex: (1) if both secretions are of the same sex, the offspring shows the highest degree of maleness or femaleness in both body and soul; (2) if the dominant male or female component came from the parent of that sex, offspring of slightly reduced bravery or modesty result; whereas (3) if the

[27] *Nature of Man* 6 (6. 44. 3–10); cf. Jouanna, *Nature de l'homme*, 240–1.

[28] In *Regimen*, on the other hand, *psychē* in the discourse on spermatology denotes the seed which contains the constitutive elements of the future being, viz. water and fire; cf. n. 33 below.

[29] *Diseases 1* 5 (6. 148. 2): τὴν ψυχὴν μεθεῖναι; *Internal Affections* 27 (7. 236. 21), 39 (7. 262. 9–10, 23), 40 (7. 264. 19): τὴν ψυχὴν ἀφεῖναι. Cf. the expression κίνδυνος περὶ τῆς ψυχῆς: *Joints* 31 (4. 146. 6–7). *Epidemics* 6, 5, 2 (5. 314. 14) states that 'the human soul grows until death'.

[30] e.g. *Diseases 1* 5 (6. 146. 17), 18 (6. 172. 12): ἐκψύχειν; cf. ἀψυχεῖν, ἀψυχία, λιποψυχεῖν, λιποψυχία. For a list of passages see Maloney and Frohn, *Concordance*.

[31] See Maloney and Frohn, *Concordance*, s.v. λιποθυμέω, λιποθυμία.

[32] The terminology is ambiguous. While in chs. 6, 7, 25 and possibly the beginning of 28 (6. 500. 25–502. 4) *psychē* (ψυχή) refers to the seed, later in ch. 28 (6. 502. 6) it certainly refers to the soul component of the embryo, while *sōma* (σῶμα) refers to its body component. In the present passage (ch. 28: 6. 502. 9–12) I understand ψυχή to refer to the soul component as well. If this is correct, at the end of ch. 29 (6. 504. 7–13) ψυχή has the same meaning, and the analogy of the fusion of cold and burning charcoal is being used to explain how a weak (female) and a strong (male) soul combine to form a unity. See, however, Robert Joly, *Hippocrate: Du Régime*, Corpus Medicorum Graecorum, I, 2, 4 (Berlin, 1984), 253 ad 144, 24 and 146, 11.

dominant component was from the parent of the opposite sex, the off-spring are effeminate males or daring females.[33]

With regard to the origin of ethnic characteristics of body and mind, the following theory is put forward by the author of *Airs, Waters, Places*: the inhabitants of different places differ in the appearance and consti-tution of their bodies and the character of their minds, because these depend on the seasons and the physical nature of their country.[34] Thus, where the seasons are similar, the land low, and the winds and waters warm, or the earth rich and well-watered, neither bodies nor souls will be able to endure strain; such bodies are broad and fleshy, and such souls sleepy and dull, timid, and not acute in the arts.[35] Where, on the other hand, the seasons vary greatly and the country is mountainous and rough, the people are tall, and have a nature that is suited to hard work and bravery;[36] or where the country is barren and exposed to wind and sun, the people are thin and tense, inclined to industry and attentive-ness, sharper in the arts, braver and cleverer in war, and their character and disposition tend to be stubborn and rather wild.[37] Two causes are adduced for the stimulating effect of a harsh climate: (1) corruption of the seed at the time of its original coagulation in the uterus; (2) shock of the mind (*gnōmē*) and violent change of the body in life.[38]

Regimen and *Airs, Waters, Places* stress, however, that although the character of the soul is in the first instance biologically or

---

[33] *Regimen* 1, 28–9 (6. 502. 4–504. 7). Cf. Erna Lesky, *Die Zeugungs- und Vererbungslehren der Antike und ihr Nachwirken* (Wiesbaden, 1951), 86–8. However, in this chapter the Hippocratic author is interested in the effect of the seed's particular mixture of water and fire on sex determination and sex-related characteristics of body and soul, not intersexuality: Robert Joly, *Recherches sur le traité pseudo-hippocratique Du Régime* (Paris, 1960), 83–4; see also G. E. R. Lloyd, *Science, Folklore and Ideology* (Cambridge, 1983), 90–4. Since the male component of the seed is engendered mainly from fire and the female from water, the sex of the child can be influenced by each parent's diet prior to the secretion of the seed: *Regimen* 1, 27 (6. 500. 1–14). How spe-cific somatic characteristics are transmitted is explained in *Generation* 8 (7. 480. 7–482. 2): since the seed comes from all parts of both parents' body, the child resembles in each of its parts that parent who contributed a larger quantity of seed from the correspond-ing part.

[34] *Airs, Waters, Places* 12–24 (2. 52. 10–92. 13): to denote the psychic, the author uses different Greek expressions: ἦθος (character) (2. 52. 18, 62. 15, 84. 9, 90. 6, 9, 92. 7); γνώμη (mind) (62. 17, 64. 4, 84. 11, 90. 3); τρόπος (temper) (90. 13); ὀργή (disposition) (90. 7, 92. 7), and ψυχή (soul) (72. 12; 84. 15, 20; 90. 17). For a detailed discussion of these chapters and similar views in *Herodotus* see Jouanna, *Hippocrate*, 308–29. Cf. Walter Müri, 'Bemerkungen zur hippokratischen Psychologie', in *Festschrift Edouard Tièche* (Bern, 1947), 71–85, at 71–4.

[35] *Airs, Water, Places* 19 (2. 72. 11–12), 24 (2. 86. 15–88. 6, 90. 13–92. 2).

[36] Ibid. 24 (2. 86. 10–14).   [37] Ibid. (2. 90. 3–7, 92. 3–10).

[38] Ibid. 16 (2. 62. 17–18. 3), 23 (2. 84. 1–17); cf. ibid. 16 (2. 64. 3–4): changes stimulate the mind.

environmentally determined, it is also shaped by the effects of culture and habit.[39] Both accounts postulate a parallelism of body and soul: certain factors have the same effect on both. *Regimen* furthermore explains the corresponding influence of inheritance on body and soul by the fact that male and female seed, as well as the *sōma* and *psychē*, consist of the same material—namely a particular mixture of fire and water which determines the sexual potentiality of the seed, the constitution of the body, and the intelligence of the soul.[40]

II

There are several accounts of sense perception in the Hippocratic Collection. Hearing, for example, is explained by the resounding quality of the empty, and hollow space of the inner ear, and the dry, hard bone and membrane surrounding it.[41] Seeing is attributed to the reflecting quality of the thin, clear membranes of the eye, which are supplied with moisture from the brain.[42] Olfaction occurs on account of the brain's moistness, as it perceives smells that it draws up together with air.[43] Although most of these accounts mention a connection between the particular sense-organ and the brain,[44] the role of the brain in perception seems undecided. In vision the only involvement of the brain mentioned is its supplying the eye with the reflective fluid. Smells are said to spread to the brain, and to be perceived there because of the brain's location directly in front of the sponge-like connection to the nose, and because of its moistness. According to *Fleshes*, it is precisely this moistness which excludes the brain from hearing, for what is moist does not resound.[45] *Places in Man*, on the other hand, explains that only sounds that reach the brain are heard clearly, whereas in the inner ear they produce nothing but noise.[46]

These accounts, then, with the possible exception of the explanation

---

[39] *Regimen* 1, 28 (6. 502. 19–23); *Airs, Waters, Places* 16 (2. 64. 6), 23 (2. 84. 18). In fact, nourishment or custom can override biological or environmental determination: *Regimen* 1, 28 (6. 502. 7); *Airs, Waters, Places* 16 (2. 64. 18–22), 24 (2. 88. 4–6).

[40] *Regimen* 1, 27 (6. 500. 1–5), 32 (6. 506. 14–510. 23), 35 (6. 512. 20–522. 16).

[41] *Places in Man* 2 (6. 278. 14–18); *Glands* 13 (8. 568. 7–8): hollow space, *Fleshes* 15 (8. 602. 19–604. 6): hollow space, surrounding hard bone and membrane. According to *Diseases* 2 4 (7. 10. 24–12. 3), the 'empty' space is filled with air.

[42] *Places in Man* 2 (6. 278. 21–280. 4); *Fleshes* 17 (8. 604. 21–606. 6); cf. *Diseases* 2 1 (7. 8. 6–10).   [43] *Fleshes* 16 (8. 604. 7–8).

[44] Ear: *Places in Man* 2 (6. 278. 16–18); eye: ibid. (6. 278. 21–3); *Fleshes* 17 (8. 604. 21–2); nose: *Places in Man* 2 (6. 278. 19); *Fleshes* 16 (8. 604. 7–11). Cf. Alcmaeon of Croton, 24 A 5 (DK 1. 212. 6–7).

[45] *Fleshes* 16 (8. 604. 7–8): the brain smells; 15 (8. 604. 2–6): the brain does not hear.

[46] *Places in Man* 2 (6. 278. 15–18).

of hearing in *Places in Man*, give a physical account of perception. Other treatises, notably *Sacred Disease* and *Regimen*, are more concerned with questions of cognition.[47] In order to provide a natural explanation for the different symptoms of an epileptic seizure, the author of *Sacred Disease* includes an explanation of the causes of intelligence (*phronēsis*) and coherent movement, the two main functions disturbed during the attack. He comes to the conclusion that these are both dependent on an unimpeded flow of air to the brain, and its free distribution from there to the cavity, the lung, the hollow vessels, and, via these, the rest of the body.[48] While air's contribution in the cavity and lung is restricted to cooling, air that enters the hollow vessels contributes by giving intelligence and movement to the limbs. This latter process occurs as follows: the external air, reaching the brain still pure and unspoiled, and before it becomes warm and moist through contact with blood and flesh, leaves there its best part and what is intelligent (*phronimon*) and has judgement (*gnōmē*); the brain endows this intelligence with comprehension (*synesis*); the eyes, ears, tongue, hands, and feet perform what the brain determines.[49] The author obviously wants to differentiate between what happens in the brain and in the rest of the body. The brain mediates between the messages from the outside, transmitted through the air, and the actions of the body. Once the brain has made these impulses comprehensible, actions of the parts follow immediately, as long as the air as medium of intelligence reaches them.[50] The author seems to distinguish different degrees of participation in intelligence: (1) The brain

---

[47] For a discussion of the mind–body relationship in the *Sacred Disease*, esp. chs. 14–17, see H. W. Miller, 'A Medical Theory of Cognition', *Transactions of the American Philological Association*, 79 (1948), 168–83; F. Hüffmeier, 'Phronesis in den Schriften des Corpus Hippocraticum,' *Hermes*, 89 (1961), 51–84, esp. 51–61; Jackie Pigeaud, *La Maladie de l'âme* (Paris, 1981), 33–41, and *idem*, *Folie et cures de la folie chez les médecins de l'antiquité Gréco-Romaine* (Paris, 1987), 47–63. For a detailed interpretation of *Regimen* 1, 35 see Hüffmeier, 'Phronesis', 77–82; J. Jouanna, 'La théorie de l'intelligence et de l'âme dans le traité hippocratique du Régime; ses rapports avec Empédocle et le Timée de Plato', *Revue des études grecques*, 79 (1966), pp. xv–xviii, and Pigeaud, *Folie*, 41–7; see also Joly, *Recherches*, 84.

[48] *Sacred Disease* 7 (6. 372. 4–374. 20). At 372. 19–21 I follow the sentence division of Grensemann and propose reading κοίλας instead of κοιλίας (MSS), secluding with Diller ἐς τὸν ἐγκέφαλον (cf. H. Grensemann, *Die hippokratische Schrift 'Über die heilige Krankheit'* (Berlin, 1968), 72): 'but the air that enters the hollow vessels contributes and thus provides intelligence and movement to the limbs'. I understand 'intelligence (*phronēsis*) and movement (*kinēsis*)' of the limbs as signifying intelligent, i.e. purposeful and coherent movement; for a different interpretation see van der Eijk in n. 9 above, 221.

[49] *Sacred Disease* 16 (6. 390. 10–392. 3). At 6. 390. 14 I follow Littré and Pigeaud, *Maladie de l'âme*, 34, in preferring the reading of Θ: πρήσσουσι, to ὑπηρετοῦσι (M): ὑπηρετέουσι (C).

[50] *Sacred Disease* 16 (6. 390. 11–16). Cf. Pigeaud, *Maladie de l'âme*, 35–7, and *idem*, *Folie*, 57–8.

receives the intelligence transmitted through the air first and in its purest state. This enables it to interpret the messages coming from the air.[51] (2) The air, after having left its acumen in the brain, then provides certain other parts with their intelligence and movement via the vessels, and thus enables them to act according to the brain's interpretation. Such parts are the eyes, ears, tongue, hands, and feet.[52] (3) Still other parts do not participate in intelligence at all: in the cavity and the lung the air's contribution is limited to cooling; the diaphragm and the heart, on account of their solid and thin structure, do not receive air, and thus have no intelligence. However, precisely because of this structure, they sense the physical effects of emotional vibrations and react to them.[53]

According to *Sacred Disease*, then, the brain, because of its privileged relationship to air, is the source of mental activity. Moreover, it is also the source of sense perception, judgement, and the emotions, and thus the cause of their disturbance as well.[54] Whereas intelligence is lost if its medium, air, does not reach the brain and the parts whose actions depend on it, activities that take place in the brain or have their origin there are impaired when the brain itself changes in any way from its normal condition. Thus perception is blurred when the brain shifts its position, while emotional disturbances result from a corruption of the brain by bile or phlegm.

In *Regimen*, on the other hand, intelligence (*phronēsis*) or unintelligence is linked to the soul, and depends upon its[55] particular mixture of

---

[51] *Sacred Disease* 16 (6. 390. 10–13, 15–18). Literally: 'the brain is the interpreter of what comes from the air'. The idea that messages from the outside are transmitted to the brain through the air occurs only here in the Hippocratic writings. In my opinion, this does not mean that the air by itself is considered to be intelligent or endowed with meaning. Rather, it seems to be the author's attempt to express the fact that thought, in so far as it is intelligent, is the result of external stimuli, and that coherent behaviour depends on the proper interpretation of these stimuli. Elsewhere, sense perception is said to provide the necessary connection to the external world, e.g. *Regimen* 1, 35 (6. 516. 9–19, 518. 4–7). Cf. Paola Manuli and Mario Vegetti, *Cuore, sangue e cervello* (Milan, 1977), 45–51. Van der Eijk, 'Hart en hersenen', 221, stresses the distinction made in *Sacred Disease* between the brain's comprehension (*synesis*) of external stimuli and the body's awareness (*phronēsis*) of and reaction to these.

[52] *Sacred Disease* 16 (6. 390. 18–20, 13–16); cf. ibid. 7 (6.372. 21). The inclusion of eyes and ears in this list is curious. The author seems to mean directed perception.

[53] Ibid. 7 (6. 372. 18–19), 17 (6. 392. 4–394. 2); cf. n. 97 below.

[54] Ibid. 14 (6. 386. 15–388. 6).

[55] Precisely what the relationship is between the body's and the soul's mixtures of fire and water is unclear: at 6. 512. 21–2 the soul's intelligence is said to depend on the mixture of fire and water *in the body*, while 6. 514. 6–7 refers to the *soul's* mixture of fire and water. Cf. Giuseppe Cambiano, 'Une intérpretation "matérialiste" des rêves, du Régime IV', in M. D. Grmek (ed.), *Hippocratica* (Paris, 1980), 87–96, at 89–90. For a similar confusion between the realms of body and soul cf. *Regimen* 2, 60 (6. 574. 10–13): excessive cold is said to lead to a coagulation of the moisture *in the body*, and to constipation, 'for the moisture *of the soul* is overpowered'.

fire and water: fire provides movement, and water nourishment. When the moistest fire and the driest water mix, each has what it needs of the other element, so the fire has no need to wander about in search of nourishment, nor is the water dull from lack of movement. Therefore, since what needs least from elsewhere is most attentive to what is present, the soul that has such a mixture is most intelligent and has the best memory.[56] Sense perception takes place when the sensations coming into the body through sight, hearing, and touch meet the soul on its revolutions (*periodoi*), mix with it, shake it, and thus are sensed by it.[57] Intelligence, it seems, depends both on the number of sensations the soul meets, perceives, and judges and on its attentiveness to these. Both the soul's perceptive capability and its constancy depend upon the speed of its revolution. If the revolution is slow, the soul's attention to each sensation is more constant, but it perceives less, since most sensations, especially those of sight and sound, are so fast that they escape its notice. If its movement is fast, the soul approaches the sensations faster and perceives them more quickly, but is less constant, as it moves on rapidly to new sensations.[58] Another factor seems to be the relative density of the soul. If water dominates in the mixture, such a soul not only moves more sluggishly, but is also thicker and less easily shaken by sensations, while a fiery soul is more easily stimulated.[59] In both extreme cases perception is disturbed: if the soul is too slow and too thick, no sensations register, and its emotions and thoughts, being cut off from the outside, do not correspond to reality.[60] If it is too fast, too many sensations register in too fast a succession, so that the soul loses all retentiveness and enters a dream-like state of rapidly succeeding images.[61]

In the author's opinion, the most intelligent soul is the soul that registers most, but still stays attentive to everything. Since this conditon is naturally fulfilled only by the soul whose mixture consists of perfectly balanced water and fire—that is, fire with the greatest admixture of water and water with the greatest admixture of fire—the mixtures of other souls are to be corrected by regimen: through food and exercise the amount of fire and water in the body can be regulated. Thus the soul's intelligence, as the author points out several times, is directly related to and can be influenced by the conditon of the

---

[56] *Regimen* 1, 35 (6. 512. 20–514. 7); cf. ibid. 3 (6. 472. 16–18).

[57] Ibid. 1, 35 (6. 516. 9–19); cf. ibid. 2, 61 (6. 574. 19–576. 6) and Joly, *Du Régime*, 279 ad 184, 9–16. The soul seems to move in three concentric circuits around the body cavity, which are equated with the hollow vessels that the fire, in giving structure to the body, created: *Regimen* 1, 9 (6. 484. 12–14), 10 (6. 486. 3–7).

[58] *Regimen* 1, 35 (6. 514. 9–15, 516. 7–19 and 6. 518. 10–13, 518. 20–520. 4).

[59] Ibid. (6. 516. 19, 520. 4).   [60] Ibid. (6. 518. 4–7).

[61] Ibid. (6. 520. 17–20). Jouanna, 'La théorie de l'intelligence', p. xvi, calls this condition an 'indigestion of sensations'; Pigeaud, *Folie*, 46, compares it to a kaleidoscope.

body.[62] The soul's *disposition*,[63] on the other hand, is not dependent upon its mixture of fire and water, but rather on the passages through which it travels, and therefore cannot be influenced by diet.

A further connection between soul and body is revealed by dreams, for during dreams the soul has a prognostic function. As long as the body is awake, the soul serves the body; its attention is divided between 'hearing, sight, touch, walking, the activities of the whole body'. But when the body is asleep and does not perceive, the soul remains awake and performs all the actions of the body as well as its own: it 'knows everything, sees what is to be seen, hears what is to be heard, walks, touches, grieves, and ponders'.[64] At that time the soul, not being distracted by movements that befall it either directly through sense perception or indirectly through the activities of the body, sees what goes on inside the body, and announces through dreams the sufferings of the body before they become apparent.[65] Whenever dreams show things as they should be, this announces health, since the soul is not being troubled and distracted by changes inside the body.[66] But if what is dreamt is different from the normal state, this points to disturbances in specific parts of the body, according to the analogy between macrocosm and

[62] *Regimen* 1, 35 (6. 516. 19–518. 2,11,19); cf. ibid. (6. 520. 10–14 and 6. 520. 20–522. 2): an inflammation of the blood drives a 'fast soul' to folly; cf. *Prorrhetic* 2 2 (9. 8. 16–20). Furthermore, a perfect soul loses all intelligence if the balance between its fire and its water is upset (6. 514. 7–9), while a soul that is unbalanced towards fire will be most intelligent with the proper moistening regimen (6. 522. 15–16).

[63] *Regimen* 1, 36 (6. 522. 22–524. 4): 'irascibility, indolence, craftiness, simplicity, quarrelsomeness, and benevolence'.

[64] Ibid. 4, 86 (6. 640. 3–16). While knowing, grieving, and pondering (ἐνθυμεῖσθαι) seem to be actions of the soul, seeing, hearing, touching, and walking are actions of the body that affect the soul; cf. ibid. 1, 35 (6. 516. 9–19) and 2, 61 (6. 574. 19–576. 6). I understand 'the activities of the whole body' at 6. 640. 7–8 in apposition to these actions, not as a different category.

For a discussion of the soul's role in *Regimen* 4 and possible shamanistic influences, see Cambiano, 'Une intérpretation matérialiste', *passim*; Joly, *Recherches*, 168–78, and *idem*, *Du Régime*, 296–301. Cf. also Xenophon, *Cyropaedia* 8, 7, 21 and Dodds, *Greeks and the Irrational*, 135.

[65] *Regimen* 4, 87 (6. 642. 2–4); cf. ibid. 3, 71 (6. 610. 10–11). Cf. also *Epidemics* 6, 8, 10 (5. 348. 1–5): the patient knows the incidents of her disease by means of her mind (*gnōmē*). The author adduces this case to show that the mind's awareness (*synnoia*)—I follow the punctuation of W. D. Smith, *Hippocrates*, VII, Loeb Classical Library (Cambridge, Mass., 1994), 281—can experience emotions such as misery and joy, fear and confidence, hope and despair independently, i.e. without the mediation of the sense-organs or input from external reality. Whether this is a sign of the mind's concentration on what happens inside the body or of a pathological seclusion from external reality, as in *Regimen* 1, 35 (6. 518. 4–7), is not clear. Cf. D. Manetti and A. Roselli, *Ippocrate, Epidemie, libro sesto* (Florence, 1982), 174–5; Pigeaud, *Maladie de l'âme*, 44–5.

[66] *Regimen* 4, 88 (6. 642. 11–17), 89 (6. 644. 12–15); cf. ibid. (6. 650. 17–652. 1), 90 (6. 652. 23–654. 8), 91 (6. 658. 6–9), 92 (6. 658. 13–17).

microcosm established in book 1, chapter 10.[67] Rarely, dreams concern the soul itself: for example, if a person dreams of fighting or disputing, this indicates that his soul is troubled by a secretion from the flesh, which is entering its circuit in the wrong direction;[68] if the heavenly bodies seem to wander about without reason, this points to a disturbance of the soul due to mental preoccupation: the person should relax and watch spectacles, preferably comedies, or whatever else he most enjoys.[69] Dreams of habitual actions point to a desire of the soul for these.[70] Two kind of dreams announce folly: to dream of the stars pursuing some 'Thing' that is rapidly receding, or of crossing rivers, of hostile hoplites, or of strange monsters.[71]

In other Hippocratic treatises, intelligence is related to the blood.[72] According to *Breaths*, when the blood is cooled in sleep, and becomes more sluggish, different 'opinions' (*doxai*)—that is, dreams—linger. When, on the other hand, the blood suddenly increases due to drunkenness, 'the souls and the thoughts (*phronēmata*) in the souls change, and they become forgetful of present evils and hopeful for future goods'. When the blood is completely disturbed, all intelligence is lost, for 'all learnings and recognitions are a matter of habit', and therefore lost when we depart from what is habitual—namely, the regular movement of the blood.[73] Here, blood and the soul are explicitly related:

[67] Cf. J. Jouanna, 'L'interprétation des rêves et la théorie micro-macrocosmique dans le traité Hippocratique du Régime: sémiotique et mimesis', in K. D. Fischer, D. Nickel, and P. Potter (eds.), *Text and Tradition: Studies on Ancient Medicine and its Transmission*, (Leiden, 1998), 161–74.

[68] *Regimen* 3, 71 (6. 610. 5–11); 4, 88 (6. 642. 19–644. 3), 93 (6. 660. 18–20).

[69] Ibid. 4, 89 (6. 648. 19–650. 4). Mental preoccupation (μερίμνη or φροντίς), which in *Epidemics* 6, 5, 5 (5. 316. 8–9) is compared to a walk, seems to cause violence to the soul, just as walks do to the body; cf. *Regimen* 2, 62 (6. 576. 7–8). This is the only explicit instance of 'psychotherapy' in the Hippocratic Collection; cf. Pedro Laín Entralgo, *La Medicina Hipocrática* (Madrid, 1970), 341–2.

[70] *Regimen* 4, 93 (6. 660. 15–16). To dream of eating and drinking announces the body's need and the soul's desire for certain foods: ibid. (6. 660. 8–16); cf. *Diseases 4* 39 (7. 558. 15–560. 5): the four humoral reservoirs communicate to the body particular needs which are experienced by the person as a desire for the appropriate food.

[71] *Regimen* 4, 89 (6. 648. 6–8) and 93 (6. 662. 2–4). To judge from the dietary prescription, the first instance of folly is clearly caused by too much fire (6. 648. 8–18).

[72] *Breaths* 14 (6. 110. 16–18): 'no constituent of the body in anyone contributes more to intelligence (*phronēsis*) than does blood'. *Diseases 1* 30 (6. 200. 11–12): 'the blood in man contributes the greatest part to his intelligence (*synesis*)—some people say everything'. While in *Breaths* a disturbance of the normal blood flow by air is adduced as the cause of epilepsy (6. 112. 13–114. 12), in *Diseases 1* a deviation from the blood's normal consistency and movement through bile accounts for the mental aberration of phrenitis (6. 200. 11–18).

[73] *Breaths* 14 (6. 112. 5–13). Cf. Hüffmeier, 'Phronesis', 62–8. J. Jouanna, *Hippocrate: Des Vents, De l'Art*, Collection des Universités de France (Paris, 1988), 122 n. 1, refers to

intelligence, which is said to consist in learnings and recognitions acquired by habit, is located in the soul, whose condition depends on the state of the blood.

III

In the treatises discussed so far, mental phenomena are related to air and the brain (*Sacred Disease*), to the movement of blood (*Breaths, Diseases 1*), and to the soul and its revolutions around the body cavity (*Regimen*). Numerous other passages describing or alluding to psychopathology provide further evidence of what the psychic is.

As will have become obvious, when the agent and/or the process of mental activity are impaired, mental disturbance results. Thus, when air does not reach the brain or is interrupted in its movement through the vessels, this causes loss of intelligence and spastic movements, the signs of an epileptic attack.[74] Corruption of the brain itself leads to emotional disturbance.[75] These opinions expressed in *Sacred Disease*, regarding the importance of air and of the brain for mental phenomena, are corroborated by the evidence of numerous other passages where a disturbance of mind, perception, or movement results from an alteration of the brain or from suffocation. Thus, according to *Glands*, if the brain is irritated, the mind (*nous*) is deranged, and the person suffers from apoplexy. If it is affected by an excess of fluid, judgement (*gnōmē*) is disturbed, and 'the patient goes about thinking and seeing alien things; he bears this kind of disease with mocking laughter and grotesque visions'.[76] When the brain is in an unclean state—that is, full of bile or phlegm— the patient has an intense headache, is deranged, and his vision is

the belief that 'dark' wine is transformed into blood. For wine contributing to mental derangement cf. e.g. *Regimen* 1, 35 (6. 522. 1); 4, 89 (6. 648. 10–11); *Regimen in Acute Diseases* 17 (2. 360. 10–11); *Prorrhetic* 2 2 (9. 8. 18–20).

For alteration of the intelligence caused by changes in the blood cf. the two types of *mania* in *Regimen* 1, 35 resulting from too slow or too fast motion of the soul (6. 518. 4–7 and 6. 520. 17–20).

[74] *Sacred Disease* 7 (6. 372. 4–374. 20). Hippocratic terminology for mental disorders is discussed by Pigeaud, *Folie*, 17–18, and Vincenzo Di Benedetto, *Il medico e la malattia* (Turin, 1986), 45–50.

[75] *Sacred Disease* 15: corruption of the brain by phlegm leads to a quiet kind of raging; bile, on the other hand, makes the person noisy and restless (6. 388. 13–16). If the brain changes because it is heated by bile, the person is seized with fear, whereas nausea, anguish, and amnesia result when the brain is chilled and contracted by cold phlegm (6. 388. 17–24); cf. the '*mania* towards the too slow' of souls with a high water content in *Regimen* 1, 35 (6. 518. 4).

[76] *Glands* 12 (8. 566. 11–568. 3). Other affections of the brain are *paraphrosynē* and *mania*: ibid. 15 (8. 570. 11–14).

impaired.[77] When it is shaken[78] or receives a blow,[79] the patient loses hearing, sight, speech, and/or intelligence. Injury[80] or inflammation[81] of the brain leads to derangement and/or spasms—it is explicitly mentioned that these seize the side of the body opposite to the affected part of the brain.[82] Suffocation resulting, for example, from interception of the movement of air around the liver, the diaphragm, or the heart—this happens when the uterus leans against these parts,[83] when a person receives a blow in the area of the stomach or the liver,[84] or when the liver expands against the diaphragm[85]—impairs vision and hearing, and the person becomes speechless and deranged.[86] Mental derangement can also result from suffocation due to a swollen throat,[87] from superficial breathing in painful pneumonia,[88] or from choking on thick sputum.[89]

In some treatises, again, disturbance of intelligence and movement is attributed to the blood. When bile enters the vessels, it heats the blood and alters its normal consistency and motion. The blood then heats the rest of the body, and 'the person loses his wits and is no longer himself'.[90] In this case, both the heat of the fever[91] and the change in the blood

---

[77] *Diseases 3* 2 (7. 118. 19–120. 2), 3 (7. 120. 17–21). In *Diseases 2* 12 (7. 20. 4–5) diplopia and in ibid. 15 (7. 28. 3–4) hemianopsia are described.

[78] *Coan Prenotions* 489 (5. 696. 2–5); cf. *Aphorisms* 7, 58 (4. 594. 10–11); see also *Sacred Disease* 14 (6. 388. 6–11).

[79] *Diseases 1* 4 (6. 146. 8–10); *Aphorisms* 7, 14 (4. 580. 10–11); Epidemics 5, 60 (5. 240. 8–10); in ibid. 7, 32 (5. 400. 22–402. 5) a blow above the left temple results in aphasia.

[80] *Diseases 1* 4 (6. 146. 10–12); *Coan Prenotions* 490 (5. 696. 5–7).

[81] *Places in Man* 32 (6. 324. 6–13); *Epidemics* 5, 50 (5. 236. 11–20); *Wounds in the Head* 19 (3. 254. 3–6); *Prorrhetic 2* 14 (9. 40. 3–5).

[82] *Wounds in the Head* 13 (3. 234. 8–11), 19 (3. 254. 6–9); *Epidemics* 5, 28 (5. 228. 2–4).

[83] *Diseases of Women* 1, 7 (8. 32. 10–12); 32 (8. 76. 5–10); 2, 127 (8. 272. 9–11), 201 (8. 384. 1–3, 12–14; 386. 4–5); 203 (8. 388. 18–390. 2).

[84] *Epidemics* 5, 39 (5. 230. 21–3). [85] *Internal Affections* 48 (7. 284. 10–286. 14).

[86] These symptoms may also be due to an overheating of the brain, cf. *Diseases of Women* 1, 32 (8. 76. 10–12): phlegm melts and flows down from the head, presumably because the uterus's interception of air around the liver prevents it from reaching and cooling the brain; cf. Lonie, *Hippocratic Treatises*, 325 ad 47, 1. If, on the other hand, the uterus settles at the loins, the head is not affected by suffocation: *Diseases of Women* 2, 201 (8. 386. 11–12). Cf. also *Internal Affections* 48 (7. 284. 8–9): bile is said to settle in the liver as well as the head. [87] *Diseases 3* 10 (7. 128. 16–130. 1).

[88] Ibid. 15 (7. 136. 11–15). [89] *Regimen in Acute Diseases* 5 (2. 260. 3–264. 3).

[90] *Diseases 1* 30 (6. 200. 11–18): phrenitis; cf. *Regimen* 1, 35 (6. 520. 11–14, 20): inflammation of the blood leads to *mania* in fiery souls. Cf. also *Diseases 1* 18 (6. 172. 12–13): a sudden migration of blood causes loss of consciousness; *Breaths* 14 (6. 112. 18–25): irregular movement of blood results in erratic movements of the body, loss of sight and hearing, and insensitivity to pain. In *Diseases 2* 3 (7. 10. 6–8) mental derangement results from overheating of blood in the head. For involvement of the head cf. *Diseases of Women* 1, 41 (8. 98. 6, 100. 3–10): If the lochial discharge is diverted to the head, symptoms include headache, impairment of hearing, delirium, and manic derangement.

[91] For heat as the cause of mental derangement see *Places in Man* 33 (6. 324. 14–16); *Aphorisms* 5, 16 (4. 536. 14–16); cf. *Epidemics* 4, 2 (5. 144. 15): bile leads to *mania*; cf.

account for the derangement; elsewhere, derangement results from an excess of blood.[92] Conversely, when the blood is cooled and coagulated by phlegm or dark bile, and its movement becomes too slow, paralysis, apoplexy, and finally death result.[93]

Only rarely does mental disturbance seem to be related directly to the liver, the diaphragm, or the heart. This is, however, the case in *phrenitis*, an acute disease that, besides involving pain in the abdomen and a high fever, is always accompanied by mental aberration.[94] In the treatise *Girls* the area around the heart is said to be 'critical and prone to mental aberration and madness' (*mania*): when, because of impeded menstruation, the heart fills up with an excess of fluid, this causes pressure, and when the stagnant blood putrefies, suicidal attempts, fear, and distress result.[95]

Diseases 2 22 (7. 36. 21–22); *Sacred Disease* 15 (6. 388. 14–16). Black bile is related to raging as well: *Epidemics* 5, 2 (5. 204. 8–9); 40 (5. 232, 1–5). According to *Diseases 1* 30 (6. 200. 18–23), in melancholics there is more raging and derangement than in phrenitics in so far as dark bile is stronger than normal bile; cf. *Airs, Waters, Places* 10 (2. 50. 12–14): *melancholia* is caused by the thickest and most acrid part of bile and blood left behind when their humid and watery parts are dried up. Elsewhere patients affected by black bile 'pluck off bits of wool, pick their noses, answer shortly whatever is asked, but of their own account say nothing sensible': *Regimen in Acute Diseases (Appendix)* 8 (2. 424. 14–426. 5).

[92] By implication, *Aphorisms* 5, 65 (4. 558. 6–10); 6, 21 (4. 568. 7–8): varicose veins or haemorrhoids resolve *mania*; cf. also *Epidemics* 2, 5, 23 (5. 132. 8–9); 3, 17, case 11 (3. 134. 1–15). In *Epidemics* 2, 6, 32 (5. 138. 19–20), and *Aphorisms* 5, 40 (4. 544. 16–17) the collection of blood at the nipples is a sign of mania; cf. *Epidemics* 2, 6, 19 (5. 136. 11–12), where intelligence (*synesis*) is attributed to the thick vessel in the nipples. In *Girls* (8. 466. 15–19) excess of blood in the heart results in mental disturbance; cf. *Epidemics* 3, 17, case 2 (3. 108. 6–112. 12): symptoms following suppressed lochial discharge include a melancholic affection of the mind.

[93] *Diseases 2* 6 (7. 14. 8–20): dark bile; 8 (7. 16. 14–22): phlegm; *Regimen in Acute Diseases (Appendix)* 5 (2. 404. 10–406. 11): dark bile, sharp fluids. For the relation of loss of power over a part to dark bile cf. also *Aphorisms* 7, 40 (4. 588. 8–9); *Prorrhetic 2* 40 (9. 68. 19–22). Cf. *Breaths* 13 (6. 110. 6–13): cold air in the body produces loss of sensation and paralysis.

[94] *Affections* 10 (6. 216. 21–218. 12): pain over the hypochondrium towards the liver, bile settling in the diaphragm; *Diseases 3* 9 (7. 128. 5–9): pain in the diaphragm; *Diseases 2* 72 (7. 108. 25–110. 13): diaphragm swollen and painful (φρενῖτις, P. Potter in *Hippocrates*, V, Loeb Classical Library (Cambridge, Mass., 1988), 226: φροντίς MSS). According to *Prognostic* 7 (2. 126. 3–5), inflammation and throbbing in the hypochondrium indicate derangement; cf. *Prorrhetic 1* 22 (5. 516. 4–5); in *Epidemics* 6, 6, 5 (5. 326. 2), on the other hand, mental derangement is said to resolve pain in the sides. Elsewhere in the *Epidemics* psychological symptoms are associated with pain in the hypochondrium or spleen (e.g. *Epidemics* 1, 13, case 3 (2. 688. 13–15); 7, 89 (5. 446. 7–12)), while the abatement of abdominal swelling is linked to the return of reason (e.g. ibid. 1, 13, case 3 (2. 690. 2)).

[95] *Girls* (8. 468. 7–8, 9–13). Similarly, involvement of the heart in inflammation causes loss of feeling, paralysis, loss of heat, and finally death: *Coan Prenotions* 395 (5. 672. 10–14). If cold fluxes reach the heart, the liver, or the vena cava, a person becomes epilep-

IV

From the above and other similar descriptions, it appears that intelligence and the emotions, as well as sensation and movement, in both normal and abnormal states depend upon the condition of the part of the body to which they are related. In short, psychic phenomena are given a somatic explanation. Conversely, psychological factors influence somatic processes. Thus, according to *Humours*, to different emotional states, such as fear, shame, grief, pleasure, or passion, the appropriate part of the body answers with its action—for example, sweating of the skin, palpitation of the heart.[96] Similarly, in *Sacred Disease* the feeling of tension in the heart and diaphragm following strong emotions is explained mechanically, as a reaction to vibrations created by the emotions.[97] Or again, in a case of breathlessness and pain in the right hip after lifting a heavy weight, the patient, besides observing dietary precautions, should refrain from shouting and excitement, presumably because there is a tear in the lung which would be aggravated by any vibration:[98] for 'excitement makes the heart and lung contract, . . . calmness expands and relaxes the heart'.[99]

Emotional states also have an effect on the fluids: in order that the patient may regain his colour, and for the sake of his humours, one should provoke excitement, desire, and fear.[100] Fear, itself provoked by bile, produces a rush of hot blood to the head, which overheats the brain

tic and paralysed: *Regimen in Acute Diseases (Appendix)* 5 (2. 404. 10–406. 11). That the heart's heat is critical for life is evidenced by instructions to except the heart when cooling the body, e.g. *Diseases 3* 14 (7. 134. 19).

On the association of *phrenes* and the heart with psychic phenomena see Volker Langholf, *Medical Theories in Hippocrates* (Berlin, 1990), 40–6, 50–1.

[96] *Humours* 9 (5. 490. 5–8). For an interpretation of the whole chapter see Pigeaud, *Maladie de l'âme*, 41–7.

[97] *Sacred Disease* 17 (6. 392. 5–12, 15–394. 2); cf. ibid. 6 (6. 370. 14–18): the heart reacts with palpitations to the vibration of the vessels caused by their sudden cooling through phlegm. Cf. *Nature of Bones* 19 (9. 194. 21–196. 7): the heart is located in a narrow space in which the vessels converge; therefore that area of the thorax is most sensitive. According to *Ancient Medicine* 22 (1. 632. 5–634. 4) parts that are full of blood and dense, or broad and extended, are very sensitive. The same is true of parts that are little protected by flesh: *Diseases 1* 26 (6. 192. 16–18), *pleuron*; cf. *Wounds in the Head* 2 (3. 188. 8–190. 13), the brain at the bregma; or that on account of their porosity or moisture are permeable: *Nature of the Child* 15 (7. 494. 11–13), 21 (7. 512. 12–13). On the other hand, a patient whose body is in good general condition does not notice his first becoming ill: *Diseases 1* 15 (6. 166. 12–13). For αἰσθάνεσθαι as the sensing and reacting of inanimate substances see *Sacred Disease* 13 (6. 384. 20–386. 3): everything, including ceramic pots and the tissues of the human body, senses and reacts to the south wind; cf. *Ancient Medicine* 15 (1. 606. 10–13), and J. Jouanna, *Hippocrate: De l'ancienne médecine*, Collection des Universités de France (Paris, 1990), 138 n. 5.

[98] *Epidemics* 6, 4, 4 (5. 306. 13–308. 6).   [99] Ibid. 5, 5 (5. 316. 5–7).
[100] Ibid. 2, 4, 4 (5. 126. 7–8).

and makes the person shout and cry out.[101] Sense perceptions, too, influence the fluids: sight and sound are among the factors that have an effect on the temperature of bile and phlegm.[102] This theory is developed further in *Regimen*: sight, sound, speech, and worry are work for the soul which causes it to move, and thus become warm and dry: when the soul has used up its own fluid, it consumes the fluid of the body, thereby making the person lean.[103] Finally, if the soul is troubled even more by its preoccupation, disease results.[104]

The Hippocratic physician is well aware that both body and soul are involved in many pathological processes, and that in prognosis, diagnosis, and treatment mental and emotional as well as somatic factors have to be taken into account.[105] In case descriptions, symptoms of body and mind are frequently recorded side by side.[106] Mental disturbance is

---

[101] *Sacred Disease* 15 (6. 388. 24–390. 9); in *Internal Affections* 48 (7. 286. 14–16) fear seems to cause bile to settle in the liver and the head (7. 284. 8–9). Cf. *Epidemics* 6, 5, 5 (5. 316. 6): excitement draws what is warm and moist towards the head.

[102] *Diseases 1* 23 (6. 188. 12–13); *Affections* 1 (6. 208. 12–13): sight, smell, and sound.

[103] *Regimen* 2, 61 (6. 574. 18–576. 6). In seeing, and presumably worrying, the soul is moved by its attention (6. 574. 21); in hearing, and presumably speaking, because it is shaken (6. 574. 23); cf. *Regimen* 3, 78 (6. 622. 18–19): a voice exercise is recommended as a means of evacuating moisture from flesh that is too dense; *Regimen* 2, 63 (6. 578. 20–4): running certain races is said to be exercise for the inner parts of the soul, probably because they require special attention (W. H. S. Jones, *Hippocrates*, IV, Loeb Classical Library (London, 1931), 354 n. 2), or because they cause vibration. Idleness, on the other hand, makes the body moist and weak, because the soul, being at rest, does not consume moisture from the body: *Regimen* 2, 60 (6. 574. 4–5).

A similar idea is expressed in *Epidemics* 6, 5, 5 (5. 316. 8–9): 'a walk of the soul is preoccupation in men'. For a comprehensive summary of various interpretations of this passage see Manetti and Roselli, *Epidemie*, 110–11, and Joly, *Du Régime*, 279–80.

Humours 9 seems to associate exertion of the soul with searching, studying, seeing and speaking (5. 488. 18–19), and affections of the mind (*gnōmē*) with sight and hearing (5. 490. 1–2).

For the idea that the soul, when heated, consumes the body cf. *Epidemics* 6, 5, 2 (5. 314. 14–15). See, however, Manetti and Roselli, *Epidemie*, 107–8, for a different reading of the passage. [104] *Regimen* 4, 89 (6. 648. 19–650. 4).

[105] e.g. *Humours* 7 (5. 488. 7–8): abscessions arise 'either from fluids, or from melting of the body, or from the soul' (I read ἢ ψυχῆς for καὶ ψυχῆς with Littré); cf. *Epidemics* 3, 17, case 11 (3. 134. 2) and case 15 (3. 142. 7): the symptoms arise 'from grief'. *Epidemics* 1, 10 (2. 670. 7–9) includes among diagnostic signs 'talk, manner, silence, thoughts, sleep or absence of sleep, the nature and time of dreams, pluckings, scratchings, tears'; *Epidemics* 6, 6, 14 (5. 330. 2–8) includes mind (*gnōmē*) and habit (*tropoi*); cf. *Epidemics* 6, 8, 7 (5. 346. 6–7); 9 (5. 346. 16–17); *Humours* 2 (5. 478. 6–13), 4 (5. 480. 7–482. 9). According to *Aphorisms* 2, 33 (4. 480. 5–6), 'in every disease it is a good sign when the patient's intellect (*dianoia*) is sound and he enjoys his food; the opposite is a bad sign'.

[106] e.g. *Diseases of Women* 2, 133 (8. 282. 15); 174 *bis* (8. 356. 2) and see especially the case histories of *Epidemics* 1, 13 (2. 682. 3–716. 14) and 3, 1 (3. 24. 2–66. 11) and 17 (3. 102. 11–148. 5). Cf. Pigeaud, *Maladie de l'âme*, 393–5, and idem, *Folie*, 14–15; van der Eijk, 'Hart en hersenen', 220.

Sometimes symptoms are primarily psychological, e.g. the phobias of *Epidemics* 5, 81 (5. 250. 10–13), 82 (5. 250. 14–17) = ibid. 7, 86 (5. 444. 13–16), 87 (5. 444. 17–21); cf. ibid. 85 (5. 444. 1–12); ibid. 3, 17, case 15 (3. 142. 5–146. 6).

expected from certain somatic conditions,[107] and may point to the—usually fatal—outcome of the disease.[108] On the other hand, certain afflictions of the body resolve mental symptoms.[109] If a condition of the body is caused by factors other than humoral, such as 'drink, venery, grief, anxiety (*phrontides*), or sleeplessness', treatment should be directed towards these, not the fluids.[110] Dietary prescriptions are given in accordance not only with the particular imbalance of fluids in the body, and the phases of the disease process, but also with the patient's spirit (*psychē*).[111] In short, the physician has to know that 'the souls and bodies of men differ much from each other, and have the greatest influence' on the healing process. Therefore it is important not only to understand mental and physical reactions as a guide to the severity of the disease, but also to know the individual disposition of the patient's body and soul, since some are more inclined than others to fever and mental disturbance.[112]

V

Turning now to the general question of what is mind, what is body, we may begin by noting that for the Hippocratic physician mind and body are two distinct, yet related aspects of human nature. According to *Regimen*, both *sōma* and *psychē* consist of the same substances. The

---

[107] e.g. *Regimen in Acute Diseases* 8 (2. 426. 8–12), 9 (2. 440. 7–11); *Aphorisms* 7, 40 (4. 588. 8–9). *Prorrhetic 1* 32 (5. 518. 3–4): urine without a deposit announces derangement, while urine with one resolves it: *Epidemics* 6, 6, 10 (5. 328. 10). Derangement is frequently associated with convulsions, e.g. *Aphorisms* 6, 56 (4. 576. 19–21), cf. ibid. 4, 67 (4. 526. 3–4); *Prorrhetic 1* 20 (5. 516. 1–2), 36 (5. 518. 11–14), cf. *Coan Prenotions* 475 (5. 690. 11–12), 228 (5. 634. 16–17), 294 (5. 648. 20–1); *Regimen in Acute Diseases* 10 (2. 446. 9–448. 6 and 450. 3–454. 1); ibid. (2. 450. 6–9): derangement *or* spasms. In *Epidemics* 2, 2, 8 (5. 88. 3–8) the absence of any change of aspect or mind (*gnōmē*) in a case of paralysis is noted; cf. ibid. 7, 8 (5. 378. 19–24).

[108] e.g. *Aphorisms* 4, 50 (4. 520. 9–10); 7, 7 (4. 580. 1), 9 (4. 580. 4), 10 (4. 580. 5–6), 14 (4. 580. 10–11), 18 (4. 582. 2); *Coan Prenotions* 88 (5. 602. 12–14), 478 (5. 692. 4–5): in fatal cases the mind (*dianoia*) is numbed. In *Epidemics* 7 it is frequently recorded whether the patient is 'in his mind' (ἔμφρων) at the time of his death, e.g. ch. 15 (5. 390. 2); cf. ch. 5 (5. 376. 12–13): the patient becomes insensitive to touch in his feet shortly before dying. In *Aphorisms* 6, 26 (4. 570. 1–2); cf. *Coan Prenotions* 129 (5. 610. 3–4), 539 (5. 706. 19–708. 1); in *Epidemics* 2, 5, 2 (5. 128. 9–13); 6, 6, 5 (5. 326. 2), on the other hand, mental derangement resolves a somatic condition.

[109] e.g. *Coan Prenotions* 474 (5. 690. 10–11); *Epidemics* 4, 58 (5. 196. 10–11); *Aphorisms* 6, 21 (4. 568. 7–8).

[110] *Regimen in Acute Diseases (Appendix)* 16 (2. 476. 4–8); *Regimen* 4, 89 (6. 648. 20–650. 2).

[111] *Affections* 46 (6. 254. 17–19); cf. *Ancient Medicine* 10 (1. 592. 7–10, 13–18): food has an effect on both body and mind (*gnōmē*). According to *Aphorisms* 2, 38 (4. 480. 17–18), food and drink pleasant to the patient are to be preferred even if slightly inferior in strength.   [112] *Prorrhetic 2* 12 (9. 32. 20–34. 1, 7–15); cf. ibid. 4 (9. 14. 23–4).

characteristics of both are shaped in a similar fashion by external influences and inheritance. Statements in other treatises indicate that the same pathogenic factor results in different symptoms according to whether the body or the mind is affected.[113] However, the division is not absolute: symptoms change from mental to somatic, and vice versa, as a disease moves from one part of the body to another.[114] Furthermore, there clearly exists a reciprocal relationship between phenomena of the two types: body affects mind, mind affects body.

Sōma comprises the different parts of the body, solid and fluid, viewed as a system. Once life has been engendered through the presence of heat, which starts respiration and nourishment in the seed, its continuation is ensured by the intake of food and air from the outside, and a proper balance of heat and moisture within the body. Processes attributed to the body are respiration, digestion, absorption and evacuation of food and drink, menstruation and lactation, production and emission of seed, conception, birth, and growth. These take place through the interaction of the body's parts with each other, and are mostly self-regulated by the 'mechanics' operating within the body (attraction, pressure, heat). Nourishment, however, also depends on a 'person's' response to appetite, by which the body's needs are communicated.[115] Similarly, seed is produced when the body is heated through sexual activity.[116]

The Greek word ψυχή (*psychē*) is not very frequent in the Hippocratic Corpus, and its usage varies from treatise to treatise, or even within the same work. In its widest sense, *psychē* is the life principle that disappears from the body at death, or temporarily in fainting. More nar-

---

[113] *Epidemics* 6, 8, 31 (5. 356. 1–3): if the infirmity affects the body, patients tend to become epileptic, if the mind (*dianoia*), melancholic; cf. *Aphorisms* 5, 16 (4. 536. 14–16): the relaxing effects of heat include debility of the cords, dullness of the mind (*gnōmē*), and fainting. According to *Epidemics* 2, 3, 18 (5. 120. 1–5), sudden disappearance of swellings at wounds results in convulsions, if the wounds are at the back of the body, in *mania*, pain in the sides, or dysentery if they are at the front; cf. *Aphorisms* 5, 65 (4. 558. 6–10). As Singer, 'Some Hippocratic Mind–Body Problems', 135, points out, such passages show that the mind–body division is only one among many divisions: symptoms depend on the particular part of the body affected; cf. Littré's commentary (4. 559–60) on the medical difficulty of the front–back division and his tentative explanation that if the disease matter attacks the spinal cord, convulsions result, while *mania* etc. are the outcome if the attack is to the head, sides, or the body cavity.

[114] e.g. *Epidemics* 3, 17, case 5 (3. 118. 12–13): mental derangement commences upon the cessation of pain in the right thigh. Elsewhere, mental symptoms are prevented (e.g. *Epidemics* 2, 3, 18 (5. 120. 1–2)) or resolved by somatic symptoms: see n. 109 above, and vice versa n. 108. Cf. Di Benedetto, *Il medico e la malattia*, 53.

[115] *Diseases 4* 39 (7. 558. 15–560. 5) (cf. n. 70 above). When the patient is deranged, he does not eat: *Diseases 1* 34 (6. 204. 7–8); cf. *Epidemics* 3, 17, case 15 (3. 142. 10–11): the patient drinks only when he is reminded; *Coan Prenotions* 136 (5. 610. 18).

[116] *Generation* 1 (7. 470. 11–16).

rowly, in *Regimen* it refers to the male and female seed as the vehicle of life.[117] In the same treatise, *psychē* is identified with the mental component of the human being. As such, it is the agent of intelligence and character, and is related to sense perception and dreams. This *psychē* is associated with heat,[118] and seems to travel inside the body along the same passages as the blood. In *Breaths* 'souls' which contain 'thoughts' are explicitly related to the particular conditions of the blood. Finally, when used in contrast to the body, *psychē* corresponds to expressions for mind (*nous, dianoia, gnōmē*). The word *psychē*, then, signifies either life principle or mental principle—whether function or agent. As the latter, it corresponds to the brain or blood as the site of mental events.

But what is the mental or psychic? It may first be noted that intelligence, the emotions, sensation, and movement are often grouped together in both clinical descriptions and theoretical statements, and that both individually and as a group these phenomena are frequently related to certain somatic principles, such as the brain, the breath, or the blood.[119] Furthermore, whereas intelligence and the emotions are clearly referred to as 'mental',[120] sensation and movement vary in their attribution to either the mind or the body, and in their significance as mental or bodily signs.[121] On the somatic level, both depend upon the soundness of the part directly involved,[122] while on the psychic level,

---

[117] See n. 33 above. For further interpretations of the meaning of ψυχή in *Regimen* cf. Hüffmeier, 'Phronesis', 69–75; Joly, *Du Régime*, 253–4 ad 146, 11.

[118] For the 'heat of the soul' (τὸ τῆς ψυχῆς θερμόν) see *Regimen* 2, 38 (6. 534. 7–8), 56 (6. 568. 12–13), 60 (6. 574. 7), 62 (6. 476. 23). Cf. also the expression σύμφυτον θερμόν, ibid. 2, 62 (6. 576. 15), and Joly, *Du Régime*, 279 ad 184, 23. While the essence of the soul is heat (cf. *Regimen* 1, 10 (6. 486. 7–9)), it needs moisture for nourishment: *Regimen* 2, 56 (6. 568. 12–13), 62 (6. 576. 23–578. 1); cf. ibid. 2, 38 (6. 534. 7–8), 60 (574. 6–8), and the expression 'moisture of the soul' (τὸ τῆς ψυχῆς ὑγρόν) (6. 574. 12–13).

[119] The association of psychic phenomena with the brain, the air, and the blood has counterparts in pre-Socratic thought (Alcmaeon of Croton, Diogenes of Apollonia, Empedocles).

[120] *Sacred Disease* 14 (6. 386. 15–388. 11) and Pigeaud, *Maladie de l'âme*, 38–41. In the case descriptions of *Epidemics* 1 and 3, when intellectual and emotional disturbances abate, the patient is said to 'regain his senses' (καταvoεῖν). In general, the absence or presence of psychological disturbance is most frequently expressed in terms that refer to the mind, e.g. *Epidemics* 7, 11 (5. 386. 14–15); cf. n. 74 above.

[121] Seeing, hearing, and feeling take place by means of the body, while the perception, comprehension, and interpretation of the messages thus perceived are psychic activities. Looking, listening, speaking, and walking are actions of the body in which the *psychē* partakes by being attentive and giving directions according to the sensations perceived; cf. esp. *Regimen* 4, 86 (6. 640. 3–16) and *Sacred Disease* 16 (6. 390. 10–392. 3).

[122] Cf. Gundert, 'Parts', 456–8, and D. Gourevitch, 'L'aphonie hippocratique', in F. Lasserre and P. Mudry (eds.), *Formes de pensée dans la Collection hippocratique*, (Geneva, 1983), 297–305.

awareness and coherence of sensation and action depend upon the
integrity of the part in man that provides intelligence. Thus, according
to *Breaths*, disturbance and corruption of the *phronēsis*-providing blood
during an epileptic attack results in uncontrolled movement and the loss
of the sensations sight, hearing, and touch.[123] Similarly, not to react to
external stimuli, or to misinterpret them, or not to be aware of one's
actions or physiological processes is considered to be a sign of disturbed
intelligence.[124] *Phronēsis*, finally, itself the result of either a particular
mixture of fire and water, the access of air to the brain and the parts, or
the regularity of the blood flow, makes a person appear intelligent by
sensing, feeling, and acting according to what is appropriate and habitual, appropriateness being defined by the person's social environment,
habit determined by his individuality. When the patient is aware of and
recognizes those about him, when he understands and remembers what
is said or done by himself or others, when he responds properly to questions, his mind is in order, and he is 'within himself'.[125] If, on the other
hand, the patient's behaviour is unrelated to his social environment, or
seems incomprehensible, or if it shows some deviation from his individual habit, this is considered to be a sign of disease, and frequently
attributed to a disturbed mind. Examples of such behaviour are: to talk
too much or not at all;[126] to exhibit unmotivated or exaggerated moods
and emotions, as in the case of the man who 'spoke more aggressively

[123] *Breaths* 14 (6. 112. 18–25). According to *Aphorisms* 2, 6 (4. 470. 17–18), insensitivity to pain is the sign of a diseased mind. While in *Breaths* and *Sacred Disease* epileptic
seizures are explained as a disturbance of the same principle that provides *phronēsis*,
according to *Epidemics* 6, 8, 31 (5. 354. 19–356. 3), epilepsy results from a weakness of
the body (not the mind); cf. ibid. 7, 8 (5. 378. 19–24): the patient is 'in his mind' even
though his body is paralysed.

[124] e.g. *Diseases* 2 21 (7. 36. 3–4); *Internal Affections* 48 (7. 284. 19–21): the patient
removes pieces of wool from his blanket believing them to be lice; cf. other cases of
unmotivated movements of the limbs, e.g. *Regimen in Acute Diseases (Appendix)* 8 (2.
424. 14–426. 2); *Epidemics* 7, 25 (5. 396. 20–1); ibid. 3, 17, case 15 (3. 142. 8–9). Ibid. 1, case
12 (3. 64. 15); *Coan Prenotions* 136 (5. 610. 17–18); *Diseases* 2 21 (7. 36. 4; cf. 9): the patient
urinates unawares. Elsewhere, on the other hand, insensibility to touch and the retention
of urine and stool followed by incontinence are attributed to injury of the spinal cord,
e.g. *Prorrhetic* 2 16 (9. 42. 9–16); *Joints* 48 (4. 212. 6–17).

[125] *Epidemics* 1, 13, case 4 (2. 692. 9–10); *Internal Affections* 48 (7. 286. 11–13); cf. *Diseases* 2 22 (7. 36. 19–20). In *Epidemics* 7, 11 (5. 384. 19, 386. 20–1), the patient, albeit
showing many signs of emotional disturbance, 'recognized everyone and all objects', and
'showed recognition and answered what was asked'; cf. ibid. 7, 3 (5. 370. 10–13): the
patient was aware of his loss of memory. By implication: ibid. 7, 5 (5. 374. 6–8); 3, 17, case
13 (3. 138. 11, 140. 6–7); and *Breaths* 14 (6. 112. 7–8).

[126] Too much or incomprehensible talk is frequently mentioned in the case descriptions of *Epidemics* 1 and 3; cf. *Internal Affections* 29 (7. 242. 26–244. 1). For silence and
withdrawal cf. *Regimen in Acute Diseases (Appendix)* 8 (2. 426. 2–4); *Epidemics* 3,
17, case 14 (3. 140. 18); case 15 (3. 142. 7–8; cf. 146. 5); 1, case 6 (3. 52. 7–8); 7, 25 (5. 396.
21).

and greeted people more warmly than the occasion warranted';[127] to act out of character;[128] or to be simply 'outside oneself'.[129]

The Hippocratic writers share the implicit assumption that there exists a 'self' upon which the experience of individual identity rests, and identify this as the mind. This personal identity, furthermore, is established through a collection of typical behaviours which guarantee its continuity and relate it to the external world.[130] Empirically, the mind has a reality in its own right. Where, however, an explanation of the mind is called for, as, for example, in cases of its dysfunction, the psychic is interpreted in terms of the body, its structures, and its processes, or not at all.[131] There is never any indication in the Hippocratic writings that *psychē*, either as life principle or as mental principle, represents an entity with a separate existence of its own. In sum, mind and body in the Hippocratic writings, while distinguished empirically by being related to different types of phenomena, are both ultimately accounted for by the same explanatory model: human nature (*physis*), which embraces the totality of bodily structures, physiological processes, and psychic events.[132]

[127] *Epidemics* 7, 10 (5. 382. 2–3); cf. ibid. 25 (5. 396. 9–10), 11 (5. 384. 5–14). Such patients shout, sing, weep, laugh; are distressed, dejected, in anguish, and then again optimistic; jump suddenly out of bed and are not to be managed, e.g. ibid. 1, 13, case 2 (2. 686. 6–7), case 8 (2. 702. 16); 3, 1, case 11 (3. 62. 5); 17, case 2 (3. 112. 11), case 11 (3. 134. 10), case 15 (3. 142. 9); 7, 89 (5. 446. 7–8), 25 (5. 396. 23).

[128] e.g. *Prorrhetic 1* 44 (5. 522. 6): 'An insolent answer from a polite person is a bad sign.' In *Epidemics* 4, 15 (5. 152. 18–20) the patient uses foul language and behaves in an unruly fashion, although he is 'not that type'; cf. ibid. 3, 17, case 11 (3. 134. 7).

[129] e.g. *Epidemics* 7, 85 (5. 444. 7 and 10); *Diseases 1* 30 (6. 200. 16); cf. *Epidemics* 7, 1 (5. 366. 1–2, 4–5), 45 (5. 412. 19–414. 3). There is no indication in the Hippocratic texts that the expressions to be 'within oneself' (ἐν ἑωντῷ) or 'outside oneself' (ἐξ ἑωντοῦ) are to be taken literally in the spatial sense that the soul has left the body or has returned to it.

[130] Cf. Müri, 'Bemerkungen', 74–8; Jackie Pigeaud, 'Écriture et médecine hippocratique', in *Texte et Langage*, i (Nantes, 1978), 134–65, esp. 144–63.

[131] Cf. I. E. Drabkin, 'Remarks on Ancient Psychopathology', *Isis*, 46 (1955), 223–34.

[132] To put it differently: the Hippocratic physician, although distinguishing between somatic processes and psychic events neither thinks in terms of a mind–body dualism, nor understands the mental as a mere epiphenomenon of the body; rather, both are manifestations of the same principle, *physis*:

Mind and body are presumably a pair of opposites and, as such, the expression of a single entity . . . concerning the ultimate nature of which nothing can be said except that it vaguely expresses the quintessence of 'life'. This living being appears outwardly as the material body, but inwardly as a series of images of the vital activities taking place within. They are two sides of the same coin, and we cannot rid ourselves of the doubt that perhaps this whole separation of mind and body may finally prove to be merely a device of reason for the purpose of conscious discrimination—an intellectually necessary separation of one and the same fact into two aspects, to which we then illegitimately attribute an independent existence. (Carl Gustav Jung, 'Spirit and Life', in *Collected Works*, viii (London, 1960), 236 (§619)

I am very grateful to Heinrich von Staden for his critical comments on an earlier draft of this paper.

2

The Defining Features of Mind–Body Dualism in the Writings of Plato

The works of Plato are unique on a number of counts, not least that they contain the first fully articulated account of the relationship between soul (*psychē*) and body (*sōma*) in Western literature. The picture that emerges is not without its complexities, not to say apparent self-contradictions; so we might usefully begin our examination with a brief, scene-setting discussion of what we know of the two notions before Plato's time.[1]

Notoriously, for the early Greeks (as portrayed, for instance, in the works of Homer) the body, at least at death, constitutes one's 'real' self. One's life principle (literally 'life', *psychē*) may have been held to be different from the body, and even to survive the death of that body, but this was small consolation; what survived did so in a miserable and undesirable state in Hades, whatever the virtue of one's life on earth. By the sixth century, with the advent of Orphism into certain sectors of Greek thinking, the *psychē* started to be seen as having a better claim than the body to the title of one's real self. Not only was it held to survive the body, it was deemed to be that whereby we are both physically alive and also alive as rational, hence responsible agents.[2] And its ontological status was such that it was the potential subject of eternal reward or punishment for the quality of life lived, bodily existence being relegated to the status of some sort of temporal way station.[3]

[1] For purposes of this essay I shall assume the following: (a) that the works of Plato fall into three main groups, characterizable as 'Socratic', 'middle', and 'late'; and (b) that the views of soul found in the Socratic group are more or less those of the historical Socrates, those in the latter two groups more or less those of Plato. I have also opted throughout for the older translation of *psychē* as 'soul' rather than 'mind', the principal reason being that this translation seems to me better to catch the sense of *psychē* as the 'person' or 'genuine self' that seems to have been what Plato was at some pains to affirm.

[2] Heraclitus, 22 B 107 (DK 1. 175. 1–3) and 22 B 118 (DK 1. 177. 4–5).

[3] For a careful study of metempsychosis in early Greek thought and in its non-Greek origins see Walter Burkert, *Lore and Science in Ancient Pythagoreanism*, trans. Edwin L. Minar, jr. (Cambridge, Mass., 1972), 120–65.

While Orphism was regarded by many as the religion of the poor, and its promises of satisfaction hereafter some sort of proto-Marxian opium of the people, it did in fact have a number of sympathizers among the intelligentsia, including Pindar, Empedocles, and Socrates. It seems clear, for example, that Socrates too thought soul had a stronger claim than did body to the title of our real self, so much so that he seems to have held that our self and our soul are one and the same.[4] As such, the soul was for Socrates self-evidently more *important* than the body, and for this reason a natural object of much greater *care* than the body. Indeed, 'the care of the soul' has been defined as the very heart of Socrates' philosophy.[5] As for its nature, he seems to have agreed with the Orphics, Pythagoreans, Heraclitus, and others that the soul is the ground of our rational and moral as well as our biological self.[6]

On the detail of his thinking about the soul–body relationship there is some unclarity. At one point he talks, apparently approvingly, of having heard a philosopher say that the body is the 'tomb' of the soul.[7] As I have put it elsewhere, 'According to this view the soul is undoubt-edly meant to be the real self, with the body serving only as a shell. As a doctrine it is fairly consistent, for "desires" are attributed to the soul alone; the body is treated as literally "dead weight" (*tethnamen*) and apparently plays no part in the operations of the person as such.'[8]

Elsewhere he talks of the body's being a possession of the soul.[9] It does not appear, however, that he is talking about arithmetical posses-sion, in the way that a violinist possesses a violin, but something closer to biological possession, in the way that a violinist possesses a *hand* that manipulates the violin. Nevertheless, the argument as we have it is not wholly clear,[10] and *Alcibiades* I is, in addition, only doubtfully a Platonic dialogue. Fortunately, Socrates returns to the notion in a dialogue that is undoubtedly Platonic, the *Charmides*. And here he if anything goes further than he does in *Alcibiades* I. If I may paraphrase from an earlier account: At *Charmides* 156d ff. we have a discussion concerning health, where Socrates propounds views which he claims to have learned from a doctor who had served the Thracian king, Zalmoxis. The passage is worth quoting in full:

---

[4] *Alc.* I, 130c5–6, and (by implication) *Protag.* 313a–b; see T. M. Robinson, *Plato's Psychology*, 2nd edn. (Toronto, 1995), 12. The notion is also clearly affirmed at *Phd.* 115c and *Rep.* 469d6–9. Alternatively, he may have held that the self consists of the soul using the body as an instrument (*Alc.* I, 130a1–3); the doubtful status of the dialogue in ques-tion, however, makes it difficult to be sure of this.

[5] John Burnet, 'The Socratic Doctrine of the Soul', *Proceedings of the British Academy*, 7 (1916), 235–59.

[6] See e.g. *Euthyd.* 295e4–5, *Charm.* 157a1–b1, *Crito* 47d3–4.

[7] *Gorg.* 493a1–5.   [8] Robinson, *Plato's Psychology*, 16.   [9] *Alc.* I, 131a ff.

[10] For a discussion of the details, see Robinson, *Plato's Psychology*, 9.

This Thracian told me that in these notions of theirs, which I was just now mentioning, the Greek physicians are quite right as far as they go, but Zalmoxis, he added, our king, who is also a god, says further, 'that as you ought not to attempt to cure the eyes without the head, or the head without the body, so neither ought you to attempt to cure the body without the soul. And this,' he said, 'is the reason why the cure of many diseases is unknown to the physicians of Hellas, because they disregard the whole, which ought to be studied also, for the part can never be well unless the whole is well.' For all good and evil, whether in the body or the whole man, originates, as he declared, in the soul, and overflows from thence, as if from the head into the eyes. And therefore if the head and body are to be well, you must begin by curing the soul—that is the first and essential thing.

What is one to make of the concept of soul as it seems to emerge from this passage? If the Thracian doctor's language is meant to be anything like exact, the relationship of soul and body is clearly not one of simple numerical addition, the combination equalling the self or complete person. The key to the relationship (and to the concept of soul itself) seems to be in the phrase 'because they disregard the whole'. This 'whole' could conceivably refer to either (a) the whole *body* or (b) the whole *person*—that is, body and soul combined.

If (a) is the case, Greek doctors are being castigated for despising courses in general physiology; they fail to realize that ailments of particular organs can be adequately diagnosed only in the light of a more general appreciation of the operations of the human body as a whole. However, this hardly squares with the sentences immediately preceding and immediately following, in which clear allusion to 'soul' occurs. So the reference is presumably to (b), and the doctors are being taken to task for failing to appreciate that many ailments are in fact (as we would now say) psychosomatic; potions and poultices will do little to cure the stomach cramp that stems from overpowering guilt feelings or anxiety, and the physiotherapist should know when to give way gracefully to the psychiatrist.

This, if true, is a piece of medical insight antedating a good deal of supposedly modern findings in the field of psychology, but the notion of soul which it seems to entail appears at least as remarkable in its acuteness. For not only is 'soul' being claimed to be the whole person, the relation between soul and body is apparently being claimed to be that of whole to part (in the particular sense, it seems, of biological whole to biological part, such as head to eye, or body to head).[11]

The relationship is in effect one of entailment, and much closer to a monistic account of the soul–body relationship than to a dualistic one. And if the notion of (living) body makes no sense except within the

[11] Ibid. 4–5.

broader context of the soul of which it forms a part, in the way that a living eye (as distinct from a preserved museum piece) makes no sense except in the broader context of the head of which *it* forms a part, the conclusion also seems to follow that the 'broader contexts' in question should be the first concern of investigators, at the risk of putting the cart before the horse if they do otherwise. In the case of medical practice, the approach must be, as we would now say, holistic, the *holon* ('whole') in question being the soul of which body forms a part; or, to put it in Socrates' own direct terms, to cure the *soul* (157a1 ff.), is an indispensable preliminary to any curing of the *body*.

The view is, on the face of it, unique and remarkable; and the type of monism it appears to espouse reverses the normal description (in which *body* is the universally accepted context into which *mind* somehow has to be fitted), and offers us an astonishing alternative, rich in possibilities. Unfortunately, Socrates (or Plato) either failed to see these possibilities, or rejected them in favour of those stemming from an alternative, more overtly dualistic theory. Certainly, but for one possible analogy at the cosmological level in the *Timaeus*,[12] the notion never recurs in the dialogues.

Whether any single one of the above views was that of the historical Socrates, we do not know. To me, the fact that Plato ascribes all three at different times to Socrates suggests that Socrates himself had some difficulty grappling with the problem, offering various tentative solutions—ranging from the purest (arithmetical) dualism of *Gorgias*, 493a1–5, to the mitigated dualism of *Alcibiades* 1 (if it is a genuine Platonic dialogue) to the uniquely formulated monism of the *Charmides*—at different times in his discussions. Of the three, the first is likely to have been the dominant one, however, if the evidence from the myth of the *Gorgias* is to be counted as firm evidence of the views of Socrates himself.[13] Here the soul in the afterlife is in effect a 'counter-person', enjoying all other characteristics of the person in this life except materiality. As such, it is the fully autonomous soul-as-self of the *Protagoras*, a soul that may in space-time periodically 'possess' a physical body, but for which a physical body is no more *part* of it than a violin is 'part' of a violinist. It is also, it seems, *itself alive*, as well as being a *principle* of life, and the life it possesses may also possibly have been thought by

---

[12] At *Tim.* 36d–e Plato talks of the world's body as being fitted by the demiurge within its *soul*, not—as might have been expected—vice versa.

[13] With the exception of the *Gorgias* and *Protagoras*, the dialogues in which myths figure prominently are commmonly considered to be more overtly Platonic in content. Whether such myths were a feature of the conversations of the historical Socrates is very hard to know, but their presence in two major dialogues largely considered to be Socratic in content is to me a small suasion in favour of believing that they were.

Socrates—following again an Orphic pattern of thought—to be either very long-lasting or even eternal.[14]

The word 'possibly' needs to be stressed here, because the Socrates of the *Apology* comes across as agnostic in the matter of an afterlife. If this is the genuine Socrates talking, references in other dialogues to an afterlife may be to an aspect of Orphism accepted (apparently) by Plato, rather than by Socrates himself. On the other hand, there is nothing intrinsically unlikely about Socrates' having himself wavered over the matter, expressing different views at different times; and in this he would not have been the last great philosopher to do so.

As far as the soul's and the body's well-being, or otherwise, is concerned, each, he says in the *Gorgias*, can be characterized by genuine health, pseudo-health, or sickness, a good doctor being needed to cure the pseudo-health, or sickness, of the body, a good judge, or legislator to cure the pseudo-health, or sickness, of the soul. The term he uses for those performing the latter service—*psychēs iatroi* ('healers of the *psychē*')—is a striking neologism, and has of course taken on a brand new life in our own time.

As for what constitutes the specific sickness of the soul, this he says is *vice*, whose cure will be brought about by repressing the *soul's* unsound desires in the way a sick body is cured by the reining in of *its* unsound desires. Sometimes, he says, this may involve drastic measures, such as cautery or surgery, the cautery or surgery for the soul consisting of the heaviest penalties of the *law*.

There are, I think, a number of interesting features about this view. The first is its apparent assumption of a parallelism between soul and body in structure and activities that *prima facie* runs counter to the asymmetry apparently involved in any theory of soul alone as being the real person. The second is its apparent assumption that *both* soul and body are characterized by 'desires' of various types, so much so that it could be dubbed an early version of the 'double-person' theory of the individual (by contrast with the 'person with an instrument' theory). The third is the assumption, common also to the 'person with an instrument' theory, that the soul is the ground of our moral/social/political activity. And the fourth is the notion that 'repression' of certain desires of the soul is valuable therapy.

The *Gorgias* is, by common admission among scholars, a dialogue written very near the end of Plato's 'Socratic' period, and it is possible that many of the above ideas are in fact his own or, if not that, at any

---

[14] The notion of the body as a (temporal) tomb for the soul implies at least the soul's greater *longevity* than the body; and at *Meno* 86a8–b2 Socrates seems satisfied that the slave's supposed pre-knowledge of geometrical truths is in fact evidence for the soul's immortality.

rate adumbrations of his own. However this may be, in the *Phaedo*, written shortly after the *Gorgias* and at the beginning of Plato's so-called metaphysical period, we see, I think, the first clear instance of Plato *himself* grappling with the heritage of Socrates on the question of soul and body. The dramatic setting is Socrates' death cell, during the last hours leading up to his drinking of the hemlock. Simmias and Cebes, Socrates' main interlocutors, are astonished at his cheerfulness in face of death, and equally astonished at his reason for such cheerfulness: that is, his conviction that his real self—his soul—will survive his bodily death, and live on in the state of happiness that is the reward for a life of virtue. Under questioning, Socrates makes it clear that his Orphism, if that is what it is, involves reason as well as simply faith, and a whole series of arguments is set forth to demonstrate, as far as it seems to him possible, that the soul which survives is in fact immortal. The arguments as such, while fascinating, can be passed over here. More important are the many notions of soul that emerge from the dialogue, and some of the problems that they generate.

Socrates' early remarks suggest that he sees the soul as some sort of 'inner person' distinct from the body and reacting in various ways to it. So bodily sensation is said to 'trouble' the soul, which should do its best to 'avoid' it, 'bid farewell' to it, and 'become alone and by itself'. The trouble caused by the body is largely in the cognitive and moral sphere. Among the evils of the body that Socrates numbers, for example, are its 'folly' and 'stupidity', which must be combatted by a soul that he clearly sees as being among other things a principle of cognition (he goes so far at one point as to call it 'intelligence' in a context where the word 'soul' itself would have been a perfectly appropriate locution). That it is also a potential source of moral harm to the soul emerges with clarity when he talks of it as 'contaminating' the soul by its presence, 'filling it up with its lusts' and 'bewitching it with its passions and pleasures'.

Some of these thoughts are, of course, very much in line with what have emerged in earlier dialogues: soul and body are distinct substances, the soul is one's real self, the soul is our source of cognitive and moral activity. Receiving somewhat heavier stress is the notion of the body as an active agent for harm in the body–soul nexus. It is no longer apparently a 'possession' in the neutral way in which an instrument, say, is a possession, but rather something more akin to a counter-person, with its own peculiar pleasures, pains, and desires, all of them at best a nuisance to the soul and at worst something likely to cause significant harm. At one point it is summed up and written off roundly as 'evil'.

This is in fact a much stronger version of what was earlier on, in discussion of the *Gorgias*, called the 'double-person' theory of the individual. What makes it stronger? The first thing is its stress on the soul as being as much a cognitive agent as a moral agent, though, given the generally intellectualist tone of Socratic moral theory, perhaps not too much should be made of this. The second, and more important, thing is the sense of all-out warfare between soul and body and the interests of soul and body; they are no longer viewed as being simply interestingly analogous in their structure and activities. The warfare, it should be added, is seen as being literally to the death; soul will only achieve the life that is authentically its own when finally separated from the body. Meantime, the truly good and just individual will do his utmost to live as though not possessing a body at all.

This somewhat dispiriting, but historically very influential, view of the body–soul relationship is the one that most people carry away from a first reading of the *Phaedo*, and it is true that it is the dominant view in the dialogue. It does, however, sit side by side with other, in many ways conflicting, versions of the soul–body relationship that Plato seems content for the moment to leave unreconciled. At one point in the discussion, for example, he quotes with apparent approval the Orphic doctrine of the body as being a prison-house for the soul (82e2 ff.), a notion analogous to the earlier notion of the body as being a simple physical possession, though now with greater stress on its power to constrain. Elsewhere he talks of the soul in ways that suggest some sort of ectoplasmic fluid permeating and coextensive with the body, an entity which, if sufficiently 'contaminated' or 'infected' by the body, may return to earth later as what most people call a ghost. And elsewhere still (specifically in the first and final arguments for immortality) he talks of soul strictly in terms of its being a life principle or life-carrier; any 'personal' features it may have are, for purposes of the arguments in question, ignored.

As Dodds once said, 'the Classical Age inherited a whole series of inconsistent pictures of the "soul" or "self," '[15] and a good number of these seem to have found their way into the *Phaedo*. (1) On the one hand, soul is strongly argued to be wholly immaterial, and analogous in this regard to the transcendental Forms; on the other hand, the description of it in ectoplasmic terms seems to be a carry-over from an earlier age when it was thought of in more overtly physicalist terms. (2) On the one hand, it is strongly argued to be strictly a unity, without parts, and immune to change, again analogous in this regard to the transcendental Forms; on the other hand, it is seen as our most genuine self, complete with all the complexity and change that go with cognition, desire, decision making, and a whole range of potential pains and pleasures. (3) On the one hand, it is seen as twinned, unnaturally, for an earthly life-

---

[15] E. R. Dodds, *The Greeks and the Irrational* (Berkeley, 1951), 179.

time with a body that is in most respects inimical to its true happiness and interests, which lie in a discarnate, immaterial existence elsewhere; on the other hand, as a life principle, it seems to have as its very essence the animating of the physical. And (4), on the one hand, the soul and the self are said to be one and the same; on the other hand, Socrates talks—possibly loosely—on occasion as though both body *and* soul are possessions of a third entity which—whatever it is—is the *genuine* self.

These varying notions of soul are, on the face of it, not easy to reconcile; but the problem of their reconciliation—if he saw it as a problem—was clearly for Plato of less importance than the main points he was at pains to reinforce, summarizable as follows. Soul is by its nature of greater importance than body in the body–soul nexus; there is an overriding need to care for our genuine self—the soul—over our would-be self—the body; the same soul that is life principle/life-carrier is also itself alive—a person constituting the genuine self and endowed with cognitive faculties and moral sensibility; and the happiness of the soul lies not in anything provided by the world of space-time, but in eternal contemplation of the transcendental Forms.

The conclusion of all this is that for the Socrates of the *Phaedo* the soul–body relationship is in essence *unnatural*. Evidence for this he finds in what seem to him the divergence, and in many instances out-and-out conflict, between 'bodily' desires (for food, drink, and sex) and the desires of the soul (for knowledge and goodness), and between 'bodily' pains and pleasures (attaching to the above-mentioned bodily desires) and the pains and pleasures of the soul (attaching to the above-mentioned desires of the soul). There is no conflict within soul as such, because soul is a simple substance; 'inner' conflict is invariably between body and soul.

In so writing, Plato is at the extreme limit of psychological dualism; in no other dialogue does he express himself in such stark and uncompromising terms about the relationship of soul and body. The degree to which he himself, at the time of writing the dialogue, believed such trenchant dualism to be a genuine description of what is the case or the degree to which it served the *dramatic* purpose of accounting for Socrates' cheerfulness in the face of death will never be known. But one thing we do know. In the dialogue almost certainly immediately subsequent to the *Phaedo*—the *Republic*—he has already moved on to a much more sophisticated description of the soul–body relationship. And to that dialogue we now turn.

In the *Republic* many of the senses of 'soul' that emerged in the *Phaedo* recur, but something very new is a description of it as divided into three parts: reason, 'spiritedness', and gut desire. With this move, Plato has edged away from that *bi*-partition of soul into reason and gut impulse which (with the exception of one argument in the *Phaedo* based on the assumption of its unity and indivisibility) had characterized his antecedent thinking. Whether, however, he progressed or regressed in attempting to separate our non-rational impulses into 'spiritedness' and gut desire has divided, and will probably continue to divide, readers of the dialogue. For many people the 'spiritedness' of which he speaks is not obviously distinguishable from the other non-rational desires, despite his attempts to argue to the contrary; and it is not difficult to argue that it is in fact *invented* as the (implausible) counterpart to one item in the well-known (and much more defensible) political analogue of the soul described at length in the *Republic*—the tripartite state. Whatever the case, tripartition of soul has rightly or wrongly come to be thought of by many as one of the core doctrines of Platonism, and some time should be spent examining it.

One immediately striking feature of the theory is the way in which all three parts of the soul are described in semi-autonomous terms; each has its own desires, pleasures, and pains, often described in such 'personal' detail that one sometimes feels that it is a theory of three inner individuals, not of three parts of one substance. On the assumption, however, that this, like earlier talk of an apparent difference between soul and self,[16] is not to be understood literally, the crucial point emerges that tensions we all feel are not, after all, as the *Phaedo* might have led us to suppose, tensions between soul and body, but tensions *within the soul itself* (a point which, as it happens, is adumbrated in the *Gorgias* (493a1–5), and to which Plato now returns).

Along with this restatement of earlier theory on the nature of our tensions (a statement couched originally in terms of bipartition rather than tripartition of soul, but still the same statement) comes an apparent revaluation of the parts of the soul in terms of the role they each perform. While, on the one hand, Plato is still prepared to say, early on in the dialogue (before the new theory of tripartition has in fact been mentioned), that 'in an individual's soul one element is better, one worse' (431a4–5), by book 9, when his tripartite psychology has been fully articulated, all three parts of soul are now fully recognized as possessing a necessary and worthwhile role in the sound functioning of the whole (586e4–587a1).

A final and critical feature of his reassessed psychology, and a feature that, as it happens, was also foreshadowed in the *Gorgias*, is his apparent abandonment of his *Phaedo* theory of what constitutes *health* of soul and body. For health—seen as a core metaphor for justice—is now carefully described, along the lines of contemporary Greek medicine, as a

---

[16] See above, p. 43.

balance of items within the organism, be that organism the body or the soul. Speaking in the scrupulously functionalist and teleological terms elaborated at the end of book 1, Socrates describes how the right functioning (= health) of the body involves the right functioning of each of the parts composing it; in his own terminology, each part does the job it is meant to do. In like manner, in the just (= healthy) soul health/justice consists in each of the three parts of soul doing the job it is meant to do.

If the rational part of the soul is still for Plato very much the most important part, and possibly the only part that is immaterial and immortal,[17] the necessary role of the other two parts *ici bas* has taken Plato a giant step beyond views propounded earlier on in the *Phaedo*. The body is now no longer viewed as some sort of material counter-person, complete with desires of its own, in opposition to the immaterial person that is the soul. *All* desires are in fact, says Plato, a feature of the *soul*; though many of these will be correctly described as operating *via* the body. And all such desires, if correctly canalized, can be directed to serve the ends of our rational—and ultimately most genuine—selves.

Such canalization, it turns out, is very much a feature of what Plato means by education. This, not surprisingly, consists of whatever techniques seem necessary to bring about and maintain balance among the items comprising the body, balance among the parts comprising the soul, and balance—not warfare—*between* soul and body. Plato has moved, it seems, as far away from the *Phaedo* position as one can possibly move while still calling oneself a psycho-physical dualist.

While that is broadly speaking true, it remains true in regard to only one aspect, albeit a critical one, of Plato's overall theory of soul and body. Other features of the theory have not changed noticeably. Soul and body continue to be thought of as really, not simply logically, distinct; their putative 'addition' would continue to make two. The one continues to be in both the long and the short run more important than the other, despite the revaluation of drives associated with the bodily condition; even physical education is said to be only incidentally for the good of the body, and primarily—in conjuction with *mousikē*—for the good of the *soul*.[18] And in yet another attempt to prove soul's immortality (608c ff.), in which—given so much that was said in the *Phaedo*—one might have expected a clear statement that it is only soul-as-*reason* which is in fact immortal, the discussion is peculiarly unclear; still unwilling, perhaps, to jettison the Orphic view of soul as being a complete person in the life beyond, not just a disembodied intellect, Plato offers an argument of possibly studied ambiguity, in which it has proved very

---

[17] On this point see however below, pp. 52–3.   [18] *Rep.* 411e–412a.

difficult to be sure whether he believes that what survives as a unity is merely soul-as-reason or whether he believes that it is some unified entity comprising within it in some non-material manner all that constituted what was once the tripartite soul.[19] In a word, despite the palpable progress, in the *Republic*, in Plato's thinking about the soul, many facets of the problem of its nature, constitution, and relationship to the body still remain, by the dialogue's end, in a state of (possibly intentional) ambiguity.

Ambiguity is not radical doubt, however, and in the *Timaeus*, which I now think to be a dialogue written near the beginning of Plato's final period of writing,[20] he returns to the topic of soul on a grand scale, arguing at length that all living things are by definition ensouled, and that since the cosmos is a living thing, it too must be ensouled. The latter hypothesis is an intriguing one, and cannot be discussed here, except in passing. As far as human soul is concerned, it is again said to be tripartite, and again apparently, to judge from the wealth of political metaphors drawn directly from the *Republic* discussion, by reference to the same political analogue as in the *Republic*. And again the three parts are located in head, thorax, and belly, respectively.

But there are some differences worth noticing. There is now no doubt which part of soul survives and is immortal; it is reason alone. And the composition of reason, be it that Reason which constitutes the totality of world soul or the reasoning part of human soul, is now described as being in some measure *material*. The move is on the face of it a paradoxical one, given Plato's earlier concerns, in the *Phaedo* and *Republic*, to stress the complete immateriality of (rational) soul. But it does in fact come to grips with a fundamentally problematic aspect of all theories of so-called naïve psycho-physical dualism, and that is the way in which a physical and a wholly non-physical substance are supposed to make contact and cohere. If it could be shown that soul is in some respect immaterial and in some respect also material, this will presumably have done something to minimize that problem. Or so, at any rate, we can speculate; Plato himself does not confront the problem in quite such terms, but rather in terms of his own basic metaphysics and epistemology. The result, however, is the same; even our rational, immortal soul is now thought of as being in some respect material, and as a result its immortal life is described as being, not an eternal immaterial existence among the Forms, but an everlasting material existence of ensoulment, in space and time, of the stars and planets.

---

[19] In *Plato's Psychology* I have argued for the view that he inclined towards the Orphic view; for the counter-case see R. A. Shiner, 'Soul in *Rep.* X, 611', *Apeiron*, 6 (1972), 23–30.

[20] Robinson, *Plato's Psychology*, pp. xiv–xv.

Whether wittingly or unwittingly, Plato appears to have here pulled together two apparently divergent views of soul—the one material, the other immaterial—that emerged first in the *Phaedo*, and in such a way as to give credence to both. Fashioned deliberately by the demiurge in such a way as to possess (a) an 'intermediate' type of reality between the absolute reality of the transcendental Forms and the semi-reality of objects in space-time, and (b) 'intermediate' versions of those features of Sameness and Difference which allow us to offer basic epistemological judgements, (rational) soul is now by its very structure shown to have a natural affinity for *both* of Plato's universes and an ability, under optimal circumstances, to achieve a maximal understanding of each. In the case of the world of Forms, this understanding will be at the level of knowledge; in the case of the world of space-time, at the level of true opinion.

Along with this remarkable clarification of soul's 'amphibian' status (a status implicit in Orphic accounts of transmigration, but now defended for the first time by Plato as a belief—like the belief in immortality—that is supportable by explicitly philosophical argument) comes an equally remarkable and little-noticed attempt to make overall sense of the fact of ensoulment as such, be it human, animal, or vegetal. Passing over (if not explicitly rejecting) standard Orphic accounts of ensoulment as being the result of either some collective 'Fall' or individual sin, or both, and picking up the idea first adumbrated in the Myth of Er (*Republic* 10) that *we* are responsible for the life we are born into—'God is not to blame'—Plato argues that in the beginning the demiurge created all souls equal. Though there is some small doubt about the detail of his argument,[21] he appears to say that the first generation of humans created by the demiurge and his helper-gods was totally male. As they died off and were duly reincarnated, those among them who had lived a 'cowardly' and, in more general terms, morally unsatisfactory[22] life were reincarnated as women(!); those who had lived at various levels of *stupidity* were reincarnated as various types of bird or animal.

If the above implies what it appears to imply, Plato's researches into

---

[21] At 90e6–7 he writes in such a way as to suggest that the differentiation into male and female was instituted by the demiurge at the very beginning; and the same might be said of an earlier passage at 41e–42a. But this seems to be a slip on Plato's part, running clean counter as it does to the general drift of the argument, in which all are given an equal chance at the beginning by the demiurge (41e4). See also the evidence of 91d7 (*andrōn*, 'males'), where he appears to be continuing a discussion of the various punishments meted out to erstwhile males, and along with it that of 42b3–c1, where once again only males appear to be in question.

[22] Literally, 'unjust'. The sense, however, as in the *Republic*, seems to be a very broad one, covering the whole range of non-virtuous action.

the nature of soul and body have led him into a description of the whole of the natural world as being in its various classes (including, it seems, among humans the entire class of women) different instances of what might be called 'appropriate degradation' for the housing of the souls of males undergoing punishment of one form or another as described above. It is a bizarre and distressing twist on the theory of transmigration that I have been unable to track down to any clear source, Orphic, Pythagorean, Zoroastrian, or Hindu, and hence *faute de mieux* tentatively posit as either Plato's own or possibly that of the renegade Pythagorean Philolaus, on whose (lost) works there is some reason for believing that much of the *Timaeus* was based. What began as a strong statement of the fairness of the demiurge in regard to all humans has led Plato into very strange terrain, where the problems elicited may well have come to be perceived by him as being perhaps greater than those he thought he was solving. If a particular Serengeti lion is the reincarnation of a particular Masai warrior, does it possess both a lion-soul and the warrior's human soul or only a lion's soul, or only the warrior's soul? All answers to the question create problems for one who believes, as any adherent of the doctrine of transmigration must, that a 'good' life as a lion (whatever that can possibly mean) warrants a step up on the ladder of lives—to the level of, say, a woman—or a 'bad' life as a lion warrants a step down, perhaps to the level of a squirrel or a snail.

As for the overall notion of 'appropriate degradation', in the case of women this seems to refer to features of both body *and* soul; they are, says Plato elsewhere in the dialogue, less physically strong[23] than males, and in the immediate context (and elsewhere in the dialogues) he also avers, as we have seen, that they tend in soul towards morally unacceptable behaviour, especially cowardice. The conclusion here, as distressing as the conclusions drawn above, appears to be that Plato— adopting an unambiguous stance in a controversy that is still with us— thinks that there is a 'natural' difference between male and female human souls analogous to the difference in their bodily strength, and that the difference is one involving the natural moral superiority of the male. In keeping with earlier Socratic doctrine that the worst thing one can do to a person is to make that person *morally worse* as a person, Plato has now come up with an argument (of sorts) to show that the appropriate punishment for the soul of a man who has demonstrated moral fault is to run the risk—by association—of yet further moral degradation by being incarnated in the body of a creature of intrinsically less moral worth than himself—that of a woman.

[23] Cf. 42a2. But the reference could be to the supposedly greater moral goodness of males; the comparative adjective *kreittōn* is, here as elsewhere, ambiguous as to whether it is to be understood as meaning physically stronger or morally better, or both.

It would be easy, but perhaps too easy, to write off the above as being purely 'mythical' and nothing that one so sophisticated as Plato could possibly have subscribed to. For, in a later dialogue, the *Laws* (944d8–e2), he says, after mentioning how Caeneus of Thessaly had once been a woman but had been transformed by a god into a man, 'Were the reverse process, transformation from man to woman, possible, that in a way would be of all penalties the properest for the man who has flung his shield away.' Whether or not he is in this statement suggesting a move away from the doctrine of metempsychosis, and in particular the remarkable version of the doctrine to be found in the *Timaeus*, his feelings about women being creatures of appropriate moral degradation to serve as prison-houses for cowardly males undergoing punishment have clearly in no way changed.[24]

It would be unfortunate to leave the *Timaeus* on such a dispiriting note, however, since it also happens to be a dialogue in which some remarkably penetrating things on psychosomatic disorder are said. After a brief discussion of bodily ailments, Timaeus continues (86b1–87a7):

Such is the manner in which disorders of the body arise; disorders of the soul caused by the bodily condition arise in the following way. It will be granted that folly is disorder of the soul; and of folly there are two kinds, madness and stupidity. Accordingly, any affection that brings on either of these must be called a disorder; and among the gravest disorders for the soul we must rank excessive pleasures and pains. . . . For the most part of his life he is maddened by these intense pleasures and pains; and when his soul is rendered sick and senseless by the body he is commonly held to be not sick but deliberately bad. . . . the truth is that sexual intemperance is a disorder of the soul arising, to a great extent, from the condition of a single substance [the marrow: T. M. Robinson] which, owing to the porousness of the bones, floods the body with its moisture. We might almost say, indeed, of all that is called incontinence in pleasure, that it is not justly made a reproach, as if men were willingly bad. No one is willingly bad; the bad man becomes so because of some faulty habit of body and unenlightened upbringing, and these are unwelcome afflictions that come to any man against his will.

Again, where pains are concerned, the soul likewise derives much badness from the body. When acid and salt phlegms or bilious humours roam about the body and, finding no outlet, are pent up within and fall into confusion by blending the vapour that arises from them with the motion of the soul, they induce all manner of disorders of the soul of greater or lesser intensity and extent. Making their way to the three seats of the soul, according to the region they severally invade, they beget divers types of ill-temper and despondency, of rashness and cowardice, of dulness and oblivion.

[24] For further evidence of Plato's stance on the matter see (depressingly) *Laws* 781a–d.

After a brief discussion of bad education, familial and political, he concludes (87b3–8):

> ...that is how all of us who are bad become so, through two causes that are altogether against the will. For these the blame must fall upon the parents rather than the offspring, and upon those who give, rather than those who receive, nurture. Nevertheless, a man must use his utmost endeavour, by means of education, pursuits, and study, to escape from badness and lay hold upon its contrary.

It is a remarkable short essay on (to coin a phrase) somato-psychic (as distinct from psychosomatic) disorder, and the relationship between such disorder and ongoing moral responsibility. It also has the distinction of being, despite its insights and importance, very little read, even by those claiming some knowledge of Plato. And close on its heels comes a brief account of psychosomatic disorder, a portion of which again (of no small interest to those involved in education!) deserves quotation (87e6–88a7):

> When the soul is too strong for the body and of ardent temperament, she dislocates the whole frame and fills it with ailments from within; she wastes it away, when she throws herself into study and research; in teaching and controversy, public or private, she inflames and racks its fabric through the rivalries and contentions that arise, and bringing on rheums deludes most so-called physicians into laying blame on the unoffending part.

Just how far Plato has apparently come in these matters can be gauged by a brief glance back at the *Gorgias*, where, as we saw, soul and body are viewed as strictly parallel entities, each with its appropriately and meticulously defined states of health and sickness, and each curable in a manner appropriate to its form of sickness, psychic or somatic; if at the time he had views on any putative contact between the two, his silence on the matter is palpable.

Not, of course, that soul and body do not continue to operate for Plato as parallel substances, along with the concomitant claim that of the two one is intrinsically more important than the other (89d4–7). In concluding his discussion of psychosomatic and somato-psychic disorder, for example, he remarks that the best preventive medicine consists in physical motion or exercise for the body and non-physical exercise (= contemplation) for the soul. It is a doctrine of *mens sana in corpore sano*, and like so much else in these closing passages of the *Timaeus* has become so familiar as to seem simply truistic. But in its day such thinking was revolutionary.

In another critical respect Plato's views also appear to have changed with the years, and that is in regard to the very definition of soul itself. In the *Phaedrus*, a dialogue written, I believe, not too long after the

Timaeus, Plato comes up with a remarkable new definition of (rational) soul as 'self-moving motion' (245c–246a). And with this definition—dry and lifeless as it may at first sight appear—he finally, after a lifetime of writing on the general topic, comes to grips with the question that many a sceptical friend must have posed: namely, why 'soul' is needed to account for any living thing at all, human or otherwise. Could not the atomists have been right all along, all that exists being the transient conjunctions of randomly moving bits of matter in space? In his carefully formulated reply Plato reiterates his view of the causal connection of movement and life, a living thing being distinguished from a non-living one by its power of (in some weak sense of the term) 'self-motion'. In this all Greeks, however unsophisticated, would have agreed with him. But the next argument would have left all but a few of them far behind, for he then argues that there is a *cause* or trigger for such (misleadingly named) self-movement, and that this cause or trigger is the *genuine* self-movement of (*rational*) soul.

Such genuine self-movement being for Plato self-evidently without a beginning in time, he then goes on to argue that the rational soul is both immortal and—more significantly, perhaps, in terms of its implications for action—eternal. For up to now Plato had argued that soul had a temporal beginning—indeed, that the point in time of its formation by the demiurge was the first point *of* time. Within this general framework, soul was seen as the creation and servant of a god/gods who served as the arbiters of its actions. At a stroke, the entire picture is called into question with the new definition, for rational soul is an uncreated entity, it appears, and as eternal as the gods themselves.

As so often, however, in Plato, a new and provocative idea goes hand in hand with a relatively conservative one barely, if at all, compatible with it. Instead of the expected survey of the possibly explosive implications for action of the newly formulated definition, Plato offers us a famous mythical description of the soul in terms of a charioteer and two horses that is in large measure a repetition of the tripartite soul theory of the *Republic* and the *Timaeus*.[25] And in the same context he describes reincarnation in the time-honoured terms of a fall, though now the world beyond is in fact his own world of Forms, and the incarnate soul itself is described as being like an oyster in a shell, in much the same way as, earlier on, in the *Phaedo*, it had been described as being imprisoned (*Phaedrus* 250c6; *Phaedo* 82e3). As for conduct, nothing is said to suggest that the new definition of rational soul has changed Plato's basic

---

[25] It is, however, not purely repetition. The fact that the good horse and the charioteer are practically indistinguishable in terms of their (rational) desires and actions suggests that Plato is on the verge of returning to his former belief in the basic *bi*partition of soul into reason and impulse.

stance on the matter; our prime concern, in a world where we are told, confusingly, both that 'all *soul* has the care of all that is inanimate' (246b6) and that *Zeus* 'orders and cares for all things' (246e5–6), our primary obligation remains the care for a morally sound (= 'balanced') soul, a soul that is in its rational aspect at any rate our real self. Though even on this latter point we are left by Plato in a state of by now familiar ambiguity. For the discarnate soul of the *Phaedrus* myth looks very much like the soul as described in so many other eschatological myths of Plato—that is, a soul such that all of its features appear to survive, not just its reason. And Plato, as in previous dialogues, offers no hint of any desire to clarify the situation, or of whether he even considers clarification desirable. For this we have to wait till the tenth book of what may well have been his last work, the *Laws*.

Here he restates his position, first set out in the *Phaedrus*, that the source of all motion is eternal self-moving soul, but this time the claim has been broadened to cover *all* soul, not simply—as the *Phaedrus* argument in context appeared to imply—rational soul. It is also stressed that the 'movement' in question is not simply the physical movement associated with organic life; the 'movements' of soul are now for the first time listed comprehensively as 'wish, reflection, foresight, counsel, judgment, true, or false, pleasure, pain, hope, fear, hate, love, and whatever kindred, or primary motions there might be' (897a1–4).

An ambiguity in the *Phaedrus* concerning the soul's ontological status has been crucially resolved. There, it will be remembered, Plato wrote of soul and Zeus in a manner suggesting that both were independent eternal entities, neither contingent upon the other, and each of them apparently performing an identically comprehensive 'caring' role in the total scheme of things. Now it is clarified that soul, while being self-moving and eternal, is so in a context of eternal dependence for its eternal *genesis* upon a transcendental divine principle. What had appeared at first sight to be a case of the eternally non-contingent status of (rational) soul has now been clarified as the eternally *contingent* status of *all* soul. But even here, to the end, Plato remains teasingly enigmatic. If, as seems at least possible, the transcendental divine principle is itself supposed to be a soul, the universality of his contingency claim is in turn apparently called into question.

This takes us into areas of Platonic metaphysics that would have to be discussed elsewhere, but enough has already been said to make the point that, to the end, Plato is an explorer in the area of philosophical psychology, as in so many other areas of speculation. Nowhere, it seems to me, is this clearer than in the *Laws*, which in terms of his views on soul and body is almost a compendium of the views he has elaborated over a writing lifetime. I say 'almost', because the tripartition of soul is a view that exists now only as a set of *disiecta membra* of the original idea; the old bipartition into reason and impulse that served Plato so well until the writing of the *Republic* seems to have returned as his favoured model of psychic structure. Apart from this—and of course the remarkable view of soul as self-moving mover first elaborated in the *Phaedrus*—the picture of soul is very much that found in earlier dialogues, where, as I have put it elsewhere,[26] 'life is a process of purification (from the body) and assimilation to the divine (716c–e); the soul is the true self and enjoys personal immortality (959b3–4); the just are rewarded in a future life, and there are sanctions reserved for the wicked; a basic substantial distinction of soul and body is taken for granted, and 'pleasures' are once again treated with distrust' (672d8–9, 727c1 ff., etc.); and elements of the soul are again unqualifiedly described as being 'good' and 'bad' (904b2–3), despite the careful revaluation of these views in *Republic* 9 and the *Philebus*.

A further view of soul in the *Laws* is worth a mention, and that is the notion that as a life force it consists of some sort of *Stoff* permeating and guiding the physical universe as a whole and all living entities within it. As such, it is ethically and intellectually neutral, only taking on ethical and intellectual colour when it operates 'with wisdom as its helper' or when it 'companies with folly' (897b1–3). The view is in many ways a slightly refined version of the somewhat ectoplasmic view of soul that first occurred in the *Phaedo*, and it takes its place in the *Laws* as one of a number of competing views that present themselves for our comparative inspection, in much the same way as they first did in the *Phaedo*.

For some readers of Plato, this apparent willingness to return to his youthful views, contradictions and all, bypassing so much in the way of careful correction and elucidation that had characterized such dialogues as the *Republic*, *Timaeus*, and *Phaedrus*, has been a source of scandal. So much so that one author, finding the whole dialogue a parody of Plato's philosophy, has argued that it is in fact not Plato's work at all.[27] But the conclusion is an extravagant one. Far from working to Plato's disadvantage, the clear unwillingness he shows to reduce to some sort of artificial order a set of concepts of soul that are probably intrinsically irreconcilable is probably better seen as a sign of his philosophical strength. Certainly, the fact that in some of his middle and later dialogues he made such apparent progress on so many matters suggests that he grew increasingly aware, if he was not aware from the beginning, of some of the problems involved in his earlier formulations of the nature of soul and the nature of the soul–body relationship. That in old age he felt the need to question whether what had seemed like progress

---

[26] Robinson, *Plato's Psychology*, 145.
[27] G. Mueller, *Studien zu den platonischen Nomoi* (Munich, 1951), 190.

in those dialogues really *was* so *may* of course be a sign of increasing senile decrepitude on his part. But it seems equally, if not more reasonably, assignable to a determination on his part, when in doubt, to leave his options open; the determination, in fact, of a man who, whatever the topic, opted to the end to express himself on the matter in the open-ended form of dialogue, not the dogmatic form of treatise.

Nowhere, it seems to me, is this more evident than in a passage at *Laws* 898e8–899a4. Having spent a lifetime discussing various aspects of the soul–body relationship, he returns to the topic for one last time, possibly just before his death. Taking the sun as his example of an ensouled object, he mentions three possible ways in which its soul might control its body: from within, as does 'our own soul'; from without; or by 'guiding' it in some other mysterious way 'stripped of body and in possession of other wonderful powers'. To the end he is wrestling with the problem that lies at the heart of all psycho-physical dualism, the problem of relating a physical substance to an immaterial one, and to the end he openly admits his bafflement. It is a splendid memorial to his intellectual honesty.

3

Aristotle's Psycho-physiological Account of the Soul–Body Relationship

PHILIP J. VAN DER EIJK

I. INTRODUCTION

Aristotle's remarks on the soul and its relationship to the body, perhaps more than those of any other ancient philosopher, continue to be welcomed as stimulating contributions to contemporary debate in the philosophy of mind and the cognitive sciences. Indeed, no modern reader with an interest in philosophical psychology will fail to be impressed by the high degree of conceptual sophistication Aristotle displays on such topics as perception, awareness, memory, dreaming, imagination, desire, thinking, and on the involvement of physical factors in all these processes, his work at times presenting striking similarities to some of the approaches taken in the modern debate.

Yet, somewhat paradoxically, it has thus far proved impossible to reach scholarly agreement on a definition of Aristotle's theory of the soul in terms of any of the positions on the mind–body problem currently recognized (dualist, materialist, functionalist, etc.).[1] And this is not just a problem that arises from the more general difficulty of matching an ancient philosopher to a modern philosophical view. For, when it comes to summing up the Aristotelian position by piecing together the relevant statements the philosopher makes in a variety of contexts in his psychological, biological, ethical, and rhetorical writings, the evidence does not always point in the same direction.

Thus a superficial reading of Aristotle's works may easily give the

---

[1] The secondary literature on Aristotle's position on the mind–body problem and its relevance to contemporary issues is very large indeed. The recent collection of essays edited by M. C. Nussbaum and A. Oksenberg Rorty, *Essays on Aristotle's De Anima* (Oxford, 1992), gives an impression of the various approaches, and contains an extensive bibliography on the subject. An introductory selection of essays with analytical bibliography is offered by J. Barnes, M. Schofield, and R. Sorabji (eds.), *Articles on Aristotle*, iv: *Psychology and Aesthetics* (London, 1979). See also G. E. R. Lloyd and G. E. L. Owen (eds.), *Aristotle on Mind and the Senses* (Cambridge, 1978).

impression of a philosopher who on the one hand seems to reduce the soul to a kind of highly sophisticated programme of functions embedded in the physical material of the body—a set of capacities a living body can exercise—yet on the other hand does not seem to abandon altogether the distinction between soul and body as two discrete entities, and seems to reserve a special status for the intellect as something that somehow transcends the psycho-physical unity of the living, ensouled body. And while on the whole he seems to present the soul as something abstract, a form or pattern, we will see that on some occasions he seems to be suggesting that it is actually a spatially extended entity which is located somewhere in the body, and *in* which certain things take place. Further, although he usually presents the conjunction between the soul and the body as a harmonious, co-operative relationship, there are also passages where he seems to assume a tension between the two, in which the one fails to 'master' the 'disobedient' other.

One explanation for these difficulties has been to say that Aristotle has not fully succeeded in making up his mind on the mind–body problem, and is torn in different directions by conflicting tendencies in his philosophical personality—tendencies that are, at least partly, related to the intellectual traditions in which he stood. In the spirit of the present collection of essays, one might consider describing this tension in terms of the 'metaphysician' versus the 'physician'. On the one hand, Aristotle inherited from his philosophical predecessors (especially Parmenides and Plato) a profound interest in metaphysics, an area for which he coined the term 'first philosophy',[2] and in which the subject of the soul, with its lofty connotations of immortality and transcendence, occupied a prominent place. This may have led him to the assumption of an incorporeal and immortal intellectual power, the *nous*, which enters the natural soul–body composite 'from outside' (*thyrathen*),[3] and whose activity does not involve a bodily substrate. It certainly led him to the firm belief—within his psychology no less than in his philosophy as a whole—in the fundamental supremacy of form over matter, of the soul as a formative, 'active' principle over the body as a material, 'passive' substrate, and—in his biological investigations of the structure and behaviour of ensouled living beings—of formal explanations 'from the top down' over material explanations 'from the bottom up'. Thus, even in Aristotle's detailed discussions of the suitability of certain bodily parts for the 'psychic' functions a living being has to perform—for example, the hand's suitability for touching, grasping, handling all sorts of objects, and performing a variety of complex operations—he rarely

---

[2] e.g. *De anima* (*An.*) 403b16; *Physics* 192a36.
[3] *Generation of Animals* (*GA*) 736a28.

fails to point out that these bodily parts are made of certain material and possess their particular shape because of the purpose (*telos*) for which they exist—namely the exercise of a 'psychic', that is, vital function, which in turn serves a higher purpose in the wider framework of the natural world of which the organism is a part.

At the same time, Aristotle was also the son of a physician. Even though he himself did not engage in medical practice, as far as we know, he certainly had a vivid interest in medical theory, and was well aware of Hippocratic and other bio-medical doctrines.[4] These doctrines influenced him in several ways, and he reviewed them elaborately in his biological and physiological writings.[5] These writings have a very down-to-earth perspective, concerned as they are with the technical and at times repulsive nitty-gritty of anatomy and physiology, from the most advanced to the most primitive kinds of life. Yet, 'there are gods here, too,' as Heraclitus said,[6] and for the natural philosopher there are 'formal' principles to be discerned and goals to be identified in the domain of biology, just as in the more consciously rational spheres of human action and cognition, or in the ethereal realms of the movements of the celestial bodies. For, in Aristotle's view, the soul is at work in plants and primitive animal species no less than in man. Indeed, his biological writings can be seen as one sustained testimony to his great interest in the variety of manifestations of psycho-physiological activity which the animal (and plant) kingdoms display, and to his tireless efforts to explain the physical make-up of animals (and plants)—their structure and bodily 'parts'—in relation to the psychic powers they serve (nutrition, reproduction, perception, desire, locomotion, etc.), or, in other words, to account teleologically for the structure of the 'organic bodies', the 'matter' to which the soul is related as the 'form'—and indeed the purpose, or *telos*.[7]

---

[4] On Aristotle's acquaintance with medical theory see C. Oser-Grote, *Aristoteles und das Corpus Hippocraticum* (forthcoming). See also the bibliography listed in P. J. van der Eijk, 'Aristotle on "Distinguished Physicians" and the Medical Significance of Dreams', in P. J. van der Eijk, H. F. J. Horstmanshoff, and P. H. Schrijvers (eds.), *Ancient Medicine in its Socio-cultural Context* (Amsterdam and Atlanta, 1995), ii, 447–59.

[5] These are *History of Animals* (*HA*), *Parts of Animals* (*PA*), *Generation of Animals*, *On the Movement of Animals* (*MA*), *On the Progression of Animals*, and the *Parva Naturalia*, as well as the lost work *On Plants*. To some extent also *On the Soul* belongs to these works, although its status is somewhat ambiguous. For a discussion of the relationship between psychology, physiology, biology, and zoology in Aristotle's works see P. J. van der Eijk, 'The Matter of Mind: Aristotle on the Biology of "Psychic" Processes and the Bodily Aspects of Thinking', in W. Kullmann and S. Föllinger (eds.), *Aristotelische Biologie: Intentionen, Methoden, Ergebnisse* (Stuttgart, 1997), 231–58, esp. 232–5.

[6] *PA* 645a22–3.

[7] Cf. G. E. R. Lloyd, 'Aspects of the Relationship between Aristotle's Psychology and his Zoology', in Nussbaum and Oksenberg Rorty (eds.), *Essays*, 147–68.

Furthermore, as these biological writings—and to some extent also his *Ethics*—testify, Aristotle's medical interests may also have made him more amenable to a recognition of what may go wrong in the soul–body relationship, and of the different levels on which things may go wrong. For although Nature, as Aristotle puts it, arranges everything for the best, some species of animals are 'more perfect' than others in the psychic organizational apparatus with which they are endowed; and within one species, some individuals, or 'types' of individuals (such as, within the human species, the so-called melancholics),[8] are less perfect than others; and, of course, one and the same individual can have his better or worse moments when it comes to the exercise of his psychic faculties. The analysis of these degrees of perfection, of the mechanisms of error and degeneration, and their categorization in terms of imperfections that are 'natural' (*kata physin*) or 'unnatural' (*para physin*), occupy a significant amount of Aristotle's attention, and lead him to consider a wide range of causal factors, many of a physical, material nature. What role, if any, these factors play in the normal, successful operation of these psychic functions is not always made clear. But the overall picture suggests that Aristotle believes that bodily agents can be both impeding and facilitating factors at all levels of 'psychic' activity, including the workings of the intellect, that they may engender a certain element of tension in the otherwise so harmonious relation between the soul and the body, and that this imbalance needs to be corrected by a number of dietetic, moral, and educational measures in order to fit the human being for the kind of life that is appropriate to it.[9]

Against this background of biological and medical interests, Aristotle's seemingly 'dualist' remarks on the soul, especially on the status of the intellect, have often been explained as an uncomfortably persisting Platonizing tendency, which can be paralleled by similar tendencies in Aristotle's philosophical anthropology in the *Nicomachean Ethics*. For, in Aristotle's moral and social philosophy, man is on the one hand portrayed as a being of flesh and blood, who is naturally inclined to take part in society and to engage in social relationships with others, but on the other hand is said to aspire to the divine, by abandoning all temporal and ephemeral concerns and focusing on the exercise of his intellect in a solitary life of philosophical contemplation.[10] Underlying these tensions we may, perhaps, perceive a basic conflict in Aristotle's views on such existential questions as man's place in the world and his relation-

---

[8] On this see p. 76 below; see also P. J. van der Eijk, 'Aristoteles über die Melancholie', *Mnemosyne*, 43 (1990), 33–72.

[9] On this see the excellent discussion by T. J. Tracy, *Physiological Theory and the Doctrine of the Mean in Plato and Aristotle* (The Hague and Paris, 1969).

[10] *Nicomachean Ethics* (*EN*) X. 7–8.

ship to the natural and the supernatural. On the one hand, his biological interests lead Aristotle to regard man as a 'rational animal' and to approach him, as it were, 'from the bottom up'—that is, as the culmination of an elaborate *scala naturae* ascending from plants via various levels of animals to the human being. Yet there are also passages where he portrays man as fundamentally and categorically different from animals, and akin to the gods, possessed by a strong inclination to abandon, or at least to ascend temporarily from, his natural body, and to immortalize himself.[11] Such existential conflicts, familiar from Plato's *Republic* and *Phaedo*, lead a more subdued life in Aristotle's philosophy, but they are by no means absent, and it is a matter of debate whether Aristotle himself—quite apart from his interpreters—considered them as finally resolved.[12]

It is an intriguing question whether these conflicting tendencies represent different stages in Aristotle's philosophical development, as scholarship of the mid-twentieth century used to assume, or whether they coexisted side by side during the whole of his philosophical activity, as seems to be the more current view; but I will not attempt to answer this question in the present essay.[13] An important source of the problem

[11] e.g. *EN* 1177b26 ff.; 1178b24 ff.

[12] Thus Aristotle's notion of 'innate pneuma', a material substance in the body mediating between the soul and the body and being somehow related to the ethereal fire of the universe (*GA* 737a1), has sometimes been explained as an effort to solve this problem.

[13] For a convenient summary of the older discussion—initiated by F. Nuyens (*L'Évolution de la psychologie d'Aristote* (Louvain, 1948)) and applied to the *Parva Naturalia* by H. J. Drossaart Lulofs (*Aristotelis De insomniis et De divinatione per somnum* (Leiden, 1947)) and I. Block ('The Order of Aristotle's Psychological Writings', *American Journal of Philology*, 82 (1961), 50–77)—see W. W. Fortenbaugh, 'Recent Scholarship on the Psychology of Aristotle', *Classical World*, 60 (1967), 316–27. The compatibility of 'instrumentalism' and 'hylomorphism' was stressed by C. Kahn, 'Sensation and Consciousness in Aristotle's Psychology', repr. in Barnes, Schofield, and Sorabji (eds.), *Articles*, 1–31, and by C. Lefèvre, *Sur l'évolution d'Aristote en psychologie* (Louvain, 1972), and *idem*, 'Sur le statut de l'âme dans le De Anima et les Parva Naturalia', in Lloyd and Owen (eds.), *Aristotle on Mind*, 21–67, and for the *Parva Naturalia* by J. Wiesner, 'The Unity of the De somno and the Physiological Explanation of Sleep', ibid. 241–80, and H. Wijsenbeek-Wijler, *Aristotle's Concept of Soul, Sleep, and Dreams* (Amsterdam, 1976). See also W. F. R. Hardie, 'Aristotle's Treatment of the Relation between the Soul and the Body', *Philosophical Quarterly*, 14 (1964), 53–72; T. J. Tracy, 'Heart and Soul in Aristotle', in J. Anton and A. Preus (eds.), *Essays in Ancient Greek Philosophy*, ii (Albany, NY, 1983), 321–39; G. Verbeke, 'Doctrine du pneuma et entéléchisme chez Aristote', in Lloyd and Owen (eds.), *Aristotle on Mind*, 191–214; E. Hartman, *Substance, Body and Soul: Aristotelian Investigations* (Princeton, 1977); D. K. W. Modrak, *Aristotle: The Power of Perception* (Chicago, 1987); and G. Freudenthal, *Aristotle's Theory of Material Substance: Heat and Pneuma, Form and Soul* (Oxford, 1995). This is not to say that developmental approaches to Aristotle's psychology have entirely disappeared: see e.g. W. Welsch, *Aisthesis: Grundzüge und Perspektiven der Aristotelischen Sinneslehre* (Stuttgart, 1987), and I. Block, 'Aristotle on the Common Sense: A Reply to Kahn and Others', *Ancient*

lies in the fact that Aristotle's extant writings do not give us a complete picture of his views, and, furthermore, at least a number of the apparent contradictions are due to the fact that differences in contextual strategies require him to comment on different aspects of the same topic. For, when writing about the soul, Aristotle is not always wearing the same hat; he himself is clearly aware of this when he says that it is different to approach the subject of the soul from a biological rather than a metaphysical or indeed an ethical or rhetorical point of view[14]— a difference that manifests itself not only in the questions that are being asked, but also in the degree of exactitude that can be achieved and the amount of technical detail that needs to be covered. Thus Aristotle's main psychological works, the *De anima* and parts of the *Parva naturalia* (a series of short essays on sensation, memory, sleep, dreams, and respiration which follows on the *De anima*), present an investigation that is explicitly conducted within the framework of natural philosophy—that is, physics, physiology, and biology—which has important implications for the kind of remarks we can expect him to make. His approach here, although heavily laden with philosophical terminology, is a bit like that of modern physiological psychology, focusing as it does on how organisms behave and react to the stimuli they are subjected to and on their various cognitive performances. There is hardly any discussion of issues concerning 'the self', 'personhood', 'identity', 'character', or the more general aspects of moral psychology. The *Nicomachean Ethics* is more informative on such subjects, but the difficulty is that the hierarchy of soul 'parts' there is rather different from that of *De anima*, and it is not easy to see how the two accounts are to be reconciled.[15] A further complicating factor is that it is not always easy to distinguish between passages in which Aristotle is speaking about how things are and passages in which he is discussing how things should be.

In the light of these considerations, the modern scholarly approach is to start from the assumption that Aristotle's remarks in various contexts are complementary, and that we must simply accept the fact that on some occasions he remains silent on aspects of the material on which he is on other occasions quite explicit, or indeed on subjects that receive so much attention on some occasions that we may be surprised on other occasions not to find them mentioned. Whether, in this scenario, all the

---

Philosophy, 8 (1988), 235–50. The problem is slightly different in the case of the apparently dualistic psychology of Aristotle's (lost) dialogues, most notably the *Eudemus*. However, these survive only in fragments and in indirect reports that are probably coloured by the Platonizing perspective that set in in the Hellenistic Peripatetic school.

[14] Cf. *EN* 1102a24 ff.; *PA* 641a18–b10; *An.* I 1.

[15] See e.g. *EN* I 13 and VI 2. On the psychological theory of the *Ethics* and the *Rhetoric* see W. W. Fortenbaugh, *Aristotle on Emotion* (London, 1975).

apparent difficulties would ultimately have been soluble if his works had survived intact, or if he had chosen to arrange what he wanted to say in a different way—indeed, in such a way as to give a clear answer to the questions raised above—is unfathomable. Still, the problems should not be overstated, and there certainly are a number of reasonably coherent psychological tenets that can be taken as characteristic of Aristotle's views on the soul–body relationship, and which distinguish him from most of his predecessors and contemporaries.

II. HYLOMORPHISM

Perhaps the most fundamental tenet of Aristotle's theory is his opinion that soul and body are not separate entities, but two mutually complementary and inseparably connected aspects—the 'form' (*morphē*, *eidos*) and the 'matter' (*hylē*)—of one and the same entity—namely a living being.[16] Consequently, Aristotle holds, the philosophical analysis of all activities of a living being (*qua* living being) must take account of both their formal and their material aspects. I refer to 'aspects', because they are not to be seen as physically separable 'parts', but can be distinguished only in our thinking and talking about them:[17] in reality, they form an inseparable unity. Accordingly, the soul is called 'the first *entelecheia* of a natural body that has the potential to live' (*An.* 412a27–8). *Entelecheia* is a technical term connoting both 'essence' and 'fulfilment': it is the full realization of what something is intended to be. The soul is called the *first* entelechy, because Aristotle makes a distinction between possessing a vital function (such as perception) and using it (which would be the 'second' entelechy): it is the possessing of these vital functions that distinguishes a living being from a corpse, which is a body 'in name only'; even if the living being does not use such a vital function— for example, when it is asleep—it still possesses it.[18]

Thus the soul is not just the life force, but also the dynamic structure and the organizational pattern according to which, and for the purpose of which, the physical body is shaped, constituted, and internally arranged.[19] This is, in rough outline, the 'hylomorphic' view of the body–soul relationship for which Aristotle is well known, and which makes his theory look so surprisingly modern. It also implies not only that the conjunction between the body and the soul is necessary for life to exist, but also that it is a natural and good relation: it is how the natural world and natural living beings are intended to be. This means

---

[16] The following account is primarily based on *An.* II 1, esp. 412a19–21 and 27–8.
[17] Cf. *An.* III 9, 432a22 ff.   [18] *An.* 417a21–b2.   [19] *PA* 645b15–28.

that the tension, or indeed the downright hostility and alienation, between the soul and the body, which is so characteristic of much of Plato's theory, is absent in Aristotle. Not only does the body need the soul in order to exist, but the soul needs the body's structures in order to operate: 'psychic' powers such as perception and locomotion need the sense-organs and limbs to become operational, and these sense-organs and limbs must be suitable. The connection between a specific psychic power and a specific bodily organ is not arbitrary, but entirely intentional and adequate.

Furthermore, as I have suggested above, Aristotle has a remarkably broad notion of the soul: it encompasses plants, animals, and humans, and comprises a wide variety of 'powers' (*dynameis*) or 'parts' (*moria*), ranging from nutrition, growth, reproduction, locomotion, perception, desire, moral discernment, and imagination to opinion and theoretical thinking. For Aristotle, to have a soul means to be alive and to have the capacity to exercise the vital functions appropriate to the category of living beings to which an individual belongs; in addition, the form–matter distinction can be applied to all the vital functions that a living being must possess and perform in order to live—that is, to all the various levels of 'psycho-physical' activity that can be discerned. This also explains why, in the context of 'psychology', a significant amount of Aristotle's attention is given to functions of living beings that have no 'mental' or 'cognitive' aspect at all.[20] In fact, a considerable part of Aristotle's biological writings are devoted to a discussion of the nutritive and locomotive faculties of the soul—that is, those functions of living beings that enable them to stay alive, to reproduce themselves, and to cope with the world around them.

These 'parts' or powers of the soul are related to one another in a pyramid-like pattern: organisms that have the higher soul faculties automatically have the lower ones as well, in the way that a quadrangle automatically comprises a triangle and a straight line.[21] Thus plants have only the vegetative 'part' of the soul (*threptikon*), which comprises the powers of nutrition and reproduction; animals have in addition the sensitive 'part' of the soul (*aisthētikon*), which comprises perception, locomotion, imagination (*phantasia*), and desire; and man has besides all these the intellectual part of the soul (*noētikon*), the power to think both practically and theoretically. Thus man has a different kind of soul from animals, and man and animals have a different kind of soul from plants.

Aristotle is less clear on the question of whether and, if so, how the 'higher' soul functions influence the operation of the lower ones. Do

---

[20] For an account of the nutritive part of the soul see Freudenthal, *Aristotle's Theory*.
[21] *An.* II 3, esp. 414b28 ff.

humans perceive differently from animals? Do animals feed themselves differently from plants? Obviously they do so in the sense that they have different bodily parts and perhaps different digestive mechanisms, but this need not be a significant or relevant difference. In the case of cognition, however, the question seems more pertinent, since the perception or recognition of objects would seem to be informed by knowledge about such objects. For example, does man perceive differently from animals because his intellect allows him to direct his attention, to steer his perception, to see things *as* certain things, to 'interpret' perceptual data? Aristotle does not discuss this point explicitly, but he would probably say that although the act of perception *itself* is not influenced by the power to think, 'indirectly' (*kata symbebēkos*) human perceptions may be different from animal perceptions in so far as thoughts may be associated with them, and/or perceptual content may be informed by memories and reflections.[22] The boundaries between the sensitive and the intellectual part of the soul are not always clearly drawn by Aristotle, and it is precisely here that faculties such as the 'central sense-organ' (*kyrion aisthētērion*)[23] and the 'imagination' (*phantasia*)[24] are operative. Although these both belong to the sensitive part of the soul, and are thus not confined to humans, the operations they perform are complex: the central sense faculty is responsible for co-ordinating the individual senses, for sensational awareness, for judging the truth of our perceptions, and for deciding between conflicting sense-data; it is also responsible for perception of the so-called common sensibles, such as number, size, shape, movement, and rest. 'Imagination' is a faculty that produces an awareness of things by presenting them as objects of perception or (in the case of humans) thought, and stimulates action by presenting them as objects of desire or avoidance; furthermore, it 'represents' items that are no longer there, as in the cases of memory and dreaming. In humans it serves as a kind of bridge between sense and intellect, in that it presents perceptual data to the intellect as material for thought, on the basis of which the intellect abstracts and forms concepts and ideas.[25]

---

[22] Cf. *De memoria* (*Mem.*) 450a13 ff.; *De sensu* (*Sens.*) 437a15–17.

[23] Also rather misleadingly called the 'common sense faculty'. There is an extensive secondary literature on this notion. See e.g. Modrak, *Aristotle*, 55–80; Kahn, 'Sensation and Consciousness'; Welsch, *Aisthesis*, 256–380. For further references see P. J. van der Eijk, *Aristoteles: De insomniis, De divinatione per somnum* (Berlin, 1994), 77 n. 89 and 138.

[24] Much, again, has been written on this notion; see e.g. M. Wedin, *Mind and Imagination in Aristotle* (London, 1988); G. Watson, '*Phantasia* in Aristotle's De anima 3.3', *Classical Quarterly*, 32 (1982), 100–13; M. Schofield, 'Aristotle on the Imagination', repr. with a postscript in Nussbaum and Oksenberg Rorty (eds.), *Essays*, 249–78; D. Frede, 'The Cognitive Role of *Phantasia*', ibid. 279–96. For further references see van der Eijk, *Aristoteles: De insomniis*, 155.   [25] Cf. *An.* 431b2–3.

A further corollary of the hylomorphic theory is Aristotle's insistence that all 'affections of the soul' (thoughts, sensations, emotions, etc.) take place in a material body, and have a material aspect. This position, on which he dwells at considerable length at the beginning of the *De anima*, seems to have a programmatic significance: he illustrates it by means of the example of the definition of the emotion 'anger',[26] suggesting that the correct, complete account of anger should state both the formal definition of anger (e.g. 'a desire for retaliation') and its material definition (e.g. 'a boiling of the blood and the hot material around the heart'). Psychology, then, is in fact psycho-physiology.

To be sure, in the following chapters of the *De anima* the account of the various psychic powers which Aristotle identifies remains fairly formal and abstract, and we do not get a very detailed account of their physiological aspects; but if we take the *Parva naturalia* and some of the zoological works (especially *Parts of Animals* and *Movement of Animals*) into consideration, a more detailed picture of the physiological structures and processes involved emerges.[27] An interesting feature of Aristotle's theory here is that bodily factors are not described just because they are involved in the process—as, for example, the eye in seeing—but also with respect to their suitability to serve as the material correlates to the activities of the soul—for example, the predominance of the watery element in the eye is related to the transparency that is required for seeing.[28] This shows that organic matter is for Aristotle not an empty concept or an unqualified stuff devoid of any qualities of its own. The living body consists of materials, parts and structures, fluids and tissues, all of which are so constituted and shaped that they are suited to carry out the functions of the organism as a whole.

A more difficult question is precisely *how* he thinks the bodily processes he envisages as being related to the 'mental' processes they accompany are related, and whether he considers such bodily processes as in any sense relevant to the understanding of these mental processes.[29] Thus, to return to the example of anger, Aristotle does not give a clear answer to the question whether the boiling of hot material around the heart is causative of the emotion anger, or the result of it, or a physical manifestation of it. At various places in his writings dealing with the psycho-physical aspects of emotions, he seems to allow all three possi-

---

[26] *An.* 403a3–b16.

[27] On the complementary relationship between these works see Kahn, 'Sensation and Consciousness', 20.   [28] See *Sens.* 438b19 ff.

[29] On this question see M. Burnyeat, 'Is an Aristotelian Philosophy of Mind still Credible? A Draft', in Nussbaum and Oksenberg Rorty (eds.), *Essays*, 15–26, and R. Sorabji, 'Intentionality and Physiological Processes: Aristotle's Theory of Sense-perception', ibid. 195–226; see also J. Sisko, 'Material Alteration and Cognitive Activity in Aristotle's De Anima', *Phronesis*, 41 (1996), 138–57.

bilities, but this raises serious philosophical questions about the kind and direction of interdependence between mental and bodily states.[30]

This question also arises on the level of individual 'psychic' faculties, when Aristotle applies a number of philosophical concepts familiar from other parts of his work. Thus 'vision' is the actualizing form, 'eye' the matter:[31] the eye cannot see without the power of vision—indeed, without this power it is no longer an eye 'except in name only'; on the other hand, the power of vision cannot reside in just any random material, and from Aristotle's analysis of the physiology of the eye, as we have seen, it becomes clear that the material make-up of the eye is particularly suited to the fulfilment of its function. However, what actually happens in the process of seeing is less clear. All perception is said to be a process in which the sense 'takes on the form of the sense object without its matter'.[32] This is compared to the way in which wax takes on the shape of a signet ring without taking on the actual gold or silver of which the ring is made.[33] In the case of visual perception, the eye is 'set in motion' by the visible object via the medium of the transparent air.[34] Whether Aristotle believes that the eye literally becomes red when it perceives a red object is debated by scholars,[35] but it seems undisputable that Aristotle assumes that a physical reaction of some sort does take place. But whether, and how, this physical process is causally related to the process of seeing is less obvious. In another passage, Aristotle brings his familiar potentiality–actuality distinction to bear on the process of perception by saying that the sense-faculty 'becomes' what the sense-object actually is.[36] He also compares the process to the chords of a lyre, each of which produces its own sound when struck, or with a flammable substance that needs the activity of something else to set it on fire.[37] These comparisons seem to indicate that the sense-organ must not only have a certain suitability for its function, but must also, so to speak, be tuned in a manner that makes it able to react to the stimulus in a way that generates the response appropriate to it: the external stimulus just acts as the catalyst.[38]

---

[30] Cf. van der Eijk, 'Matter of Mind', 257 and n. 99 on *MA* 701b17 ff. It is of course possible to interpret a statement such as 'fear causes shivering' in the sense that 'fear' and 'shivering' are mental and physical aspects of two different states, of which the one leads to the other. The fact that such a statement contains two incomplete descriptions of these two states might then be accounted for by considerations of relevance. But there are no explicit remarks by Aristotle to this effect.   [31] *An.* 426a13.

[32] *An.* 424a18–20.   [33] *An.* 424a19–21; *Mem.* 450b1.   [34] *An.* II 7.

[35] See the discussion by Sorabji, 'Intentionality and Physiological Processes'.

[36] *An.* II 5, esp. 418a3–6.   [37] *An.* 424a32; 417a8.

[38] This account of perception is interpreted by some scholars in the sense that the actualization of sense perception is the realization of forms that are already immanent in the sense-faculty: thus perceptions do not come 'from without' (although they are triggered by external factors), but are in fact internal processes within the sense-organs themselves. See Welsch, *Aisthesis*, and W. Bernard, *Rezeptivität und Spontaneität der Wahrnehmung bei Aristoteles* (Baden-Baden, 1988).

As for the bodily agents involved in the exercise of the various psychic functions, Aristotle's discussion of the nutritive part of the soul also refers to nutritive and digestive mechanisms, the role of heat in the processing of food, several kinds of 'burning' and 'quenching', and the disposal of waste products (*perittōmata*).[39] His discussion of sense perception takes account of the sense-organs—the eyes, ears, nose, tongue, and flesh—and discusses their physical make-up in respect of their suitability to the functions they serve.[40] Apart from these peripheral sense-organs, Aristotle also posits a central sense-organ located in the heart, and he claims that the peripheral sense-organs cannot operate independently of this cognitive centre: when the central sense-organ is inactive, as in sleep, the peripheral sense-organs are incapacitated.[41] Moreover, an operational connection between the peripheral senses and the central sense-organ is necessary for sensory awareness, because the impulse or signal must be transmitted from the peripheral sense-organ to the heart in order to be actually noticed: only when a stimulus arrives at the common sensorium does the animal become 'aware' of it, and it is perfectly possible that some stimuli that are weaker than others 'escape' notice (*lanthanein*).[42] How such stimuli reach the heart is a matter of some debate among interpreters, as the textual evidence is not free of ambiguities. It seems that Aristotle attributes an important role here to the blood, although other factors, such as heat, the condition of the flesh, and perhaps also 'air' (*pneuma*) may play a role as well; but the precise modalities of this transmission remain unclear.[43] There are resemblances to earlier medical thought here,[44] which may be why Aristotle seems to presuppose that his audience is familiar with the physiological details.

Yet, although the heart is clearly the cognitive and nutritive centre, it is quite in keeping with his hylomorphic theory that Aristotle, in contrast to some Hippocratic writers and Plato, is remarkably vague on the *place* in the body where all the psychic faculties are located. As I have said, he makes it clear that the 'parts' of the soul are not spatially distinguishable

---

[39] This is the subject-matter of the latter section of the *Parva Naturalia*, the treatises *On Length and Shortness of Life*, *On Youth and Old Age* (*Juv.*), and *On Respiration* (*Resp.*).

[40] See P. Webb, 'Bodily Structure and Psychic Faculties in Aristotle's Theory of Perception', *Hermes*, 110 (1982), 25–50; T. K. Johansen, *Aristotle on the Sense-Organs* (Cambridge, 1997). For the rationale underlying the various accounts of sense perception in Aristotle's psychological and biological works see van der Eijk, 'Matter of Mind', 235.

[41] *De somno et vigilia* (*Somn.*) 455a13–b3.

[42] These 'unnoticed' sense perceptions form the basis of Aristotle's theory of dreams, on which see van der Eijk, *Aristoteles: De insomniis*.

[43] For a discussion of this problem and further references see ibid. 81–7.

[44] See the discussion by Beate Gundert in Ch. 1 above; apart from the Hippocratic writings, mention should also be made of the medical writer Diocles of Carystus, who was probably a contemporary of Aristotle, and who may have influenced Aristotle in his use of *pneuma* (cf. Freudenthal, *Aristotle's Theory*, 113 and 121).

in the way Plato allocated the rational part to the brain, the spirited part to the chest, and the appetitive element to the liver. Rather, they are to be seen as powers, or faculties, in whose exercise a number of bodily components are involved, a co-ordinated system. It is of some importance to stress this, because in the history of ideas Aristotle's position on the question of the physical location of the intellect has often been defined as 'cardiocentrist'. Now it is true that the heart, as the centre of bodily heat and as the seat of the common sensorium, plays a vital part at least in nutrition and perception, and perhaps even in thinking; and it is also true that Aristotle sometimes seems to assume that the soul is somehow a distinct entity—for example, when he speaks of experiences that are 'peculiar to the soul'[45] as opposed to experiences that are 'common to the soul and the body',[46] or when he says that certain stimuli 'arrive at the soul' or 'reach the soul',[47] or when he refers to 'the part of the body that has soul in it'[48] and the part of the body that 'partakes in thinking'.[49] These phrases seem to suggest that the soul is, after all, a separate entitity—indeed, a spatially extended entity, which is located at a particular place in the body (e.g. in or near the heart) and *in* which certain things take place.[50] On two occasions he even seems to equate the soul with fire, when he speaks of the 'kindled soul'.[51] Nevertheless, in *De anima* he specifies explicitly that heat, or fire, is a 'contributory cause' (*synaition*), not the cause itself.[52] At any rate, the role of heat in all this is paramount: heat is indeed 'the most serviceable thing to the activities of the soul'.[53]

It is important, though, to bear in mind that what Aristotle locates in the heart is the 'principle of perception' or the 'principle of the soul', not the soul itself, nor indeed the intellect, which would by definition defy any allocation to a specific bodily part or organ.[54] This brings us to our next heading.

III. THE INTELLECT AND HYLOMORPHISM

It would seem, again, to be fully in keeping with his hylomorphic theory if Aristotle assumed that the intellect too involved physical activity—

---

[45] *Somn.* 453b12.   [46] *An.* 433b19–21; *Sens.* 436a8; cf. *PA* 643a35.

[47] *An.* 408b16–18; *De divinatione per somnum* 464a10–11.

[48] *Mem.* 450a27–8; 450b10–11.   [49] *PA* 672b28 ff.

[50] Cf. also the expression 'in the soul' in *An.* 431b5.

[51] *Juv.* 469b16; *Resp.* 474b13. See Freudenthal, *Aristotle's Theory*, 20–2.

[52] *An.* 416a9–15.   [53] *PA* 652b10.

[54] It is certainly no coincidence that although Aristotle does talk of the 'nutritive place' (*threptikos topos*) (*Somn.* 457a32) and the 'perceptive place' (*Mem.* 453a24), he—as opposed to the author of the pseudo-Aristotelian *Problemata* XXX 1 (954a35)—nowhere uses the term *noeros topos*.

that is, that the activity of the intellect consisted in the function of certain suitable physical structures and processes. And it would also not be unreasonable if here, too, he assigned a principal role to the heart; for the heart is, after all, the place of the common sensorium, which seems so closely related to intellectual activity.

However, as is well known, on this point Aristotle wavers. For he sometimes says that the intellect is separable from the body, that it is the only 'part' of the soul that can aspire to immortality, and the only faculty whose activity, thinking, takes place without the involvement of a bodily substrate.[55] Apart from the questions of how this can be and what sort of activity it is, there is also the problem that on many other occasions Aristotle seems to be suggesting that the activity of thinking, and the ability to think, can be significantly affected, both positively and negatively, by the bodily conditions under which it is operating—that is, by the anatomical structure of certain bodily parts, or by the body as a whole, or by incidental physiological and pathological states that inter-fere with the normal state of affairs.[56]

Thus Aristotle indicates on several occasions that differences in the quality of the blood make for differences in intellectual powers, the best blend being blood that is warm, thin, and pure.[57] He also remarks that the brain's failure to cool the bodily heat may lead to mental distur-bances (*paranoiai*).[58] And the fact that man is the most intelligent living being is said to be indicative of the fine blend between the warmth of the heart and the coldness of the brain that characterizes the human species.[59] The presence of a warm, moist residual substance in the neigh-bourhood of the diaphragm is said to 'cause confusion' (*tarattein*) and 'change' to the intellect.[60] Similarly, the intellectual process of recollec-tion is said to be impeded by moisture around the perceptive place.[61] And it is suggested that incidental conditions such as strong emotions, diseases, and sleep may 'overshadow the intellect' (*epikalyptesthai ton noun*).[62] Age too is said to affect intellectual powers: very young people do not have the power to think, being similar to animals; and old age is accompanied by a deterioration of intellectual powers.[63] Even environ-

---

[55] *An.* 413a6: intellect is the *entelecheia* of nothing bodily. On the immortality of the intellect: *An.* 430a17–18, 22–3; *GA* 736b28–9. It is true that *An.* III 5 restricts the immor-tality to the so-called active intellect, but it seems that this distinction between active and passive intellect is an *ad hoc* solution, and the restriction is not made in other con-texts where the *nous* is presented as different from the other parts of the soul in respect of its relation to the body.

[56] For a more elaborate discussion of all these passages see van der Eijk, 'Matter of Mind'.   [57] *PA* 648a2 ff.; 650b19 ff. See van der Eijk, 'Matter of Mind', 248–9.

[58] *PA* 653b5.   [59] *GA* 744a30.   [60] *PA* 672b28 ff.

[61] *Mem.* 453a15–31.   [62] *An.* 429a5–8.

[63] *HA* 588a31 ff.; *Politica* (*Pol.*) 1270b40; *An.* 408b19–31.

mental factors such as climate and geographical region are said to affect intelligence.[64] People who are born blind are said to be more intelligent than those who are born dumb or deaf, apparently because their auditive faculties have been better trained, and because hearing is conducive to 'intellect and prudence' (*nous* and *phronēsis*).[65] Furthermore, thinking is described as the result of a process of 'bodily motion coming to a standstill', which is compared with the transition from drunkenness (or sleep) to sobriety (or awakening).[66]

Perhaps the two most illuminating passages are contexts in which Aristotle refers to material factors that cause man to be more intelligent than other living beings, and some humans more than others. First, in *De anima* 421a22 ff., he suggests that there is a direct connection between degrees of softness of the flesh and degrees of intelligence in human beings. The passage is dealing with the sense of smell, and Aristotle remarks that man has a very weak, unarticulated sense of smell in comparison with many other animals: he is only capable of labelling smells as pleasant or unpleasant. The situation is slightly better with taste, he says, for man's sense of taste is more accurate than his sense of smell, because taste is a form of touch, and, as regards touch, man is the most accurate of all animals.[67] He then continues:

This is also the reason why man is the most intelligent of all animals (*phronimōtaton*). A sign of this is that within the species of man as well it is in relation to this sense-organ that an individual is well or poorly endowed (with intelligence), but not in relation to any other sense-organ: for people with hard flesh (*sklērosarkoi*) are poorly endowed with intelligence (*aphyeis tēn dianoian*), while people with soft flesh (*malakosarkoi*) are well endowed with it (*euphyeis*).

Here Aristotle distinguishes not only between different species of animals, but also between different members (or types of members) of one species. Man is more intelligent than other animals because of the accuracy of his sense of touch, which is supported by the fact that within the human species individuals with soft flesh (which is obviously conducive to touch) are by nature more intelligent than those with hard flesh. Thus variations in intellectual capacities are here directly related to variations in the quality of the skin. Just *how* they are related does not emerge from this passage, but the text points to a relation of efficient causality between touch and intelligence. Perhaps it has something to do with the fact that touch is the fundamental sense which is closely connected with, if not identical to, the 'common sense faculty',[68] which in turn is most closely related to intellectual activity; hence variations in the performance of this faculty might also bring about variations in

---

[64] *Pol.* 1327b20 ff.   [65] *Sens.* 437a15–17.   [66] *Physics* 247b1 ff.
[67] Cf. *HA* 494b17; *PA* 660a12.   [68] *Somn.* 455a23, also referred to at *PA* 686a31.

intellectual performance. Another possibility is that a delicacy of the skin is somehow conducive to a thinness and agility of the blood, which in its turn, as we saw, influences the degree of intellectual activity. But at any rate, the relation seems entirely 'mechanical', and the explanation is an explanation 'from the bottom up': there is no mention of a purpose that is served by this mechanism.

The following passage from *Parts of Animals*, which deserves to be quoted in full, puts the connection between physical structure and cognitive ability in a teleological perspective:

Man, instead of forelegs and forefeet, has arms and the so-called hands. For man is the only animal that stands upright, and this is because his nature and essence is divine. The activity of that which is most divine is to think and to be intelligent; but this is not easy when there is a great deal of the upper body weighing it down, for weight hampers the motion of the intellect and the common sense. Thus, when the weight and the corporeal condition (of the soul) become too great, the bodies themselves must lurch forward towards the ground; consequently, for the purpose of safety, nature provided quadrupeds with forefeet instead of arms and hands. All animals that walk must have two hind feet, and those I have just mentioned became quadrupeds because their soul could not sustain the weight bearing it down. In fact, compared with man, all the other animals are dwarf-like. . . . In humans, the size of the trunk is proportionate to the lower parts, and as they are brought to perfection, it becomes much smaller in proportion. With young people, however, the contrary is true: the upper parts are large and the lower are small. . . . In fact, all children are dwarfs. The genera of birds and fishes, as well as every animal with blood in it, as I have said, are dwarf-like. This is also the reason why all animals are less intelligent than man. Even among human beings children, for example, when compared to adults, and those among adults who have a dwarf-like nature— even though having some exceptional capacity—are nevertheless inferior in respect of their possession of intelligence. The reason, as has already been said, is that in many of them the principle of the soul is sluggish and corporeal. If the heat which raises the organism up wanes still further and the earthly matter waxes, then the animals' bodies wane, and they are many-footed; and finally they lose their feet and lie full length on the ground. (*PA* 686a25 ff.)

In this passage, we are given an anatomical and physiological reason why man is the most intelligent living being. It is suggested that the activities of thinking and of the common sense may be impeded by the position of the body; indeed, it is also suggested that structural differences in anatomy and physiology between species—and between individual members of one species—make for differences in intellectual abilities. Yet there is a clear formal, teleological explanation for this, and the distribution of intelligence over the various kinds of animals is here presented as something in itself good and purposive: even though it is material factors such as the position of the body, the predominance of certain elements (such as earth), and so forth that are said to be responsible for the fact that some animals are more intelligent than others, and within the human species some members more intelligent than others, nevertheless, all these variations are entirely natural and not to be understood as disturbances of the natural order.[69]

It becomes clear from these passages that variations in bodily factors are causally related to variations in intellectual performances. Most of the passages deal with comparisons between different kinds of animals or between different members within a kind. Some of the variations are incidental, and can apparently happen to anyone; others have a more permanent character, and seem linked to certain 'types' of individuals within a species. And some of these variations seem to be entirely mechanical, while others are purposive and functional within the wider framework of Nature.

Yet it would probably be a misunderstanding of the Aristotelian position to take these physical factors as the material aspects of intellectual activity in the same hylomorphic sense in which the boiling of blood is the material aspect of anger, or the alleged colouring of the eye jelly is the material aspect of seeing. It seems, rather, that the bodily factors mentioned are conditions that facilitate, support, or disturb intellectual activity without actually constituting the process itself in any way. As such, their influence may be subsumed under the heading 'the dependence of the intellect on (mental) appearances (*phantasmata*)', which is a point Aristotle alludes to several times:[70] he concedes that although the intellect itself works separately from the body, it requires a supply of *phantasmata*—appearances (or images) generated by perception and hence of a physical nature—whose condition affects the intellect's thinking capacity and performance. The remarks about physical factors influencing the workings of the intellect may be referring to this supply of *phantasmata*, and thus imply only an indirect physical influence on the workings of the intellect. If this is correct, it would be wrong to speak of 'degrees of intelligence' in Aristotle's theory—that is, of intelligence as a quantifiable variable: for variations in intellectual performance and intellectual power would be the result of something which itself does not belong to the intellectual part of the soul, but rather to the sensitive part of the soul supplying the intellectual part with *phantasmata*.

Aristotle's position seems to be that the intellect functions ideally

---

[69] A similar perspective is offered later on in the same chapter, where Aristotle discusses the fact that man has hands. It is not that man is most intelligent because he has hands, he argues (against Anaxagoras), but that man has hands because he is the most intelligent living being, and can make use of them sensibly (*PA* 687a2–23).

[70] *An.* 431a16–17, 431b2, 432a3–14; *Mem.* 449b31 ff.

under circumstances in which the body is in a state of equilibrium, a right balance between warm and cold, and other physical factors.[71] This allows the intellect to reflect on the *phantasmata* with which it is presented, and to abstract noetic images from them. This is suggested by the passage in *Physics* 247b1 ff. already alluded to, where thought is described as the result of a process of 'bodily motion coming to a standstill'. As Theodore Tracy summarizes:

[K]nowledge is acquired and activated only when the body, and the sensory system in particular, *calms down*, being freed from disturbance and brought to a state of stable equilibrium in all respects, i.e. to a state of maturity, health, sobriety, and moral excellence. Some of these may be produced by natural processes alone; others, like health and moral excellence, may require assistance from the physician and trainer, the moral guide and statesman.[72]

As emerges from a study of Aristotle's works on sleep and dreams, one of these 'natural processes' is the restoration of the balance between warm and cold in the body which occurs when the process of digestion (the material cause of sleep) is completed; another accompanying process is the separation of the blood into a thinner, clearer part and a thicker, more troubled part;[73] another, arising in the case of drunkenness, is the dissolution of movement and confusion brought about by *pneuma*.[74] How exactly these processes interact with and influence cognitive processes, Aristotle does not make very clear; but he certainly believes that healthy bodily conditions are conducive to a successful operation of the intellectual part of the soul.

Yet even if there is no genuine contradiction in Aristotle's theory here, one may still find his insistence on the incorporeality of *nous* difficult to understand—if not philosophically unsatisfactory.[75] To explain this as an awkward Platonic relic which does not fully fit into his own system begs the question why Aristotle, who does not shy away from severe criticism of Platonic doctrines in other areas, did not reject it. For

---

[71] It should be stressed, though, that the passage in *An.* 421a22 ff. about the *malakosarkoi* suggests that there is also a more positive side to this bodily influence. For the possibility that bodily factors may also make for exceptionally good intellectual performance see van der Eijk, 'Matter of Mind', 254–5.

[72] Tracy, *Physiological Theory*, 276.

[73] On the physiological explanation of sleep in *Somn.* see Wiesner, 'Unity of the De somno'.   [74] *De insomniis* 461a23–5.

[75] For a recent attempt to explain why *nous* must be incorporeal see C. Kahn, 'Aristotle on Thinking', in Nussbaum and Oksenberg Rorty (eds.), *Essays*, 375–9. One of the reasons why Kahn's answer does not satisfy me is that it does not explain why the distinction between 'the principle of *nous* as such and concrete acts of human thought' (376; cf. 367) does not also apply to the principle of perception as such versus concrete acts of human perception; yet Aristotle does not claim the same kind of incorporeality for the principle of perception (which is located in the heart).

one might argue that there is absolutely no need for a 'ghost in the machine' like *nous*, and that it is perfectly possible to think of the soul's equilibrium—including that of the intellect—in entirely material terms, as a balance of opposite qualities, comparable to the way in which the Hippocratic author of *Regimen* (to whom Aristotle seems indebted in a variety of ways)[76] defines the activity of the intellect as a certain blend or proportion between fire and water.

Any answer to this question must remain speculative, but it seems plausible that Aristotle was worried about the apparently mechanistic and deterministic implications of this bio-medical approach to the soul. For in all his psychological enunciations, he gives the impression that living beings are like mechanical systems that react to stimuli, and whose behaviour is explicable in terms of cause and effect. Of course, the word 'mechanical' should not be taken in the sense that these psycho-physical processes are not directed to particular goals or goods, for it is abundantly clear from the whole of Aristotle's thought that he believes they are directed to such goals. Yet this does not alter the fact that Aristotle's hylomorphic theory seems, precisely because of its biological character, to reduce the soul to a 'set of capacities' which leave very little room for any arbitrariness or subjectivity—indeed, subjectivity itself would also be defined in terms of a physical structure, such as the heart, being affected in a certain way; and there are passages in *Parts of Animals* which attribute to the size of the heart and the quality of the blood the role of determinants in the moral disposition of the animal concerned.[77] Even in his account of action and locomotion in the *Movement of Animals*, Aristotle draws a picture of appearances (*phantasmata*) presenting themselves to the moving agent, and discerning faculties such as judgement (*doxa*) and thinking (*nous*) performing decisory actions which have been 'prepared' under the influence of certain psycho-physical processes. All this gives a rather 'instrumental' impression, which is not in any way mitigated by the teleological assumption that in such cases the physical factors, such as the blood, are 'informed' or 'programmed' by the form of the specific psychic organization that is appropriate to that particular species, and which has been allotted to that species by Nature.

All this seems to bring Aristotle uncomfortably close to determinism—a position which he emphatically rejects elsewhere in his works, especially in the *Nicomachean Ethics*, where he repeatedly emphasizes that human beings are not machines, and that what we decide to do is 'up to us' (*eph' hēmin*) because the 'principle' (*archē*) of action, 'choice'

[76] *On Regimen* I 35–6 see Ch. I above: see also van der Eijk, 'Matter of Mind', 253–4.

[77] *PA* 667a11 ff. On the blood see above, p. 68, and the monograph by F. Rüsche, *Blut, Leben, Seele* (Paderborn, 1930).

(*proairesis*) or will, is 'within us'.[78] Yet here (in book VII), too, in his
analysis of weakness of the will and of a failure to act according to
reason, Aristotle concedes that the functioning of this faculty can be
affected by bodily conditions (such as drunkenness), natural constitu-
tions, or dispositions that have become established by a pattern of
living.[79] An example of people in whom these cognitive and decision-
making faculties are permanently impeded are the so-called melancholics, who represent a constitution type characterized by a set of
abnormal bodily features somehow related to the presence of black bile,
a bodily fluid whose existence Aristotle probably accepted on the
authority of a medical tradition, and which was particularly associated
with mental disorders.[80] In Aristotle's view, melancholics are somehow
degenerate, and in a way that naturally disables their cognitive abilities
and hence their moral self-control. To put it crudely, their souls are constrained by their bodies, because the *krasis* ('mixture') or *physis* ('physical constitution') of their bodies is unbalanced.[81] They are referred to
several times in Aristotle's discussion of pleasure and weakness of will[82]
as an example of a structural psycho-physical condition which is to be
avoided: not only is it within human control to make judgements and
decisions, to act according to them, and to create and maintain the circumstances in which such judgements and decisions can be taken, it is
also within human control to avoid circumstances (such as drunkenness,
or a life-style devoted to bodily pleasure) that may temporarily impede
or gradually erode the exercise of the very faculty of free will.

The example of the melancholics illustrates both Aristotle's indebtedness to the medical tradition and a possible reason why he may have
felt compelled to offer something more. The significance of the physiological aspects of the doctrine of the mean and of the medical background to Aristotle's ethical theory is that the exercise of free will,
rational deliberation, and theoretical thinking can only take place in
favourable physiological circumstances.[83] These ideal bodily conditions
bring about a condition of equilibrium on the basis of which an incorporeal process can best take place. Just as mechanical or material explanations are ultimately unsatisfactory to Aristotle, and just as he feels the
need for a formal principle, a *telos* that goes beyond the mechanical
structure and serves as the explanation why a mechanism is such as it
is and not otherwise, and why it is orientated in a particular direction,
likewise, in the explanation of living beings, and of man in particular,
Aristotle may well have felt that what is needed is something that goes

---

[78] For an overview of the Aristotelian position see R. Sorabji, *Necessity, Cause and
Blame* (London, 1980).   [79] e.g. 1147a14 ff., 1147b7, 1148b25 ff., 1152a15, 1154b10.
[80] See van der Eijk, 'Aristoteles über die Melancholie'.   [81] Cf. *EN* 1154b12.
[82] *EN* 1150b25; 1152a18, 27; 1154b12.   [83] See Tracy, *Physiological Theory*.

'beyond' the natural, psycho-physical, composite unity of a human being—indeed something divine, the *nous*, which both emerges from and overrides the bodily *krasis*, something that is both connected with it and goes beyond it—and must do so in order to retain its independent status as an explanatory principle. Aristotle is here carefully balancing the two aspects of what it is to be a man: namely an animal and a being related to the divine. This takes us back to the beginning of our discussion about the tension in Aristotle's anthropology. For, while to detach the essence of man completely from his physical make-up would run counter to Aristotle's biological approach to man as a natural living being, the ultimate implication of his view on the divinity of *nous* is that the fullest realization of what it is to be a human being is to go beyond the limits of corporeality and mortality, and to become, if only temporarily, a god.

4

Body, Soul, and Nerves: Epicurus, Herophilus, Erasistratus, the Stoics, and Galen

HEINRICH VON STADEN

Psychē is *sōma*

Epicurus

The *psychē* therefore is a *sōma*

Cleanthes, Chrysippus

Corpus est anima

Zeno of Citium

It is striking that polarities such as corporeal–incorporeal, mortal–immortal, matter–form, transient–eternal, and generated–ungenerated—all of which are deployed to draw lines of demarcation between body and soul from the classical period to later antiquity—are not central to the more influential early Hellenistic theories of body and soul. Despite their radically divergent versions of the world and of human beings, Epicurus, many Stoics, and the more significant early Hellenistic physicians share a constellation of convictions concerning soul and body which is not receptive to boundary lines of such a kind (even if some features of their beliefs continue to resonate with those of their precursors). The belief cluster shared by Hellenistic philosophers and physicians includes, for example, that all *psychē* is *sōma* but not all *sōma* is *psychē*; that only what is spatially extended, three-dimensional, and capable of acting or being acted upon exists; that the soul meets these criteria of existence; that this corporeal *psychē*, like the rest of the body, is mortal and transient; that the *psychē* is generated with the body; that it neither exists before the body nor exists eternally after its separation from the body—that is, the soul does not exist independently of the body in which it exists.

These beliefs are prompted in part by the difficulty of accounting for interaction between soul and body if soul is an incorporeal entity and body is corporeal; it is thought easier to account for interaction between matter and matter, or, as most ancient Greeks put it, between a body (*sōma*) and a body. Epicurus, the Stoics, and Hellenistic physicians do not, however, always present the same motivations and justifications for these shared beliefs. Nor do they agree on many significant points. And they do not always use identical or even similar strategies to address some fundamental questions prompted by the beliefs which they hold in common. Crucial among such questions is: If the soul is a corporeal 'body', how does soul differ from body? This question acquired renewed urgency after Herophilus's and Erasistratus's discovery of the nerves and after their meticulous dissections of the human brain in the third century BC. In particular, the discovery of the sensory and motor functions of the nerves, and of the relation of sensory and motor nerves to the brain, posed a challenge to Platonic, Pythagorean, and Aristotelian theories of the soul and of its relation to the body. The nature and scope of the challenge will be addressed below (sections II–V), but first the theory of Epicurus, one of the earliest Hellenistic exponents of the cluster of beliefs to which I have referred, merits re-examination.

I. EPICURUS (*c*.341–270 BC)

The extant remains of Epicurus's answer to the question of the difference between soul and body are riddled with stylistic, syntactic, and lexical obscurities, with theoretical and logical lacunae, and with other hermeneutic obstacles; but it displays three recognizable, central moves. The first is a response at the level of matter: yes, *psychē* is *sōma* and hence material, but the soul is constituted of atomic matter that is different from that of the rest of the body ('body' here understood as the atomically constituted 'aggregate', *athroisma*, of the total organized matter—tissues, bones, liquids, etc.—of a living being, viewed as an entity).

The second is a reply at the level of capacities and susceptibilities— that is, of *dynameis* ('faculties', 'powers', 'potentialities') and *pathē* ('affections', 'feelings', 'passions', 'affects'). *Psychē too* is body, but it has distinctive capacities and susceptibilities (by virtue of its distinctive matter), and it therefore can act and be acted upon in ways that set it apart from the rest of bodily matter.

A third response is represented by the distinction between the body as material container and its material contents, or, more specifically, between the container and the differentiable parts of its physical contents, among which is the *psychē*: without the body as the 'covering' or 'sheltering' mechanism, there can be no contained parts such as soul. A controversial passage in Epicurus's *Letter to Herodotus* illustrates these and further features of his theory:[1]

(1) The *psychē* is a fine-textured (*leptomeres*) body (*sōma*),
(2) which is spread [sown, diffused] along the whole of the aggregate (*athroisma*);
(3) [*psychē* is a body] most similar to pneuma that has a certain blending (*krasin*) of warmth,
(4) and [*psychē* is a body] in one way similar to the former [i.e. to pneuma], in another to the latter [i.e. to warmth],
(5) but it [the fine-textured body, i.e. *psychē*] is[2] the part [*to meros*, sc. of the bodily aggregate] which, by virtue of the fineness of its parts, has acquired a great difference even from these themselves [i.e. from pneuma and warmth],
(6) yet it [this part of the aggregate, i.e. *psychē*] is liable to co-affection, more so with the former [pneuma], but also with the rest of the aggregate;
(7) the capacities (*dynameis*) of the soul make all of this evident, and so do its affections (*pathē*), motilities (*eukinēsiai*, ease of motion, mobilities), acts of thinking, and the things deprived of which we die;
(8) and one must hold on to (the fact) that the *psychē* bears the greatest responsibility for sense perception (*aisthēsis*): *psychē* would not have acquired *aisthēsis* if *psychē* were not somehow covered by the rest (*loipou*) of the aggregate (*athroismatos*).

Several details in this passage have become controversial, in part as a consequence of a desire on the part of modern interpreters to force it into agreement with later passages (in the scholia, in Lucretius, and in

---

[1] *Letter to Herodotus* 63–4. All translations from Greek and Latin in this essay are my own.

[2] Some interpreters have assumed that an existential (rather than a predicative or copulative) reading of 'is' (*esti*) is the only possibility here: 'there exists', '(the part) exists'. They overlook, first, that *psychē* has been the subject throughout, and therefore can naturally continue as subject without stylistic or syntactic offence (linked by 'and/but it is': *esti de*); second, that Epicurus has not been talking about parts, and that the definite article *to* ('there exists *the* part') would therefore be jarring if one read the passage as a theory of the parts of the soul (Woltjer, followed by Von der Mühll and Arrighetti, is aware of this, and therefore emends 'the' (*to*) to 'a' (*ti*): 'there is a [part]'—an emendation rendered unnecessary by the interpretation reflected in my translation); and third, that *esti* ('it is'), while transmitted with an accent (suggesting an existential use of the verb 'to be'), regularly loses the status of an enclitic not only when it expresses existence but also when, as here, it is the first word in a sentence, regardless of the sense (existential, predicative, copulative) in which it is being used. See Herodian, in I. Bekker, *Anecdota Graeca* (Berlin, 1821), III, 1148–9; Rafael Kühner and Friedrich Blass, *Ausführliche Grammatik der griechischen Sprache*, 3rd edn. (Hannover and Leipzig, 1890), I. 1, 344.

the doxographer Aëtius) which deal with the parts and elements of the soul.[3] Taken on its own, and in its own context, however, the passage from Epicurus seems to offer a unitary account of the relation of *psychē* to body, and to proceed relatively coherently through the steps enumerated in the translation offered above.[4] Two features of the passage that would seem to support this interpretation have often been overlooked:

1. 'The rest of': having called *psychē* a *sōma*, Epicurus refers (8 above) to what we normally call 'the body' (i.e. to the entity that represents the physical structure and the total organized material substance of the living being) as 'the rest of the aggregate' (*to loipon athroisma*, 6, 8 above). His repeated use of the expression 'the rest of' the aggregate in the immediately following part of the *Letter to Herodotus* underscores not only the conceptual and ontological accommodation of the soul as a part (*meros*, 5) of that bodily 'aggregate' which is the living being, but also that what is at issue in this passage is, in the first place, the relation of *psychē*, as part of the body-aggregate, to 'the rest of the body', rather than the question of the parts of the soul. The latter point is reinforced by the fact that Epicurus starts out by stating, without qualification, that the soul (and not 'a part of the *psychē*', let alone 'the irrational part of the *psychē*') is a body most similar to a certain kind of pneuma (1–3). He likewise concludes (7) by saying that the capacities, etc., of the soul—that is, as a whole (and not the capacities of 'a part' or of 'the parts of the *psychē*')—render all aspects of his account evident; and then, even as he proceeds to a new point, he immediately re-emphasizes that the relation of *psychē* to 'the rest of the body-aggregate' remains at issue, thrice reintroducing this phrase in the subsequent section of the *Letter to Herodotus* (64–5).

2. Similarity and difference are explicitly deployed throughout the passage in order to illuminate the relation of soul, as a whole, to body

---

[3] Cf. scholium on Epicurus, *Letter to Herodotus* 66, in Hermann Usener, *Epicurea* (hereafter Us.) (Leipzig, 1887), no. 311; Lucretius 3, 136–369; Aëtius, *Placita* 4, 3, 11 (no. 315 Us.). See A. A. Long and D. N. Sedley, *The Hellenistic Philosophers* (2 vols., Cambridge, 1987), ii. 65–6; Julia Annas, *Hellenistic Philosophy of Mind* (Berkeley, 1992), 137–51. In order to justify her claim that Epicurus in the passsage cited above (*Letter to Herodotus* 63–4) is primarily presenting his theory of the soul-elements (i.e. of the four types of soul-atoms of which the soul is composed), Annas resorts to methodologically questionable strategies, such as the claim (137) that Epicurus here 'so understates' his own doctrine 'as to be seriously misleading'.

[4] G. B. Kerferd, 'Epicurus' Doctrine of the Soul', *Phronesis*, 16 (1971), 80–96, revived the earlier view (advocated by Richard Heinze and others) that Epicurus here presents a unitary account of *psychē*. But a close reading of the text on its own terms suggests that Epicurus's explicit emphasis here is on the similarities and differences between *psychē*, pneuma, and the body-aggregate (see below). For a different view see e.g. Long and Sedley, *Hellenistic Philosophers*, ii. 65–6; Annas, *Hellenistic Philosophy of Mind*, 137 ff.

as a whole, rather than to offer, as most recent interpreters have argued, an identification and analysis of the parts or elements of the soul. The different parts are not identified here, let alone enumerated, by Epicurus. A scholiast of uncertain date and later Epicureans such as Diogenes of Oenoanda understood the parts of the soul to be the 'rational' (*logikon*) part, located in the chest, and the 'irrational' (*alogon*) part, diffused throughout the body, corresponding, respectively, to Lucretius's *animus* and *anima*; but Epicurus himself introduces no such distinction in this passage.[5] Nor does Epicurus here set out to identify, let alone analyse, the elements (*stoicheia*) of the soul (which later sources identify as 'the smoothest and roundest atoms' or as 'fire-like, air-like, pneuma-like elements, and a fourth nameless element'[6]).

In the passage cited, at least four claims concerning similarity and difference are relevant for present purposes. First, *psychē* is a fine-textured body most similar to pneuma, notably to pneuma that has a certain blending (*krasin*, 3) of warmth. Epicurus, unlike the Stoics, does not say that the soul is pneuma. Nor does he say (here, at least) that pneuma is one of several constitutive elements of the *psychē*. Nor does he claim that any one part of the *psychē* has a special relation to pneuma. Rather, it is *psychē* as a whole that is a body 'most resembling' a certain kind of pneuma—namely pneuma with or having a blend of warmth (3).

Furthermore, according to Epicurus, this fine-particled psychic body (*sōma leptomeres*, 1) as a whole in one way (or: on the one hand) is similar to pneuma, in another way (or: on the other hand) is similar to the warm (4). Again, it is a partial similarity, not identity, that is claimed for the relation of the corporeal soul as a whole to pneuma.

Third, this psychic body not only is similar to pneuma and heat, however; it also must differ from them, for if it did not, it would simply be warm pneuma, not soul. The claim of difference is necessary, in part to explain why atomic interactions can—and often do—produce pneuma and heat without necessarily constituting *psychē*. Indeed, the fine-particled psychic body 'is the part' of the body-aggregate 'which . . . has acquired a great difference', and it is, specifically, very different 'even from pneuma and heat themselves' (5). The difference is succinctly, if not satisfactorily, specified: the soul's fineness of parts (*leptomereia*, 5), to which Epicurus referred already in the first sentence of the passage cited, sets it greatly apart even from the very things it most resembles—namely from pneuma and the warm (5) or, more precisely, from 'pneuma that has a blending of the warm' (1). Here it becomes

---

[5] Diogenes of Oenoanda 37, 1, 5–7; Lucretius 3, 136–76; scholium on *Letter to Herodotus* 66 (no. 311 Us.); Aëtius, *Placita* 4, 4, 6.

[6] Scholium (see n. 5); Aëtius, *Placita* 4, 3, 11 (no. 315 Us.). Cf. Plutarch, *Adversus Coloten* 20 (*Moralia* 1118D–E; no. 314 Us.).

more fully evident that Epicurus's previous, repeated emphasis on resemblance (rather than identity) must be taken at face value: unlike identity, similarity always entails partial difference; and a specification of difference (here the exceptionally fine material texture of the soul) could help to complete an account of the nature and limits of the resemblance. Epicurus does not specify precisely wherein the 'great similarity' (3–4) lies. Nor does he, unlike his followers, in the extant evidence identify more exactly the nature of the fine parts of which the soul's matter is constituted, although he makes amply clear that the soul, like any complex atomic structure, is itself compounded of 'parts'.

Fourth, this 'great difference' (5) between soul's body (by which I mean the body (*sōma*) of which the soul is constituted), on the one hand, and the warm pneuma it most resembles, on the other, nevertheless does not preclude the possibility of this fine-particled soul-body being co-affected with the rest of the body-aggregate (6), notably with that which it most resembles within the rest of the body-aggregate—that is, with pneuma (*toutōi mallon*, 6).

This passage, taken in its entirety, thus appears to be centrally structured by a series of delineations of difference and similarity between *psychē* as a whole and body as a whole, rather than by the definition of the parts of the soul that most critics have tried to find in it. The reading offered here might be further confirmed by the evidence which, in conclusion, Epicurus summons for 'all of this' (7) before he subsequently moves on to a new point concerning the relation of the corporeal *psychē* to the rest of the body in the specific cases of sentience of injury or mutilation and of death. 'The capacities of the soul', he says, 'make all of this evident, and so do its affections, motilities, acts of thinking, and the things deprived of which we die' (7). This enumeration stretches to include everything for which the *psychē* might be held responsible, culminating in a privative definition of life itself ('the things deprived of which we die'), rather than specifying the two Epicurean parts of the *psychē*—rational and irrational—and then mentioning their respective capacities or affections. First place among the evidencing instances is assigned to 'the capacities (*dynameis*) of the soul', again without any qualification or subdivision of the *psychē*. Epicurus thus seems to signal in conclusion, too, that he has been talking of the soul as a whole without qualification, and not of any particular part or element of the *psychē*.

As will become evident below, both in philosophy and in medicine *dynamis* ('capacity', 'faculty', 'power', 'potentiality') plays an increasingly conspicuous role in post-classical Greek models of the relation of the soul to the body. Among the distinctive capacities of the *psychē* explored by Epicurus to define his view of the relation of body to soul, none is more prominent than sensation and perception or sentience (all of which are designated by *aisthēsis*). There are, of course, well-known epistemological reasons for this—*aisthēsis*, as the first of the three criteria of truth, is a corner-stone of Epicurus's *Kanōn*[7]—but my primary concern here is whether his discussions of *aisthēsis* reveal anything further about his views on the relation of soul to body.

In the passage from the *Letter to Herodotus* cited above, Epicurus attributes 'greatest' or 'very great'—but not sole—responsibility for sentience to the *psychē* (8), implying that something, or some things, other than the *psychē* bear co-responsibility, albeit lesser responsibility, for sentience. Indeed, the co-responsible entity is subsequently identified as 'the rest of the body-aggregate': '*psychē*', says Epicurus, 'would not have acquired [the greatest responsibility for] *aisthēsis*, if *psychē* were not somehow covered [sheltered] by the rest of the aggregate' (8). But Epicurus does not limit himself to claiming that, by 'covering' the soul, the body makes sentience (and, as other passages suggest, all animate functioning) possible. He also insists that the relation of body to *psychē* is characterized by close interaction, by interdependence, and by co-affection, as the case of *aisthēsis* in particular reveals:

The rest of the aggregate, having provided it [the *psychē*] with this responsibility [sc. for *aisthēsis*], itself in turn acquired from it [from the soul] a share in such an accidental property (*symptōma*)—though not a share of all the attributes which the soul has obtained and possesses. For this reason, when the soul has been removed, it [sc. the rest of the body-aggregate] does not have *aisthēsis*. You see, it [the body-aggregate] did not itself possess this capacity [*dynamis*, sc. *aisthēsis*] in itself. Rather, it [the body-aggregate] had been preparing it [sc. this sentient capacity] for another thing [sc. the soul] which had come into being simultaneously with it [sc. with the body-aggregate]. And it [the soul] through the capacity [sc. *aisthēsis*] which had been brought to perfection with and in it in accordance with its motion, instantly achieved the accidental property capable of [or enabling] sensation (*symptōma aisthētikon*) for itself, and it [the soul] was giving [this property] to the other [sc. to the rest of the body-aggregate] too, as I said, in accordance with their contiguity and co-affection [*sympatheia*, mutual sensibility].[8]

In addition to the chain of reciprocally enabling characteristics, capacities, and activities of soul and body, two features of this passage are noteworthy. First, the soul's capacity (*dynamis*)—here *aisthēsis*—is described as an accidental property of the soul. In a subsequent part of the *Letter to Herodotus* Epicurus, arguing against the incorporeality of the soul, says that the *psychē* 'could not act or be acted upon in any respect, if it were of such a kind [sc. incorporeal]; but now both these accidental properties [*symptōmata*, sc. acting and being acted upon] are

---

[7] Diogenes Laertius 10, 31–2. Cf. Epicurus, *Letter to Herodotus* 38–9; *idem, Kyriai doxai* 23–4.   [8] *Letter to Herodotus* 64.

self-evidently discernible in the soul'.[9] Such passages suggest that not only sensation, but all capacities and susceptibilities of the *psychē* are its accidental properties, produced in part by the contiguity and mutual co-affectability of soul-atoms and body-aggregate-atoms.

Indeed, soul is itself an accidental property of certain combinations of certain kinds of atoms, and the body too is a relatively stable complex of properties of certain combinations of certain atoms—properties over and above the primary attributes of their constituent atoms.[10] Although the soul, its distinctive capacities, and its distinctive susceptibilities are all accidental properties of atomic compounds in the body, neither the soul itself nor any of its capacities is a merely passive epiphenomenon causally determined by atomic motions.[11] Rather, the soul itself also acquires a causal efficacy distinct both from that of its constituent atoms and from that of the rest of the body-aggregate: the soul can operate causally and intentionally upon the component atoms of our body-aggregate and can overcome, modify, or restrain some of the natural inclinations 'accidentally' produced by the combinations of atoms that constitute the rest of our body-aggregate.

Soul and body are, then, two mutually dependent 'bodies' defining a living thing. To function as soul and as body, respectively, they need each other. Without the rest of the body-aggregate, the fine-particled body which is *psychē* cannot function as soul—indeed, without the rest of the body, the soul does not exist, and the atoms that might have become soul are simply dispersed insentient atoms. And without the corporeal soul, the rest of the body is a mere corpse or merely dispersed insentient atoms. Obvious epistemological motivations apart, the reasons for the centrality of sentience or sense perception (*aisthēsis*)—itself an accident of atomic combinations and motions—in Epicurus's account of the body–soul relation become clear. *Aisthēsis* provides a paradigmatic case-study in the relations between soul and body: sentience becomes possible only through the interaction of the mutually dependent body and soul, yet is necessary to both.

[9] *Letter to Herodotus* 67.
[10] On secondary attributes of complex entities, including essential permanent attributes and (non-essential) accidents, see *Letter to Herodotus* 68–73; Lucretius 1, 445–82. On the primary attributes of atoms (shape, size, weight) see *Letter to Herodotus* 54–6.
[11] Apparently, unlike Democritus, Epicurus takes the secondary or 'phenomenal' attributes of compound bodies to be real; these attributes are not merely arbitrary constructions placed upon configurations of atoms and the void by our cognitive apparatus. Not only are phenomenal properties real—and sense impressions of them normally true—but the *psychē*, through its responses and volitions, has a causal capacity that is real, ultimately derived from, yet standing over and above, the underlying matrices of atomic motions. See Epicurus, *On Nature* 34, 21–30. Cf. also Lucretius 2, 251–93 on the 'swerve' and human autonomy.

II. HEROPHILUS (*c*.330–250 BC)

Among the roughly 300 scattered extant remains of the theories of Herophilus, several suggest a keen interest in some of the problems explored above. Herophilus retains a distinction between soul and body, but, like many of his contemporaries, including Epicurus and the Stoics (see section IV below), he believes that *psychē* is corporeal. And, like Epicurus and the Stoics, he draws a line of demarcation between the corporeal soul and the rest of the body both in material terms and in terms of powers or capacities. He shares their belief that the material substance of the *psychē* is, in some respects, different from that of the rest of the body; and, like the Stoics, he claims that the substance of the soul is pneuma.[12] Furthermore, he redefines the line of demarcation between this corporeal soul and the rest of the body by sharply limiting the ascription of 'capacities' or 'powers' or 'faculties' (*dynameis*) to the *psychē*, and by making nature (*physis*) rather than the soul responsible for functions which Plato, Aristotle, and others had previously ascribed to the soul. This redefinition of the soul and of the range of its activities was, it seems, a direct consequence of Herophilus's discovery of the nerves, which had far-reaching consequences for models of the soul—and of soul–body relations—both in medicine and in philosophy.

Like his philosophical contemporaries, Herophilus takes up the perennial issue of the localization, within the ensouled body, of individual psychic functions or parts. In particular, he addresses the popular question of the bodily location of the ruling part or command centre (*hēgemonikon*) of the *psychē*. In the recurrent Greek *agōn* between the heart and the head, he sides with the proponents of the brain (Alcmaeon, Democritus, Diogenes of Apollonia, the Hippocratic treatise *Sacred Disease*, Plato, etc.) against the advocates of the heart (Empedocles ('blood around the heart'), Aristotle, Epicurus, the Stoics, etc.). Herophilus's remarkable anatomical explorations, based in large measure on systematic human dissection and probably, to some extent, on human and animal vivisection, not only allowed him to confirm that the brain is the centre of all psychic activity, as several predecessors had claimed, but also to specify more precisely than any precursor the location of the soul's central 'ruling part': it is in 'the ventricle of the brain which is its base' or, as he puts it elsewhere, in 'the ventricle in the

---

[12] Galen, *De sententiis* (= *De propriis placitis*) 145b, in H. von Staden, *Herophilus: The Art of Medicine in Early Alexandria* (hereafter *Heroph.*) (Cambridge, 1989), 323–4, seems to ascribe the view that the substance of the soul is pneuma to Hippocrates, Erasistratus, and Herophilus, while emphasizing that each viewed the distribution of soul-pneuma differently; see the forthcoming edition (Corpus Medicorum Graecorum (hereafter CMG)) of *De sententiis* by Vivian Nutton.

cerebellum [which] exercises most control'[13]—that is, in the so-called fourth ventricle.

The means by which the *psychē*'s ruling centre interacts with the human body are the nerves, for whose discovery Herophilus was responsible. The nerves are 'offshoots' or 'sprouts' (*blastēmata*) of the cerebellum, and all action of the body is brought about through them (but see below on 'natural activities').[14] There is good evidence that he distinguished sensory nerves (*neura aisthētika*, 'nerves that make *aisthēsis* possible' or 'that belong to sensation') from motor nerves. The latter he calls 'voluntary nerves' (*neura prohairetika*, 'nerves that make choice possible'), probably to differentiate the voluntary motions (*kinēseis prohairetikai, hai kata prohairesin kinēseis*) and activities for which the *psychē* is responsible from involuntary (*aprohairetōs*) movements in or of the body, such as the pulse and respiration, which he also calls 'natural activities' (*physikai energeiai*; see below),[15] and which are not functions of the soul.

Just how the nerves interact with the *psychē* to transmit information from the command centre in the ventricle of the cerebellum to various parts of the body, or vice versa, is not altogether clear from the extant evidence, but there are some tantalizing hints. In the case of vision, one problematic ancient source, Calcidius, claims that, according to Herophilus, the optic nerve contains 'natural pneuma' (*spiritus naturalis = pneuma physikon*?), and this is consistent at least with Herophilus's identification of the substance of *psychē* with pneuma[16] (although 'natural' strikes me as possibly suspect, especially in view of Herophilus's collocation of 'natural' with involuntary activities such as respiration and the pulse). It also suggests a model in some respects similar to Chrysippus's subsequent image of an octopus or spider web,

---

[13] Galen, *De usu partium* (hereafter *UP*) 8, 11 (I, 484 Helmreich), *Heroph.* T138; Tertullian, *De anima*, ed. J. H. Waszink (Amsterdam, 1947), 15, 2–5 (*Heroph.* T139). See also *Heroph.* 314–15 (T137a–e).

[14] Rufus of Ephesus, *De nominatione partium hominis* 149–50, ed. C. Daremberg and C. E. Ruelle (Paris, 1879), 153; *Heroph.* T125.

[15] Rufus of Ephesus(?), *De anatomia partium hominis* 71–5 (184–5 Daremberg/Ruelle; *Heroph.* T81): 'voluntary nerves' (*neura prohairetika*). Galen, *De tremore, palpitatione, convulsione et rigore* 5, in *Claudii Galeni opera omnia*, ed. C. G. Kühn (hereafter K) (20 vols. in 22, Leipzig, 1821–33), 7.605–6; *Heroph.* T141: nerves are responsible for voluntary motions. Rufus of Ephesus(?), *Synopsis de pulsibus* 2 (220–1 Daremberg/Ruelle; *Heroph.* T149): the pulse attends us involuntarily (*aprohairetōs*) and naturally (*physikōs*), whereas other motions are within our power of choice (*prohairesis*). See also *Heroph.* 320–2 (T143a–c): the lungs' activity occurs naturally (*physikōs*), and its 'natural activity' is the drawing in of breath (*pneuma*) from outside.

[16] Calcidius, *In Platonis Timaeum comment.* 246, ed. J. H. Waszink (Leiden and London, 1962), 256–7; *Heroph.* T86. On some of the affinities with Stoic theory see the pioneering contribution by Friedrich Solmsen, 'Greek Philosophy and the Discovery of the Nerves', *Museum Helveticum*, 18 (1961), 150–97; repr. in *idem, Kleine Schriften* (3 vols., Hildesheim, 1968–82), I. 536–82.

according to which the soul's pneuma flows between its ruling part and each sensory organ, with the difference that, in Herophilus's view, such 'messages' are transmitted from the cerebellum through the sensory nerves, whereas Chrysippus locates the ruling part of the soul in the heart (see section IV below). It should, however, be kept in mind that no ancient author confirms Calcidius's attribution of *spiritus naturalis* to Herophilus; nor is similar evidence extant for senses other than vision.

The scanty extant evidence is even more problematic in the case of the voluntary or motor nerves. It is not certain, *pace* Solmsen,[17] that Herophilus resorted to a similar model—pneuma transmitting messages through the motor nerves—to account for the way in which the soul's command centre, from its seat in the cerebellum, governs the body's voluntary motions. Galen, for one, makes no mention of 'motor pneuma' (or of pneuma at all) when he criticizes Herophilus for failing to recognize 'that the body (*sōma*) of the nerves (*neurōn*) is not itself the cause of motion but rather its instrument (*organon*), whereas its moving cause is the faculty (*dynamis*) which extends through the nerves; here I reproach Herophilus for not having distinguished faculty from instrument'.[18]

Galen's criticism is put forward in full knowledge of the fact that Herophilus was not averse to one of Galen's favourite explanatory devices—namely 'capacities' or 'powers', or 'faculties' (*dynameis*): Galen knows and reports that Herophilus, too, recognized a number of such capacities that are responsible for bodily activities. Some of these Herophilean *dynameis* are, significantly, depicted as 'natural capacities' that operate independently of the nerves and of the *psychē*. Thus a 'motor faculty' or 'kinetic capacity' (*dynamis kinētikē*) flows from the heart through the arterial coats and thereby enables the arteries to dilate and contract—a 'capacity' which, Galen seems to suggest, Herophilus also called 'vital faculty' or 'life-enabling power' (*zōtikē dynamis*), and which he described as capable of varying degrees of strength. Similarly, Herophilus describes the lungs as having a natural desire to expand and contract.[19]

---

[17] Solmsen, 'Greek philosophy', 571–4.

[18] Galen, *De tremore, palpitatione, convulsione et rigore* 5 (7. 605–6, K; Heroph. T141); cf. Paul Potter, 'Herophilus of Chalcedon: An Assessment of his Place in the History of Anatomy', *Bulletin of the History of Medicine*, 50 (1976), 45–60, at 52.

[19] On the capacity or faculty that makes the pulse possible according to Herophilus see Galen, *De pulsuum differentiis* 4, 2 and 4, 6 (8. 702–3, 733 K; *Heroph.* T155, T144), and *idem, An in arteriis sanguis contineatur* 8, ed. D. J. Furley and J. S. Wilkie, in *Galen on Respiration and the Arteries* (Princeton, 1972), 176–8 (*Heroph.* T145a). On the 'vital dynamis' and its strength see Galen, *De pulsuum differentiis* 3, 2 (8. 645 K; *Heroph.* T164); on 'kinetic dynamis' see pseudo-Galen, *De historia philosopha* 103, in H. Diels (ed.), *Doxographi Graeci* (Berlin, 1879), 639 (*Heroph.* T143c).

Other 'capacities' or 'faculties' are, however, specific to the soul, such as sentience and the voluntary 'kinetic powers' in the motor nerves, in the muscles, and generally in the 'nerve-like class' of bodily parts (probably including tendons and ligaments).[20] These powers are, significantly, all associated with the nerves. While the *psychē* is not alone in manifesting itself in the body through distinctive capacities—nature (*physis*) does so too—Herophilus believes that the soul possesses powers or faculties peculiar to it, and that these operate and extend through the nerves. Yet he equally clearly attributes certain kinetic affections, such as tremors, to lesions or dysfunctions of bodily parts themselves, rather than to impairment of the relevant capacity flowing to them through the nerves; it is this feature of Herophilus's theory that arouses the displeasure of Galen, who, as will be shown in section V, believes there is little that could not be explained by some or other 'faculty'.[21]

Herophilus's differentiation, within living beings, of activities produced by capacities of the *psychē* from 'natural' capacities and their activities signals that he circumscribes the soul's distinctive powers and activities much more narrowly than had, for example, Plato and Aristotle. This more restrictive view of *psychē*, of its *dynameis*, and of its 'ruling part' is centrally informed by Herophilus's exploration of the hindbrain, by his discovery of the nerves, and in particular by his distinction between motor and sensory nerves. Furthermore, he uses 'nature' (*physis*) to draw lines of demarcation between *psychē* and the rest of the body in ways which, as will be shown below (section IV), display a significant affinity with Stoicism after Herophilus: sentience and voluntary movement are the domains of *psychē*, whereas vegetative and other involuntary functions—digestion, respiration, pulsation—are domains of nature. For nature's activities, the soul is not responsible. (This view bears obvious resemblance to the Stoic distinction between soul and nature which within Stoicism, to my knowledge, is first attested for Chrysippus (281 or 277–208 or 204 BC), i.e. well after Herophilus's *floruit*; see section IV below.)

The fragmentary remains of Herophilus's works leave unclear, however, how Herophilus understood the relations between the pneuma which is the substance of the soul, the soul-pneuma in the nerves, the finely divided soul-pneuma which, according to a problematic testimonium,[22] is present in all parts of the living body's constituents (i.e. not

---

[20] *Heroph.* T143c (see n. 19), T141 (see n. 18), T81 (see n. 15), and 240–1.

[21] *Heroph.* T141 (see n. 18). For Galen's uses of *dynamis* see below, sec. V.

[22] If a problematic Latin translation of Galen's *De propriis placitis* (*De sententiis*) is to be trusted, it appears that Herophilus believes that the pneuma which is soul 'is divided' into small parts, such that there is no one of the constituent parts of the body in which it is not present. Herophilus thus apparently resorts to very fine 'division' to

only in the nerves or in the cerebrum), and the non-psychic pneuma that is present, for example, in the lungs and, mixed with blood, in the arteries.

Furthermore, while the features of Herophilus's theories singled out thus far elucidate the relation of the soul to the body principally by providing details on how a corporeal *psychē* functions in and with the body, they tell us less about the nature of the body itself. In the extant evidence Herophilus's apparent retention of humoral pathology suggests that he might subscribe to the traditional theory of the four elements, but this is not brought to bear upon the question of the line of demarcation between body and soul.[23] Nor does his influential tripartite classification of bodies (*sōmata*) as healthy, diseased, and neither (*oudetera*) offer much from this perspective.[24] Indeed, about the elemental constituents of the body, and how they differ from or resemble the elemental constituents of the soul-pneuma, Herophilus seems to have exercised *epochē* (or at least his customary caution): he is among the physicians, observes Galen, 'who did not dare declare themselves at all concerning the nature of the primary bodies (*ta prōta sōmata*) of the body'.[25] This is in keeping, epistemologically and methodologically, with Herophilus's claim that it is by nature undiscoverable whether or not cause exists, and that causal statements can hence be made only *ex hypothesi*.[26] His slightly younger contemporary Erasistratus, by contrast, was much more confident that a valid account of the body, of its processes, and of its relation to the soul can be achieved: therapeutics and semiotics might be conjectural endeavours, he said, but in aetiology and physiology one can achieve certain knowledge (*epistēmē*).[27]

depict the soul as present throughout the body (whereas Epicurus characterizes the fine-particled atomic soul as a body that is in the state of being 'spread' or 'sown', or 'diffused' (*diesparmenon*) over the entire rest of the body-aggregate, and whereas the Stoics, as will be shown in sec. IV, describe the corporeal soul as thoroughly 'blended' with the entire body). See *Heroph.* 323–4 (T145b).

[23] See *Heroph.* 242–6, 311–13 (T130, T132–4).

[24] *Heroph.* 89–98, 103–8, 112–14, and T42–8.

[25] Galen, *Methodus medendi* 7, 2 (10. 461–2 K); *Heroph.* 588 (T293).

[26] *Heroph.* 115–25, 130–4 (including T50a–b, T58, T59a). For a somewhat different interpretation see R. J. Hankinson, 'Saying the Phenomena', *Phronesis*, 35 (1990), 194–215; but the suggestion that Anaxagoras, rather than the Aristotelian and medical traditions, represented the major methodological inspiration for a third-century BC physician practising in Alexandria, stretches the historical imagination, also in view of the fact that the relevant fragment of Anaxagoras (H. Diels and W. Kranz, *Die Fragmente der Vorsokratiker*, 6th edn. (3 vols., Berlin, 1952), 59 B 21a (2. 43. 13–18)) is not attested by classical and Hellenistic authors. It never appears before Sextus Empiricus (*Adversus mathematicos* 7, 140), and all but one manuscript of Sextus's text—albeit a superior manuscript (N)—omit the fragment.

[27] Ps.-Galen, *Introductio* 5 (14. 684 K): the *epistēmonikon* part of medicine vs the *stochastikon* = fr. 32 in Ivan Garofalo, *Erasistrati fragmenta* (hereafter *Eras.*) (Pisa, 1988).

III. ERASISTRATUS (*c*.320–240 BC)

Erasistratus makes the innovative claim, startling in its historical context, that a corporeal *psychē* is always present throughout the living body of an animal by virtue of being materially present as a feature of one of the three constitutive parts of the basic matter out of which the body as a whole is constructed. Erasistratus believes that the 'principles (*archai*) and elements (*stoicheia*) of the body as a whole are the *triplokiai* ("triple webs", "triple braids", "triple twining") of arteries, veins, and nerves'.[28] Every part of the body, including all muscles, tendons, organs, skin, vessels, and presumably bones, consists of such elemental 'triple twists', woven everywhere 'just like a rope plaited [twisted] from three cords [thongs] that differ from one another in their nature'.[29] The capacities and functions of arteries, veins, and nerves can thus be exercised throughout the body. Even perceptible nerves themselves are composed of such imperceptible nerve–artery–vein interwoven triple strands.[30] This elemental constitution of the body, Erasistratus believes, is central to the relation of the soul to the body.

Most, but not all, ancient sources suggest that Erasistratus, like Herophilus, attributed to the nerves alone the ability to receive and transmit the soul's messages throughout the body or to communicate information to the soul's ruling part. In Erasistratus's amalgam of teleology and mechanism,[31] each of the duct systems represented in the triple strands—the arterial, venous, and nervous systems—has a distinct source, material content, function, and purpose; and each is supplied with its content by mechanistic processes. An informing principle of these mechanistic processes is that matter 'follows toward that which is being emptied' or vacated (*pros to kenoumenon akolouthia*, henceforth *PTKA*): that is, the principle that if matter is vacated from any contained space, other matter will rush in to take its place, since a massed void is impossible (even if dispersed or 'disseminated', or interstitial, void were possible).[32] The sources—

---

[28] Ps.-Galen, *Introductio* 9 (14. 697 K; *Eras.* fr. 86).

[29] Galen, *De naturalibus facultatibus* (hereafter *Nat. fac.*) 2, 6 (2. 96 K) = *Galenus, Scripta minora* (hereafter *Scr. min.*), ed. J. Marquardt, I. von Müller, and G. Helmreich (3 vols., Leipzig, 1884–93), III, 171 = *Eras.* fr. 89; *idem, UP* 7, 8 (3. 538 K; I, 392 Helmreich; *Eras.* fr. 88); *idem, De anatomicis administrationibus* (hereafter *Anat. adm.*) 2, 11 (2. 337 K; I, 254 Garofalo; *Eras.* fr. 90); *idem, An in arteriis sanguis contineatur* 4 (4. 716 K; 158 Furley and Wilkie; *Eras.* fr. 46); Anonymus Londinensis XXI, 23–8 (*Eras.* fr. 87); Soranus, *Gynaecia* 3, 4 (CMG IV, 94 Ilberg; *Eras.* fr. 60).

[30] Galen, *Nat. fac.* 2, 6 (2. 103 K; *Scr. min.* III, 176 Helmreich).

[31] See H. von Staden, 'Teleology and Mechanism: Aristotelian Biology and Early Hellenistic Medicine', in W. Kullmann and S. Föllinger (eds.), *Aristotelische Biologie: Intentionen, Methoden, Ergebnisse*, (Stuttgart, 1997), 183–208.

[32] Galen, *De facultate purgantium medicamentorum* 1 (11. 324 K; *Eras.* fr. 93); *idem, Nat. fac.* 2, 1 and 2, 6 (2. 75, 99 K; *Scr. min.* III, 155, 173 Helmreich; *Eras.* frs. 95–6); *idem,*

brain, heart, liver—of the three duct systems *prima facie* might suggest an echo of Plato's *Timaeus*, but Erasistratus's theory introduces themes and explanatory principles that are a far cry from Timaeus's 'likely story'. According to Erasistratus, the nerves distribute soul-pneuma (*pneuma psychikon*) from the brain (or, as he apparently originally believed, from the dura mater), the arteries distribute life-pneuma or vital pneuma (*pneuma zōtikon*, 'pneuma that makes life possible') from the left ventricle of the heart in accordance with the *PTKA* principle, and the veins carry blood as nourishment from the liver to the entire body, again by *PTKA*.[33] But what is the origin of soul-pneuma, and how does it differ from 'the body' and from other kinds of pneuma in the body?

All pneuma in the body has the same ultimate source, being derived from the external air through respiration. After each exhalation, external air rushes into the lungs (in accordance with the *PTKA* principle).[34] From the lungs, by the same principle, some of the air, in the form of pneuma which is not yet further differentiated, moves through the 'vein-like artery' (i.e. the pulmonary vein) into the left ventricle of the heart, whenever the ventricle expands after each contraction. In this cardiac ventricle the pneuma becomes refined into vital pneuma or 'life-pneuma' before being 'sent off' or thrust into the aorta with each contraction of the left ventricle.[35] The contraction of the ventricle in turn causes the aorta to dilate. Since the left cardiac ventricle is empty after contraction, undifferentiated pneuma moves into it again from the lungs via the 'vein-like artery' (in accordance with the *PTKA* principle), thus dilating the ventricle once more. The cycle continues, the systole of the left cardiac ventricle apparently always coinciding with the diastole of the arteries, and vice versa. Each fresh increment of vital pneuma expelled from the left ventricle into the arterial system pushes along the immediately adjacent vital pneuma, thereby setting off a wave-like

---

Anat. adm. 6, 16 (2. 648–9 K; *Eras.* fr. 49A). Cf. J. T. Vallance, *The Lost Theory of Asclepiades of Bithynia* (Oxford, 1990), 62–79 (from whom I gratefully take over the convenient abbreviation 'PTKA', which avoids some of the pitfalls inherent in the scholarly tradition of referring to Erasistratus's theory as 'the *horror vacui* principle').

[33] Galen, *De placitis Platonis et Hippocratis* (hereafter *PHP*) 7, 3, 6–11 (CMG V 4, 1, 2, 440–2 De Lacy; *Eras.* fr. 289); *idem, In Hippocratis Aphorismos* 6, 50 (18A. 86 K; *Eras.* fr. 288). Cf. *Eras.* frs. 101–8, 112–12B.

[34] Anonymus Londinensis XXIII; Galen, *An in arteriis* 2 (4. 706 K; 148 Furley and Wilkie; *Eras.* fr. 101). See Vallance, *Lost Theory*, 67–74; Furley and Wilkie, *Galen on Respiration*, 26–37.

[35] Galen, *An in arteriis* (4. 714 K; 156 Furley and Wilkie; *Eras.* fr. 102); *idem, De locis affectis* 5, 3 (8. 316 K; *Eras.* fr. 105); *idem, De pulsuum differentiis* 4, 2 and 4, 17 (8. 702–3, 759–60 K; *Eras.* frs. 110, 205); *idem, PHP* 1, 6, 3 (78 De Lacy; *Eras.* fr. 203). See C. R. S. Harris, *The Heart and the Vascular System in Ancient Greek Medicine from Alcmeon to Galen* (Oxford, 1973), 177–233.

ripple of dilatation that moves with lightning speed through the arteries in each diastole.[36]

The arterial system carries some of the vital pneuma to the brain (or, in one version, to the meninges, and perhaps more specifically to the dura mater), where it becomes still more highly refined, namely into soul-pneuma, which is the soul.[37] The sparse extant evidence does not offer an account of how this refinement takes place (but Erasistratus's theory that the large number of convolutions in the cerebellum can be correlated with the superior cognitive capacity of the human species is suggestive, especially in light of the fact that one of the two main functions of the *psychē*, in his view, is precisely cognition; see also below, section V).[38] Nor do the extant remains of his works specify exactly what the physical (as opposed to functional) difference between 'vital' and 'psychic' pneuma is, other than to imply that psychic pneuma is more refined, inasmuch as it is produced out of vital pneuma. The only quality that Erasistratus explicitly assigns to pneuma of any kind is 'fineness', which, he says, characterizes vital pneuma.[39] The association of pneuma with fineness (or with 'fineness of parts', 'fineness of texture', *leptomereia*) is not uncommon from Aristotle on. As pointed out above, Epicurus compares soul to a 'fine-particled body' (*sōma leptomeres*) which closely resembles pneuma; later, Chrysippus again calls the constitutive elements of pneuma (air and fire) fine-particled (*leptomeres*).[40] There is no sign that Erasistratus shared the Stoic principle of tensile movement or tension to differentiate one kind of pneuma from another (see section IV below); but, given his emphasis on the fineness of vital pneuma, it is not unlikely that he shared with Epicurus the use of degrees of 'fineness of parts' as a way of distinguishing soul-pneuma from other kinds of pneuma.

Since nerves are one of the three constitutive parts of the constitu-

---

[36] This movement of vital pneuma from the heart into the arteries is irreversible because, as Erasistratus apparently proved experimentally, the function of the heart valves—which he describes in considerable anatomical detail—is to ensure the irreversibility of the various flows from and into the heart. Galen, *PHP* 6, 6, 4–19 (396–8 De Lacy; *Eras.* fr. 201). See H. von Staden, 'Experiment and Experience in Hellenistic Medicine', *Bulletin of the Institute of Classical Studies*, 22 (1975), 178–99; idem, 'Cardiovascular Puzzles in Erasistratus and Herophilus', in *XXXI Congresso Internazionale di Storia della Medicina* (Bologna, 1988), 681–7.

[37] Galen, *De usu respirationis* 5 (4. 502 K; 122 Furley and Wilkie; *Eras.* fr. 112); idem, *PHP* 2, 8, 38 (164 De Lacy; *Eras.* fr. 112B).

[38] Galen, *PHP* 7, 3, 9–10 (440–2 De Lacy; *Eras.* fr. 289); idem, *UP* 8, 13 (3. 673 K; I, 488 Helmreich).

[39] Galen, *UP* 8, 8 (3. 540 K; I, 393 Helmreich; *Eras.* fr. 104).

[40] Epicurus, *Letter to Herodotus* 63; Hans von Arnim, *Stoicorum veterum fragmenta* (hereafter *SVF*) (4 vols., Leipzig, 1903–25), 2. 473 (155, 32–6). Cf. Aristotle, *De anima* I 2, 405a622 (on Diogenes of Apollonia); idem, *Meteorologica* III 1, 370b6, 8.

tive element (*triplokia*) of the entire body, they are present everywhere in the body. Soul, as psychic pneuma, therefore, is likewise corporeally present throughout the body. This would explain, for example, why Erasistratus says that psychic and vital capacities are both present in the heart, even while insisting that only vital pneuma is produced in the left cardiac ventricle (and that only blood, which has neither a vital nor a psychic but only a nutritive capacity, enters into and is expelled from the right cardiac ventricle).[41] Since the heart, like all parts of the body, is itself constituted of the braided triple strands, the heart's nerves can transmit any sensation—for example, of pain—to the soul's ruling part in the brain through their psychic pneuma. Neither the vital pneuma nor the blood in the heart could communicate such a sensation to the brain, because psychic pneuma alone is capable of sensation.

Sensation and perception, however, are not the only capacities displayed by psychic pneuma. Like Herophilus, Erasistratus makes both cognition and voluntary motion the primary distinctive activities of soul-pneuma.[42] In the case of voluntary movement of the muscles, psychic pneuma—borne from the brain to the muscles through the motor nerves (*neura kinētika*)—causes the contraction of the muscles by inflating them: when filled with pneuma, the muscles increase in width, but decrease in length, and therefore contract, before relaxing again by a reverse process.[43] The physicalism that dominates early Hellenistic explanations of soul, of its interactions with the body, and of its distinctive capacities and activities is amply evident in this example, too.

Erasistratus thus makes soul-pneuma, distributed through both sensory and motor nerves, responsible primarily for the living being's cognitive and motor activities, while fencing off the soul from responsibility for other 'life functions', such as the pulse, respiration, digestion, and reproduction. He shares this more narrowly circumscribed version of the soul and of soul–body interaction with Herophilus (and, as will be shown in section IV, with some Stoics), perhaps without, however, sharing the hierarchical Herophilean and Stoic distinction between nature and soul. Rather, '[Erasistratus] says that the living being is managed (*dioikeisthai*, "administered") by two materials (*hylai*): on the one hand by blood as nutriment, on the other hand by pneuma as auxiliary (*synergon*) for the natural activities (*physikai energeiai*)'.[44] This might suggest that Erasistratus, unlike Herophilus and the Stoics, views all bodily activities enabled by pneuma as 'natural activities', whether

---

[41] Galen, *De pulsuum differentiis* 4, 17 (8. 760 K; *Eras.* fr. 205). This is strikingly similar to the pulse definition of the Herophilean Chrysermus; see *Heroph.* 526.

[42] Nerves alone carry psychic pneuma, and the only functions of nerves are sentience and voluntary motion.   [43] Galen, *De locis affectis* 6, 5 (8. 429 K; *Eras.* fr. 54).

[44] Ps.-Galen, *Introductio* 9 (14. 697 K; *Eras.* fr. 86).

they are 'vital' (pulse) or 'psychic' (sentience and cognition, voluntary motion).

Be this as it may, Erasistratus's overall view seems to be that the living body itself continuously, mechanistically, produces a corporeal soul, in the form of 'psychic pneuma', in the brain from initially 'non-psychic' matter (vital pneuma), which in turn ultimately is continuously derived from an inanimate part (air) of the immediate environment of each living being by means of the mechanistically operative respiratory cycle, and that this soul is distributed as 'psychic pneuma' throughout the body by motor and sensory nerves.

IV. STOICISM

Like Epicurus, each of the early Stoics (Zeno, Cleanthes, and Chrysippus) developed arguments for the corporeality of the *psychē*. Some argued from the interaction of body and soul (e.g. only bodies can interact and be co-affected, but body and soul interact and are co-affected, therefore soul is body), others from the separation of body and soul (e.g. death is the separation of soul from body, but nothing non-bodily can be separated from body, since nothing non-bodily touches body; the soul both touches and is separated from body; therefore the soul is body).[45]

Significant though these problematic arguments are, more immediately relevant to the subject of this book are the Stoic responses to the problem of defining the difference between soul and body, within a theory that insists on the corporeality of both. These responses display many resonances with the theories explored above. They agree with Epicurus, for example, that soul, while a corporeal thing sharing in three-dimensionality, is in fact distinct from the body, particularly in so far as the *psychē* is uniquely responsible for cognitive, moral, and voluntary motor activities. And just as Epicurus maintained that an individual is an arrangement of matter—namely of invisible, indivisible atomic 'bodies', some of which constitute his bones, flesh, blood, etc., while others are responsible for the many 'psychic' capacities and susceptibilities displayed by the body (that is, by the body constituted by the bones, flesh, blood, etc.) so the Stoics claim that an individual is an arrangement of two interactive things, each of which is a 'body' (*sōma*),

---

[45] *SVF* 1. 137, 518; 2. 773–4, 790–1; see also Alexander of Aphrodisias, *De anima mantissa*, Supplementum Aristotelicum II. 1 (Berlin, 1887), 113–18 Bruns; Malcolm Schofield, 'The Syllogisms of Zeno of Citium', *Phronesis*, 28 (1983), 31–58; A. A. Long, 'Soul and Body in Stoicism', *Phronesis*, 27 (1982), 34–57; Annas, *Hellenistic Philosophy of Mind*, 37–70.

but one of which is again primarily responsible for 'psychic' capacities displayed by the body as a whole or by its parts. The Stoics further agree with Epicurus that the soul is not immortal, although some Stoics, unlike Epicurus, claim that the soul can survive the destruction of the body temporarily, and thus that it can exist independently of the body at least for a while after death (but the Stoics agree with Aristotle's and Epicurus's anti-Platonic view that the soul does not exist prior to the body—i.e. prior to any body for whose capacities or functions it is responsible).[46] Furthermore, like Epicurus, Herophilus, and Erasistratus, the Stoics make pneuma central to their accounts of the *psychē*. Despite these many shared commitments, the Stoic approach to the body–soul relation is distinctive in a number of crucial respects.

In order to explore how, according to Stoic theory, the corporeal soul and the living being's body as a whole resemble or differ from each other, modern scholars have had recourse to five fundamental ontological distinctions introduced by the Stoics in their analysis of the nature of matter and of the relations between different types of matter. I shall argue, however, that the first four of these distinctions, while not irrelevant, and while in part clarifying the *relation* of soul to body, do not account for the *difference* between soul and body.

(1) God versus matter: in the Stoics' universe, which is a material continuum, all matter (*hylē*), including that of every discrete body, is said to be pervaded by 'god', whom they also describe as 'fire', 'the fiery craftsman', or 'intelligent pneuma', and who therefore himself is corporeal too.[47] This pervasive conjunction of god and matter invariably results in 'qualified body'—that is, body with certain qualities (*sōma poion*).[48] Some interpreters have seized on this distinction to try to define the relation of soul to body in terms of 'god' and 'matter'. They emphasize in particular that the Stoics explicitly locate the human *psychē* in a version of the universe according to which there is considerable continuity between humans and the rest of nature. The universe itself, like us, is an ensouled

[46] On the coming into being and passing away of the soul see Eusebius, *Praeparatio evangelica* 15, 20, 6 (*SVF* 2. 809). Eusebius also reports that, according to the Stoics, the souls of the virtuous (*spoudaioi*) survive after death (at least up to each periodic cosmic conflagration), whereas the souls of the foolish or senseless (*aphrones*) survive only for a brief, fixed time. Eusebius does not attribute this view, however, to any specific early or late Stoic by name, but simply reports that 'they [the Stoics] say that . . .'.

[47] Alexander of Aphrodisias, *De mixtione* 10, Supplementum Aristotelicum II. 2 (Berlin, 1892), 224–7 Bruns (136 ff. Todd; *SVF* 2. 310, 475); Aëtius, *Placita* 1, 7, 33 (*SVF* 2. 1027). Cf. *SVF* 1. 155 (*quomodo mel per fauos*), 157, 161; 2. 414, 1042.

[48] Cf. *SVF* 2. 320 (Plotinus, *Enneads* 2, 4, 1). Being 'qualified' is one of four metaphysical aspects under which the Stoics believed that a given entity could be viewed: as substrate (*hypokeimenon*), as qualified (*poion*), as disposed (*pōs echon*), and as relatively disposed (*pros ti pōs echon*). See Simplicius, *In Aristotelis Categorias* 4 (ad 1b25); *Commentaria in Aristotelem graeca* 8 (Berlin, 1907), 66. 32–67. 8 Kalbfleisch (*SVF* 2. 369).

material continuum; it, too, is a living being.[49] Furthermore, the human *psychē*, though distinctive in certain respects, is not materially different from the world's *psychē*, in so far as both, at least according to Chrysippus, are pneuma of a certain sort. Structurally and functionally, too, the human soul and the cosmic soul display similarity, each operating through a 'ruling part' (*hēgemonikon*) located in its hottest part (in the heart and in the ether or sun, respectively).[50]

Because the conjunction of god and matter is a universal condition of matter, however, there presumably is no difference, in this respect, between a stone, an ivy leaf, a lion, and Socrates: all four, like all other discrete bodies and their parts, whether animate or inanimate, are matter pervaded by god; all four, consequently, are 'qualified bodies'. Indeed, given the pervasive, universal conjunction of god and matter, the soul's pneuma is itself qualified body, no less so than is the entity normally referred to as an animal's 'body'. In and of itself, the distinction between god (or divine, 'intelligent pneuma') and matter, while in certain respects analogous to the relation of soul and body, therefore does not account for the difference between the corporeal soul and the rest of the body: both the soul and the body of a person are conjunctions of god and matter, and, as such, both are qualified bodies.

(2) The related Stoic distinction between a rarefied active body (sometimes identified with pneuma or with the weightless elements air and fire, and at times understood to be coextensive with 'god') and a dense passive body (identified with the inactive or inert elements earth and water, which have absolute weight and are at times understood as coextensive with the material substrate of objects, *hylē*)[51] likewise has been taken to be promising for present purposes. But it too leaves central

[49] Diogenes Laertius 7, 142–3 (*SVF* 2. 633); Plutarch, *De Stoicorum repugnantiis* 39 (*Moralia* 1052C–D; *SVF* 2. 604). Cf. Cicero, *De natura deorum* 2, 58 (*SVF* 1. 172); Sextus Empiricus, *Adversus mathematicos* 9, 75 (*SVF* 2. 311).

[50] Diogenes Laertius 7, 138–9, 147 (*SVF* 2. 634, 1021). Cf. Cicero, *De natura deorum* 1, 39 (*SVF* 2. 1077). The special cosmic status of vital heat perhaps illustrates the considerable influence of biology on Stoic physics: the coherence of the cosmos at times is said to be due to a pervasive faculty (or cosmic soul or world mind, both of which are at times identified with celestial fire), which makes intelligent use of its own cohesive power to hold together all parts of the universe. See David Hahm, *The Origins of Stoic Cosmology* (Columbus, Oh., 1977), 60–6, 76–8, 136–84.

[51] Galen, *De plenitudine* 3 (7. 525 K; *SVF* 2. 439); Plutarch, *De communibus notitiis* 49 (*Moralia* 1085C–D; *SVF* 2. 444). Cf. Aristotle, *De generatione et corruptione* 2, 329b24–32. All animals, plants, and inanimate compounds on earth are composed of the four traditional elements earth, air, fire, and water: Stobaeus, *Eclogae* 1, 10, 16c (I, 129–30 Wachsmuth; *SVF* 2. 413). Galen (*De plenitudine* 3 (7. 525–7K)) attributes to the Stoics the distinction between 'pneumatic substance' and 'material substance' (*pneumatikē* vs *hylikē ousia*): pneumatic substance (air and fire) has the cohesive power (*synhektikē dynamis*) that *makes* all things hold together, whereas material substance (earth and water) *is* held together. See n. 59 below.

questions unanswered. For one thing, all soul might be pneuma, but not all pneuma is soul. As the pervasive presence of pneuma in inanimate (i.e. soulless) natural objects and in soulless artefacts shows, pneuma might be a necessary condition of the existence of *psychē*, but it certainly is not a sufficient condition. In and of themselves, then, the distinctions between active principle and passive principle, between rarefied body and dense body, between pneuma (or fire and air) and inert elements (water, earth) will also not account adequately for the difference between soul and body, even though they are all essential to understanding the nature of both *psychē* and *sōma*.

(3) A further fundamental Stoic distinction concerning the relation of matter to matter appears to be more useful. Chrysippus's theory of mixture, in part in critical response to Aristotle's, allows for three kinds of relations between physical substances: juxtaposition or 'joining' (*mixis parathesei* or *kath' harmēn*), fusion (*synchysis*), and blending (*krasis*).[52] An example of juxtaposition is a mixture of beans and grains of wheat: their surfaces are in contact, but each preserves its own substance and quality. Fusion, by contrast, occurs when the substances and qualities mixed together are mutually destroyed, and another, different body, with different properties, is generated out of them, as in the case of a compound medical drug. The original substances and qualities of the ingredients can never be recovered from the fused new body, which has powers that none of the ingredients has by itself. In the case of blending, the blended substances and their qualities are mutually coextended throughout the entity, 'passing through' one another everywhere, so that there are no parts of the blended mixture that do not participate in everything contained in the mixture (hence 'blending' is not 'juxtaposition'). Yet each of the original substances remains preserved with its qualities (hence 'blending' is not 'fusion'). Indeed, each of the original substances, with its original properties, is in principle recoverable from a 'blended' mixture. Water, some Stoics argue, can, for example, be artificially separated from the wine with which it has been blended.[53]

A prime Stoic example of this third type of relation, blending (*krasis*), is the relation between body and soul.[54] A living animal is a product of a thorough blending, throughout the animal, of body and soul. The animal thus has no part which is only soul and no part which is only body: it is, throughout, an ensouled body. But, because the living crea-

---

[52] Alexander, *De mixtione* 3 (216–17 Bruns; 114–16 Todd; *SVF* 2. 473). Cf. *SVF* 2. 471–2. Robert B. Todd, *Alexander of Aphrodisias on Stoic Physics* (Leiden, 1976), esp. 30–65; Richard Sorabji, *Matter, Space, and Motion* (Ithaca, NY, 1988), 79–105; M. J. White, 'Can Unequal Quantities of Stuffs be Totally Blended?', *History of Philosophy Quarterly*, 3 (1986), 379–89.   [53] Stobaeus, *Eclogae* 1, 17, 4 (I, 155 Wachsmuth; *SVF* 2. 471).
[54] See n. 52 (*SVF* 2. 473 (p. 155, 24–9)). Cf. Iamblichus, *De anima*, in Stobaeus, *Eclogae* 1, 49, 33 (I, 368 Wachsmuth; *SVF* 2. 826).

ture is not a product of fusion, its body and its soul, while coextended, always retain their distinctive properties.

Differentiating 'blending' from 'fusion' and 'juxtaposition' therefore helps to clarify the Stoic view of the nature of the relation of the corporeal soul to the body. Yet the notion of 'blending', in and of itself, does not offer any demarcation between soulless and ensouled bodies: a soulless mixture of water and wine represents 'blending' no less than does an ensouled mixture of *psychē* and body. Nor does the theory of 'blending' answer the more specific question, how does the corporeal soul differ from the corporeal body? Nor, for that matter, does it specify which distinctive properties *psychē* and body each preserves when they are 'blended', as they are in all animals. Here two further Stoic taxonomic principles might be helpful.

(4) The Stoics also differentiate (i) a body that is a collection of separable entities (e.g. an army or a chorus) and (ii) composite bodies composed of contiguous parts that are joined together so as not to separate (e.g. a house or a ship) from (iii) natural bodies that are 'in a unified condition' (*hēnōmena*), such as stones, plants, and animals.[55] The latter are all 'unified' in the sense that they have a natural internal principle of unity that renders them single entities: they are all 'held together' by the cohesive power of pneuma. From such Stoic examples of unified bodies it seems to follow that unity, like pneuma and blending, while not a sufficient condition of ensouled life, is a necessary condition (or at least a necessary manifestation?) thereof. Unified bodies therefore in turn need a principle of differention that would account for the differences between, for example, a unified but soulless rock, a natural living tree, and an ensouled human being.

(5) The Stoic solution is, in part, a natural hierarchy of unified bodies, within which the place of each class of natural, unified bodies is determined by the degree of tension (*tonos*) that characterizes the movement of its cohesive pneuma: the greater the tension, the more complex and adaptable the unified functioning of the relevant body, and hence the higher its place within the natural hierarchy.[56] To put it differently, the more complex and diverse the capacities and the behaviour of a living thing, the greater the degree of unification it requires to be a single, coherent functioning being. It is precisely the increased tension of its pneuma that ensures such a higher degree of coherent unified functioning in the more complex being. The tension itself is produced by a

---

[55] Sextus Empiricus, *Adversus mathematicos* 9, 78 (*SVF* 2. 1013) and 7, 102. Cf. *SVF* 2. 366–8.
[56] Diogenes Laertius 7, 138–9 (*SVF* 2. 634); Nemesius, *De natura hominis* 1 (38–42 Matthaei; 2–4 Morani). Cf. *SVF* 2. 407, 440–1, 447–8, 458, and next note.

simultaneously operative dual capacity of pneuma to expand and contract, to move 'outwards' and 'inwards'.[57] Pneuma is a dynamic continuum always marked by tension because of the thorough blending
(*krasis*) of its two constituents, one of which is hot (fire), the other cold
(air). Any given portion of pneuma consequently is both hot and cold,
in part expanding from heat, in part simultaneously contracting from
cold, thus always displaying the complex motion known as 'tensile
movement' (*kinēsis tonikē*) or simply as 'tension' (*tonos*).[58]

According to Chrysippus, the lowest form of unified functioning is a
state (*hexis*, 'holding itself in a certain condition') exemplified by natural
entities that cohere but do not have their own principle of movement,
such as stones, which are naturally 'held together' by cohesive pneuma
(*synhektikon pneuma*, 'pneuma capable of holding [things] together').[59]
Plants, by contrast, are made to grow and reproduce by pneuma in a
state of greater tension than that of *hexis*—namely by 'nature' or by
'natural pneuma' (*pneuma physikon*, 'pneuma capable of, or enabling,
physis'); unlike stones, plants, by virtue of 'nature', have a principle of
movement which allows them to grow 'out of' themselves.[60] *Psychē*,
whose pneuma displays a still greater degree of tension than nature,
enables animals not only to cohere and to grow, but also to perceive and
to move purposively, and hence to act; ensouled beings alone are
purposeful self-movers.[61] The unity of each of these types of body—

---

[57] Nemesius, *De natura hominis* 2 (70–1 Matthaei; 18 Morani); Alexander, *De mixtione*
10 (224 Bruns; 136 Todd; *SVF* 2. 442). Cf. *SVF* 2. 458; n. 56 above. According to Galen,
PHP 5, 3, 8 (306 DeLacy; *SVF* 2. 841), Chrysippus claimed that the pneuma that constitutes the soul's ruling centre (*hēgemonikon*) 'has acquired two parts and elements and
conditions, blended with each other throughout the whole: the cold and the hot or, if one
wishes to call them by different names, i.e., from their substances, air and fire'. On Galen
as a source for Chrysippus's views on the soul see Teun Tieleman, *Galen and Chrysippus
on the Soul: Argument and Refutation in De Placitis Book II–III* (Leiden, 1996), p. xv.

[58] See n. 51–2, 57. According to Galen, *De plenitudine* 3 (7. 525–7 K; *SVF* 2. 439–40),
the Stoics argued that, because of their highly tensile motion, air and fire hold both themselves and other things together (by being blended with the latter), whereas earth and
water, having less tension, are in need of being held together.

[59] Cf. Galen, *De plenitudine* 3 (7. 525 K; *SVF* 2. 439); Plutarch, *De Stoicorum repugnantiis* 43 (*Moralia* 1053F; *SVF* 2. 449); Galen, *Nat. fac.* 1, 3 (2. 8 K; *Scr. min.* III, 106
Helmreich = *SVF* 2. 406); Plutarch, *De communibus notitiis* 49 (*Moralia* 1085C–D; *SVF*
2. 449); Alexander, *De mixtione* 10 (223–4 Bruns; 134–6 Todd; *SVF* 2. 441). Cf. *SVF* 2. 368,
393, 458, 714, 716, 1013.

[60] Ps.-Galen, *Introductio* 13 (14. 726 K; *SVF* 2. 716). Cf. *SVF* 2. 368, 458, 714, 1013. See
n. 61.

[61] Origen, *De principiis* 3, 1, 2–3 (*SVF* 2. 988); see also n. 60. Parallel to the hierarchical distinctions between 'soul: animals', 'nature: plants', and 'state: stones' is perhaps a
distinction between three kinds of innate (*emphyton*) or connate (*symphyton*) pneuma:
psychic pneuma (responsible for *aisthēsis* and *kinēsis*), natural pneuma, and cohesive
pneuma; see ps.-Galen, *Introductio* 13 (14. 726 K) and 9 (14. 697 K; *SVF* 2. 716); the attribution of the latter passage to Stoics remains problematic, however. On the correlation

inanimate stones, living plants, ensouled animals—is, then, due to the cohesion and tensile motion imparted by a corporeal constituent, pneuma, throughout each of them. Each is, of course, also characterized by complete blending (*krasis*) of its active and passive elements throughout, and each is also matter pervaded by god; but, as suggested above, their natural unity is more than a function of blending or of being qualified body: it also requires the cohesive power of pneuma.

It is historically plausible that Chrysippus's radical distinction between nature and soul, between *physis* and *psychē*, was prompted by Herophilus's distinction between 'psychic' and 'natural' capacities within a living being (see section II above) and by Erasistratus's distinction between 'psychic' and 'vital' functions (section III above). This is especially likely given the fact, first, that both Herophilus and Erasistratus, like Chrysippus, identified the substance of the soul with pneuma while recognizing that not all pneuma in the body functions as soul, and second, that Chrysippus, exactly like the Hellenistic discoverer of the nerves, uses this distinction—soul versus nature—to limit soul functions to cognition and voluntary motor activity. As pointed out in section III, the same limitation is visible in the fragments of Erasistratus too.

In early Stoicism, the soul thus is not just pneuma but connate pneuma (*pneuma symphyton*) at a sufficiently high tensile level to allow it to function as soul-pneuma (*pneuma psychikon*, perhaps, taking the *-ikos* suffix in one of its well-attested meanings,[62] 'pneuma that makes *psychē* possible'). Thoroughly blended with the body throughout the ensouled entity, this psychic pneuma renders the body capable of sentience (*aisthēsis*), impression (*phantasia*), impulse (*hormē*), and in the case of humans, also capable of rational thought.[63] Sensory awareness of an external object and the impulse to avoid or pursue it in turn provide the 'psychic' conditions of animal locomotion. From antiquity to the present, the distinctive capacities[64] of the *psychē* in this Stoic

of 'state', 'nature', and 'soul' with inanimate being, the plant kingdom, and the animal kingdom, respectively, see also Sextus Empiricus, *Adversus mathematicos* 9, 81 (*SVF* 2. 1013).

[62] See P. Chantraine, *Études sur le vocabulaire grec: Études et commentaires*, xxiv (Paris, 1956), 91–171; A. N. Amman, *-IKOS bei Platon* (Bern and Freiburg, 1953).

[63] Philo, *Quod deus sit immutabilis* 41 (*SVF* 2. 458). On the relation of *phantasia* (a direct or indirect product of *aisthēsis*) to *hormē* (which, in later Stoicism, is often used interchangeably with *kinēsis*) see also Stobaeus, *Eclogae* 2, 7, 9 (II, 86–7 Wachsmuth; *SVF* 3. 169). Cf. Brad Inwood, *Ethics and Human Action in Early Stoicism* (Oxford, 1985), 55–6, 224–42.

[64] Stobaeus reports that Iamblichus in his *De anima* said that 'the philosophers [descended] from Chrysippus and Zeno and all those who conceive of the soul as body conclude that the capacities (*dynameis*) are qualities in the [material] substrate, while the soul is a substance already underlying the capacities' (Stobaeus, *Eclogae* 1, 49, 33 (I, 367 Wachsmuth; *SVF* 2. 826). It remains unclear to what extent this is an authentically Stoic formulation.

model have therefore been characterized—in a striking analogy to Herophilus's and Erasistratus's theories—as subsumable under sentience and motion, *aisthēsis* and *kinēsis*. The psychic pneuma that carries these capacities accordingly at times is subdivided into 'sensory pneuma' and 'motor pneuma'[65]—a subdivision that corresponds very closely to Erasistratus's views on the pneuma carried in the nerves (see above, section III). The question whether such a characterization of psychic capacities (*dynameis*) is fully compatible with various Stoic theories of the parts (*merē*) of the *psychē* (such as Chrysippus's theory of an eight-part *psychē*, each part consisting of the same kind of psychic pneuma and extending like the tentacles of an octopus or like a spider's web from the ruling part of the *psychē*, in the heart, to its local organs such as the eye, ear, nose, tongue, larynx, genitals, etc., and each part transmitting information to and from the ruling part) deserves closer scrutiny; but this would lead us too far afield here.[66]

More directly pertinent is that the frequent tendency, ancient and modern, to interpret the Stoic view of the capacities and 'functions' of the soul primarily in terms of cognition and voluntary motion, while perhaps at times misleading, and while certainly not applicable to all Stoics, rightly points to the fact that *some* Stoics, conceivably in response to Herophilus's and Erasistratus's accounts of the nervous system (see sections II–III above) and of the role of pneuma within the nervous

---

[65] Ps.-Galen, *Introductio* 13 (14. 726 K; *SVF* 2. 716—but see n. 61 above), subdivides the powers of *psychikon pneuma* into two: it makes animals sentient (*aisthētika*) and moved (*kinoumena*) with respect to every motion (*pasan kinēsin*). A later Stoic, Hierocles, also defines *aisthēsis* and *hormē* (see n. 63) as the two things that distinguish the animal from the non-animal: *Elementa ethica*, ed. Hans von Arnim, Berliner Klassiker Texte, 4 (Berlin, 1906), 4, 38 ff. Cf. Philo, *Legum Allegoria* 1, 30 (I, 68 Wendl; *SVF* 2. 844). It should perhaps be noted that Alexander of Aphrodisias's criticism of those who believe that the soul has only a single *dynamis* (*De anima mantissa*, 118–19 Bruns), though included by von Arnim among the Stoic testimonia (*SVF* 2. 823), does not refer to any Stoic explicitly.

[66] On the theory of an eight-part *psychē* see Chrysippus, *De anima I*, reported by Galen, *PHP* 3, 1, 9–11 (170 De Lacy; *SVF* 2. 885). Aëtius, *Placita* 4, 21, 1–4 (*SVF* 2. 836), attributes the octopus image to Chrysippus. Calcidius, *In Platonis Timaeum Comment.* 220 (232–3 Waszink; *SVF* 2. 879), seems to attribute the image of a tree trunk (*ex trabe*) and its branches (*ramos*) to Chrysippus. See also Iamblichus, as reported by Stobaeus, *Eclogae* 1, 49, 33 (I, 368, 12–20 Wachsmuth; *SVF* 2. 826). On the primacy of the heart— a view also shared, in a variety of refractions, by Epicurus and by several of the Stoics' precursors, including Empedocles ('blood around the heart') and Aristotle—see Calcidius, *In Platonis Timaeum Comment.* 220; Galen, *De fetuum formatione* 6 (4. 698 K; *SVF* 2. 761); *PHP* 2, 5, 9–13 (130 De Lacy; *SVF* 3, Diogenes 29): speech (*logos*), since it is sent out through the windpipe, proves that thought (*dianoia*) resides in the region of the heart. It is not inconceivable that Chrysippus's model was, in part, prompted by Herophilus's and Erasistratus's theory that pneuma is distributed from the ruling part of the *psychē* through the nerves (with the crucial difference, however, that Chrysippus, like other Stoics, locates the ruling part in the heart, whereas Erasistratus and Herophilus locate it in the brain; see above, secs. II–III).

system, *sometimes* circumscribed the functions of the soul much more narrowly than had many of their philosophical precursors. The living body with which, upon its birth, highly tensile psychic pneuma becomes thoroughly blended is itself previously already cohesive and capable of digestion, nutrition, and growth—that is, prior to receiving any soul-pneuma whatsoever: in the womb, this living but soulless body was previously held together and granted vegetative functions by pneuma at the lower tensile level of 'nature' (*physis*)—that is, by natural pneuma (*pneuma physikon*). Only upon parturition is psychic pneuma accordingly formed and blended with an already living but not yet ensouled body. The embryo itself, whether human or animal, though alive and manifestly capable of teleologically directed development, according to this theory is a *psychē*-less being, functioning in ways similar to living plants.[67]

Many living things thus do not have soul, and *psychē* hence is not, as it is, for example, in Aristotle, primarily what differentiates a living body from a non-living body; rather, the possession of psychic matter differentiates more complex living bodies (animals, including humans) from less complex ones (embryos, plants).

The physicalism of the Epicurean and Stoic versions of the *psychē*, their emphasis on the capacities (*dynameis*) of the soul as setting it apart from the rest of the body, their central deployment of pneuma to account for *psychē* and its activities, and the Stoics' distinction, within the *psychē*, between its sensory and kinetic pneuma, all display strong affinities with Hellenistic medicine, and, in particular, with Erasistratus's theories. Affinity is, of course, no guarantor of influence, and the tendency to account for all affinities by means of a 'genealogy of influence' can be methodologically insidious.[68] Furthermore, when dealing with a given Stoic theory that bears resemblance to a medical theory, it should also not be overlooked that 'Stoic' in the ancient sources can cover a considerable chronological spectrum, that the question whether a given theory is attributable to Zeno, Cleanthes, Chrysippus, or a later Stoic is often intractable, and that Zeno (331–262 BC), for example, was an almost exact contemporary of Herophilus, whereas Chrysippus (281 or

---

[67] The most extensive extant Stoic account of reproduction is that of Hierocles (c.AD 100), who tries to account for the transition, at birth, of the living being from an embryo governed by nature (*physis*) to a living being (*zōion*) governed by *psychē* (*Elementa ethica* 1, 5–33; 4, 38–53). Cf. Plutarch, *De Stoicorum repugnantiis* 41 (*Moralia* 1052F; *SVF* 2. 806): Chrysippus says that 'the foetus in the womb is nourished by nature just like a plant. But when it is born, its pneuma, being chilled (*psychomenon*) and hardened (*sto-moumenon* ("tempered", like steel)) by the air, changes and it becomes a living being (*zōion*); the *psychē* therefore has been named after this "chilling" (*psyxis*).' See also Plutarch's objections, *Moralia* 1053C–D.

[68] See H. von Staden, 'Affinities and Elisions: Helen and Hellenocentrism', *Isis*, 83 (1992), 578–95.

277–208 or 204 BC) was a good forty to fifty years younger than Erasistratus and Herophilus. The affinities traced above are historically suggestive, nevertheless, and, especially by the time of Chrysippus, the discovery of the nerves would have been well known.

From the corporeal theories of the *psychē* explored thus far, it is perhaps not a long step to the denial of the very existence of the *psychē*—a denial attributed in antiquity to both philosophers and physicians of the third-century BC, notably to early followers of Aristotle and of Herophilus. If 'soul' is a certain kind of 'body' or matter, and if such matter, along with the nerves and 'nature', can do much or all of the explanatory work previously done by 'soul', why does one still need the concept 'soul'? Thus Andreas, a third-century BC Ptolemaic court physician (*c*.270–217 BC) and a remarkable student and follower of Herophilus, is said to have asserted that '*psychē* does not exist', and that what traditionally is called 'soul' is simply the body 'disposed a certain way' or 'in a certain condition'.[69] If all human structures and functions are explicable in corporeal terms, in terms of the interaction of matter with matter, as Epicurus, Herophilus, Erasistratus, and the Stoics seem to believe, the descriptive and explanatory utility of the concept 'psyche' becomes arguable. Indeed, 'psyche' can become a source of misunderstanding and confusion, particularly given the historical, semantic, and metaphysical freight—including the sharply valorized polarities mentioned at the outset—which it inevitably brings in tow. This, it seems, is at least one reason for Andreas's view that, while there might be different kinds of body, different forms of life, and different capacities, activities, and dysfunctions displayed by different types of matter within living bodies, *psychē* is not necessary for accounting for any of these, or for the differences between them.

Psychē is a tenacious concept, however, and the vast body of Galen's extant writings—in which both *psychē* and *sōma* occur more often than in any other Greek author—illustrate its central role in philosophy and medicine of the Roman imperial period.

V. GALEN

For all his ardent polemics against Erasistratus, Chrysippus, and other Hellenistic figures, and for all his professions of Platonism, Galen's view

---

[69] See e.g. Tertullian, *De anima* 15. On Dicaearchus, the Peripatetic philosopher, see also Sextus Empiricus, *Pyrrh. Hyp.* 2, 31; Cicero, *Tusc.* 1, 11, 24 (cf. 1, 22, 55); *idem, Acad. prior.* 2, 39, 124. But the evidence concerning Dicaearchus is not without its difficulties; see Fritz Wehrli, *Die Schule des Aristoteles*, 2nd edn., i (Basel and Stuttgart, 1967), Dicaearchus, frs. 7–12. On Andreas see *Heroph.* 472–7.

of the relation of body to soul is more strongly indebted to the physicalist strain in many of his early Hellenistic precursors' theories of *psychē* and, in particular, to the discovery of the nerves, than has hitherto been acknowledged. The theories explored above (sections II–IV) may well have prompted him, despite his avowed Platonism, explicitly and repeatedly to suspend judgement or to express ambivalence on questions such as the immortality of the soul, its substance, its incorporeality, the number of its 'forms' or parts, the scope of its activities, and its transmigration, and to display terminological and doctrinal equivocation when it came to Plato's tripartition of the soul and to several other key features of Plato's theories of the *psychē*. Any interpretation of Galen's theory of the body–soul relation that focuses only on the strong Platonic heritage indubitably visible, for example, in his *On the Opinions of Plato and Hippocrates* therefore runs the risk of being seriously misleading. In a late work, *On My Own Opinions*, Galen still explicitly asserts that he cannot answer the question what *psychē* is or how it appears in the body, or exactly why soul is separated from body under various conditions. And even in his twin treatises on errors and passions or affections of the soul, he leaves central issues unresolved, as Pierluigi Donini has shown.[70] Yet Galen freely deploys the word *psychē*, making the soul central to his conception of the living body, and he offers numerous detailed comments on interactions between soul and body and, similarly, on the structure, capacities, activities, dysfunctions, and instruments of the soul.

Fundamental to Galen's view of the body–soul relation are his views on humours (*chymoi*), blendings or temperaments (*kraseis*), capacities (*dynameis*), bodily instruments (*organa*), forms or parts of the soul (its *eidē* or *merē*), and the localization of various parts or forms or capacities of soul. The body is 'proximately composed' of the four humours (blood, black bile, yellow bile, and phlegm), whose proper blend (*krasis*, *eukrasia*) is different in different parts of the body, so that the brain, the heart, and the liver, for example, each has its own proper blend. Because the different faculties or capacities (*dynameis*), and activities (*energeiai*) characteristic of a living thing are centred in different parts or organs of the body, the humoral blend or temperament of, for example, the brain, the heart, and the liver will each have a profound effect on the capacities that reside in these organs, and this will in turn affect the corresponding activities. This interactive relation between humoral blend or temperament and the soul's capacities is a central feature of Galen's view of the body–soul relation, and indeed he devoted an extant trea-

---

[70] P. Donini, 'Tipologia degli errori e loro correzione secondo Galeno', in Paola Manuli and Mario Vegetti (eds.), *Le opere psicologiche di Galeno* (Naples, 1988), 65–116.

tise precisely to this subject (*That the Soul's Capacities Follow the Body's Temperaments*).[71]

At times Galen depicts some of a living being's capacities as belonging uniquely to the soul and others as belonging uniquely to nature, therein following the model developed by Herophilus and by some Stoics. Galen does not apply this 'soul–nature' distinction consistently to the explanation of activities or functions in living bodies, but where he does uphold the distinction, as in *De symptomatum differentiis*, the 'natural activities' of a living being are said to include appetite or 'striving', digestion, the distribution of nutriment, the generation of blood, the pulse, and the excretion of residues (i.e. of useless bodily 'leftovers'), whereas the 'psychic activities' are restricted—exactly as in the theories of Herophilus, Erasistratus, and some Stoics—to cognitive and voluntary motor activity.[72]

The 'natural activities' in the body are explicable, Galen argues, in terms of four capacities or faculties that belong to 'nature', not to the soul, and that are present in each part of the body: the attractive, retentive, alterative, and secretory capacities.[73] It is these natural capacities, using different bodily parts as instruments to different effects, that account for all the natural activities in the body; to explain them, recourse to the soul is unnecessary. Every natural capacity for an activity (*energeia*) is said to be a connate power of the natural instruments (*organa physika*) in which it shows itself (e.g. in the liver, in the arteries, in the veins).[74] An inanimate analogy introduced by Galen is that of a

---

[71] Galen, *Quod animi mores corporis temperamenta sequantur* (4. 767–822 K; *Scr. min.* II, 32–79 Müller). See Luis Garcia Ballester, 'La "Psique" en el somaticismo medico de la antiguedad: la actitud de Galeno', *Episteme*, 3 (1969), 195–209; Geoffrey E. R. Lloyd, 'Scholarship, Authority and Argument in Galen's *Quod animi mores*', in Manuli and Vegetti (eds.), *Le opere psicologiche*, 11–42; R. J. Hankinson, 'Galen's Anatomy of the Soul', *Phronesis*, 36 (1991), 197–233.

[72] Galen, *De symptomatum differentiis* 3 (7. 55 K). For Galen's division of activities (*energeiai*) into natural (*physikai*) and psychic (*psychikai*) see also e.g. *De sanitate tuenda* 6, 2, 15 (CMG V 4, 2, p. 170, 30–2 Koch); *De motu musculorum* 1, 1 (4. 372. 11–15 K); *De crisibus* 1, 14 (9. 612–13 K; 108, 6–7 Alexanderson); *De temperamentis* 2, 1 (1. 576–7 K; 43, 2–4 Helmreich); *De sententiis* (4. 759 K). See also *Nat. fac.* 1, 1 (2, 1–2 K; *Scr. min.* III, 101 Helmreich): animals share with plants growing and being nourished, which are the works (*erga*) of nature (*physis*), whereas sensation and voluntary motion, which are the works of *psychē*, are peculiar (*idia*) to animals; hence animals are governed simultaneously by nature and *psychē*, whereas plants are governed by nature alone.

[73] Galen, *De propriis placitis (De sententiis)* (4. 759 K); *Nat. fac.* (2. 1–214 K; *Scr. min.* III Helmreich), *passim*; *Sympt. diff.* 4 (7. 63 K). But see also *idem*, *In Hippocratis Epidemiarum III. comment.* 1, 17 (CMG V 10, 2, 1, p. 46, 12–15 Wenkebach): the liver is the *archē* of the *psychē* called vegetative (*phytikē*) as well as (*te kai*) natural (*physikē*), whose four powers are attraction, retention, alteration, and secretion, and by virtue of which the processes of being nourished and of growing exist in bodies.

[74] *Loc. aff.* 1, 7 (8. 66 K).

magnetic stone, which always has in itself a power or capacity to attract iron to itself.

The capacities or faculties that render the soul distinct from the body, by contrast, are not innate in their organs or instruments, but 'flow to the soul's instruments from its *archē* [sc. the brain], similar to the light of the sun [radiating out]' (see below).[75] When Galen is not defending the Platonic tripartite structure of the soul, he often groups these psychic capacities and their corresponding activities under two headings: *aisthēsis* and *kinēsis* (again, in striking agreement with Herophilus, Erasistratus, and some Stoics), with the occasional addition of a third category—namely 'activities that belong to the ruling part (*hēgemonikon*)' of the soul.[76] Adding 'capacities and activities of the ruling part' to the two dominant Hellenistic faculties of the *psychē*—sentience and motion—perhaps was intended, first, to account for forms of cognition higher than sensation and perception, such as memory and thought, and, second, to resolve the problem of how to account for the distinctive nature of mental activities if the soul's two principal capacities—sentience and voluntary motion—manifest themselves throughout the body.

Bringing his characteristic diaeretic procedures to bear upon the soul's capacities and activities, Galen further subdivides each of the two classes of cognitive activity: the sensory activities of the soul are subdivided into the individual activities of each of the five senses, while the activities of its ruling centre are subdivided into those that belong, respectively, to impression (*phantasia*), thought, and memory (*De symptomatum differentiis*), or into impression, memory, recollection, knowledge, thinking, and discursive thinking (*De placitis Hippocratis et Platonis*), or into thinking, remembering, reasoning, and choosing (*De locis affectis*).[77]

Galen further differentiates the soul's 'hegemonic' activities from its other activities by calling the former 'functions [which the soul performs] by itself', whereas the sensory and voluntary motor activities of

---

[75] *Loc. aff.* (8. 66–8 K).

[76] e.g. *Sympt. diff.* 3 (7. 55 K). On the somewhat different perspectives that emerge in books 2–3 of *PHP* see Tieleman, *Galen and Chrysippus*, pp. xxxi–xxxvii.

[77] *Sympt. diff.* 3 (7. 55–6 K); *PHP* 7, 3, 2 (438–40 De Lacy); *Loc. aff.* 2, 10 (8. 126–7 K). Cf. *UP* 8, 6 (3. 641 K); *Loc. aff.* 3, 9 (8. 174–5 K). For the diseases corresponding to these capacities of the soul see Jackie Pigeaud, 'La psychopathologie de Galien', in Manuli and Vegetti (eds.), *Le opere psicologiche*, 153–83. The influential localization of *phantasia* in the anterior ventricles, of thought in the third ventricle, and of memory in the cerebellum (or, more generally, in the hindbrain) does not seem to appear in Galen; Aëtius of Amida 6, 2 (CMG VIII 2, p. 125, 16–20 Olivieri) ascribes it to the physician Posidonius, and Nemesius of Emesa also is familiar with it (*De natura hominis* 6; 12; 13 (173, 9–11; 201, 7–9; 204, 5–207, 9 Matthaei; 56, 2–4; 68, 11–13; 69, 16–71, 2 Morani).

the soul are relational: they exist 'in relation' to the sentient and moved parts of the living being (the latter being moved by the soul's kinetic capacity 'in accordance with *hormē*', as in Stoicism). The capacities of the ruling part of the soul are also distinctive in so far as they render human beings capable of culture: 'There are capacities in the ruling part for all *technai*.'[78] Although Galen therefore often shares the Herophilean, Erasistratean, and Stoic restriction of soul to cognitive and voluntary motor functions, the additional ascription of a rich variety of cognitive capacities to the ruling part of the *psychē* allows him to accommodate under his notion of 'psyche' a very wide range of mental functions that are distinct from sense perception yet distinctively cognitive and hence psychic.

Elsewhere, however, Galen uses quite different models to account for the various activities that characterize living things—models which, to some extent, are on a collision course with the features of his theory discussed so far. From Plato's *Republic*, for example, Galen at times adopts the proof that the soul is tripartite, and from Plato's *Timaeus* the location of the centre of the three parts of the soul in the head, the heart, and the liver, respectively. In *De Placitis Hippocratis et Platonis* Galen describes a living being after birth as governed by three principles (*archai*), one each in the head, the heart, and the liver.[79] The works (*erga*, 'functions') of the one in the head are, by itself, the higher cognitive activities described above and, in relation to the other parts of the body, sensation and voluntary motion. The works of the one in the heart are, by itself, the proper tension (*tonos*) of the soul, to help maintain the right blend or temperament (*eukrasia*), to be constant in the things that reason commands, and, in states of passion, to provide the 'boiling' of the innate heat; in its relation to other things, it functions as the source both of heat for the individual parts and of pulsating motion for the arteries. The capacity—Galen here implicitly identifies, it seems, an *archē* as a *dynamis*—seated in the liver has as its works all things having to do with nourishing the living being, notably (at least in us and in all other blooded animals) the generation of blood, and, ultimately, to supply the substances whose mixture form the body's blend or temperament (*krasis*). It is to this third capacity that the enjoyment of pleasures and its excesses (intemperance, incontinence) also belong.[80]

---

[78] *De consuetudinibus* 4 (*Scr. min.* II, 25 Müller; CMG suppl. III, 26 Schmutte). For 'by itself' (*kath' heautēn*) vs 'in relation to' (*to pros ti*) see e.g. *PHP* 7, 3, 2 (438, 29–33 De Lacy).

[79] *PHP* 7, 3, 2 (438–40 De Lacy). Not only the Platonic theory of tripartition, notably as developed in the *Timaeus*, but also Erasistratus's use of the brain, the heart, and the liver as the sources (*archai*) of the three duct systems responsible for human life is visible in this Galenic model (see sec. III above). [80] *PHP* 7, 3, 3 (440 De Lacy).

This Platonically inspired application of anatomical geography to psycho-physiology is, of course, reconcilable to a great extent with Erasistratus's theory of the sources of psychic pneuma, vital pneuma, and blood (see section III above). But Galen's Platonic view that the lower functions too—not only heat and pulse, but also the vegetative, nutritive, reproductive, desiderative functions (especially desires for food, drink, and sexual pleasure)—are activities of the *soul*, and that human beings share this desiderative kind of soul with plants, is hardly compatible with the Galenic views traced above, and especially not with his distinction between *physis* and *psychē*—that is, between human capacities, activities, and instruments that belong to 'nature' and to 'soul' respectively.

Galen thus at times accepts Plato's attribution of desiderative soul to plants, but he also seems to have found the more restrictive Hellenistic accounts of the range of the soul's activities plausible. This leads to vacillation and to occasional expressions of indifference. In *Methodus medendi*, for example, Galen says that it makes no difference whether one calls the faculty or capacity (*dynamis*) emanating from the liver 'desiderative' (*epithymētikē*, in allusion to Plato's theory of the third and lowest part of the soul), or 'natural' (*physikē*, in allusion to Herophilus and the Stoics), or 'nutritive' (*threptikē*, in allusion to the lowest part of the soul in Aristotle's psychology).[81] In *De usu partium* he similarly observes, 'I leave to others the question whether it should be called "nature" or "nutritive faculty"', and in *De propriis placitis* he confesses that he adapts his terminology according to his audience: 'Among Platonists I refer to that which governs plants as "soul" [sc. as did Plato and Aristotle], but among physicians as "nature" [sc. as did Herophilus].'[82] And in *De naturalibus facultatibus* he advocates the adoption of 'customary usage' in this matter, by which he means calling sensation and voluntary motion 'the works of *psychē*' (peculiar to animals), but growth and nutrition 'the works of nature' (shared by plants and animals), while conceding that those who ascribe the latter activities to a vegetative-nutritive part of the soul are essentially saying the same thing.[83] So per-

---

[81] *Methodus medendi* 9, 10 (10. 635, 14–15 K). On the question whether plants have desiderative *psychē*, see e.g. Galen, *In Platonis Timaeum* 3, 2 (CMG suppl. I, 10–13 Schröder), on Plato, *Tim.* 76e7–77c5; *PHP* 6, 2, 7–3, 7; 6, 4, 1–3; 6, 8, 54; 9, 6, 63 (368–74, 384, 418, 584 De Lacy). Cf. Phillip De Lacy, 'The Third Part of the Soul', in Manuli and Vegetti (eds.), *Le opere psicologiche*, 43–63.

[82] *UP* 4, 13 (3. 308–9 K; I, 226, 18–25 Helmreich); *De sententiis* (= *De propriis placitis*; see forthcoming edition by Vivian Nutton); cf. *PHP* 6, 3, 7 (374 De Lacy), on the varying names given to the governing principle that resides in the liver and in plants.

[83] *Nat. fac.* 1, 1 (2. 1–2 K; *Scr. min.* III, 101 Helmreich). Galen's frequent tolerance of a non-standardized terminology to describe the soul, its parts, and its potentialities does not appear to be motivated by his repeatedly expressed view that standardization of

vasive was Herophilus's and Erasistratus's un-Platonic, un-Aristotelian restriction of the soul's powers and activities to cognition and to voluntary motion—a restriction which, as suggested above, was a direct result of their discovery not only of the nerves but also, in particular, of the distinction between sensory and motor nerves—that Galen here refers to Herophilus's (and Chrysippus's) nature–soul distinction as 'customary usage' and even urges its adoption.

Despite multiple unresolved tensions within his theory, despite his uncertainty and vacillation concerning the boundaries of 'soul', and concerning the line of demarcation between 'soul' and 'nature', Galen uniformly insists on certain features of the relation of soul to body. He consistently underscores, for example, that 'whatever the substance of the *psychē* may be', the *psychē* uses pneuma as its 'first instrument' (*organon*) and various bodily parts as its secondary instruments.[84] Psychic pneuma in the nerves, Galen further elaborates, is neither the substance (*ousia*) of *psychē*—as Herophilus, the Stoics, and Erasistratus apparently had thought—nor its dwelling place (*oikos*), but its primary instrument 'both for all the sensations/perceptions (*aisthēseis*) of the living being and, in addition, for its voluntary motions'.[85]

As in the four early Hellenistic cases explored above (sections I–IV), so too in Galen's theory, pneuma therefore is crucial to an understanding both of the *difference* between soul and body and of the *relation* between the two. For all his professions of Platonism, Galen ascribes a central role to pneuma in his accounts of body–soul interaction, a role which betrays not only Galen's strong awareness of Hellenistic theories in general (and of the views of Archigenes and other Pneumatists), but in particular the considerable impact upon Galen of one of his arch-enemies, Erasistratus.

I offer only a few examples of affinities between central features of Galen's psycho-physiology and Erasistratus's:

terminology is unnecessary, provided that clarity (*saphēneia*), the greatest virtue of scientific language, and univocity are achieved; rather, in the case of the *psychē–sōma* relation, a lacunose, vacillating (even though richly detailed) theory lurks behind his shimmering nomenclature.

[84] *PHP* 7, 3, 21; 7, 3, 27; 7, 3, 30 (444, 4–8; 444, 31–3; 446, 11–13 De Lacy); *De usu respirationis* 5 (4. 501–2, 509 K; 120, 130 Furley and Wilkie); *De symptomatum causis* 2, 5 (7. 191 K); *De locis affectis* 3, 9; 4, 3 (8. 175, 233 K); *In Hippocratis Epidemiarum VI comm.* 5, 5 (CMG V 10, 2, 2, p. 271, 9–11 Wenkebach); *De simplicium medicamentorum temperamentis ac facultatibus* 5, 9 (11. 731 K).

[85] *PHP* 7, 3, 21; 7, 3, 30 (444, 4–8; 446, 11–13 De Lacy). At times Galen is equivocal on the precise role of pneuma in the case of voluntary motion; see Mario Vegetti, 'I nervi dell' anima', in J. Kollesch and D. Nickel (eds.), *Galen und das hellenistische Erbe* (Stuttgart, 1993), 63–77 (esp. 68), who also emphasizes the mechanical analogies used by Galen to explain some activities and affections of the soul; R. J. Hankinson, 'Greek Medical Models of Mind', in S. Everson (ed.), *Psychology* (Cambridge, 1991), 194–217.

(1) Like Erasistratus, Galen distinguishes between vital (*zōtikon*) and psychic (*psychikon*) pneuma.

(2) Galen and Erasistratus both describe the arteries as ducts for vital pneuma (but, in Galen's view, not only for vital pneuma).

(3) Both depict the nerves as the ducts for psychic pneuma.

(4) They both make the left ventricle of the heart the locus where vital pneuma is produced.

(5) Both regard the arterial system as responsible for distributing vital pneuma from this ventricle to the entire body, including the brain.

(6) Both depict the brain, in turn, as the place where psychic pneuma is produced.

(7) Galen and Erasistratus both subdivide 'psychic pneuma' into sensory and voluntary motor pneuma.

(8) They likewise both subdivide the nerves into sensory and motor nerves (for the two types of psychic pneuma).

(9) Both Galen and Erasistratus depict the brain as the source of all nerves and of the nerves' psychic capacities, the heart as the source of all arteries and of the arteries' ability to pulsate, and the liver as the source of all veins and of the 'natural faculty' or 'capacity'.

(10) They both regard the right ventricle of the heart as containing only blood (i.e. not pneuma).[86]

Galen's accounts of vital and psychic pneuma admittedly are much more detailed than Erasistratus's, perhaps in part because of conditions of transmission and reception, and in certain significant respects—for example, his ubiquitous emphasis on 'capacities' or 'faculties'—Galen sharply departs from Erasistratus's mechanistic version of the soul's activities. But that Galen, who quotes extensively from Erasistratus's works (albeit with polemical intent), on the whole is considerably indebted to the Erasistratean model seems probable, also in view of many other largely unacknowledged correspondences between their theories.

Galen says he does not know what *psychē* is, and he explicitly professes agnosticism (or remains silent or inconsistent, or obscure) on many other issues that might have helped clarify exactly how and where he draws a line of demarcation between soul and body. He does, however, offer a partial answer to a question of significance for present purposes (a question to which we found no adequate answer in the extant remains of Erasistratus's and Herophilus's writings): if psychic pneuma is essential to the activities of the soul, when and how does non-psychic pneuma become psychic pneuma? Or, to put it in Erasistratean terms, how does our breath become our soul?

[86] *UP* 1, 16 (3. 45–6 K; I, 32–3 Helmreich). Cf. *PHP* 7, 3, 2–3 (438–40 De Lacy).

Galen's version of the generation of psychic pneuma—the distinctive bodily matter used uniquely by *psychē* as its tool—offers a further example of the impact of detailed anatomical exploration on theories of body–soul interaction. Perhaps on the basis of his dissections of artio-dactyls (notably of the pig), Galen accepts Herophilus's erroneous at-tribution to humans of a *rete mirabile*, a small but dense, united network of contiguous 'webs' (*plegmata*) of vessels at the base of the brain, 'like a complex labyrinth' inside the cranium, surrounded by the dura mater and formed from the internal carotid arteries when the latter break up into numerous branches before reuniting into two arteries that proceed to the brain.[87] He likewise confirms Herophilus's observation of choroid plexuses in humans (i.e. highly vascular portions of the meninges that project into the ventricles of the brain).[88] Ever a committed, 'complete' teleologist,[89] Galen reflects at length on the purpose of these vascular complications of the arterial flow of vital pneuma to the brain. Why does vital pneuma not proceed more directly to the brain, instead of having to pass through these dense vascular networks? He concludes that the purpose of the *rete mirabile* and of the choroid plexuses is, above all, to prolong the sojourn of vital pneuma in this part of the arterial system, so as to ensure that vital pneuma here becomes further refined or elabo-rated (*katergazesthai*, 'to be worked on') and undergoes further change (*metabolē*) before it is 'breathed out' into all the ventricles of the brain, where it finally becomes psychic pneuma.[90] Vital pneuma thus is the 'proper material' (*hylē oikeia*) used for generating psychic pneuma. Galen's favourite anatomical analogies are the convoluted vascular 'spirals' that lie before the testes (to ensure the refinement of blood into *sperma*) and the length of the vessels that go to the female breasts (to ensure the refinement of blood into milk). 'For wherever nature wishes to refine or elaborate matter, it arranges for it to spend a long time in its instruments of concoction.'[91] In his discussion of the ventricles of the brain, Galen adds further details: the two anterior ventricles (i.e. the lateral ventricle or internal cavity of each cerebral hemisphere) pre-elaborate and prepare in advance psychic pneuma for use by the brain,

---

[87] *Heroph.* T121; Galen, *De pulsuum usu* 2 (5. 155–6 K; 200 Furley and Wilkie); *UP* 9, 4; 16, 10 (3. 696 ff., 4. 333 K; II, 10 ff., 420 Helmreich).

[88] *Heroph.* T124; Galen, *Anat. adm.* 9, 3 (2. 719–20 K; 808–10 Garofalo).

[89] See R. J. Hankinson, 'Galen and the Best of All Possible Worlds', *Classical Quar-terly*, 39 (1989), 206–27; *idem*, 'Galen's Theory of Causation', in W. Haase and H. Temporini (eds.), *Aufstieg und Niedergang der römischen Welt*, II 37, 2 (Berlin, 1994), 1757–74.

[90] Galen, *PHP* 7, 3, 23–9 (444–6 De Lacy). Cf. *idem*, *Praesagitione ex pulsibus* 1, 1 (9. 210 K).

[91] *UP* 9, 4 (3. 699–700 K; II, 12, 5–8 Helmreich). See also *UP* 16, 10 (4. 322–3 K; II, 420 Helmreich); *De usu pulsuum* 2 (5. 155–6 K); *PHP* 7, 3, 29 (446 De Lacy).

while the ventricle of the cerebellum (fourth ventricle) subsequently receives this pre-refined psychic pneuma from the anterior ventricles via a 'canal' (i.e. the third ventricle, which Galen is not sure actually *is* a ventricle).[92]

Galen's detailed anatomical knowledge of the fine structure of the brain thus emboldened him to develop an elaborate theory of how and where the primary bodily instrument specific to the *psychē*—psychic pneuma—is generated. But, faced with the question of the substance or essence of the soul itself, or of how the soul first enters the body, anatomy responds with silence, and Galen with agnosticism.

If the main purpose of the arteries is to maintain the natural, innate heat of the body, a secondary purpose is 'to nourish the psychic pneuma' with vital pneuma.[93] As often, Galen's teleological approach permits multiple ends. A similar dual purpose is ascribed to breathing in *De causis respirationis*, *De usu respirationis*, and elsewhere: 'Usefulness is the most important of the causes of breathing, viz. on the one hand, preserving the balance (*symmetria*) of the innate heat, on the other, nourishing the substance of psychic pneuma.'[94] The former is achieved by the larger portion of inhaled air, which goes to the lungs and thence, in part, to the heart and the arteries, while the latter is effected by a smaller portion of inhaled air, which goes through the nostrils past protective barriers to the brain.[95] Both the pneuma reaching the brain directly through respiration and the vital pneuma arriving through the mediation of the arterial system thus serve as nourishment for psychic pneuma, much the way, says Galen, that air nourishes fire.[96]

Exactly wherein the greater 'refinement' that constitutes the difference between psychic and vital pneuma lies, remains unclear, as does the precise nature of the material threshold—as opposed to the anatomical and functional threshold—between psychic and vital pneuma. But it is evident that Galen, like Herophilus and Erasistratus, tries to harness a detailed knowledge of anatomy and physiology to an explanation of the materials and mechanisms by which the soul interacts with the body.

A famous Galenic analogy, introduced in the context of respiration, but applied to voluntary motion, neither mitigates the obscurities nor fills the lacunae, but it illuminates his general approach. The choice made by the soul's ruling part in the case of voluntary motion is like

---

[92] *UP* 8, 10–11 (3. 663–5 K; I, 481–2 Helmreich).

[93] *UP* 1, 16 (3. 46 K; I, 33, 7–8 Helmreich).

[94] Galen, *De causis respirationis* 2 (4. 466 K; 240 Furley and Wilkie). Cf. *idem, De usu respirationis* 5, 1–3; 5, 8 (4. 501–5, 510 K; 120–6, 132 Furley and Wilkie).

[95] Ibid.

[96] Ibid. Some pneuma is also produced by vaporization of the blood, effected by the innate heat. See Galen, *Methodus medendi* 9, 2 (10. 742 K); O. Temkin, 'On Galen's Pneumatology', *Gesnerus*, 8 (1951), 180–9; Vegetti, 'I nervi dell' anima', 70.

that made by a charioteer who moves the reins and the horses: the nerves through which the motor pneuma runs are the reins, the muscles moved by the pneuma-carrying nerves are the horses, and the 'use' (*chreia*) is the desired end—that is, the motion—just as victory is the end of chariot racing (and there would have been no choice without such an end in mind).[97] This example again illustrates the extent to which Galen's view of the relation of soul to body is informed by Herophilus's and Erasistratus's anatomical and physiological versions of the body: more than four centuries after the discovery of the nerves, the activities of the soul remain intimately linked to soul-pneuma in the nerves.

Galen's account of perception, in which the influence of the early Stoics, notably of Cleanthes, also seems evident, offers a further illustration of the extent to which his philosophical heritage is reshaped by anatomical and physiological considerations. Adopting a literal, physicalist version of the Stoic notion of *typōsis* ('act of imprinting, stamping, impression') to explain how the external object of perception is registered by the soul, Galen introduces his principle that the alterability or modifiability of a substance stands in a direct relation to the softness of its matter, and hence to its malleability or plasticity. Galen argues that, while all nerves are soft, the softer nerves are affected by sensation, whereas the harder nerves, capable of imparting or effecting action, belong to motor activity:

Each of the sense-organs individually needs a soft nerve: *nerve*, because this is the instrument (*organon*) of sense perception, and *soft*, because, for sense perception to occur, the sense-organ must somehow be arranged and affected by that which has impinged upon it from outside [sc. the perceptible object]; but the soft is better suited to being affected, the hard to acting upon something.[98]

The sensory nerves, carrying sensory pneuma between the brain and the sense-organs, thus themselves have to be affected in order to transmit sensory messages to the brain, where sensory impressions are physically imprinted and stored. Galen here leaves the relation between the affected soft nerves and their content (pneuma) murky, but he leaves no doubt that while sense perception is an activity of the soul, it takes place only through modifications or alterations of the soft bodily matter of the nerves.

Galen further observes that the brain 'in its substance, is very similar to the nerves, whose principle (*archē*) it was always destined to be, except that it is so much softer than they'—and this is a necessary quality, says Galen, in an instrument (*organon*) of the *psychē* in which all sense perceptions, impressions (*phantasiai*), and thoughts (*noēseis*)

---

[97] Galen, *De causis respirationis* (4. 469 K; 244 Furley and Wilkie).
[98] *UP* 8, 5 (3. 633 K; I, 458–9 Helmreich); see 8, 6 (3. 636–9 K; I, 461–3 Helmreich).

end up.[99] It is this very soft brain-matter in which imprints are left by perception, and in which, if the imprints are sufficiently clear, memory, thought, and so on take place. Yet here too, Galen steadfastly refrains from explicitly identifying the brain-matter itself with the soul or with its substance.

The material through which the soul works, its bodily instruments, its bodily capacities and activities, and the physical processes by which the soul acts and is affected therefore are described in unprecedented detail by Galen, but 'psyche' itself remains indeterminate and elusive.

Yet neither theoretical nor terminological indeterminacy prevented Galen's theory from becoming immensely influential for many centuries. And neither can obscure the considerable, if in part mediated, indebtedness of this self-professed second-century Platonist's accounts of body–soul interactions to early Hellenistic physicalist models of *psychē* and *sōma*, notably to the versions developed by his admired anatomical precursor Herophilus, by his formidable physiological adversary Erasistratus, and, in part under their influence, by some Stoics.

The discovery of the nerves entailed the first significant erosion of the vast territory ruled by the soul in Platonic and Aristotelian philosophy, an erosion accompanied by an expansion of the rule of 'nature', visible not only in medicine but also in philosophy. While few ancients joined Herophilus's politically well-connected pupil Andreas in radically questioning the explanatory utility of the very concept 'soul', and while Platonic, Pythagorean, and Aristotelian theories of soul and body remained immensely influential, the momentous restriction of the soul's activities and affections to those conducted through the nerves, along with the detailed physicalism, often richly informed by anatomy and physiology, that dominated many Hellenistic accounts of the soul's substance and of its interactions with the ('rest of the') body, rendered even as self-confident, assertive a Platonist as Galen uncertain and equivocal concerning key aspects of the relations between body and soul. Galen's tenacious authority ensured the transmission not only of this ambivalence to the early modern period, but also of the early Hellenistic link between the nerves and the soul—a link which in the long run posed a greater threat to the soul than it did to the body.[100]

---

[99] *UP* 8, 6 (3. 636 K; I, 461, 4–9 Helmreich).

[100] I am deeply grateful to Paul Potter and to other contributors to the volume for many helpful comments on this essay.

5

Body and Soul in Saint Paul

THEO K. HECKEL

It is often said that the physician cares for the body, the priest for the soul. But no more than the physician has soulless bodies to deal with, does the priest meet bodiless souls: believers have both body and soul. And yet it has often seemed, especially in Protestant theology, that the bodily side of belief could be ignored, leading many theologians to attempt to make Christianity a purely inward phenomenon: religion was concerned with the individual soul, and could justifiably leave social and political spheres aside. Right from the beginning of the Protestant movement, from Martin Luther himself, this unfortunate innerness seemed to be destined. Citing Saint Paul, the German reformer says, in his famous text 'On the Freedom of the Christian' (1520), that the freedom of the individual believer is neither outward nor bodily.[1] Indeed, it is with the Apostle of the Gentiles that we come to the root of the question of what the body means for Christian existence.

The texts of Paul that concern us here are letters which represent one half of a dialogue: the New Testament contains only Paul's side of the dialogue; not even the specific questions to which he is replying are known. Before we move to their interpretation, one point about the special form of these sources must be clarified. Paul is writing in a particular situation; he is carrying on a correspondence, not promulgating a worked-out system. But because the New Testament presents the letters completely without context, these answers have taken on the character of a timeless pronouncement, in spite of the fact that Paul is clearly involved in a specific exchange of ideas. His theology is not brought forth as a complete system, but rather develops step by step as he replies to his questioners and seeks to win their agreement.[2] An essay

---

[1] Martin Luther, *Studienausgabe*, ed. H.-U. Delius (Berlin, 1992), ii. 267; cf. Eberhard Jüngel, *Zur Freiheit eines Christenmenschen: Eine Erinnerung an Luthers Schrift*, 2nd edn. (Munich, 1981), 58–9.

[2] Cf. Rudolf Bultmann, *Theologie des Neuen Testaments*, 9th edn., ed. O. Merk (Tübingen, 1984), 191–2; Jürgen Roloff, *Die Kirche im Neuen Testament* (Göttingen, 1993), pp. 87–8; James D. G. Dunn, *The Theology of Paul the Apostle* (Grand Rapids,

with the title 'Body and Soul in Saint Paul' runs the risk of inadvertently changing this dialogue into a system. In my opinion, such a change would inevitably result in a falsification of the truth, for the intellectual comprehensiveness of such a system would have to be supplied by the interpreter himself, by going beyond what Paul says, and possibly misrepresenting him. Thus I have chosen to present Paul's views by reconstructing and interpreting the original *dialogue*.

In recent scholarly discussion, much attention has been given to the concepts 'body' (*sōma*), 'soul' (*psychē*), 'understanding' (*nous*), and 'inward man' (*esō anthrōpos*), terms belonging to Paul's standard collection of anthropological categories. In any attempt to understand how Paul addressed the body–soul problem, however, little is to be gained by investigating these categories individually, since the problem encompasses them all together, and thus reappears each time an attempt is made to examine any one of them separately.[3]

The body–soul problem is particularly evident in sections of the Letters to the Corinthians. In fact, scholars have long noticed that in certain passages of these letters the apostle's use of anthropological terms goes much farther than is usual with him towards a body–soul dualism of the Platonic type. This apparent Platonic dependence goes against everything else we know about the apostle's intellectual character. Thus scholars have attempted to minimize the significance of this Platonizing episode, or have simply ignored it. Rudolf Bultmann is undoubtedly correct when he emphasizes that 'It would be methodologically incorrect to base an interpretation on these passages'.[4] But even if the interpretation of Paul's anthropology is centred on other sources, still, it cannot completely ignore these striking texts. How is the apostle's use of Platonic terminology on this occasion to be explained?

To say that Paul merely supports Old Testament monism against pagan body–soul dualism does not suffice. If the matter were that simple, the apostle would not have needed to hold an extended dialogue on the subject with the Corinthians. Somehow the Corinthians' questions stimulated the apostle to explain his theology in philosophical terms, to distinguish between body and soul. In his response, he came to open up a third path between the Old Testament and Platonic views of man.

Paul did not have as easy a time with the Corinthians as some modern interpreters have believed. The body–soul discussion with the Corinth-

---

Mich., 1998), 11–26. The practice of taking catchwords and giving them a new theological interpretation is typical for Paul: see Theo K. Heckel, *Der Innere Mensch* (Tübingen, 1993), 102–6, 173–5.

[3] e.g. Bultmann, *Theologie*, 202–3 (§17), 205 (§18).   [4] Ibid. 203.

ians involved him in a process whose consequences he could not foresee. Bultmann feels compelled to warn us:

Since Paul's ability to reason abstractly is not developed, and he therefore cannot distinguish between soma in the absolute sense of an essential category, and the phenomenon of the material body, he connects the idea of somatic existence in its perfection with a mythological doctrine of the resurrection (1 Cor. 15).[5]

In this way Bultmann attempts to dispose of the passages which contradict his interpretation of Paul's conception of the body as human essence. According to him, any anthropology that sounds dualistic is in the last analysis the result of Paul's limited ability for abstract thought. But here we must defend the apostle against his interpreter. Paul had good reasons to distinguish the body from the soul, even though he never intended to separate them from one another.[6]

The dialogue between Paul and the Corinthians has a special meaning for us today, too, as we may learn by examining the history of its influence. Indeed, the effects of popular Platonic body–soul dualism continue to be felt down to our own time. Even some hymns give evidence of it:

> The soul may live, free of lamentation,
> The body sleeps until the day of judgement.[7]

And this is not just a specifically German misunderstanding of the tradition. In the novel *Moby-Dick*, Herman Melville has his hero Ismael say:

Methinks my body is but the lees of my better being. In fact take my body who will, take it I say, it is not me. And therefore three cheers for Nantucket; and come a stove boat and stove body when they will, for stave my soul, Jove himself cannot.[8]

Thus, the task of reconstructing the dialogue out of Paul's answers in order to understand his arguments promises to repay our pains. It is not only in this book that we come from Greek philosophy and wish to gain access to Paul the Jew. In general, as Europeans, we are immeasurably closer to the Corinthians' assumptions than to Paul's. Paul's answers to the Corinthians nearly 2,000 years ago can in a way be understood as if they were directed to us today.

[5] Ibid. 199.
[6] Cf. Samuel Vollenweider, 'Der Geist Gottes als Selbst der Glaubenden', *Zeitschrift für Theologie und Kirche*, 93 (1996), 163–92, at 187.
[7] 'Nun laßt uns den Leib begraben', text by M. Weiße, 1531, in *Evangelisches Kirchengesangbuch* (Munich, n.d.), n. 174/5.
[8] Herman Melville, *Moby-Dick; or, the Whale* (New York, 1851), ch. 7 (fin).

In what follows, I shall attempt to present the body–soul problem in Paul by reconstructing the course of the dialogue he held with the Corinthians. In preparation, I first introduce the two participants in the dialogue, the apostle Paul and the Corinthians (section I). The dialogue, as far as it is preserved, develops in two exchanges, or rounds. From the first response of the apostle, known from the First Letter to the Corinthians (section II), followed new questions from the Corinthians. To these the apostle responded in the Second Letter to the Corinthians (section III). This experience with the Corinthians also leaves a trace in the care with which Paul takes up the same subject again in the later Letter to the Romans. A brief look at this document closes the essay (section IV).

I

The spiritual home, the language, and the theological background of Paul are permeated by the Septuagint, the Greek translation of the Hebrew Scriptures with some additions. But the apostle does not limit himself to expounding these Scriptures; he has experienced in the life of Christ something completely new, and it is this most especially that he is reporting. His letters are evidence of the intellectual achievement through which he has been able to win a language for Christian theology.

Paul's missionary activities extended far beyond his physical and spiritual home. In the port city of Corinth he founded the first Christian community, and even after this first conversion the apostle maintained contact with his flock. He visited Corinth several times, and wrote several letters, of which Corinthians 1 and 2 have survived. Historically, the dialogue about body and soul grew out of an interrogation of Paul by the Corinthians. Although the Corinthians are called 'opponents'[9] in the scholarly literature, in all probability their questions arose out of a positive desire for explanation, rather than out of any love of argument for its own sake. Anyone who refuses to take these questions seriously can solve the problems they contain more quickly than the apostle was able to; but if we take them seriously, and make use of this opportunity to learn to understand the Corinthians better, we will also come to understand Paul better.

The content of the questions posed by the Corinthians can be ascertained with a fair degree of precision from Paul's answers. In 1 Corinthians, Paul introduces the various topics he discusses with the formula:

---

[9] On the term see Wolfgang Schrage, *Der erste Brief an die Korinther* (Zurich, 1991), i. 39.

'now concerning' (*peri de*). In so doing, he must be referring back to written questions he has received from Corinth.[10] These questions were not unmotivated, but reveal themselves as problems arising naturally from Paul's earlier theological pronouncements. Whether they are misunderstandings of his teachings or not, Paul chooses to treat them as not improbable examples of such.

We must exercise care in attempting to form a picture of life in the Corinthian community on the basis of these questions. Clearly they are not the product of purely theoretical difficulties, but in most cases the positions the Corinthians are presenting to their apostle for judgement derive from important practical considerations. We may be confident that there were at least some Christians in Corinth who thought in these ways; for purposes of simplicity in this essay, in any case, I shall speak of these explicit views of the Corinthians as the Corinthian position in general. Many features of the correspondence with the Corinthians, such as the form of the individual questions, the terminology, and the pattern of the arguments which are reflected in Paul's answers, provide us with a consistent picture of their philosophical thought. Similarities with many of the ideas of Philo and other Alexandrian thinkers are striking.[11] Although an amalgam of divergent intellectual currents, at the core of the Corinthians' thought appears to be a particular form of the Platonic tradition which I shall call 'religious Platonism'. This religious Platonism is characterized by a special interest in the myths and images Plato weaves into his dialogues. Any serious discussion of Plato's philosophical ideas, on the other hand, is noticeably absent.[12] Some recent theological studies have brought the significance of this religious Platonism in Christian thought in Corinth clearly to light.[13] Paul, in his replies, takes up the questions posed by the Platonizing Corinthian community.

II

The First Letter to the Corinthians contains a first discussion of the significance of the body. From Paul's responses, the original questions of the Corinthians can be largely determined. The Corinthians start the discussion of body and soul by posing questions to the founder of their community. The intellectual background of these questions can be ascertained only indirectly. The Old Testament, in any case, can be excluded

---

[10] Ibid. i. 90–1.   [11] Ibid. 60–1.   [12] Heckel, *Der Innere Mensch*, 28–9, 38–41.
[13] Gerhard Sellin, *Der Streit um die Auferstehung der Toten* (Göttingen, 1986), 202–9: some of the 'opponents' have a connection to Alexandrian Judaism. Although there is no direct connection to Philo (97), the Platonic background is similar (141–3).

as the source of the Corinthians' position. More likely, we may suspect, is a more or less radical misunderstanding of Paul's own theology.

We may assume that the Corinthians had heard from Paul's sermons how the baptized will one day arise with Christ. Now if this future resurrection is vouched for through the spirit, how should the body have anything to do with it? From this question comes the assertion of 1 Corinthians 15: If the Christian community represents the Body of Christ, as Paul was wont to say, then such a Body cannot be understood as anything very concrete, or of the flesh. Indeed, the Corinthian position denies the human body any meaning at all in the life of a Christian. Therefore anything that involves the body is theologically and ethically irrelevant. So even harlotry can be placed in the category of *adiaphoron* 'indifference' (1 Cor. 6: 12–20), and the provision of adequate food for all members of the community at the communion can be seen as unimportant (1 Cor. 11: 17–34). Some Corinthians evidently were not so much interested in such care of the living as in the proxy baptism of the already deceased (1 Cor. 15: 29). But this is not what Paul means. He takes up a position against such Christians, whom he accuses of wanting to live a worldless holiness in an unholy world.

In dealing with the concept of 'body' (*sōma*), Paul begins from the Body of Christ. This starting position explains the objections and alterations which the apostle makes to the Corinthians' Platonically coloured view of body. The community as body, although admittedly intangible, is not without significance: its unifying force is visible in the proclamation of the gospel, and the communion at which the Lord's words are remembered: 'This is My body.' The body is the instrument of the Word—that is what the Body of Christ, as it exists in the person of the community, and the body of the individual Christian have in common. This shared significance explains why Paul can use the same term 'body' (*sōma*) both collectively for the community and individually for its members.[14] Since the body is an instrument of the Word, but not its receiver, Paul is apparently willing to divide body and soul.

It is this perceived division that gives rise to all subsequent problems. It was not Paul's intention to take over with these words the associated

---

[14] Cf. Ernst Käsemann, *Paulinische Perspektiven* (Tübingen, 1969), 198–204. The origin of the expression 'Body of Christ' in Paul is debated: Roloff (*Kirche*, 107–8), among others, traces it back to literature on the Holy Communion: *pace* Andreas Lindemann, 'Die Kirche als Leib', *Zeitschrift für Theologie und Kirche*, 92 (1995), 140–65; Dunn (*Theology*, 548–52), derives it from the Greek political metaphor of a body with many limbs. Lindemann ('Kirche', 162–5) also suggests that the apostle's 'democratic' orientation influenced him to adopt a political metaphor. However, the difficulty with applying the concept 'democratic' to Paul is evident from the very nature of his apostolate, which he legitimates not on the basis of 'democracy', but on Christological grounds; cf. Gal. 1: 15–16; 1 Cor. 15: 9–10.

division meant by Plato. He wanted to establish a different kind of division, for which, however, he was forced to employ the existing terms. In his new definitions the apostle raises the words to the heights of his own theology, by dividing understanding (soul) from action (body). But as the Pauline usage fell into obscurity, the whole construction slipped into the Platonic mode: out of a division came a separation of the redeemable soul from the sinning body. The Corinthians ask Paul to comment on the meaning of bodily existence for the individual. The apostle emphasizes the meaning of the corporeality of Christian life.

I would like to present Paul's argumentation in 1 Corinthians under three heads: first, the Old Testament arguments derived from the theology of creation; next, the Christological heightening of this Old Testament argumentation; finally, I shall attempt to estimate the importance of Paul's transformation of the spatial division he inherited into a chronological division.

First, Paul is able to argue from the Scriptures and to present a reason based on the theology of creation for his insistence upon the significance of the body. In this, he is completely in the spirit of the Old Testament. To give a fuller account of the body and soul in the Old Testament is not possible in the framework of this essay, but one may say in summary that the widely divergent conceptual and theological models put forth there stand in remarkable unanimity in their contrast to Platonic theories of the soul: indeed, questions of a Platonic kind receive no response in these writings at all. This, of course, is the result of the Old Testament's strict body–soul monism, which contains no place for a bi- or tripartite human nature.[15] Much more difficult to understand are the anthropological categories of the Old Testament in their own context. Generally, the categories that define the individual tend to be put in *relational* terms, whether to other human beings or to God. By contrast, statements about what is *in* the person do not occur.[16] The few passages that refer to the survival of the individual after his earthly death (e.g. Psalm 73: 23–8; Daniel 12: 2) emphasize only that his relationship to God continues. Reference to any kind of soul as agent of this persisting connection is not found.

God created body and soul.[17] On this basis, Paul checks any attempt

---

[15] For details see Hans Walter Wolff, *Anthropologie des Alten Testaments*, 6th edn. (Munich, 1994); Horst Dietrich Preuß, *Theologie des Alten Testaments* (Stuttgart, 1992), ii. 117–18, 161; Eduard Schweizer, 'Body', in *Anchor Bible Dictionary* (New York, 1992), i. 767–72; Edmond Jacob, '"psyche" B: Die Anthropologie des Alten Testaments', in *Theologisches Wörterbuch zum Neuen Testament* (Stuttgart, 1973), ix. 614–29; Gerhard Dautzenberg, 'Seele . . . im biblischen Denken sowie das Verhältnis von Unsterblichkeit und Auferstehung', in K. Kremer (ed.), *Seele* (Leiden, 1984), 186–203.

[16] Cf. Preuß, *Theologie*, 124, 140.

[17] Cf. Walter Gutbrod, *Die Paulinische Anthropologie* (Stuttgart, 1934), 86.

to assign the soul alone to the divine realm, with the body—as a prison—holding the soul back from God.[18] In theological terms, Paul resists the attempt to regard sin as a phenomenon of the body. It is not the body which separates man from God, but rather man's attempt to free himself from dependence on God, and through his own deeds make himself equal to him. So the separation from God—that is, sin—involves the whole man.

Before God there is no naked soul, only whole persons: thus the person is called upon to make himself pleasing to God, a task of the whole man (2 Cor. 5: 9). Here Bultmann's much cited dictum can claim validity: 'The person does not have a body, he is body'.[19]

What interests the apostle is not the component parts of man or his static substance, but rather his embodied living functions. As Paul develops his account of the Body of Christ from the power of the Word, it is clear that he is speaking about the interactions between body and limb. Actions and dependencies, not spatial relationships, determine the relationship between body and soul. The spirit of Christ must rule in the community, as in the individual member. The body is not a static prison of the soul, but its instrument and centre of communication.

But with whom does the body communicate? Rudolf Bultmann, in his classic account, defines man as follows: Man 'is called *sōma* in so far as he can make himself an object of his own action, or experiences himself as the subject of a happening or a suffering'.[20] This definition is very formal.[21] And whoever devotes himself to harlotry in Corinth (1 Cor. 6: 12–20) also makes himself the object of his own action and experiences himself as the subject of a happening.

But Paul attacks this conception sharply. His point is not only that 'one be one with oneself',[22] but also that only he can 'be one with himself' who has become 'one with God'. This is the point of Romans 5–8: out of peace with God (Rom. 5: 1; cf. 8: 31) comes peace within the person himself (Rom. 7: 24 and 25a).

The apostle also has a Christological reason for emphasizing the significance of the body: Jesus died on the cross, body and soul. Crucifixion did not just involve Christ's soul. The death on the cross cannot be interpreted as a separation of Jesus' body and soul.[23] It is from this

---

[18] Jürgen Becker, *Paulus: Der Apostel der Völker* (Tübingen, 1989), 406.

[19] Bultmann, *Theologie*, 195.   [20] Ibid. 196.

[21] Cf. Eduard Schweizer, 'soma', in *Theologisches Wörterbuch zum Neuen Testament* (Stuttgart, 1964), vii. 1063–4 n. 410: 'This definition is not adequate, and runs the risk of suggesting the Greek view, which sees the human being as a self-centred individual.'

[22] Bultmann, *Theologie*, 197–8. But in the 'Vorbemerkung', §17, p. 193, Bultmann suggests that only the relationship with God makes a positive relationship with oneself possible.

[23] Thus Paul never speaks of the *psychē* of Christ in relation to the body of Christ.

central theological truth that Paul rejects any claim for a bodiless existence. Because of the experience at the cross, such an existence cannot
be. The body works towards the outside, the Body of Christ justifies the
community of believers. As the resurrected Christ continues to act in,
among other things, the community of believers, he obviously has a
body. Paul does admit that there is a change in Christ's body through
crucifixion: the body does lose its carnality, but it remains as instrument;
as spiritual body, as body subservient to spirit, it remains indispensable.

From Christians Paul expects a similar transformation of the body. At
the final judgement they will receive a 'spiritual body' (1 Cor. 15: 44).
This concept is not without difficulties; indeed, it sounds like a self-
contradiction, like an incomprehensible thought. Paul seems to have
created the term himself. What he really means by it can no longer be
definitely determined.[24] Nevertheless, the fact that he created such an
original synthesis demonstrates how inconceivable a redeemed soul
without a body was for him.[25] If the soul alone could be redeemed, then
the person could not.

The participants in the dialogue are analysing man in different ways:
the Corinthians divide him spatially, the apostle temporally. This apparently superficial difference is the mark of a profound theological split.
The Corinthians are trying to name the place where God resides in
them. As in religious Platonism in general, the argumentation is framed
in spatial terms; historical development is hardly considered. In this
point too, the intellectual proximity of the Corinthians to Philo of
Alexandria is clear: Philo's fundamental lack of historical perspective in
his interpretations has often been noted by scholars.[26] The apostle is not
content with a timeless analysis of body and soul, but attempts to transform the spatial difference into a historical one. The discussion of life in
this historical dimension comes to include death as well.

Paul sees in the Corinthians' position the danger of an anthropological ideal which Christians are really supposed to have left behind them:
an elevated form of salvation through works, the attempt to excel before
God through one's own deeds. Precisely by pointing out the freedom of
the soul from the body, some Corinthians are attempting to emphasize
the connection of the soul with God. Several of their questions show
how confident they are in exhibiting their new freedom *vis-à-vis* the
body. Their boldness ranges from the consumption of meat slaughtered
at pagan rites (1 Cor. 8: 10) to the above-mentioned harlotry.

The new position of the Corinthians is based on the knowledge that
no external force can any longer exert power over the individual's

---

[24] Cf. Sellin, *Streit*, 73, 222; Heckel, *Der Innere Mensch*, 106.

[25] This is the main point of Bultmann's account (*Theologie*, 193) of the concept 'soma'.

[26] Cf. Heckel, *Der Innere Mensch*, 48.

behaviour. Paul now says that this self-confidence is a very dangerous basis for life. It is founded on an assumption that, in epistemological terms, is equivalent to the salvation through works ideas common in certain circles with Jewish tendencies. The person who wishes to possess himself creates a self viewed as the sum of his deeds or the sum of his thoughts. This view of life must close its eyes to the future, for at the latest, with death, its powerlessness becomes apparent. Looking back, Paul defines pre-Christian existence in these terms. Two historical instances are advanced as arguments: (1) Paul's own personal Pharisee past; (2) the general pre-Christian past (Rom. 7: 7–25a). In both cases Paul speaks in the first person singular: 'I tried to justify myself before God by my deeds.' Paul now judges this, in his opinion typically pre-Christian, view as follows: 'It is not worth a straw' (Phil. 3: 8). 'I cannot make my life myself, I receive it: God creates me anew in baptism; in the Gospel I receive daily a new creation from the inside out' (1 Cor. 8 and 10; Rom. 12: 2). With this new life from God, the previous life coming out of oneself is superseded. The person has his existence not from what he does, but from his submission to God's word. In God's eyes the active person becomes the submitting person; out of the 'old person' comes a 'new person' (Rom. 6: 4–6). It is worth noting that the apostle also takes up the topic of death. He develops his view not from the idea of death as the end of life, but from the theological side: death is separation from God. He also on occasion views conversion as a death (Rom. 7: 10): the confidence of the active agent in opposition to God ends definitively: Paul feels himself absolutely passive in his relationship to God; it is precisely in this passivity that he reaches God. He begins the new life by submitting to God's word. According to Paul, the Christian has already put death as absolute passivity behind him. Thus, in the words of the baptismal formula: 'We are baptized in the death of Christ, and buried with Him' (Rom. 6: 3–4). In this way the still outstanding earthly death loses its absolute terror. Death of the body too leads to a complete passivity in relationship with God. But just as God has once given new life in baptism, so he will do the same again. Earthly death remains a great step, but conversion to Christianity through baptism is also a great step. Earthly death has been addressed and prepared for by the Christian's overcoming of his idea of himself as active partner. So this discussion of the correct understanding of the body finds its goal in the correct understanding of the resurrection (1 Cor. 15).

Somatic existence does not have to wait for death to gain meaning. Ideas of body and soul, images of body as garment or house of the soul, always pertain to the realm of the individual. If this is the point of focus, then the community which is collected by the Spirit slips out of view. But it is precisely in the context of community that the apostle speaks of body (*sōma*): the Spirit creates the community as the Body of Christ. To live in this community means to share the things of the body: whoever takes his meal without thinking of the hunger of his fellow Christians forfeits the basis upon which the communion's benefits depend (1 Cor. 11: 27–34).

III

After Paul's First Letter to them, the Corinthians returned once more to the subject of body and soul. In his first response in 1 Corinthians, Paul had used certain expressions which were inevitably misunderstood when taken in the context of a Platonic view of the soul. The Corinthians, it would seem, attempted to understand Paul's answers on the model of the Platonic soul. Here I shall present a short summary of the Platonic soul model, as it is developed in the ninth book of the *Republic*.

Plato speaks of three parts of the soul, each of which directs a set of bodily activities. In an image widely known in antiquity, Plato describes the three parts of the soul as follows.[27] Behind the shell of the visible man his soul lies hidden; Plato, so to speak, looks into this inner world and presents us with three figures representing the parts of the soul. First, he distinguishes the appetitive and spirited parts, describing each with an animal image: a many-headed hydra represents the appetites; a lion, courage. In religious Platonism, of course, the third and highest soul part was of special interest: that is, understanding (*nous*), which Plato explicitly calls 'divine'. In the Platonic model, it is an invisible man inside the man, the 'inward man', who is to steer the soul. In order to steer the soul correctly, the man inside the man requires the proper insight and wisdom, which are to be attained through philosophical instruction, the nourishment of the soul. If this nourishment is lacking, the man dies, the reason in him dies, and only the visible shell of the outward man remains; the specifically human possibility of thought is dead, the bestial part reigns, and the man becomes an ape.[28]

This Platonic model of the tripartite soul achieved a remarkable popularity in the ancient world. Philo of Alexandria refers on many occasions to this image of the inner man.[29] One of the latest books of the Septuagint, 4 Maccabees 7: 14, also betrays a knowledge of the Platonic passage. Later, this model was persistently adopted in the intellectual circles which came to be called Gnostic.[30] In the Gospel of

---

[27] Ibid. 11–26.   [28] e.g. Plato, *Republic* 9, 590b; cf. 10, 620a–d.
[29] Heckel, *Der Innere Mensch*, 42–71.   [30] Ibid. 76–88, 221–6.

Thomas, an apocryphal Jesus religion is expounded which can only be understood in reference to the Platonic soul model derived from the ninth book of the *Republic*: 'Jesus said, blessed is the lion that becomes man when consumed by man; and cursed is the man whom the lion consumes, and the lion becomes man' (Gospel of Thomas, log. 7).[31] That later Gnostics made use of this passage in creating their supposedly Christian theology is proved not only by the reports of the Church Fathers, but also by the fact that a translation of the passage from Plato is included in the Nag Hammadi texts.[32] This wide circulation of the Platonic image permits us to conclude that it was well known to the Corinthians.

Paul draws a sharp line between pre-Christian and Christian views of man. In Romans he speaks of the 'old man' who in baptism is symbolically crucified (Rom. 6: 6), but who through baptism gains a part in the new life of Christ, and thus becomes the 'new man'. About the actual existence of a Christian, it can only be said that he is *somehow* both the 'old man' and the 'new man'. This italicized 'somehow' points to the problem. Paul first tried to transform the earlier spatial division into a temporal one (see above). From this follows the Corinthians' second question: Where in this life is the decisively new character of Christian existence to be seen; where is Christ in us? This question could not be answered with a temporal division, at least not if Paul wanted to deny an absolute discontinuity between pre-Christian and Christian time. Sharply as he drew the line—he could even say 'I' died—the same 'I' still had to exist, to be the same person before and after. The individual's identity had to bridge the division. On this point Ernst Käsemann cannot be correct when he asserts: 'The idea of an immanent continuity of life is unknown to Paul'.[33] This same scholar has quite rightly persisted, however, in emphasizing that Christology is both the starting-point and the goal of Pauline theology. It is precisely for a correct understanding of the crucifixion that an identity of person exists between the crucified Jesus and the risen Christ.

In this situation the Platonic soul model seemed to fit seductively well. Paul had provided material for a Platonic interpretation. From all that we can gather from his letters, however, Paul himself was unaware of the tenets of this religious Platonism. It was different with his Corinthian correspondents. From Plato himself on, the danger that the inward man should starve and die had been expressed. In comparing his conversion to a death (Rom. 7: 10), Paul seemed to be experiencing something similar. But Paul replaced the dead inward man, Plato's 'reason', in a very different way. The apostle speaks of Christ's presence in us several

---

[31] *The Nag Hammadi Library in English*, ed. James Robinson, 3rd edn. (Leiden, 1988), 127.   [32] Nag Hammadi Codex VI 5; ibid. 318–20.

[33] Käsemann, *Paulinische Perspektiven*, 20.

times (Gal. 2: 20; cf. 2 Cor. 13: 5; Rom. 8: 10). In 1 Corinthians 2: 16 he writes: 'But we have the understanding (*nous*) of Christ.' Where else, then, should the Corinthians expect this 'Christ in us' to be located, than in the soul. This 'inward Christ', they imagined, was to take over the role of the 'inward man'. In place of human understanding came the understanding of Christ. Had not the apostle himself said exactly this?

But Paul detected the hidden anthropocentrism of the concept of the inward man. Even as reflected in the popular Platonic understanding of the Corinthians, it is clear that for them the inward man, 'reason' (*nous*), is the divine part of man: Plato had called the highest part of the soul 'divine' (*theion*).[34] This divine part of the soul was to be nourished by education and learning (*paideia*). Paul, on the contrary, rejected the idea of nourishing the reason in man by educational efforts—even if these were Christian. He sets the inward man under the influence of a daily renewal through God (2 Cor. 4: 16). He is interested not in the capabilities of an educated reason, but in a person's receptivity.

The Body of Christ is experienced in the community of Christians. Body, then, is a collective concept: The community is body; it does not just represent a collection of individuals who have bodies. This collective assumption is so jarring that even Rudolf Bultmann passes over it in silence. For Paul the question of the individual's body is clearly secondary. The apostle presses the individual anthropological concepts of the Corinthians into a collective mould. In the passage 2 Corinthians 4: 16–5: 10, this process takes place before our eyes. The metaphors of body as garment and house of the soul are oriented towards the individual. Paul expands the house metaphor with his own temple metaphor. Temple or edifice of God is not the individual Christian, but the community. From the limbs of the community arises an edifice (*oikodomē*). In 1 Corinthians, Paul uses this image of an edifice to emphasize the meaning of coherence in the community (1 Cor. 3: 16–17; 14: 26). In the final analysis, the apostle's thought here is rooted in the idea of the 'People of God', rather than being developed from the concept of the religious individual.

This same change from the individual to the 'we' of believers is also reflected in the later exposition in Romans 7: 7–8: 17. Paul first depicts from the standpoint of an individual Christian the pre-Christian situation (Rom. 7: 7–25a) and then life in the 'newness of spirit' (Rom. 8: 1–17). As he moves from pre-Christian to Christian life, he also changes from the singular to the plural. In Romans 8 he describes the 'newness of spirit' from the perspective of the community with the first person plural.[35]

---

[34] e.g. Plato, *Republic* 9, 590d; similarly *Phaedrus* 247d.
[35] Cf. Vollenweider, 'Geist', 168.

The apostle takes over the Platonic images of house and garment for the body, but he then expands them in his own way. Not only is the soul clothed with the body, but both together must be clothed again. This idea is new and probably original with Paul. It may well be possible to divide body from soul,[36] but what matters in Christianity is that both body and soul together are covered by another garment: only through this final reclothing of body and soul does salvation become possible. The body may be understood as house of the soul, but for Paul what matters is that we receive another 'house' prepared by God over the top (2 Cor. 5: 1–2).

IV

The spiritual entities conscience, inward man, and understanding are highlighted by Paul because he links the Gospel to the spreading of the word from the Cross. He addresses those parts of the person which are capable of receiving this message. In Romans 8 Paul refers back to his discussion with the Corinthians from some distance in time. Here he shows considerable care in handling the individual anthropological terms. Only in depicting the pre-Christian era does he use the metaphor of the inward man, which he calls a positive but ineffectual faculty of the person (Rom. 7: 22). It was Ernst Käsemann in particular who warned against interpreting the collective character of Paul's theology of justification from the viewpoint of the individual.[37] The special significance which Paul in particular gives to the individual in relationship to God cannot serve as the beginning point of his anthropology, but must rather be seen as its culmination:

For him [sc. Paul] man in the reign of sin could not be an 'individual', but was, as representative of this world, implicated in its violence. For Paul the 'individual' is not the premise of an anthropological theory, but rather the result of the Grace which takes him into Its service.[38]

In the depiction of positive Christian existence in Romans 8, Paul switches to the vague 'in us'. It is from the inside out that the whole person is awakened to new life (Rom. 8: 9–11). In this process the same spirit of God is active which awakened Christ from the dead. In this passage Paul draws a parallel between God's spirit and the spirit of man: It is an openness or receptivity to God's spirit that gives the human spirit its special significance.[39] This openness is the gift of the freedom that is

---

[36] Another example of this freedom with anthropological constructions is the tripartite body–soul–pneuma synthesis in 1 Thess. 5: 23.

[37] Käsemann, *Paulinische Perspektiven*, 24, 36, 117, 132–3.   [38] Ibid. 59.

[39] Cf. Vollenweider, 'Geist', 168–79.

neither outward nor bodily.[40] It is not the intellectual powers of the human mind, its wisdom, which, as in Plato, predestines it to be the ruling part of the soul. Rather, it is because God's word has the potential to change a person from the inside out that Paul is interested in human souls. And because this word so alters a person from the inside out that outward effects must follow, a Christian can only live in relationship to God within a community of persons who have all been changed by hearing God's word. This community Christians have in the Body of Christ.

[40] Cf. the Luther passage cited in n. 1 above.

6

Internalist Reasoning in Augustine for Mind–Body Dualism

GARETH MATTHEWS

Reasoning about souls is as old as Western philosophy. Thus Thales, along with supposing that water is the *archē* of all things, also reasoned that magnets have *psychē*, soul, since they move things.[1] One could extract this argument for souls from Thales' contention:

(1) A magnet can move things.

(2) Whatever can move things has a soul.

Therefore:

(3) A magnet has a soul.

Therefore:

(4) Something has a soul; that is, there are souls.

Aristotle records no argument from Thales for 'the real distinction' between soul and body, to put the point in a Cartesian way. The conclusion of the argument from Thales seems to be quite compatible with a soul's being, rather than a substance in its own right, merely an attribute, or a power, of certain bodies—a power of magnets, for example.

There is, however, an argument for the real distinction between souls and bodies in Plato; in fact, there are several. In the *Phaedo*, for example, Plato tries to give us reason to think that we can recollect knowledge of the Forms from a previous life. There follows this exchange between Socrates and Simmias:

SOC. When do our souls acquire this knowledge [i.e. the knowledge of Forms we have remembered, but had earlier forgotten]? It cannot be after the beginning of our mortal life.
SIM. No, of course not.

---

[1] Aristotle, *De anima* 405a19.

soc. Then it must be before.

sim. Yes.

soc. Then our souls had a previous existence, Simmias, before they took on this human shape. They were independent of our bodies, and they were possessed of intelligence.

sim. Unless perhaps it is at the moment of birth that we acquire knowledge of these things, Socrates. There is still that time available.

soc. No doubt, my dear fellow, but just tell me, what other time is there to lose it in? We have just agreed that we do not possess it when we are born. Do we lose it at the same moment that we acquire it? Or can you suggest any other time?

sim. Of course not, Socrates. I didn't realize what nonsense I was talking.[2]

The core of Plato's reasoning here seems to be this:

(5) We know things we have not learned in this life.

(6) If we know things we have not learned in this life, then we must have learned something before our souls took on human shape.

(7) If we learned something before our souls took on human shape, then our souls once existed apart from our bodies.

Therefore:

(8) Our souls once existed apart from our bodies.

We could add, if we like:

(9) If our souls once existed apart from our bodies, then our souls are entities really distinct from our bodies.

Therefore:

(10) Our souls are entities really distinct from our bodies.

Toward the end of the *Phaedo*, at 105d–106c, Plato offers a famous argument for the soul's immortality that also promises to underwrite soul–body dualism. He argues there that a person's soul is the principle of life and, as such, does not admit of death; it is, therefore, immortal. But, of course, one's body is far from being immortal. So, again, the conclusion is that one's soul is an entity distinct from one's body.

Although philosophical argumentation to support soul–body dualism thus has a long history, in Augustine it takes a radically new turn. In him we find, for the first time, an argument for dualism that is essentially internalist. This is reasoning from what each mind can know about itself to the conclusion that minds are non-corporeal entities.

At first thought, a shift from (i) what we can know about minds or

---

[2] *Phaedo* 76c–d, trans. H. Tredennick, in Plato, *The Collected Dialogues of Plato*, ed. E. Hamilton and H. Cairns (New York, 1963), 59–60.

souls in general—for example, that they have knowledge they have not acquired 'since taking on human form'—to (ii) what each mind knows about itself might not seem especially interesting or important. One could easily turn the Platonic arguments above into first-personal ones. Thus, I could say that my soul knows things it has not learned in this life. And I could go on to argue on this basis for the conclusion that my soul is distinct from my body. Again, I could begin with the premise that my soul is a principle of life, which does not admit of death, and reason to the conclusion that my soul is distinct from my body, which, lamentably, does admit of death.

Yet, such first-personal transformations of the previously mentioned Platonic arguments would hardly be internalist in any very interesting way. To appreciate how different the Augustinian reasoning is, we need to examine it in some detail.

The place where this internalist argumentation for mind–body dualism turns up most clearly in Augustine is in his strikingly original treatise on the Divine Trinity, *De trinitate*. Augustine's project in that work is the dauntingly difficult task of trying to make sense of the Christian doctrine that God is Three in One. His tactic, through the last half of the work, is to offer mental, or psychological, analogies to the claim that God is somehow both Three and also just One. His idea is that these mental analogies may make the doctrine of the Trinity seem less counterintuitive.[3]

Thus in book 9 Augustine offers the mind, its knowledge, and its love as 'a certain image of the Trinity' (*De trinitate* 9 12, 18). In the next book he discusses the trinity of memory, understanding, and will. In book 11 he finds a trinity in perception: namely, the form of the body perceived, the image impressed on the sense, and the will of the perceiver. And there are other psychological analogies as well. In the midst of his search for mental or psychological analogies to the Divine Trinity, Augustine presents some of his most interesting and important thinking about the human mind. The Augustinian thesis that I want to give special emphasis to from the last half of the *De trinitate* is this one:

Thesis A: The mind of each of us knows what a mind is simply and solely by knowing itself.

So far as I know, this thesis is original with Augustine. Its implications are profound. But before I trace out some of them, let me quote a few of the passages in which Augustine gives the thesis itself expression. This is, perhaps, the first relevant passage:

[3] No doubt this idea of Augustine's is unduly optimistic. I am myself inclined to agree with the quip, 'Consciousness is like the Trinity; if it is explained so that you can understand it, it hasn't been explained correctly' (R. Joynt, in 'Are Two Heads Better than One?', *Behavioral and Brain Sciences*, 4 (1981), 108).

[A]s regards the soul, we not unfittingly say that we, therefore, know what a soul is because we also have a soul. We have never seen it with our eyes, nor formed a general or special idea of it from any similarity with other souls that we have seen, but rather, as I said, because we also have a soul. For what is so intimately known, and what knows itself to be itself, than that through which all other things are likewise known, that is, the soul itself? (Ibid. 8 6, 9)[4]

Augustine's idea here is immediately appealing, even if, in the end, it is plagued with severe philosophical problems, difficulties that Wittgenstein and other twentieth-century philosophers have sought to point out. Augustine contrasts our knowledge of what a soul is, and how we can come to have the knowledge of what a soul is, with our knowledge of what an F is, where we can observe multiple Fs and determine, somehow, what it is they all have in common that makes them Fs. Augustine is certainly sensitive to the difficulty of understanding what an F is (say, a table, or a wall) from seeing many Fs (many tables, or walls) and taking note of what they have in common. He brings out these difficulties in his remarkable early dialogue *On the Teacher* (*De magistro*). But however it is that we come to understand what a wall is after seeing examples of walls, that procedure, he suggests, won't work for souls, since the only soul we can observe is our own. The good news, he supposes, is that observing our own soul, or mind, is also sufficient for knowing what a mind, or soul, is. That is thesis A.

Yet, if our own mind is the only soul we can observe, how do we know that anyone else has a mind? That is the notorious problem of other minds. Augustine realizes that thesis A raises the problem of other minds. Thus, immediately after the passage from the *De trinitate* I have just quoted, Augustine presents the argument from analogy for other minds, or souls. This passage is, so far as I know, the first statement of the argument from analogy for other minds.

For we also recognize, from a likeness to us, the motions of bodies by which we perceive that others besides us live. Just as we move [our] body in living, so, we notice, those bodies are moved. For when a living body is moved there is no way open to our eyes to see the mind (*animus*), a thing which cannot be seen by the eyes. But we perceive something present in that mass such as is present in us to move our mass in a similar way; it is life and soul (*anima*). Nor is such perception something peculiar to, as it were, human prudence and reason. For

---

[4] This passage, and all other quotations in this paper from *De trinitate* except two, follow Stephen McKenna's reliable translation in Saint Augustine, *The Trinity* (Washington, 1963). The translation is vol. 45 in the series, The Fathers of the Church.

The two exceptions are (i) the very next passage I quote (*De trinitate* 8 6, 9), which I have myself translated freshly, and (ii) ibid. 10 10, 16, where I substitute 'essence' for McKenna's 'substance'. I comment on the reason for that substitution in the body of the text.

indeed beasts perceive as living, not only themselves, but also each other and one another, and us as well. Nor do they see our soul (*anima*), except from the motions of the body, and they do that immediately and very simply by a sort of natural agreement. Therefore we know the mind (*animus*) of anyone at all from our own; and from our own case we believe in that [viz. that mind of another] which we do not know. For not only do we perceive a mind (*animus*), but we even know what one is, by considering our own; for we have a mind (*animus*). (*De trinitate* 8 6, 9)

I should make a comment here about terminology. Augustine uses both the feminine word in Latin for 'soul', *anima*, as well as the masculine word, *animus*, and also the (feminine) word for 'mind', *mens*. He seems to think of an *animus* as a specifically rational *anima*—that is, a rational soul, or mind (*mens*). Thus, focusing in the passage above especially on the rational *anima*—that is, the human mind—he shifts unselfconsciously between *anima* and *animus*. In the following books of *De trinitate* he shifts to *mens*, 'mind', as an alternative to *animus*, 'rational soul'.

Although there are many things in the passage above that deserve comment, what I want to emphasize right away is the importance of thesis A to the statement of the argument from analogy. Augustine's idea is that we know the minds of others—that they have minds, as well as what it is for them to have a mind—as an extrapolation from our own case. I know what a mind is by knowing my own mind, and I know what a mind does by observing my own mind move my own body. When I see other bodies move in ways similar to those in which my body moves, I may therefore infer that they are moved by minds similar to my own.

It is also worth emphasizing that thesis A not only helps make the argument from analogy for other minds possible; it also makes it necessary. Thus, if I know what a mind is *solely* by knowing my own mind, then, if I am to have reasonably good grounds for supposing that there are minds in addition to my own, I must have some such argument as the argument from analogy to provide those grounds.

Here are two passages from the next book of the *De trinitate* that also give expression to thesis A:

When the mind (*mens*), therefore, knows itself fully and nothing else with itself, then its knowledge is equal to it, because its knowledge is not from another nature when it knows itself. And when it perceives itself fully and nothing more, then its knowledge is neither less nor greater than itself. (*De trinitate* 9 4, 4)

When the mind (*mens*), therefore, knows itself, it alone is the parent of its own knowledge, for it is itself both the object known and the one that knows ... Hence, when it knows itself, it begets a knowledge of itself that is equal to itself. For it does not know itself as less than it is, nor is its knowledge that of another essence, not only because it is itself that which knows, but also because it knows itself. (Ibid. 9 12, 18)

When Augustine talks about the mind knowing what it itself is, he clearly means to include in that knowledge knowing what it is to be a mind, or, as we might also put it, knowing what is essential to being a mind. In book 10 Augustine inquires specifically into the nature of mind:

> But since our inquiry concerns the nature (*natura*) of the mind (*mens*), let us remove from consideration all knowledge obtained externally through the senses of the body, and attend more diligently to that which we have set down: that every mind (*mens*) knows and is certain concerning itself. (Ibid. 10 10, 14)

Three chapters earlier Augustine had surveyed the philosophical theories known to him concerning the nature of mind, or soul. Since the variety of these theories will be important to the internalist argument that Augustine presents for the incorporeality of the mind, it is well to take special note of their variety. Thus some philosophers have thought the mind to be blood, Augustine reports; others, the brain, and others the heart. He continues:

> Others believe that it consisted of very minute and indivisible bodies called atoms which meet and cling together. Others said that its substance was air, others fire. Others could not think of any substance except as a body, and since they found that the soul was not a body, they said that it was not a substance at all, but the harmony itself of a body, or the combining of the primary substances by which that flesh is as it were joined together. And, consequently, all of these have regarded the soul as mortal; for whether it was a body or some combination of the body, in either case it would certainly not live forever.
>
> But some have declared that its substance was a kind of life, altogether different from corporeal life. For they have found it to be a life that vivifies and animates every living body, and have attempted to prove, as each one could, that it must logically be also immortal, since life cannot be without life. Some add a fifth body—I do not know what it is—to the well-known four elements of this world and from it, so they say, mind comes. (Ibid. 10 7, 9)

Included in this survey is the view of the ancient atomists, who thought that the soul is a collection of fine atoms, like fire or air. The idea of the soul as a harmony of body elements is one that Plato has Simmias espouse in his dialogue *Phaedo*, at 85e–86d. And, finally, the mention of the soul as a vivifier may be a reference to the Platonic argument from the end of the *Phaedo* that I discussed earlier.

The idea of a 'fifth body' seems to puzzle Augustine. It raises for him the question of what these earlier philosophers might have understood by 'body' (*corpus*). He responds with this fascinating comment:

> [E]ither [those who speak of 'a fifth body'] use the term 'body' in the same sense as we do, namely, that of which a part is less than the whole in the extension of place (*in loci spatio*), and then we must number them among those who believe the mind to be corporeal; or, if they call every substance, or every changeable

substance, a body, although aware that not every substance is contained in the extension of place by length, width, and height, we need not dispute with them about a question of words. (*De trinitate* 10 7, 9)

Whatever Augustine may have meant exactly by 'the extension, or space, of place' (*spatium loci*), the occurrence of this phrase here is likely to remind modern readers of Descartes' conception of body as an 'extended thing' (*res extensa*), which, of course, Descartes contrasts with a mind, a 'thinking thing' (*res cogitans*).

We need to return now to Augustine's claim that 'every mind (*mens*) knows and is certain concerning itself' (Ibid. 10 10, 14). Augustine seems to include in 'knowing and being certain concerning itself' (i) knowing what it itself is: namely, a mind; (ii) knowing what it is to be a mind; and even (iii) knowing what is essential to being a mind. What does Augustine take to be essential to being a mind?

To determine what is essential to being a mind, Augustine seems to use something much like Descartes' method of systematic doubt, though, of course, he does not call it 'the method of doubt'. By seeing what he can doubt, and what he cannot, he seeks to establish, not just that he exists, but also that he understands and lives as well:

Let this remain to it, which not even they have doubted who regarded the mind (*mens*) as this or that kind of a body. For not every mind (*mens*) regards itself as air, but, as I mentioned above, some regard it as fire, others as a brain, and others as this or that kind of a body. All know, however, that they understand and live; they refer what they understand to the understanding, but refer being and life to themselves. And no one doubts that no one understands who does not live, and no one lives who does not exist. (Ibid. 10 10, 13)

Augustine's idea seems to be that attempting to doubt that one understands in itself shows that one understands, as doubting that one lives, or exists, itself shows that one lives, or exists. We are now on the road to showing that the corporealists are wrong—indeed, that they must be wrong:

For men have doubted whether the power to live, to remember, to understand, to will, to think, to know, and to judge is due to air, to fire, or to the brain, or to the blood, or to atoms, or to a fifth body . . . or whether the combining or the orderly arrangement of the flesh is capable of producing these effects. . . .

On the other hand, who would doubt that he lives, remembers, understands, wills, thinks, knows, and judges? For even if he doubts, he lives; if he doubts, he remembers why he doubts; if he doubts, he understands that he doubts; if he doubts, he wishes to be certain; if he doubts, he thinks; if he doubts, he knows that he does not know; if he doubts, he judges that he ought not to consent rashly. Whoever then doubts about anything else ought never to doubt about all of these; for if they were not, he would be unable to doubt about anything at all. (Ibid. 10 10, 14)

The effort to doubt that the mind is something that lives, remembers, understands, wills, thinks, knows, and judges thus reveals the mind indubitably doing these very things. It is in this way, Augustine thinks, that the mind knows what a mind is, even essentially is, and not by observing various minds and developing a general idea from them of what is essential to being a mind.

Might it not still be the case that these powers of living, remembering, understanding, willing, thinking, knowing, and judging are yet the powers of some corporeal thing? 'Those who regard the mind (*mens*) either as a body, or as the combination or harmony of the body', Augustine writes,

wish all these things to be seen in a subject. Thus the air, the fire, or some other body would be the substance which they call the mind (*mens*), while the understanding would be in this body as its quality. . . . And even those who do not regard the mind as a body, but as the combination or harmony of the body, are pretty nearly of the same opinion. For they differ in this respect: the former say that the mind itself is a substance, wherein the understanding is present as in a subject; but the latter declare that the mind itself is in a subject, that is, in a body of which it is the combination or harmony. (Ibid. 10 10, 15)

The idea seems to be that even those who suppose the mind is something corporeal do not deny that the mind understands, wills, thinks, knows, and judges. Augustine has, he thinks, just established that the effort to doubt these things is self-defeating. The corporealists thus agree that the mind is whatever it is that thinks (etc.), but they mistakenly identify this thinking thing with something corporeal, whether they think of it as being air, fire, or whatever.

The stage is now set for Augustine's internalist argument for the incorporeality of the mind, and hence for mind–body dualism. We begin with this, as Augustine thinks, now well-established premise:

(11) The mind knows and is certain concerning itself.

What (11) means includes, as we have said, this:

(12) The mind knows and is certain that it is a mind.

The mind recognizes that it is a mind, not by examining a number of things with minds and determining that what they have in common is a mind. Rather, the mind recognizes in itself what a mind is. This is thesis A.

Among the things that follow from (12), Augustine thinks, is this:

(13) The mind is certain that it understands, wills, thinks, etc.

That performing those mental functions is essential to being a mind follows, Augustine supposes, from trying to doubt that the mind does those things.

Augustine's reasoning continues:

(14) If (a) the mind were something *corporeal* that understands, wills, thinks, etc., then, if (b) the mind is really certain of its essence, then (c) the mind would know and be certain that it is something corporeal.

Augustine wants to use *modus tollens* on this complex conditional. That is, he wants to deny its consequent so that he can get the denial of its antecedent. But the consequent is itself a conditional, namely this one:

> if (b) the mind is really certain of its essence, then (c) the mind would know and be certain that it is something corporeal.

To get the denial of this conditional, we need its antecedent, (b), to be true, and its consequent, (c), to be false. So these are the next steps in the argument:

(15) The mind is really certain of its essence.

(16) The mind is not certain that it is something corporeal.

Augustine thinks of (15) as an implication of thesis A. As for (16), he thinks that the cacophony of wildly different corporeal and body-related theories of the mind, or soul, shows that nobody can be really certain of the corporeality of the mind. After all, some say the mind, or soul, is air; some say it is fire; some say it is the harmony of bodily elements; and so on, and so on. What all this disagreement shows, Augustine thinks, is that the mind does not know, nor is it certain, that it is something corporeal. Unlike doubts about whether the mind thinks, wills, remembers, etc., doubt about any of these hypotheses is not self-defeating. So no corporeality thesis is self-certifying. Therefore the mind is not certain that it is something corporeal.

We are now in position to deny the consequent of (14) and so to conclude, by *modus tollens*, that the antecedent is also false. Thus

(17) The mind is not something corporeal that understands, wills, thinks, etc.

But, of course, we now know for certain that the mind is something that understands, will, thinks, etc. So what is wrong with (17) is just the corporeality part. Thus

(18) The mind is not anything corporeal, and so is something incorporeal.

Here is the crucial passage in which the reasoning I have tried to regiment a bit appears:

All of these people overlook the fact that the mind (*mens*) knows itself, even when it seeks itself, as we have already shown. But we can in no way rightly say that anything is known while its essence (*substantia*) is unknown. Wherefore, as long as the mind knows itself, it knows its own essence (*substantia*). And when it is certain of itself, it is certain of its essence (*substantia*). But it is certain about itself [e.g. that it thinks, understands, wills, etc.], as what we have already said clearly demonstrates. But it is by no means certain whether it is air, or fire, or a body, or anything of a body. It is, therefore, none of these things. (Ibid. 10 10, 16)

In this passage I have departed from Stephen McKenna's excellent translation by rendering *substantia* as 'essence' rather than 'substance'. Augustine gives us licence to do this, I think, when he writes in book 5 of *De trinitate*:'The usage of our language has already decided that the same thing is to be understood when we say *essentia* as when we say *substantia*' (Ibid. 5 9, 10). The context here seems to make it quite clear that Augustine's point is that the mind couldn't just *happen* to be something corporeal. If it were corporeal at all, it would be *essentially* corporeal. But the mind knows and is certain of itself, including its own essence. The very disagreement among corporealists as to what the mind is thus serves to show that the mind is not anything corporeal. It is therefore something incorporeal. Minds are things distinct from bodies.

Augustine's mind–body dualism leaves him in a rather odd position with respect to the Christian doctrine of bodily resurrection. If the mind or soul is an incorporeal thing, why do we need to receive bodies at the resurrection? Augustine himself puzzles over this question in his 'literal commentary' on Genesis (*De genesi ad litteram*). 'Why', he asks there, 'must the spirits of the departed be reunited with their bodies in the resurrection, if they can be admitted to the supreme beatitude without their bodies?'[5] The question is pertinent because Augustine has been discussing the phenomenon of mystical visions, when, as he supposes, the soul temporarily leaves the body. Why shouldn't the soul's departure at death be simply a final release from corporeal bondage?

'This is a problem that may trouble some,' Augustine admits,

but it is too difficult to be answered with complete satisfaction in this essay. There should, however, be no doubt that a man's mind, when it is carried out of the senses of the flesh in ecstasy, or when after death it has departed from the flesh, is unable to see the immutable essence of God just as the holy angels see it, even though it has passed beyond the likenesses of corporeal things. This may be because of some mysterious reason or simply because of the fact that it possesses a kind of natural appetite for managing the body. (*De genesi ad litteram* 12 35, 68)[6]

---

[5] Augustine, *The Literal Meaning of Genesis*, trans. J. H. Taylor (New York, 1982), ii, 228. This volume is no. 42 in the series Ancient Christian Writers, ed. J. Quasten, W. J. Burghardt, and T. C. Lawler.   [6] Ibid. 228–9.

This is an oddly unsatisfactory response. For purposes of contrast, we might remind ourselves that St Thomas Aquinas is able to adapt Aristotle's metaphysics to provide a rather impressive rationale for the resurrection. Thus Aquinas supposes that the human soul, being the form from the human body, is not itself an independent substance. However, since it has essentially an intellectual operation in which the body does not share, it does have a certain independence from the body, the independence of what Aquinas calls a 'subsistent thing', as distinct from a substance (*Summa theologiae* 1a q75 a2). This independence is sufficient to guarantee the soul's persistence after death, but the essential incompleteness of a merely subsistent thing means that the soul needs a body, in the resurrection, to attain completeness. Thus the resurrection is metaphysically motivated.

By comparison, Augustine's suggestion that perhaps our soul, or mind, 'possesses a kind of natural appetite for managing the body' seems rather lame and surprisingly tentative. This very lameness and tentativeness underline the distinctness of the mind from the body that, he thinks, his internalist reasoning for the incorporeality of the mind has made plain.

The idea that we each of us know what a mind is from our own case, the assurance of mind–body dualism that Augustine bases on this idea, and the argument from analogy for other minds that it seems to make both possible and necessary, have all been major preoccupations of important twentieth-century philosophers. Remarkably, this cluster of issues has occupied philosophers on the continent of Europe fully as much as it has concerned philosophers in Britain and America.

Thus Martin Heidegger, whose *Being and Time* (*Sein und Zeit*) appeared in 1927 and quickly established itself as a modern classic, denies that an '"I" or subject' is 'proximally given'—that is, is immediately known to human existence (*Dasein*).[7] He thus denies thesis A. Moreover, he rejects any argumentation from one's own case to establish the 'I' of another on the grounds that the result would be merely: 'a Projection of one's own Being-towards-oneself "into something else". The Other would be a duplicate of the Self.'[8]

Jean Paul Sartre's *Being and Nothingness* (*L'Être et le néant*), which appeared in 1943, and which is heavily indebted to Heidegger, devotes a long chapter to the question of 'the existence of others'. Even though Sartre, like Heidegger, rejects Augustine's idea of the mind as a separate substance, and even though he, too, is critical of the argument from analogy for other minds, he, unlike Heidegger, thinks he needs to offer

---

[7] Martin Heidegger, *Being and Time*, trans. J. Macquarrie and E. Robinson (New York, 1962), 72. [8] Ibid. 162.

an argument to provide warrant for our assurance that other minds exist.

Within the analytic tradition of recent British and American philosophy these same issues have been equally prominent. I have already mentioned that they were a target of Ludwig Wittgenstein's criticisms. Norman Malcolm, an influential student and interpreter of Wittgenstein, identifies in his essay 'Knowledge of Other Minds'[9] 'the fundamental error of the argument from analogy' as the 'mistaken assumption that *one learns from one's own case* what thinking, feeling, sensation are'.[10] According to Malcolm, Wittgenstein made clear that this 'assumption' leads first to solipsism and eventually to nonsense.

What Malcolm here calls the fundamental error of the argument from analogy is very close to what I have called 'thesis A'. Rather than say it is 'an error of the argument from analogy', I prefer to say that it is an assumption that seems to demand that we have an argument for the existence of other minds to justify our assurance that solipsism is false.

The preoccupation of recent philosophy of mind with thesis A and with internalist reasoning we find prominent in Augustine's *De trinitate* is usually considered to be an attempt to deal with an inheritance we owe to Descartes. Since Descartes is much more commonly read by contemporary philosophers than is Augustine, it is not surprising that they should find in Descartes the progenitor of the ideas they want to criticize. But there are several reasons for seeing Augustine as their real target, rather than Descartes. For one thing, Augustine developed his ideas twelve centuries before Descartes was born. Secondly, and even more importantly, these ideas are much more prominent in Augustine than they are in Descartes. In particular, the argument from analogy, which Augustine presents in book 8 of his *De trinitate*, is never even stated in Descartes.[11] The problem of other minds that one actually finds in Descartes is the problem of how one knows whether *certain classes of entities*—specifically, non-human animals and automata—have minds, not how one knows that there is at least some second mind in addition to one's own. Thus, there is in Descartes no extrapolation from one's own, singular case; there is only a question about whether one can extrapolate from the general, human case to any non-human cases. Thus the issue as to whether one can argue successfully by induction from a single instance does not arise for Descartes.

[9] Norman Malcolm, 'Knowledge of Other Minds', in *Knowledge and Certainty* (Englewood Cliffs, NJ, 1963), 130–40.   [10] Ibid. 136.

[11] Readers sometimes assume that the 'hats and cloaks' passage in *Meditation* 2 is a statement of the argument from analogy. I argue that this is incorrect in 'Descartes and the Problem of Other Minds', in Amelie O. Rorty (ed.), *Essays on Descartes' Meditations* (Berkeley, 1986), 141–51, and in ch. 9 of my *Thought's Ego in Augustine and Descartes* (Ithaca, NY, 1992), 107–24.

In Augustine, then, we have a radically new argument for mind–body dualism. It is an internalist argument, in that it proceeds from what, allegedly, the mind can know concerning itself to the conclusion that the mind is incorporeal. It makes essential use of the thesis, much debated in our own century, that the mind of each of us knows what a mind is simply and solely by knowing itself. Although there are certainly striking and highly significant similarities between Augustine's philosophy of mind and that of Descartes, it seems that much of the recent criticism of the thesis that each of us knows what a mind is from our own case and of the argument from analogy that this thesis invites should be targeted at Augustine, rather than at Descartes.

7

Renaissance Theories of Body, Soul, and Mind

EMILY MICHAEL

I. INTRODUCTION

The human soul, or psyche, from ancient times to the early modern period played a double role in relation to the body. First, it was believed to be integrally linked to the human body as the locus or cause of its vital and cognitive activities; and, second, it was believed to be the vehicle, as separable from the human body, of personal immortality. Different aspects of this double role were emphasized at different times and by different thinkers. The story of the human soul's career during the Renaissance is that of the progress from general agreement on the harmony of these two roles to a common preoccupation with their reputed conflict. This story is the subject of the following study.[1]

The thesis that I wish to support is that, though the Renaissance has been largely neglected by contemporary historians of philosophy, developments of this period played a vital role in the transition from medieval to modern accounts of body, soul, and mind. Renaissance thinkers were influenced by their Scholastic predecessors, and after the Renaissance revival of ancient views, by these as well. And, in turn, Renaissance developments provided a foundation for the theories of body, soul, and mind of the early modern period.

During the Renaissance, Aristotle's *De anima* and *Parva naturalia* provided the context for discussion of the human soul in courses and works on natural philosophy and medicine, and the prevalent Renaissance account of the human soul was the Thomistic interpretation of

[1] I gratefully acknowledge that research for this paper was partially supported by a fellowship from the Ethyle R. Wolfe Humanities Institute of Brooklyn College and by a grant from the Research Foundation of the City University of New York. All translations are my own unless otherwise noted.

Aristotle's view.[2] But this was not the only account. There were, in fact, two stages of Renaissance Aristotelian views: the first in the fifteenth and early sixteenth century, the second following this. During the latter stage, a non-Thomistic view largely absent in the first stage acquired a prominent following. I will tell the Renaissance story of the human soul by discussing the source, the impetus, the nature, the development, and the influence of this non-Thomistic, late Renaissance view. To this end, I will discuss, in chronological order, the two Renaissance stages mentioned above. In the earlier stage, there were two dominant Aristotelian views of the human soul, to which we now turn.

II. THOMISM, AVERROISM, AND THE RENAISSANCE MIND–BODY SEPARATION PROBLEM

It is well known that most philosophers of the fifteenth century were Thomistic Aristotelians,[3] and that Averroism flourished in Italy, especially at the universities of Padua and Bologna.[4] I will briefly examine these two views of the human soul through two representative late

---

[2] Contemporary studies of sixteenth- and early seventeenth-century anti-Aristotelians should not obscure the fact that Aristotle's works were the principal subject-matter of philosophy courses throughout Europe at most universities until at least the middle of the seventeenth century. See e.g. the discussion of the curriculum in the 1599 *Ratio Studiorum: St Ignatius and the Ratio Studiorum*, ed. Edward A. Fitzpatrick (New York, 1933): 'In logic and natural philosophy, philosophy, and metaphysics, the doctrine of Aristotle is to be followed'(107); 'In matters of any importance let him not depart from Aristotle unless something occurs which is foreign to the doctrine which academies everywhere approve of' (168). See also *A Bibliography of Aristotle Editions, 1501–1600*, ed. F. E. Cranz (Baden-Baden, 1971); C. B. Schmitt, 'Towards an Assessment of Renaissance Aristotelianism', *History of Science*, 11 (1973); C. M. King, 'Philosophy and Science in the Arts Curriculum of the Scottish Universities in the 17th Century' (Ph.D. thesis, Edinburgh, 1974). The term 'psychologia', meaning the study of the soul, is said to have been coined by Joannes Thomas Freigius in 1575 to refer, in particular, to the problems raised by Aristotle's *De anima* and *Parva naturalia*; see K. Park and E. Kessler, 'The Concept of Psychology', in C. B. Schmitt and Q. Skinner (eds.), *The Cambridge History of Renaissance Philosophy* (Cambridge, 1988), 455.

[3] Frederick J. Roensch indicates as criteria distinguishing early Thomistic Aristotelians the adoption of key doctrines such as: one substance has one substantial form; prime matter is pure potentiality; individuation is by matter (*Early Thomistic School* (Dubuque, Ia., 1964), sec. 3). Aquinas's distinctive and thoroughgoing analysis of prime matter as pure potentiality and of each substantial form as a complete and absolute actuality had implications for the system of doctrines, from embryology to immortality, that are definitive of Thomistic Aristotelianism.

[4] For further information on Aristotelianism at Padua and Bologna, see esp. E. Renan, *Averroès et l'averroisme* (Paris, 1852), and among recent discussions articles by Luce Giard in *Revue de synthèse*, 104, 110, 115, 120 (1983–5), and in *Les Études philosophiques*, 3 (1986); L. Olivieri (ed.), *Aristotelismo veneto e scienza moderna* (2 vols., Padua, 1983); A. Poppi, *Introduzione all' aristotelismo padovano* (Padua, 1970).

fifteenth-century works, the *Expositio . . . circa tres libros De anima Aristotelis*[5] of Lambertus de Monte,[6] a dedicated Thomist and master at the University of Cologne, and the *De elementis*[7] of Alessandro Achillini,[8] a physician and professor at the University of Bologna. I will then turn to events of the late fifteenth century that undermined each of these views, and led, in turn, to widespread acceptance of an alternative Aristotelian account of the human soul.

Lambertus de Monte, presenting Thomas's interpretation of Aristotle's *De anima*, says that each individual entity is composed of, first, prime matter, which is *pure potentiality*, not really anything at all apart from form, incognizable even by God; and, second, *inhering in prime matter*, an actuality, *one* substantial form, which makes an individual what it is.[9] In each living thing, a *soul* inhering in prime matter is the one substantial form that determines the nature of a living body, and this soul has powers that activate that body. In human beings, the one substantial form is a rational soul, and *intellect* is one faculty or power of the rational soul, along with nutrition and sensation. As indicated in his diagram reproduced as figure 7.1, Lambertus distinguishes five faculties of the rational soul: namely vegetative and sensitive powers, local motion, appetite, and intellection. The first four are powers that are immersed in and activate particular organs. The last, intellection, is a psychic power that is exercised without the use of any corporeal organ.

Achillini distinguishes two human souls: an organic soul and a mind.[10] The organic soul has powers similar to those of the organic faculties in de Monte's diagram. But Achillini denies that intellection is a faculty of the human organic soul. He asserts instead that Averroës' claim that the human intellect is a separated substance that is one for all human beings correctly interprets Aristotle's view. The single human soul, separated

---

[5] Lambertus de Monte, *Expositio . . . circa tres libros De anima Aristotelis* (Cologne, 1496).

[6] Lambertus de Monte, who taught at the University of Cologne from 1455 until his death in 1499, published editions of Aristotle's *De anima* (*Copulata super libros De anima Aristotelis* (Cologne 1485, 1492); *Expositio*); and *Physics* (*Compilatio commentaria . . . in octo libros Aristotelis De physico* (Cologne, 1493, 1498)). He is of interest here as a committed follower of the interpretation of Aristotle presented by Thomas Aquinas.

[7] Alessandro Achillini, *De elementis* (Venice, 1505).

[8] Alessandro Achillini (1463–1512) was a popular writer on Aristotle's logical and scientific works, with eleven publications in twenty-four editions beginning in 1494. In addition, five editions of his collected works were published in Venice in 1508, 1545, 1548, 1551, and 1568. For a detailed discussion of Achillini's life, works, and career, see Herbert Matsen, *Alessandro Achillini (1463–1512) and his Doctrine of 'Universals' and 'Transcendentals'* (Lewisburg, Pa., 1974), 21–41.

[9] Lambertus, *Expositio*, book 2, esp. 21–2.

[10] Achillini, *De elementis*, book 2, articles 4–5, in *Opera omnia in unum collecta* (Venice, 1545).

Emily Michael

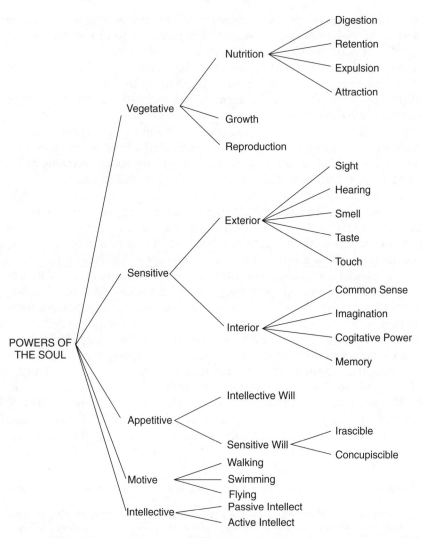

FIGURE 7.1. Aristotle's powers of the soul according to Lambertus de Monte.

from matter and common to all human beings, acts in conjunction with the cogitative power of individual human souls to produce, for each individual, intellective cognition. But the Averroist view that body and mind are two really distinct substances—that is, the Averroist distinction between a *single* eternal human mind and each human body with its mortal organic soul—entails a denial of personal immortality. Renaissance opponents saw the prevalence of this view as a serious threat to faith.

This Averroist claim was never taken lightly. Opposition arose as early as the mid-thirteenth century, when Aristotle's scientific works were introduced into the curriculum at the University of Paris along with Averroës' commentaries on them.[11] Various Averroist doctrines were regarded as heterodox; but particularly incendiary was Averroës' doctrine of the unicity of the intellect,[12] which stimulated the influential attacks of Albertus Magnus in 1256 and of Thomas Aquinas in 1270. Also in 1270, E. Tempier, bishop of Paris, condemned the principal doctrines of Averroist Aristotelians, attacking views adopted by such masters of arts at the University of Paris as Siger of Brabant and Boethius of Sweden. This controversy culminated in Bishop Tempier's Great Condemnation of 1277,[13] a concerted attempt to crush Averroism at the University of Paris. None the less Averroës' commentaries remained in use and were influential; and in the fourteenth century Averroës' doctrine of the unicity of the intellect was openly supported by, for example, Jean of Jandun, and was transported to Italy by such figures as Angelo of Arezzo and Thaddaeus of Parma.

As shown in Renan's *Averroës et l'averroisme*, Averroist monopsychism, largely suppressed elsewhere in Europe, flourished in northern Italy in the late fifteenth century.[14] And once again, as in the thirteenth century, this prompted a virulent wave of opposition, with influential attacks upon Averroës' doctrine of the unicity of the intellect in, for example, Ficino's *Theologica Platonica de immortalitate animarum* (1482),[15] Bishop Pietro Barozzi's *Decretum contra disputantes de unitate*

---

[11] Cf. Dominic A. Iorio, *The Aristotelians of Renaissance Italy* (Lewiston, NY, 1991), 37; James A. Weisheipl, *The Development of Physical Theory in the Middle Ages* (Ann Arbor, 1959), 26–8; Fernand Van Steenberghen, *Aristotle in the West*, trans. L. Johnston (Louvain, 1953), 89–114.

[12] Excellent accounts of Averroës' doctrine of the unicity of the intellect in the context of medieval monopsychism are provided in various works by F. Van Steenberghen: e.g. *Thomas Aquinas and Radical Aristotelianism* (Washington, 1980); *Maitre Siger de Brabant* (Louvain, 1977).

[13] E. Tempier, bishop of Paris, condemned 219 propositions, of which some were Averroist views, and some were held by Aquinas. See Edward Grant, 'The Effect of the Condemnation of 1277', in N. Kretzmann, A. Kenny, and J. Pinborg (eds.), *The Cambridge History of Later Mediaeval Philosophy* (Cambridge, 1982), 537–9.

[14] See Renan, *Averroës*. Monopsychism was supported in the 1480s by the Paduan professor Nicoletto Vernia (1420–99), his student at Padua from 1480 to 1482, Giovanni Pico, and such associates of Pico in Padua as Elijah del Medigo (1460–93). Monopsychism retained a following at the universities of Padua and Bologna in the sixteenth century in works of Tiberius Baccilerius, Alessandro Achillini, and Ludovicus Buccafereus.

[15] This work was written by Ficino between 1469 and 1474 and printed in 1482. P. O. Kristeller concludes that Ficino presented 'the most detailed refutation of Averroism after that of Aquinas', but that his 'critique was concerned primarily, and even exclusively, with the defense of immortality, as that of Thomas had not been' ('The Immortality of the Soul', in *Renaissance Concepts of Man and Other Essays* (New York, 1972), 33).

intellectus (1489),[16] which banned future public discussion of Averroës' controversial doctrine, and Antonio Trombetta's *Tractatus singularis contra Averroystas de humanarum animarum plurificatione*.[17] To make matters worse, this conflict was further exacerbated by a new development at the turn of the century.

With the 1495 Latin translation of Venetian humanist Jerome Donato of the *De anima* of Alexander of Aphrodisias,[18] Alexander's view that for Aristotle the human soul is mortal acquired some popularity at the Renaissance universities of Padua and Bologna.[19] Alexandrist mortalism, coupled with the monopsychists' denial of personal immortality, added fuel to a growing fire.[20] This culminated in a new dogmatic proclamation of the Church. In 1513, the eighth session of Pope Leo X's Lateran Council issued a dogmatic proclamation declaring the personal immortality of the human soul, to correct the current 'extremely pernicious errors' found in the schools, 'namely that the soul is mortal [i.e. Alexander's view] or one in all men [i.e. Averroës' view]'.[21] This Lateran

[16] For a discussion of Bishop Barozzi's relationship to the Scotists at Padua, and of their influence in the eighth session of Pope Leo X's Lateran Council, see John Monfasani, 'Aristotelians, Platonists, and the Missing Ockhamists: Philosophical Liberty in Pre-Reformation Italy', *Renaissance Quarterly*, 46 (1993), 247–76. Monfasani notes the opposition of Maurice O'Fihely, a Scotist theologian at the University of Padua, to heterodox Averroist doctrines, and Pietro Barozzi's warm support of Trombetta and especially O'Fihely, whom he recommends for a salary increase, citing 'the Scotist chair of theology, which is like a medicine for the errors on the eternity of the world, on the unity of the intellect, . . . which abound among the philosophers'. For the original letter, see M. Sanudo, *I Diarii* (Venice, 1881), V. 884.

[17] Antonio Trombetta, *Tractatus singularis contra Averroystas de humanarum animarum plurificatione ad catholice fidei obsequium Patavii editus* (Padua, 1498). Trombetta, professor of Scotistic metaphysics at the University of Padua, had an influence in the actions of the eighth session of the 1513 Lateran Council discussed below. See also A. Poppi, 'Lo scotista patavino Antonio Trombetta (1436–1517)', *Il Santo*, 2 (1962), 349–67; *idem*, 'L'antiaverroismo della scolastica padovana alla fine del secolo XV', *Studia patavina*, 11 (1964), 102–24.

[18] For further information, see F. E. Cranz, 'Alexander Aphrodisiensis', in P. O. Kristeller (ed.), *Catalogus translationum et commentariorum* (Washington, 1960), I, 77–135 and II, 411–22.

[19] See e.g. Thomas de Vio, *Commentaria de anima* (Florence, 1509), 205, and for a discussion of the early view of Thomas de Vio (later Cardinal Cajetan), P. I. Coquelle, *Thomas de Vio Cardinal Cajetanus (1469–1534)*, Scripta philosophica . . . ; (Rome, 1938), introduction. Gaspar Contarini, a fellow student of de Vio's in Padua, remarks that at that time de Vio 'viewed the opinion of Alexander of Aphrodisias as preferable to all others' (*Opera* (Paris, 1571), 180). Contarini himself later attacked this view.

[20] On Averroism and Alexandrism at the Renaissance University of Padua, see P. O. Kristeller, 'Paduan Averroism and Alexandrism in the Light of Recent Studies', in *Renaissance Thought* (New York, 1965), ii, 111–18; Charles B. Schmitt, *Aristotle and the Renaissance* (Cambridge, Mass., 1983), 22–3.

[21] *Conciliorum oecumenicorum decreta*, ed. Centro di Documentazione, Istituto per le Scienze Religiose, Bologna (Basel, 1962), 581–2.

Council also issued the unprecedented request that philosophers attack these errors and prove the soul's immortality by natural reason, not faith alone.[22] For the first time, philosophers were required to demonstrate a theological doctrine.[23] And, for the first time, a *dogmatic* Church proclamation directly attacked Averroës' monopsychism, along with the more recent and more provocative Alexandrist mortalism.

None the less, Pietro Pomponazzi, in his infamous *De immortalitate animae*,[24] published in 1516 (three years after the Fifth Lateran Council proclamation), supported Alexander's mortalistic interpretation of Aristotle's view, and claimed that we know the immortality of soul *only by faith*.[25] Pomponazzi adopted the Thomistic account of the human soul, but he claimed that from this view it follows that, according to Aristotle and reason, each human rational soul is *material* and therefore *mortal*. That is, Pomponazzi argued that the Thomistic view of the human soul *also* entails a denial of human immortality.

Here 'material' does not indicate that, as the Epicureans and Stoics claim, the human soul is a body; for Pomponazzi, like other Thomists, maintains that the rational soul is a substantial form.[26] He presumes two sorts of substantial forms. First, there are separated substantial forms, which, existing apart from matter, are *immaterial* forms, forms wholly independent of matter; and, since destruction occurs by the separation of form from matter, these separated substantial forms are indestructible. Separated forms—for example, the Heavenly Intelligences—have intellective cognition as their essential activity. Second, there are ma-

---

[22] Ibid.

[23] I am grateful to Roger Emerson for pointing out to me that Vatican I (1871) (*Acta et decreta sacrorum conciliorum recentiorum*, VII, cols. 250 and 255) provides a subsequent similar requirement of philosophers to demonstrate God's existence: 'The ... Church holds and teaches that by the natural light of reason, God ... can be demonstrated with certainty by means of created things.'

[24] Pietro Pomponazzi, *Tractatus de immortalitate animae* (Bologna, 1516); *idem*, 'On Immortality', ed. and trans. William. H. Hay, in E. Cassirer (ed.), *The Renaissance Philosophy of Man* (Chicago, 1956). For more information on Pomponazzi's works see J. H. Randall, *The School of Padua and the Emergence of Modern Science* (Padua, 1961), 87–8, and C. Schmitt, *A Critical Survey and Bibliography of Studies on Renaissance Aristotelianism, 1958–1969* (Padua, 1971). For a discussion of Pomponazzi's views, see e.g. M. Pine, *Pietro Pomponazzi, Radical Philosopher of the Renaissance* (Padua, 1986).

[25] Although at the time of the decree Pomponazzi had not argued in print that for Aristotle the soul is mortal, contemporary commentators, like those in the seventeenth century, identified the problem of immortality with his *De immortalitate*. See e.g. *Conciliorum*, 569, and the *New Catholic Encyclopedia* (New York, 1967), viii, 409. See also B. de Spina, who attacked Cajetan's mortalistic interpretation of Aristotle's psychology in *Propugnaculum Aristotelis de immortalitate animae contra Thomas Gaetanum* (Venice, 1519), and claimed that Cajetan's work was the source of Pomponazzi's interpretation.

[26] For further discussion of Pomponazzi's use of the term 'material', see my paper (with F. Michael), 'Two Early Modern Concepts of Mind: Reflecting Substance vs. Thinking Substance', *Journal of the History of Philosophy*, 27 (1989), 29–47.

terial substantial forms. These inhere in prime matter, and thereby constitute and activate a body. A material form is integral to, and has no activity apart from, a body, and, as such, it is wholly dependent on that body and inseparable from it.

Pomponazzi claims that the rational soul, like all other forms that inhere in prime matter, is inseparable and material, and so mortal, but he recognizes that Aquinas and his followers reject this view. Their argument can be represented as follows:

P1: A soul, like all substantial forms, is incorporeal, and so, since destruction of an entity is the separation of form from matter, it is the sort of entity that is indestructible.

P2: A soul can be destroyed only if it is totally dependent on the body for its activities (as is the condition of the souls of non-human animals).

P3: But the rational soul has an activity that does not depend upon the body—namely intellective cognition—and, as such, it can exist apart from the body.

C: So the rational soul is separable from the body and indestructible, and hence immortal.

This assumes that the rational soul is a third sort of substantial form, an intermediate form; for it can inhere in prime matter and activate a body, but it is also separable from the body. And in this separated state, it only thinks. The claim here is that the human soul's separability makes it an immaterial form. Pomponazzi maintains instead that the human soul is intermediate in the sense that it has activities of both separated and material forms: that is, it has intellective and organic powers, and, in this way, it is 'relatively immortal,' but it is 'unqualifiedly mortal.'[27]

Pomponazzi objects to each premise:

P1: Pomponazzi notes another Aristotelian principle of destruction of an entity: that which is generated must also be corrupted. The human soul, like all other souls, is generated and so corrupted.[28] His opponents respond that the human soul is not generated but, rather, created by God. But this will not do, for Aristotle asserts that 'man generates man'.[29]

P2: Pomponazzi contends that destruction of the soul is also implied by its dependence on organs of the body for *some* of its essential activities—for example, nutrition and sensation. A soul, as a substantial form, is a principle of the natural motion or activities of a thing, as the substantial form of a stone is a principle of its motion down-

---

[27] Pomponazzi, *De immortalitate*, ch. 9; Hay, 'On Immortality', 313.

[28] Pomponazzi, *De immortalitate*, ch. 8; Hay, 'On Immortality', 311–12.

[29] Pomponazzi (*De immortalitate*, ch. 9) cites Aristotle, *Physics* II 2, 194b13: 'the sun and man generate man'; Hay, 'On Immortality', 325.

wards and of fire upwards. Further, a form cannot alter its powers without changing its essential nature. But the human soul cannot exercise its vital and sensitive powers apart from the body, though these powers are essential to its nature. So the human soul, by its dependence on the body for some of its activities, must perish with the body.[30]

P3: This is Pomponazzi's central argument. He contends that the human soul, in *all* its activities, is dependent upon the body, and, as such, is inseparable from it. He says: 'If the human soul is dependent in all its operations on some organ, it is inseparable and material; but, in all its operations it is dependent on some organ; hence, it is material.'[31] He explains: 'The major follows from *De anima 1*, where Aristotle says "If knowing is imagination, or is not without imagination, it is impossible to be separated".'[32]

Pomponazzi points out that, fundamental to all intellective activity, is the abstraction of universals from phantasms of the imagination. He agrees that the soul, as the *subject* of intellective activity, does itself act, using no bodily organ. But required for abstraction is an image of the imagination, and to receive this image, the soul depends upon the body as a receptive object. He concludes: 'But the human soul is unqualifiedly the act of a physical and organic body, since it has no operation in which it does not depend in some way on the body; and if not as subject, at least as object; when it receives something from the body.'[33] Pomponazzi, citing Aristotle's statement that 'The soul does not know at all without some phantasm,'[34] claims that all knowing is imagination [sensation] or is accompanied by an image of imagination [intellection], and therefore that 'it is impossible to be separated'.[35] So, he concludes, the rational soul is inseparable from the body, and therefore is material and mortal. Renaissance philosophers thereafter had a soul–body separation problem.

Pomponazzi's mortalism, along with the Lateran Council action, had long-range consequences for the development of psychology. Pomponazzi's mortalistic arguments created an immediate furor, stimulating accusations of heresy and numerous replies, and, coupled with

---

[30] Pomponazzi, *De immortalitate*, ch. 8; Hay, 'On Immortality', 309.

[31] Pomponazzi, *De immortalitate*, ch. 8; Hay, 'On Immortality', 305.

[32] Pomponazzi, *De immortalitate*, ch. 8; Hay, 'On Immortality', 305.

[33] Pomponazzi, *De immortalitate*, ch. 10; Hay, 'On Immortality', 336.

[34] Pomponazzi, *De immortalitate*, ch. 9; Hay, 'On Immortality', 315; Aristotle, *De anima*, III 7, 431a16–17. Aquinas similarly states that the intellect, when it is united with a body, cannot think without the presence of a sense image ('nisi convertendo se ad phantasmata') (*Summa theologica*, Ia, 84, 7).

[35] Pomponazzi, *De immortalitate*, ch. 8; Hay, 'On Immortality', 305.

the Lateran Council proclamation, provoked numerous works demonstrating immortality.[36] Nor was this reaction short-lived.[37] For the next century and a half, personal immortality was viewed as a critical and pressing philosophical problem, and was routinely considered in the discussion of the human soul in courses and works on natural philosophy and medicine.[38]

For example, Descartes, in the preface to his *Meditations*, relating his endeavour to these Renaissance developments, describes his project as follows:

[36] Some early responses to Pomponazzi are: Hieronymus Lucensis, *Apologia pro animae immortalitate in Petrum Pomponatium Mantuanum philosophicum* . . . (Bologna, 1518); Agostino Nifo, *De immortalitate animae libellus* . . . (Venice, 1518); Bartolomeo Spina, *Tutela veritatis de immortalitate animae* . . . (Venice, 1519); A. Flandinus, *De animorum immortalitate* . . . *liber contra assertorem mortalitatis* . . . (Mantua, 1519); Crisostomo Javelli, *Solutiones rationum animi mortalitatem probantium quae in defensorio contra Niphum* . . . *a P. Pomponatio formantur* (n.p., 1523).

[37] References to Pomponazzi continued: the Coimbra commentators noted and opposed Pomponazzi's 'claim that the soul is mortal and destined to die' (Coimbra [Collegium Conimbricense], *Commentarii Collegii Conimbricensis Societatis Iesu, in tres libros De anima Aristotelis* (Coimbra, 1649), 565). M. Mersenne, discussing immortality, commends Mirandulus for his arguments against Pomponazzi's mortalism (*L'Impiété des déistes, athées* . . . (Paris, 1624), ii, 497–9). See also Edward Stillingfleet, *Origines sacrae*, 3rd edn. (London, 1666), 419.

[38] Kristeller, 'Immortality of the Soul', 29, points out that the doctrine that 'the soul is incorporeal and by nature immortal . . . became a part of standard mediaeval doctrine, more or less taken for granted by everybody, . . . but it was rarely challenged or discussed in detail'. Selected works on immortality, 1525–1667: P. N. Castellani, *Opus de immortalitate animorum* . . . (Faenza, 1525); A. Paleario, *De animorum immortalitate* (Lyons 1536); R. Odoni, *Disputatio de animo* . . . *utrum Aristoteli mortalis sit, an immortalis* (Paris, 1558); M. A. Passeri Genua, *Disputatio de intellectus humani immortalitate* (Monte Regali, 1565); F. Pendasio, *Tractatus de immortalitate animae*, MS, Vat. (1570); G. Contarini, *De immortalitate animae* (Paris, 1571); P. Martinez, *In tres libros Aristotelis De anima* . . . *animae nostrae immortalitas asseritur et probatur* (Siguenza, 1575); J. Riolan, *De immortalitate* (c.1580; published by his son in the collected works (Paris, 1610)); N. Nancel, *De immortalitate animae, velitatio adversus Galenum* (Paris, 1587); Jean de Champaignac, *Traicté de l'immortalité de l'âme* (Bordeaux, 1595); H. Pontanus, *De immortalitate animae ex sententia Aristotelis* (Rome, 1597); P. Crespet, *Discours* . . . *immortalité de l'âme* (Paris, 1604); E. Rudius, *Liber de anima, in quo* . . . *rationalis animae immortalitas efficacissimis rationibus probatur* (Padua, 1611); L. Richeome, *L'Immortalité de l'âme* (Paris, 1621); J. C. Lagalla, *De immortalitate animorum* (Rome, 1622); F. Liceti, *De animarum rationalium immortalitate* . . . (Padua, 1629); A. Oregius, *Aristotelis vera de rationalis animae immortalitate sententia* . . . (Rome, 1632); Jean de Silhon, *De l'Immortalité de l'âme* (Paris, 1634); R. Descartes, *Meditationes de prima philosophia in qua Dei existentia et animae immortalis demonstratur* 1st edn. (Paris, 1641); P. Athanasius, *Tractatus tres, primus* . . . *de animae immortalitate* . . . (Paris, 1643); A. Roccus, *Animae rationalis immortalitas* . . . (Frankfurt, 1644); K. Digby, *Demonstratio immortalitatis animae rationalis* . . . (Paris, 1651); Walter Charleton, *The Immortality of the Human Soul* (London, 1657); H. More, *The Immortality of the Soul* (London, 1662); R. Baxter, *The Reasons of the Christian Religion* . . . (London, 1667).

As regards the soul, many people have considered that it is not easy to discover its nature, and some have even had the audacity to assert that, as far as human reasoning goes, there are persuasive grounds for holding that the soul dies along with the body and that the opposite view is based on faith alone. But in its eighth session the Lateran Council held under Leo X condemned those who take this position, and expressly enjoined Christian philosophers to refute their arguments and use all their powers to establish the truth; so I have not hesitated to attempt this task as well.[39]

Descartes indicates his desire to prove the soul's immortality in personal letters to friends such as Mersenne and Regius;[40] and the first edition of the *Meditations* (1641) was entitled *Meditations on First Philosophy in which the Existence of God and the Immortality of the Soul is Demonstrated.*[41]

Kenelm Digby rails against Pomponazzi and other Renaissance mortalists:

But unawares I have gulfed myself into a sea of contradiction, from no mean adversaries: for Alexander Aphrodiseus, Pomponatius, and the learnedest of the Peripatetic school, will all of them rise up in main opposition against this doctrine of mine: showing how in our body, all our soul's knowledge is made, by the working of our fancies and that there is no act of our soul, without speculation of phantasms residing in our memory: therefore, seeing that when our body is gone, all those little bodies of phantasms are gone with it, what sign is there, that any operation can remain? And hence they infer, that seeing every substance has its Being for its operations sake, and by consequence were vain and superfluous in the world, if it could not enjoy and exercise its operation, there is no necessity or end, why the soul of a man should survive his body: and consequently, there is no reason to imagine other, than that it perishes when the man dies.[42]

Pierre Gassendi also identifies the problem addressed by his arguments for the immortality of the human mind with the problem answered dogmatically by the Lateran Council definition of the soul, which definition,

---

[39] R. Descartes, *Meditations*, in *The Philosophical Writings of Descartes*, trans. J. Cottingham, R. Stoothoff, and D. Murdoch (Cambridge, 1985–6) (hereafter CSM), II, 4.

[40] Letter to Mersenne, in *Oeuvres de Descartes*, ed. C. Adam and P. Tannery (Paris, 1897–1913) (hereafter AT), I, 177; Descartes, *Philosophical Letters*, trans. A. Kenny (Minneapolis, 1970), 19. Letter to Regius, AT III, 508, in *Philosophical Letters*, 130. See also Descartes, *Discourse on Method*, CSM I, 141.

[41] R. Descartes, *Oeuvres philosophiques 1638–42*, ed. F. Alquié (Paris, 1967), ii, introductory illustrations.

[42] K. Digby, *Two Treatises: In the One of which the Nature of Bodies; in the Other the Nature of Mans Soule is Looked into in the way of Discovery of the Immortality of Reasonable Soules* (London, 1665), 428.

he says, declares '[t]he mind [*mentem*], or that superior part of the soul, ... to be an incorporeal substance'.[43]

Pomponazzi's argument undermined comfort with the commonly accepted Thomistic defence of the immortality of the human soul. Pre-Lateran Council philosophers had the option of supporting the soul's immortality by faith, whatever reason might seem to entail; but after the Lateran Council of 1513, this strategy was ruled out. Renaissance philosophers required a new strategy to prove the soul's immortality. In response to this challenge, a *non-Thomistic Aristotelian approach* gradually acquired popularity, and, in turn, provided the foundation for the early modern accounts of mind of, for example, Gassendi, Digby, and, arguably, even Descartes. This non-Thomistic approach is the subject of the following section; to explain this approach, we turn first to two representative Aristotelians at the University of Padua.

III. PLURALISM, DISTINCTNESS, AND IMMORTALITY

I will examine a distinctive non-Thomistic approach that acquired popularity during the late Renaissance by considering the representative works on natural philosophy of two prominent and influential Aristotelians at the University of Padua, the *Librorum ad scientiam de natura attinentium*[44] of Francesco Piccolomini[45] and the *De rebus natu-*

---

[43] P. Gassendi, *Syntagma philosophicum*, in *Opera omnia* (Lyon, 1658), II, 425. Cf. J. Glanvill: 'Now the Soul's Immortality has had a general reception from the wiser and better part of Mankind . . . A council of the Church of *Rome* it self has defined it, and recommended the demonstrating of it to all Christian Philosophers' ('Of Scepticism and Certainty', in *Essays on Several Important Subjects in Philosophy and Religion* (London, 1676), 55).

[44] F. Piccolomini, *Librorum ad scientiam de natura attinentium* (Frankfurt, 1597). See also his commentary on Aristotle's *De anima* (Venice, 1602) and his philosophical dictionary, *De rerum definitionibus* (Venice, 1600). Piccolomini has also been credited (*Cambridge History of Renaissance Philosophy*, 861) with two earlier pseudonymous works, *Peripateticae de anima disputationes*, published in Venice under the name of Petrus Duodus in 1575, and *Academicae contemplationes*, published in Venice under the name of Stephanus Theupolus in Venice in 1576. There is little likelihood, however, that either work is by Piccolomini. Both authors cite Piccolomini as an influence (Theupolus, introduction; Duodus, dedication). For evidence that Duodus was an actual person, see *Dispaccio di Pietro Duodo, Ambasciatore Veneto ad Enrico IV nel 1597* (Venice, 1864). On Theupolus, see L. A. Kennedy, 'Francesco Piccolomini (1520–1604) on Immortality', *Modern Schoolman*, 56 (1979) 150, who provides evidence that Stephanus Theupolus was a patrician of Venice and a *Potestas* of the University of Padua.

[45] Piccolomini (1523–1607) was professor of natural philosophy at the University of Padua from 1560 until 1601. See Antonio Riccoboni, *De Gymnasio Patavino commentariorum libri vi* (Padua, 1598), 49; A. Lisini and A. Liberati, *Genealogia dei Piccolomini di Siena* (Siena, 1900).

ralibus[46] of Iacopo Zabarella.[47] I seek to show how this approach provided Renaissance and early modern philosophers with an alternative response to Pomponazzi's soul–body separation problem.

Iacopo Zabarella and Francesco Piccolomini, though notorious adversaries, both agree that each human being is composed of prime matter and many substantial forms, each of which determines 'partial' substances that make up one complete substance—that is, one individual.[48] Prime matter itself has some actuality; it has 'indeterminate' extension, and is determined by substantial forms of the body. Socrates' blood, bones, and flesh remain distinct, as do other homogeneous compound bodies composing his corporeal organs, so each of these bodies must have a distinct substantial form. In addition, another substantial form, a sensitive soul, makes Socrates an animal. This 'animal soul', Piccolomini claims, develops continuously from, and, Zabarella claims, is superadded to, a vegetative soul. Finally, Socrates, a composite of all these forms, is united as one substance by an ultimate substantial form—namely an intellective soul or mind, which places him in the human species. The human mind exercises only intellective activities, which it carries out without the use of any organ.

This account of the human soul as a conjunction of two really distinct souls, one organic and one intellective, is attributed, by such diverse sources as Philipp Melanchthon,[49] the Coimbra commentators,[50] and Pierre Gassendi,[51] to William of Ockham. In fact, Ockham held the non-Thomistic view of the structure of human beings described above.[52] He too maintains that prime matter has quantity, characterized as indeterminate extension, and he too distinguishes, in each human being, a substantial form of the body and two souls: an organic sensitive soul and an intellective soul or mind. This view common to Zabarella,

---

[46] I. Zabarella, *De rebus naturalibus libri XXX* ... (Venice and Cologne, 1590). See also *Commentarii* ... *in tres Aristotelis libros De anima* ... (Frankfurt, 1606), which contains the books on psychology published in 1590 in *De rebus naturalibus*. The commentary on *De anima* is incomplete, dealing only with book 1, 402a1–403b19; book 2, 412a3–419b3; and book 3, 429a10–430a25.

[47] Zabarella was professor of natural philosophy at the University of Padua from 1569 till his death in 1589. For discussion of his life, works, and writings on logic see William F. Edwards, 'The Logic of Iacopo Zabarella (1533–1589)' (Columbia Ph.D. thesis, 1960). See also Jorge L. Soler, 'The Psychology of Iacopo Zabarella (1533–1589)' (Ph.D. thesis, Buffalo, 1971), and A. Poppi, *La dottrina della scienza in Giacomo Zabarella* (Padua, 1972).

[48] Zabarella, *De rebus*, 275–86, 696–711; Piccolomini, *Librorum*, 870–80.

[49] Philipp Melanchthon, *Commentarius de anima* (Wittenberg, 1548), 12a.

[50] Coimbra, *De generatione et corruptione*, ch. 4, q. 21, art. 2.

[51] Gassendi, *Syntagma philosophicum*, II, 256.

[52] William of Ockham, *Quodlibetal Questions*, trans. A. J. Freddoso and F. E. Kelley (New Haven, 1991), quodlibet 2, qq. 10, 11. For a discussion see M. M. Adams, *William Ockham* (Notre Dame, Ind., 1987), esp. ii, 633–95.

Piccolomini, and Ockham had its source in a distinctive though now
little-known Aristotelian tradition, that of Scholastic pluralism, an
approach developed in the medieval period—in particular, by the
Franciscans.[53] All Aristotelians adopted a form–matter ontology, but
Scholastic pluralists and Thomists disagreed in their analyses of form
and matter, and this led them to such conflicting doctrines as the
following:

SCHOLASTIC PLURALISTS	THOMISTS
Matter has actuality.	Matter is pure potentiality.
A substance can have a plurality of substantial forms.	One substance has one form.
The fundamental principle of individuation is not matter, but form.	The principle of individuation is matter signed by quantity.

Pomponazzi's arguments raised a new problem for the Thomists. The
framework of the Scholastic pluralists provided Renaissance philosophers with a response to Pomponazzi's soul–body separation problem.

So Piccolomini rejects the Thomistic analysis of the human soul and
instead, like Ockham, adopts the following thesis:

T1: The human mind is really distinct from the human organic soul.

Unlike the Thomists who claim that one substance must have one substantial form, its total 'actuality', Piccolomini maintains instead that a
substance can have many substantial forms, and that each human being
has forms of the body, an organic soul, and mind, all really distinct. This
framework, postulating a human mind that is really distinct, and in this
sense separate from the body with its material and mortal organic soul,
enables him to respond to Pomponazzi's arguments against the human
soul's immortality, and provides him with a strategy to demonstrate, as
the Lateran Council requested, the immortality of the human soul.

   Implicit in Pomponazzi's arguments are the following conditions for
the immateriality and immortality of the human soul. These are the conditions attributed to separated eternal forms:

C1: The human soul is a substantial form that does not inhere in prime
      matter.
C2: The human soul is not naturally generated.
C3: The human soul has no essential organic powers.
C4: The human soul has an activity of its own that does not depend
      upon the body.

[53] Cf. Roberto Zavalloni, *Richard de Mediavilla et la controverse sur la pluralité des
formes* (Louvain, 1951); Roensch, *Early Thomistic School*.

Piccolomini contends that the organic soul, transmitted by parents, is a mortal material form, immersed in and extended throughout the body. But the human mind, created by God, is an *immaterial* substantial form; it does not inhere in prime matter; nor is it extended throughout the body, but rather is 'unextended', wholly wherever it is.[54] All the powers of the organic soul activate organs. But the mind only thinks; so it has no organic powers, and has an activity of its own. Finally, the human mind has an activity that is wholly independent of the body—namely, it reflects upon itself. And thereby satisfying C1, C2, C3, and C4, Piccolomini concludes, as the Fifth Lateran Council proclaimed, that the human intellective soul is indestructible, and hence immortal. But these claims about the nature of the human mind must be shown to be true.

Piccolomini devotes an extensive section of his *Librorum ad scientiam de natura attinentium* to the immortality of the human intellective soul. Here he argues that the immateriality of the intellective soul can be shown from its operations and its objects. Reflective operations provide the mind with an activity wholly independent of the body; self-reflection of the mind needs no corporeal organs for its action or its object. He says:

[T]hat which has the capacity to turn on itself, is free from matter; mind when it understands itself turns itself on itself; therefore it is free from matter, and by that from passivity and destruction, for faculties of matter, since they are extended through matter, are not able to turn upon themselves: This sensation does not sense itself.[55]

Piccolomini takes the view that all material forms—that is, all forms that depend on matter, whether such attributes as pink and hot or such substantial forms as the organic soul—have extension. All substantial forms dependent upon and so immersed in the body (itself a composite of form and prime matter), acquire thereby extension. But whatever is extended cannot 'turn itself on itself'.[56] An eye cannot see itself; nor can any sensation act on itself and perceive itself by itself. Seeing is the apprehension of its external exciting cause; seeing doesn't apprehend itself.[57] An extended substance must be moved from without, and so too the extended organic soul. Human beings, though, can apprehend their own sensing and, in turn, can apprehend this apprehension, and they can think, and thinking can turn upon itself and think about this thinking. This is impossible for a material faculty, a power of an extended organic

---

[54] Piccolomini, *Librorum*, 876–7.   [55] Ibid. 1268.   [56] Ibid.

[57] Piccolomini describes 'sensible species' as acts, i.e. as acts of apprehension of an external object. He takes the 'modern' view that sensations are the result of motions in a medium produced by the external exciting cause and affecting a sense-organ. He opposes the common and more conservative view, adopted by Zabarella, that sensible species are spiritual entities, analysed as forms separated from matter.

soul. Therefore, reflection must be a power of an *immaterial* soul, a soul that does not inhere in prime matter, or depend upon organs for its activity, but rather is whole and complete wherever it is, that is inorganic and unextended. But the organic soul cannot be both extended and unextended, material and immaterial. So human beings must have another really distinct immaterial soul, and this distinct soul is the human mind.

Piccolomini further argues that human beings apprehend objects that could not be perceived by a material soul. The organic soul is dependent on the body; it operates by means of organs and apprehends *singulars* through *images*. Piccolomini takes the 'modern' view that sense perception is the result of *motions*, produced by an external object. These motions affect, in turn, sense-organs, nerves, and brain, causing thereby the imagistic apprehension of the external exciting cause. But human beings also understand universal concepts, such separated substances as God and angels, the infinite, and their own cognitive activities. These non-imagistic objects cannot be received by any organ or perceived in any image; they can be understood only by an *immaterial* substantial form, a soul that is independent of the body, and this is the human mind. Similarly, sense appetites are raised only by external objects; but humans beings have a will that 'operates freely by its own choice without corporeal instruments; that is subjected to religion, averse to the perturbations of the senses, and that rules the body'.[58] Will too requires an immaterial human mind.

The human mind here depicted is a separate substantial form analogous to God and the Heavenly Intelligences, with a like kind of activity of its own. But, Piccolomini insists, the human mind is not the Averroist intellect, one for all human beings. In fact, he says, Averroës does correctly interpret Aristotle's view. But in this view, Aristotle errs; for a number of absurdities follow with regard, for example, to the human condition and to divine justice and right. Reason, guided by revelation to understand that God can create the human mind and unite it with a human body, enables us to achieve a psychology consistent with Aristotelian principles and to avoid these absurdities. Piccolomini concludes that since the individual human mind is a distinct immaterial substantial form, unextended and capable of self-conscious reflection, caused by God, with no organic activities, then it must be immortal.

Piccolomini's two-soul account is representative of the response to Pomponazzi's separation problem that was adopted by such traditional, though non-Thomistic, Aristotelians as Piccolomini's influential succes-

[58] Piccolomini, *Librorum*, 1277.

sor at the University of Padua, Fortunius Liceti.[59] Further, the Renaissance rediscovery of ancient sources stimulated the development of new approaches. Still, Aristotle's *De anima* continued as the principal inspiration for discussions of the human soul, and influential new theorists adopted, in their interpretation of Aristotle's psychology, the multi-soul account of Ockham and other Scholastic pluralists. To complete our story of the Renaissance response to Pomponazzi's soul–body separation problem, we will consider representative examples of two new Renaissance approaches—namely eclecticism and 'corporealism'.

Philipp Melanchthon (1497–1560), Luther's principal associate, was eclectic. He united Aristotle's definition and general account of the human soul with views of Galen, Cicero, and Plato.[60] Melanchthon acknowledges Ockham as the source of his own division between an organic soul and a human mind,[61] but himself claims three human souls, 'vegetative, sensitive, and rational, as Plato, Aristotle, and Galen say'.[62] He lays out his problem: science demands a like animal soul as the cause of like animal activities,[63] but faith requires an immortal human soul.[64] Melanchthon, in response, disputes the Thomistic one-soul view: '[W]e hold the vegetative and sensitive to be just entelechies, that is, agitations (*agitationes*) of certain parts of the body, or temperaments; the rational soul to be Spirit (*spiritum*),'[65] and so a soul of a different sort. Further, Melanchthon explains: 'Man generates man. But this is not according to the rational soul. Therefore it is according to *a* form of the body,' a distinct organic soul. 'For', he adds, 'the opinion of the pious . . . is that the rational soul is divinely created and infused in the body.'[66]

The organic soul, Melanchthon claims, is an 'activity' or 'continuous motion', the life itself, that is in a body,[67] and so it is integrally linked to a body as a property of it. He explains that the organic soul is both an 'accidental form', as an attribute of the body, and a 'substantial form', as that which makes an entity a living thing of a particular sort. Further, Melanchthon rejects the Thomistic view of psychic powers of, for example, Lambertus de Monte for whom vital and cognitive powers are psychic attributes, or 'accidental forms', *of the soul*, with different

---

[59] Fortunius Liceti published many works, including *De ortu animae humanae* (Genoa, 1602); *De rationalis animae varia propensione ad corpus libri duo* (Padua, 1634); *De animarum rationalium*.

[60] Melanchthon, *Commentarius de anima*. [61] Ibid. 12a.

[62] Ibid. 11b. A similar three-soul view was put forth in Scotland by William Lamb of St Andrews University, who distinguishes in human beings a vegetative soul, a sensitive soul, and a rational soul (*Theses aliquot logicae, ethicae, physicae, . . .* (Edinburgh, 1613)). See also Alexander Monroe, *Theses philosophicae* (Edinburgh, 1628), chs. 12–13.

[63] Melanchthon, *Commentarius de anima*, 7. [64] Ibid. 11b.

[65] Ibid. [66] Ibid. 12a.

[67] Melanchthon attributes this 'correct' analysis of 'entelechy' to Cicero.

powers located in different organs. From this Thomistic viewpoint, the particular activities of organs are determined by the soul; so, if the psychic power of vision were in the feet, the feet would see. Melanchthon maintains instead, as did Ockham and also Piccolomini, that particular activities of a living thing are determined by the organ empowered by a soul, which soul itself is uniformly extended throughout the body. He therefore, in explaining natural activities, focuses upon bodily parts and their functions, from which study, we, *a posteriori*, come to understand the powers implicit in the organic soul.[68] Melanchthon concludes that the sensitive soul is but an agitation or motion in a living body, and so is inseparable from the body and mortal.

But further, Melanchthon states: 'We said however before of powers (*potentiis*), which are called organic, that is, which do not exercise their powers (*vires*) except by corporeal organs, [that] they are able also to be demonstrated in beasts. . . . Moreover in man there must be another superior *potentiam*, because we have actions that are not able to be imitated by beasts.'[69] This superior power is the human mind. Melanchthon explains its distinctive actions: 'A human being counts; understands not just singulars, but also universals; has innate notions; rationally concludes one thing from another; constructs arts; judges his own reasoning, and catches and corrects errors; has reflective activities; . . . he discerns honour (*honesta*) and turpitude; he deliberates by lengthy ratiocination.'[70] But, Melanchthon contends, no extended soul and no corporeal organ can perform these activities. So human beings must have a really distinct immaterial soul, the human mind.

Melanchthon's arguments for the immateriality of the human mind, drawn from the differences between human beings and other animals, are like those of Piccolomini, except for the addition of the clearly non-Aristotelian postulation of innate ideas. This Platonic addition relieves

---

[68] After a detailed discussion of the generation of the foetus according to Galen, including the three central organs, the liver, heart, and brain, Melanchthon proceeds to discuss the external and internal bodily parts, e.g. the organs, humours, and spirits. Finally, he turns to a consideration of the psychic powers implied by the natural activities of the human body. Here he co-ordinates the powers described by Aristotelian philosophers and Galenist physicians—the vegetative, appetitive, and sensitive—with the natural, vital, and animal powers respectively; which, in turn, occupy (1) the organs of nourishment, growth, generation, (2) the humours, and (3) the sense-organs, nerves, and brain. Local motion is attributed to the sensitive soul in association with the nerves and muscles of the body.

[69] P. Melanchthon, *Liber de anima*, in *Opera quae supersunt omnia*, ed. C. G. Bretschneider (Halle, 1846), XIII, 138–9.

[70] Ibid. 139. See also Melanchthon, *Commentarius de anima*, 129, for three differences between human and animal cognition which require an immaterial human mind: viz. animals do not apprehend universals; they have no innate notions; and they have no reflective acts.

the human mind of dependence on the body for its apprehension of concepts, and makes it even more like such separated substances as God and angels. In addition, our innate idea of God can be caused only by God, so the human mind with this innate idea must be created by God.

But Melanchthon's overall account of mind is not Platonistic. He rejects Plato's concept of the rational soul, which, located in the head, has sensitive and intellective powers, because sense cognition depends on corporeal organs; so, in his view, the Platonic rational soul must be an 'entelechy', an agitation, or motion, to enable sense-organs, nerves, and brain to fulfil their functions. But this sort of soul cannot be separated from the body and be immortal. The immortal human mind, he argues, can have no organic activities; it must be purely intellective, and, as such, it is indestructible, hence immortal. Melanchthon's account of the human mind is more like that of Piccolomini, Ockham, and other Scholastic pluralists.

A 'corporealist' account, postulating a mortal *corporeal* sensitive soul and an incorporeal immortal mind in each human being, was adopted by, for example, Bernardino Telesio,[71] Francis Bacon,[72] and Tommaso Campanella.[73] Further, Galenists such as Eustachius Rudius, a late Renaissance professor of medicine at the University of Padua, distinguished two corporeal souls, identified with Galen's vital and animal spirits, and, further, an incorporeal human mind.

Pierre Gassendi (1592–1655), popularizer of Epicureanism[74] and adversary of Descartes, inherited all these views. Gassendi, a modern, rejects Aristotelian forms as unintelligible, and adopts instead an atomistic theory.[75] From *his* viewpoint, the human body is not itself a substance composed of form and matter, but a composite of many substances, each of which has, as its fundamental matter, atoms, with differing structures and arrangements. Still, in his discussion of the human soul, Gassendi's aim, arguments, and strategy are much like those of Piccolomini and Melanchthon. He indicates his problem. First, the human soul, like the souls of other animals, must be corporeal.[76] But, further, a

---

[71] Bernardino Telesio, *De rerum natura* (Naples, 1586), 177–86.

[72] Francis Bacon, *The Advancement of Learning*, 1st edn. (London, 1605), book 3, ch. 4.

[73] Tommaso Campanella, *Prodromus philosophiae instaurandae*, ed. T. Adami (Frankfurt, 1617), 83; *idem, Universalis philosophiae, seu metaphysicarum rerum iuxta propria dogmata, partes tres* . . . (Paris, 1638), 148b.

[74] Gassendi's popular *Philosophiae Epicuri syntagma*, a systematized reconstruction of the philosophy of Epicurus, was first published as an appendix to his *Animadversiones in decimum librum Diogenis Laertii* (Lyons, 1649). On the life of Epicurus see also *idem, De vita et moribus Epicuri* (Lyons, 1647). The remainder of the *Animadversiones*, although certainly indebted to Epicurus, represents Gassendi's own thought.

[75] Gassendi, *Syntagma Philosophicum*, I, 249, 335.   [76] Ibid. II, 250–1.

Lateran Council definition declares the human soul to be incorporeal and immortal.[77] In response, Gassendi, acknowledging a debt to Ockham and the Paduan philosopher Fortunius Liceti, seeks to show really distinct (1) observable corporeal parts of the human body; (2) a subtle invisible substance, a corporeal human soul; and (3) an incorporeal substance, the human mind.

Gassendi argues in support of a corporeal soul:[78]

P1: The soul is perceived to produce corporeal effects, such as heat, pulsation, respiration, sensation, reproduction, digestion.

P2: To produce corporeal effects, the soul must act, by its motion, upon other parts of the body.

P3: But that which, by its motion, acts upon and moves parts of a body must itself be corporeal.

C: Therefore, the soul must be corporeal.

He objects to the view that the soul is an activity or motion, as Melanchthon supposes; for to move the body, the soul must be a *thing* that acts. But Gassendi adds that we know of the corporeal soul only through the evidence of natural activities for which it must be presupposed; but to know the nature of the soul itself, we must wait until we have a microscope powerful enough to observe this subtle body directly. His corporeal soul can be charitably regarded as analogous to the currently assumed structure of molecules that make the body work.

But, Gassendi claims, besides a corporeal soul, human beings must have a second soul, an incorporeal mind. This, he says, follows from the distinctive activities and objects of human cognition. First:

Certainly nothing could be more absurd than to think that a dog, for example, says to himself, I imagine that I imagine or something else of this sort. When we observe our imagining itself, we proceed by a power and perceive by an operation which is superior to the phantasy itself.[79]

For self-conscious reflection, a higher-level perceiving agent is required: 'This job is wholly above a corporeal faculty', which 'is not able to proceed in the direction of itself, but only towards other objects different from itself.' So, 'part of the surface of the finger is not able to [touch itself nor] act on itself. This is the reason that sight cannot see itself or know its vision or apprehend that it sees; nor can any other faculty which is corporeal do the like; and moreover, neither can imagination, which

---

[77] Ibid. 425. Cf. Gassendi, *Animadversiones*, I, 554–5; II, 627, where we are told that the Council teaches that 'there is a soul in each single man, rational and incorporeal . . . which will survive after death or continue immortally', and that the Council enjoins us 'to demonstrate by natural reason the immortality of man, or the rational soul'.

[78] Gassendi, *Syntagma philosophicum*, II, 250.   [79] Ibid. 441.

is corporeal, perceive its own imagining or apprehend that it imagines.'[80] Reflective cognition is impossible for corporeal organs or a corporeal soul. This requires an incorporeal substance—namely the human mind.

Second Gassendi argues from objects of human cognition:

Animals are not able to know a universal itself, or universal natures, e.g. humanity, which are precise and distinct from all grades of singulars; and, further, animals are not able to apprehend abstractions, but concrete things only; as not colour, but the coloured thing; not savour, &c., so a dog has nothing other than the memory of singulars alone . . . while we conceive universals.[81]

The cognition of the corporeal soul cannot take place without a sense impression received by the action of an external exciting object on sense-organs, and this, in turn, sets up a motion in the nerves which affects the brain, where it has a double effect. First, the impression produces a fold or trace in the brain (a *species impressa*), and, concomitantly, it produces the experience of an image (a *species expressa*). But universals, spiritual objects, and abstract and theoretical conceptions are apprehended with no corporeal impression and no image. Human beings must therefore have an incorporeal cognitive power—namely the human mind.

Gassendi objects to the Thomistic view that human beings have one soul, which both regulates animal activities of the body and is incorporeal and immortal. This view, Gassendi argues, will not do for a number of reasons. First, if a single human soul is infused in the body by God, inherited physical traits are left unexplained. Further, the activities of sensation and understanding are inconsistent, for sensing requires corporeal organs, while understanding cannot use corporeal organs. But the same soul cannot have inconsistent powers. Therefore, human beings must have two souls, a corporeal animal soul and an incorporeal mind.

For Gassendi, the human mind is a distinct incorporeal substance united to the body, but unextended, without density or figure, whole and complete wherever it is. It is purely intellective, with no organic activities, and it can reflect upon itself, an activity that is independent of the body. Unlike the corporeal soul, which is produced by parents, the human mind is created *de novo* by God. Finally, Gassendi, citing Cicero, argues that an incorporeal substance, lacking extension or complexity, cannot be divided or dissolved, and thus, incapable of destruction, the human mind must be immortal. Tied to Gassendi's modern concept of body is this human mind, which is much like that of Piccolomini and various other Renaissance pluralists.

Piccolomini and other pluralistic Aristotelians shared with eclectics

---

[80] Ibid.   [81] Ibid.

and corporealists a common concept of a distinct, immaterial, so immortal, human mind. The pluralistic Aristotelian Fortunius Liceti, a prolific writer, with lengthy works on immortality and on the origin and nature of two human souls, lifelong correspondent of George Herbert and acknowledged as a source by Gassendi, was widely known and influential. Melanchthon was a leader in the Lutheran reform movement—indeed, its official public voice—and, through his writings, his view of the human soul had a widespread influence, particularly in Protestant countries.[82] Further, Gassendi's two-soul view and his arguments for immortality were popular throughout the seventeenth century, particularly in the scientific community, being explicitly accepted by, for example, Walter Charleton[83] and Thomas Willis[84] (Locke's teacher at Oxford) and by such *novantiqua* philosophers as David Derodon[85] and Caspar Wyss.[86] It seems quite clear that, as all these representative theories testify, the Lateran Council proclamation of 1513, along with Pomponazzi's arguments, had a direct impact on the development of psychology for nearly two centuries. Admittedly, the Thomistic analysis of the human soul, supported by the Church, remained the prevalent view throughout the Renaissance. But the more influential view was the non-Thomistic account of a distinct human body, soul, and mind of a prominent, productive, and widely read minority.

[82] See e.g. the *Philosophical Theses* of the University of Aberdeen professor Alexander Alexander, who, citing the 'Lateran sub Leo X', supports Melanchthon's view of a distinct spiritual rational soul, which must be immortal (*Philosophemata libera* (Aberdeen, 1669), 81).

[83] Walter Charleton posits—in company, he claims, with Bacon, Gassendi, and Willis—two human souls, 'one simply reasonable, the other merely sensitive' (*Natural History of the Passions* (London, 1674), preface).

[84] Thomas Willis (*Two Discourses Concerning the Soul of Brutes, which is that of the Vital and Sensitive of Man,* trans. S. Pordage (London, 1683), 'Epistle Dedicatory') writes: 'I assert a Man . . . to be indued with many distinct Souls.' Further, Willis argues that human beings have two souls, a corporeal animal soul and an incorporeal and immortal rational soul. He attributes this view to 'that famous philosopher, *Peter Gassendus,* who . . . differencing the mind of man, as much as he could from that other sensitive power of his, . . . because when he had shown this [sensitive power] to be corporeal, extensive and nascible or that may be born, and corruptible, he saith that the other [the mind] was an incorporeal substance, and therefore immortal, which is created mediately by God, and infused into the body' (40).

[85] David Derodon combines Aristotelian pluralism with views of Galen and Gassendi. He writes: 'At nos existimamus duas esse animas in quodlibet bruto scilicet vegitativam & sensitivam; tres vero in quodlibet homine, scilicet vegetativam, sensitivam, & rationalem . . . existimamus plures esse alias formas partiales, puta formas nervi, ossis, &c.' ('Moreover, we claim that there are two souls in whatever animal, namely, vegetative and sensitive; three, truly, in whatever man, namely vegetative, sensitive, and rational . . . we claim that there are many other partial forms, such as forms of nerve, bone, etc.') (*Philosophia contracta* (Geneva, 1681), 179).

[86] Caspar Wyss, *Cursus philosophici* (Geneva, 1669), 209, 309–13, 366–71.

IV. DUALISMS AND MORE MIND–BODY PROBLEMS

It might be asked of all these thinkers: If body and mind are really distinct substances, material and immaterial, extended and unextended, how can they form one unified entity, and how can they interact? During the Renaissance, however, the problem of the unity of mind and body and of their interaction went largely unconsidered by these pluralists. Perhaps they saw no problem; for, first, the soul was thought to be naturally tied to the body as the cause of its vital and sensitive activities. Further, they claimed a natural interconnection between mind and body via the cognitive capacities of the sensitive organic soul. Both the sensitive soul and the human mind think, and so can be said to function together as an information-processing system. So Piccolomini described the organic soul as a 'medium' or 'middle term' between mind and body,[87] and Pierre Charron (1541–1603), identifying in each human being 'l'esprit, l'âme, la chair', distinguished two parts of the human soul, 'the high, pure, intellectual, and divine, in which beasts have no part', and 'the low, sensitive, and bestial which, attached to the body and to matter, *is like a middle between the high and the body*'.[88] None the less, Thomistic opponents of the Scholastic pluralists from the thirteenth century onwards complained that really distinct substantial forms constitute distinct substances, which, in a single individual, would make one substance many substances, a problem of *per se* unity, and, further, that these distinct substances could not interact.

During the seventeenth century, various sorts of dualisms acquired a following. One of these was the above-noted corporealist account of a corporeal organic soul that is a part of a living body, and which, in human beings, is distinguished from a second sort of substance and soul, an incorporeal and immortal mind. Another, influenced by a different strain of Renaissance pluralism, was the view of Scotistic Aristotelians. For example, Eustachius a Sancto Paulo maintained that each living thing is a composite of, first, distinct corporeal forms of distinct homogeneous parts of a living body—for example, blood, bones, flesh, and, in addition, another really distinct, ultimate, supervening substantial form, the soul.[89] Eustachius distinguished, in human beings, a body, caused by

---

[87] Piccolomini, *Librorum*, 876–7.

[88] Pierre Charron, *De la sagesse* (Paris, 1604), 55; emphasis added.

[89] Eustachius a Sancto Paulo, *Summa philosophiae quadripartita: de rebus dialecticis, moralibus, physicis, et metaphysicis* (Paris, 1609), 185–6: 'Quaeritur utrum praeter illam formam totalem, nempe animam, admittendae sint aliae substantiales formae partiales pro varia partium illarum dispositione. Qua de re graviter inter Scotistas affirmantes, & Thomistas negantes, . . . Probabilior autem nobis videtur hac in parte Scotistarum opinio, videlicet praeter formam totalem quae est in anima, admittendas esse formas alias partiales, ut formam carnis, ossis, nervi, &c.' ('It is asked whether besides that total form,

parents, and a soul, caused by God and immortal.[90] Kenelm Digby, in
his *Two Treatises*, the first on body, the second on mind, claiming as his
principal objective the demonstration of the immortality of the human
soul, develops an eclectic dualistic account. Digby, combining a motley
mélange of theories, including atomism, Aristotle's four elements, and a
unique mechanistic account of the motions, sensations, and passions of
the body, postulated, in addition, in human beings, a really distinct incorporeal substance, the human soul or mind, which is purely intellective.[91]
Another seventeenth-century dualism was the innovative and influential distinction between mind and body proposed by Descartes.

Though Descartes' mind–body problem is commonly perceived as a
problem of the union and interaction of mind and body, Descartes
denied that these are problems. He says, in a letter to Elisabeth:

> There are two facts about the human soul on which depend all the knowledge
> we can have of its nature. The first is that it thinks, the second is that, being
> united to the body, it can act and be acted upon along with it.[92]

The union, so interaction, of soul and body, he contends, is a 'primitive
notion'. Both facts are *evident*. Descartes explains that, instead, his 'principal aim was to prove the distinction between the soul and the body'.[93]

Descartes' particular argument that mind and body are mutually
exclusive substances, initiated, for future generations, the now familiar
problems of how mind and body are united or joined, how they form
one unified entity, and how they interact. But his professed mind–body
problem, that of demonstrating the real distinctness of soul and body to
prove the separability, hence immortality, of the human soul or mind,
was inherited from his Renaissance predecessors. Descartes too, in
seeking to show that mind and body are really distinct, opposed the contemporary Thomistic Aristotelians, and adopted the 'distinct mind' strategy of the Renaissance pluralists.

But Descartes postulated not merely that body and mind are distinct,
as material and immaterial, extended and unextended, an argument

namely, the soul, there are admitted other partial substantial forms for various dispositions of the parts. This is strongly affirmed by the Scotists, denied by the Thomists . . .
The more probable, however, is seen by us [as being] on the part of the Scotistic opinion,
namely, besides the total form which is in the soul, admitting that there are other partial
forms, as a form of flesh, bone, nerve, etc.')

[90] That Descartes was aware of the Scotistic dualism of Eustachius is suggested by his
letter to Mersenne dated 11 Nov. 1640, where he says of Eustachius: 'I have bought the
Philosophy of Father Eustache of St Paul, which seems to me the best book of its kind
ever made. I would be glad to know if the author is still alive' (CSM III, 156; AT III,
232). I am grateful to Stephen Voss for the information that Descartes is known to have
read Eustachius at La Flèche (AT III, 185), and that he even thought of including some
of Eustachius's *Summa philosophiae quadripartita* in his *Principles of Philosophy* (AT
III, 233, 259–60).

[91] Digby, *Two Treatises*.   [92] Descartes, CSM, III, 217–18.   [93] Ibid. 218.

employing the principle of contradiction common among pluralists since Ockham;[94] he also claimed that mind and body are distinct as thinking and unthinking, respectively. Only the human mind experiences sense ideas, images, or thoughts; only the human mind thinks. Bourdin, in the Seventh Set of Objections to Descartes' *Meditations*, objected to Descartes' view, and instead distinguished reflective mental cognition from corporeal sensitive cognition.[95] This, Descartes responded, is a dangerous line of thought, a slippery slope, leading ultimately to the obfuscation of a clear distinction between mind and body. If body can perform some cognitive activities, then why not all? If body is capable of sense cognition, then why not reflective cognition too. The mind must be the subject of all cognition. He says:

My critic says that to enable a substance to be superior to matter and wholly spiritual (and he insists on using the term 'mind' only in this restricted sense), it is not sufficient for it to think; it is further required that it should think that it is thinking, by means of a reflexive act, or that it should have awareness of its own thought. . . . The initial thought by means of which we become aware of something does not differ from the second thought by means of which we become aware that we were aware of it, any more than this second thought differs from the third thought by which we become aware that we were aware that we were aware. And if it is conceded that a corporeal thing has the first kind of thought, then there is not the slightest reason to deny that it can have the second. Accordingly, it must be stressed that my critic commits a much more dangerous error. . . . He removes the true and most clearly intelligible feature which differentiates corporeal things from incorporeal ones, *viz.*, that the latter think but not the former; and in its place he substitutes a feature which cannot in any way be regarded as essential, namely that incorporeal things reflect on their thinking, but corporeal ones do not. Hence he does everything he can to hinder our understanding of the real distinction between the human mind and the body.[96]

Therefore, in Descartes' view, soul or mind is a distinct thinking substance, the locus of all human thought. Further, non-human animals are merely bodies; animals, unlike human beings, have no mind or soul and therefore no cognitive experience.

Descartes explains the significance of this analysis:

Here I dwelt a little upon the subject of the soul, because it is of the greatest importance. For after the error of those who deny God . . . there is none that leads weak minds further from the straight path of virtue than that of imagin-

[94] Ockham argues in support of the real distinctness of the organic (sensitive) soul and the intellective soul: 'It is not the case that what is numerically the same form is both extended and non-extended, both material and immaterial. But in a human being the sentient soul is extended and material, whereas the intellective soul is not, since it exists as a whole in the whole [body] and as a whole in each part' (*Quodlibetal Questions*, trans. Freddoso and Kelley, i, 134).

[95] Descartes, AT VII, 533–4; CSM II, 364.   [96] AT VII, 559–60; CSM II, 382.

ing that the souls of the beasts are of the same nature as ours, and hence that after this present life we have nothing to fear or hope for, any more than flies and ants. But when we know how much the beasts differ from us, we understand much better the arguments which prove that our soul is of a nature entirely independent of the body, and consequently that it is not bound to die with it. And since we cannot see any other causes which destroy the soul, we are naturally led to conclude that it is immortal.[97]

To this, Guillaume Lamy,[98] for example, objected that Descartes' soul is a principle of thought, not of life; it is not tied to the body as the cause of its natural activities. That is, Descartes' account of soul as only a thinking substance entails a rejection of the traditional role of the soul, a role that naturally joins the soul to the body, which union, in turn, makes the *per se* unity of a human being possible. Lamy complained that for Descartes the soul does not activate the body, but only thinks. But, Lamy argued, Descartes cannot then explain how soul and body are united, or how they interact.

In Descartes' view, the body, analysed as a machine, is not enlivened by a sensitive organic soul. This is a new line, denying the traditionally recognized commonality between human and animal sense experience and imagination, and, with this, rejecting corporeal sense cognition, said by Renaissance pluralists to be a 'medium' between mind and body, between *l'esprit et la chair*. Descartes' new line, as is well known, was very influential. But with this new line (i.e. bodies do not think), a strategy employed, at least in part, to resolve Pomponazzi's soul–body separation problem, Descartes raised and bequeathed to us all the egregious problems of mind–body union and interaction.

In conclusion, I have attempted to show that late Renaissance theories of the human mind, influenced by a little-known Aristotelian tradition, are of considerable interest in their own right. Further, I have argued that Renaissance Aristotelians provided the impetus and, in turn, the foundation for analyses of mind of the early modern period. If my conclusions are correct, then Renaissance Aristotelianism cannot simply be dismissed as obsolete and therefore lacking in interest. Instead, Renaissance Aristotelians, as well as Renaissance innovators, must be seen as significant contributors to our understanding and assessment of where we are and how we got here—an inviting and provocative call to historians of thought that here waits a wealth of answers, but that too little is known and much remains to be done.

[97] AT VI, 59–60; CSM I, 141.
[98] Guillaume Lamy, *De principiis rerum libri tres* (Paris, 1669), 126–7.

8

Descartes: Heart and Soul

STEPHEN VOSS

I. INTRODUCTION

'The preservation of health', writes Descartes to the Marquess of Newcastle in October 1645, 'has always been the principal end of my studies'
(AT IV, 329: CSMK, 275).[1] In a famous passage in the *Discourse on
Method*, to which we shall return, he explains why medical matters mean
so much to him.

The preservation of health . . . is undoubtedly the chief good and the foundation of all the other goods of this life. For even the mind depends so much on
the temperament and disposition of the bodily organs that if it is possible to
find some means of making men in general wiser and more astute than they
have been up till now, I believe we must look for it in medicine. . . . we might

[1] I use these abbreviations to refer to the standard edition and English translations of
Descartes' works:

AT   *Oeuvres de Descartes*, ed. Charles Adam and Paul Tannery (11 vols., Paris,
         1964–74)
CSM   *The Philosophical Writings of Descartes*, trans. John Cottingham, Robert
         Stoothoff, and Dugald Murdoch (2 vols., Cambridge, 1985–6)
CSMK   *The Philosophical Writings of Descartes: The Correspondence*, trans. John
         Cottingham, Robert Stoothoff, Dugald Murdoch, and Anthony Kenny
         (Cambridge, 1991)
Hall   *Treatise of Man*, trans. Thomas Steele Hall (Cambridge, Mass., 1972)
Olscamp   *Discourse on Method, Optics, Geometry, and Meteorology*. trans. Paul J.
         Olscamp (Indianapolis, 1965)

     I locate passages in *Principles of Philosophy* by part and article, and passages in *Pas-
sions of the Soul* by article, using the abbreviations *Principles* and *Passions*. I locate all
other passages by volume and page in AT and CSM, CSMK, Hall, Olscamp, or G. A. Lindeboom, *Descartes and Medicine* (Amsterdam, 1978), though I may use other translations, like Valentine Rodger Miller and Reese P. Miller's of the *Principles* (Dordrecht,
1983) and my own of the *Passions* (Indianapolis, 1989). For resources beyond those mentioned here see Francesco Trevisani's bibliographical essay on 1937–78, 'Descartes et la
médecine', *Bulletin cartésien*, 9, 1–22, published in *Archives de philosophie*, 44 (1981). The
work of Etienne Gilson, K. E. Rothschuh, Jacques Roger, and H. Dreyfus-Le Foyer is
particularly valuable. And see Vincent Aucante's Ph.D. dissertation 'L'horizon métaphysique de la médecine de Descartes' (Paris-IV, 1998).

free ourselves from an infinity of diseases, both of the body and of the mind, and perhaps even from the infirmity of old age, if we had sufficient knowledge of their causes and of all the remedies that nature has provided us (AT VI, 62: CSM I, 143)

Descartes' medicine is both art and science. As science, it aims to understand the structure and function of the human body—anatomy and physiology—and the causes of and therapies for its malfunctioning—pathogenesis and therapy. As art, it aims to prolong life and maintain health. Anatomy and physiology gain their character from the primary roles assigned to the heart and blood. The blood's ignition in the heart generates heat and movement in the body, and is the source of every physiological function.[2] Descartes understands illness as a malfunction of the circulatory system, which might be caused entirely mechanically or partly psychologically, and offers three kinds of therapy: mechanical, psychosomatic, and naturopathic.

To understand a human phenomenon, Descartes holds that we must first determine whether to ascribe it to soul, body, or the intimate union linking soul and body.[3] Medical knowledge in particular requires both that we distinguish the functions of body and soul and that we understand the union between them. We shall see that medicine builds essentially on a distinctive metaphysics of the soul and the physical universe (section II); on an equally distinctive physics, which directly grounds anatomy and physiology (section III); and on a certain conception of the union between soul and body (section IV), which completes the grounding of pathogenesis and therapy. Descartes' medicine rests squarely on two Archimedean points: the metaphysics of the soul and the physics of the heart.[4]

I present an account of this foundation here. I aim both to clear away the fog that often blurs it and to point out vistas often unnoticed or misperceived. The complementary topics of mechanism and teleology require especially critical scrutiny. I shall suggest two related theses about the sort of medicine these foundations support: the first about medicine as science, the second about medicine as art (section V).

---

[2] AT XI, 130–1: Hall, 20–2; AT XI, 226–7: CSM I, 316; *Passions* 8–9. See H. Dreyfus-Le Foyer, 'Les conceptions médicales de Descartes', *Revue métaphysique et morale*, 44 (1937), 237–86; repr. in Geneviève Rodis-Lewis (ed.), *La Science chez Descartes* (New York, 1987), 281–330, at 282–4; page references are to the latter printing.

[3] AT XI, 119–20: Hall, 1; AT XI, 223–7: CSM I, 314–16; AT III, 665–6, 691–2: CSMK, 218, 226–7; *Principles* I, 48; *Passions* 2–6.

[4] AT IXB, 14: CSM I, 186, and AT IV, 329: CSMK, 275 display the sort of knowledge that medicine presupposes. Etienne Gilson, *René Descartes: Discours de la méthode, texte et commentaire* (Paris, 1962), 449, singles out the soul–body distinction and the theory of the heart's movement as foundations of medicine, citing AT XI, 223–4, 245: CSM I, 314, 319.

II. THE METAPHYSICS OF SOULS AND BODIES

Each of us is a soul. The soul is a thinking thing. Its nature, essence, and principal attribute is to think. This makes possible all of its modes. Each of the soul's modes is a thought or disposition toward a thought. There is no vegetative or sensitive soul. The soul is simple, or indivisible. The soul is distinct from the body. The will is free. Let us see what these slogans amount to.

An attribute is included in a substance's essence when that substance cannot exist without it (AT VII, 219: CSM II, 155; AT III, 423: CSMK, 189). In that sense my entire essence is simply to think (AT VI, 33: CSM I, 127; AT VII, 27, 78: CSM II, 18, 54). I am then a soul, and I cannot exist without thinking.

Thought is my principal attribute: that is, it is capable of receiving or admitting all the modifications, or modes, a soul can possess (AT V, 221: CSMK, 357). Very general attributes like duration or existence aside, each of the soul's modes presupposes thought (*Principles* I, 53, 56). The concept of any mode of a thing depends on the concept of the thing's principal attribute (AT VII, 444: CSM II, 299).

Each mode is a particular thought or a disposition (AT III, 503–4: CSMK, 208) toward thoughts. Thoughts include not only intellectual functions but 'volitions' and sensory, imaginative, appetitive, and emotional 'perceptions' (AT VII, 28: CSM II, 19). In perception the soul is passive, in volition active (*Principles* I, 32; *Passions* 17–26).

There is no vegetative or sensitive soul; the soul's *only* function is to think (AT XI, 202: Hall, 113; AT VII, 27, 351: CSM II, 18, 243; AT III, 372: CSMK, 182). The soul is utterly distinct from the principle by which we are nourished and carry out all the functions we share with animals. Therefore the mind, the principle by which we think, is not a part of the soul, but the soul in its entirety (AT VII, 356: CSM II, 246); the terms 'soul' (*anima*) and 'mind' (*mens*) are interchangeable.

The soul is not multiple (AT III, 369, 371: CSMK, 181, 182). It is simple: it is indivisible, and has no parts (*Passions* 30). No doctrine of 'faculties' can be allowed to divide the soul into parts: it is the same I who wills, understands, senses, imagines, and has appetites (AT VII, 28–9, 85–6: CSM II, 19, 59; *Passions* 47, 68). Anyway, on the grounds Molière makes famous, Descartes regards the idea of a faculty as useless.

There is a *real distinction* between the soul and every body or corporeal substance, including the human body and each of its parts: if you count a soul and a body, the right answer is always 'two', never 'one' (AT VII, 78: CSM II, 54; *Principles* I, 60). As we shall see when we examine Cartesian bodies, all their modes are made possible by extension, since that is their principal attribute. Since the soul is not a body and lacks extension, it has none of the modes that bodies have.

While the soul's perceptions have determinate causes, at least some volitions do not: events may incline or incite the soul to will something, but the soul may freely decline (*Principles* I, 39; AT IV, 115–18, 173–5: CSMK, 233–4, 244–6; *Passions* 41). To that extent, volitions are causally undetermined and scientifically unpredictable.

The Aristotelians who for two millennia shaped the Western concept of science had been guided by Aristotle's position in the first chapter of *De anima*, that the study of the soul falls within the science of nature and is a proper concern for physicists—that is, positive scientists. Descartes uses the term 'science' to refer both to knowledge in general and to positive science in particular; in the latter sense, there is for him no science of the soul. Three of the above theses stand out as obstacles to any scientific psychology: the soul displays no corporeal modes; it is free; it is simple—the first two because science aims primarily to discover the causes of local motion, the last because science explains in terms of the parts of things, and what is simple has no parts. So 'nature' (*natura*) comes to amount to extended nature, and 'physics' (from the Greek *physis*, nature), the study of nature, comes to amount to the science of extended nature. Descartes' excision of the soul from nature and his exclusion of its study from positive science—that is, physics— were deeply revolutionary, to an extent we have still not fully grasped.[5]

The nature, essence, and principal attribute of a corporeal substance or body is three-dimensional extension (*Principles* I, 53; II, 4). Extension is capable of admitting or receiving the various modes of which bodies are capable; it is what makes a substance capable of those modes (AT VIIIB, 348: CSM I, 297). They are all ways of being extended, and thereby presuppose extension. Again leaving existence, duration, and the like to one side, *the modes of bodies* are determinations of shape, size, position, rest, or motion, and the possession of parts with those features, along with dispositions to have such modes (*Principles* I, 48; AT III, 503: CSMK, 208). Descartes provides an *epistemological* test for

---

[5] Gary Hatfield, in his important study 'Remaking the Science of Mind', in C. Fox, R. Porter, and R. Wokler (eds.), *Inventing Human Science: Eighteenth-Century Domains* (Berkeley, 1995), 184–231, agrees that substance dualism led to 'the divorce of psychology from its previous position within natural science' for the close followers of Newton and some Cartesians (195). But I think that he does not sufficiently acknowledge Descartes' creation of and commitment to the divorce (see 192–4); and his conclusion that 'psychology or the science of the mind was conceived as a natural science in the seventeenth, eighteenth, and nineteenth centuries' (216) can by no means be taken as a universal rule. For Descartes' conception of the scope of physics, and consequent banishment of the study of the soul from it, see AT II, 268, 542: CSMK, 118–19, 135; AT VI, 61–2: CSM I, 142–3; AT IXA, 212–13: CSM II, 274–5; *Principles* II, 64; AT XI, 315–18.

whether a supposed feature of a body counts as a mode of it: he asks whether it can be conceived 'clearly and distinctly'—that is, *mathematically* (AT VII, 63–5, 80: CSM II, 44–5, 55–6). Heat and colour, as commonly conceived, fail the test; so do substantial forms, real qualities, and faculties as philosophically conceived.

The nature and the very possibility of Descartes' physics and medicine rest on his metaphysics of nature—that is, of bodies: 'In my physics I consider nothing apart from the sizes, shapes, positions, and movements of the particles of which bodies are made up. . . . Physicians are very well aware of this' (AT III, 686: CSMK, 224).

III. THE PHYSICS OF BODIES: FOUNDATIONS OF ANATOMY AND PHYSIOLOGY

Physics aims to discover 'the true Principles of material things' and the composition and nature of various kinds of bodies (AT IXB, 14–17: CSM I, 186–8). Recognizing that all change is motion, physics derives three basic laws of motion from the immutability of God, their efficient cause (AT XI, 36–46: CSM I, 92–7; *Principles* II, 23–4, 36–44), and seven laws of collision from them (*Principles* II, 45–53). In part because the latter are ideal laws and cannot be applied without an understanding of the configuration of things, physics must also study the composition of the universe: the nature of the earth and the bodies commonly found on it, like air, water, fire, magnets, and other minerals, and the qualities of these bodies, such as light, heat, and weight; and the nature of plants, animals, and above all human beings.

The physical universe is the creation of a perfect God. In him, understanding, willing, and creating are a single act (AT I, 152–3: CSMK, 25–6; AT IV, 119: CSMK, 235; *Principles* I, 23). He has established the laws of nature so that the parts of the universe will constitute a 'very perfect world' (AT XI, 34–5: CSM I, 91).

Descartes' physics is thus grounded in theology. But it is not teleological.[6] It is enjoined from reasoning based on God's purposes (AT VII, 55–6, 374–5: CSM II, 38–9, 258; *Principles* I, 28 (French version); AT V, 158: CSMK, 341), for three reasons. First, Descartes can write that 'it does not seem to me that a finite mind can judge' 'that God always does what he knows to be the most perfect' (AT IV, 113: CSMK, 232), and his affirmations of the perfection of God's works are typically qualified, particularly by the insistence that a thing that is perfect as a part

---

[6] On teleology in Descartes see Jean Laporte, *Le Rationalisme de Descartes*, 2nd edn. (Paris, 1950), book 3, ch. 2.

of the world might be imperfect if it existed alone (AT I, 154: CSMK, 26; AT VII, 55–6: CSM II, 39; *Principles* III, 45). Moreover, the physical universe and its parts can be regarded as perfect only by reference to God's purposes, and apart from revelation these are utterly inscrutable to us (*Principles* III, 2; AT V, 158, 168: CSMK, 341, 349). Most importantly, God's purposes for a thing are extrinsic to its nature. That is why 'knowledge of a thing's purpose never leads us to knowledge of the thing itself; its nature remains just as obscure to us'.[7] For all three reasons, 'the customary search for final causes [is] totally useless in physics' (AT VII, 55: CSM II, 39). Although physics includes the study of the human body, we shall see that Descartes modifies his prohibition significantly in this unique case.

Descartes' physics is instead mechanistic. For the entire visible universe can be 'described . . . as a machine (*instar machinae descripsi*)', and throughout his writings Descartes' label of choice for the human body is 'the machine of our body'.[8] The most fundamental physiological processes—embryogenesis, heart motion, and separation of animal spirits from blood—are each said on distinct occasions to occur 'in accordance with the laws of mechanics'.[9] Descartes is a principal architect of the 'Mechanical Philosophy', and his version of it saturates his medicine. For all these reasons, it is of critical importance, far beyond our present aims, to understand precisely what *he* means by 'machine' and 'mechanics'.

From innumerable sources one can learn that Descartes conceived of a version of the mechanical philosophy which consists of a radically new paradigm, or heuristic, or framework, or method, or regulative or constitutive conception of nature. When these sources are not impossibly vague, they are mutually inconsistent. If we are after precision, I believe that the best vantage-point for understanding Descartes' intentions in adopting the language of machines is that of the young man himself at work on mechanics at the dawn of his career—though no source I know interprets him just as I shall here.

The mechanical treatises available to Descartes were all written by mathematicians, not by Peripatetic physicists.[10] The tradition originated

---

[7] AT V, 158: CSMK, 341. The same point is suggested by *Principles* III, 45.

[8] *Principles* IV, 188; AT XI, 120, 130–2: Hall, 2–5, 21–2; AT VI, 55–6: CSM I, 139; AT VII, 84–5: CSM II, 58–9. For the latter phrase in particular see *Passions* 7, 13, 16, 34; AT XI, 226: CSM I, 315.

[9] AT II, 525: CSMK, 134; AT IV, 5: Lindeboom, *Descartes and Medicine*, 107; AT VI, 54: CSM I, 139.

[10] See Alan Gabbey, 'Descartes's Physics and Descartes's Mechanics: Chicken and Egg?', in Stephen Voss (ed.), *Essays on the Philosophy and Science of René Descartes* (New York, 1993), 311–23, at 315. See also his 'Between *Ars* and *Philosophia Naturalis*', in J. V. Field and Frank A. J. L. James (eds.), *Renaissance and Revolution* (Cambridge, 1993), 133–45.

with pseudo-Aristotle's *Questions of Mechanics*, written in the Lyceum in the third century BC, multiply translated in the late fifteenth century, and widely commented on in the sixteenth and early seventeenth centuries.[11] Descartes may have studied such treatises at the Collège Royal de la Flèche, where he did not 'yet notice the true use' of mathematics, but only its application to 'the mechanical arts'.[12] Evidently, though, it was precisely through a deeper study of the *science* of mechanics with the physicist (and newly licensed physician) Isaac Beeckman that he came to understand the true use of mathematics. For by April 1619 he is promising Beeckman to put his 'Mechanics or Geometry' in order (AT X, 162: CSMK, 4). What is he referring to? When we read these words, it is clear enough that we are present at the creation of the physics whose rules Descartes will later describe as 'the principles of Geometry and Mechanics' (*Principles* IV, 203, French version). For his physics is precisely his own creative amalgam of geometry and mechanics, extant sciences respectively of extension and motion.

My suggestion, then, is that Descartes derives a model for all of science from his early work with mechanics; his role at this point in creating the mechanical philosophy is to expand the scope of an ancient and ongoing enterprise. The mechanics he encounters differs strikingly from its sister Aristotelian physics, in two ways: it specifically treats 'violent' motion, motion contrary to nature for human ends; and it treats it mathematically. Descartes comes to view the first trait as accidental: he remarks that 'the term "violent" refers only to our will. . . . In nature, however, nothing is violent' (AT V, 404: CSMK, 381). He views the second trait as essential: 'The mechanics that has been used up to now is nothing but a small part of the true physics, which took refuge with the mathematicians, since it was not welcomed by the supporters of the common philosophy' (AT I, 421: CSMK, 64). His essential step is to recognize that motion everywhere is mathematical in nature, and to assimilate motion in accordance with nature to motion contrary to nature. With that step, the prototype, mechanics, becomes a part of the new physics, and that physics comes to ground mechanics.[13] The laws of nature, 'the true Principles of material things', may now be identified indifferently with the laws of physics and the laws of mechanics (AT I, 524: CSMK, 81; AT VI, 54: CSM I, 139).

So when Descartes compares the universe to a machine, his point is

---

[11] Paul Lawrence Rose and Stillman Drake, 'The Pseudo-Aristotelian *Questions of Mechanics* in Renaissance Culture', *Studies in the Renaissance*, 18 (1971), 65–104.

[12] AT VI, 7: CSM I, 114. See Geneviève Rodis-Lewis, 'Descartes' Life and the Development of his Philosophy', in John Cottingham (ed.), *The Cambridge Companion to Descartes* (Cambridge, 1992), 21–57, at 22–31.

[13] AT I, 420–1: CSMK, 64; *Principles* IV, 203; AT X, 380: CSM I, 20–1. See Gabbey, 'Descartes's Physics'.

not that natural bodies fall under the genus machine, but that its nature can be characterized mathematically, so that the laws that govern it are mathematical. Of course, his point is not that the methods or the standards of physics ought to be those of arithmetic and geometry: mathematicians don't dissect, and physicists can be happy with moral certainty. His point is, rather, that the principles and composition of natural things are without residue geometrical and numerical.

In particular, when Descartes writes of 'the machine of our body', his phrase is not classificatory. It is a moment in his ceaseless campaign to induce readers to 'withdraw their mind from the senses' (AT VII, 9: CSM II, 8), by reminding them of what is actually involved in the human body's nature as an extended thing through a comparison with the machines which scientists had understood for 2,000 years to be amenable to mathematical study. The human body is exhaustively characterizable in terms of shape and number, and the principles that govern it and allow explanation of it are—apart from the influence of the soul— exhaustively mathematical: 'if we knew all the parts of the seed of some animal species, for example *man*, we could deduce from that alone, by entirely mathematical and certain reasons, the whole shape and conformation of each of its members' (AT XI, 277).

Since mechanics aims to discover the configuration of things useful in the traditional mechanical arts, Descartes regards it both as a science grounded in physics and as an art (*Principles* IV, 204; AT IXB, 14: CSM I, 186). In just the same way, medicine must discover the specific configuration of the human body, and succeed as art by qualifying as science.

In his physics Descartes attributes to things not only categorical modes, but immensely varied powers and tendencies. He explicitly allows the fundamental notion of 'action, that is, the inclination . . . to move', and distinguishes it from motion itself (AT XI, 44: CSM I, 96). Light, for example, is a type of action, or tendency, or striving, or pressure toward motion in the particles of some optic medium. This striving is not, of course, a thought or volition; it is a 'disposition' or 'impetus' to overcome resistance to motion (AT VI, 83–93: Olscamp, 66–74; AT XI, 84–103; *Principles* III, 55–64; IV, 28). Descartes uses homely examples to expand the range of mechanical explanation: he is convinced that clocks, fountains, church organs, and the spin on tennis balls can be analysed mechanically, even if he cannot give the analysis. In so far as colour or cardiac heat can plausibly be assimilated to spin or fermentation, it can plausibly be regarded as mechanical too.[14] Because his physics considers no categorical modes but shape, size, position, and

---

[14] See Geneviève Rodis-Lewis, 'Limitations of the Mechanical Model in the Cartesian Conception of the Organism', in Michael Hooker (ed.), *Descartes* (Baltimore, 1978), 152–70, esp. at 153–4.

motion, Descartes sometimes thinks that with enough money he could complete it himself. Because it also considers powers and dispositions, and examines not only laws of nature but configurations of things, he sometimes thinks that the task will take many centuries.[15]

Bodies are indefinitely divisible into further bodies. Indefinite divisibility is a consequence of geometrical extendedness—the very nature of body. The divisibility of extended things makes science itself possible, for science is essentially micro-reductive (*Principles* II, 23; IV, 201); in particular, it makes possible a physics that explains the features of bodies by the modes of their parts.

Physics is pursued by the same method throughout the extended realm, from the celestial to the terrestrial, from the non-living to the living, from plant to animal to human body (AT X, 360: CSM I, 9). The same explanations hold celestially and terrestrially—magnetism in stars and on earth is explained identically (*Principles* IV, 133). The same explanations hold for plants, animals, and non-living things—heat is the same quality, and fire the same phenomenon, in inanimate bodies, wet hay, and the human heart (AT XI, 202: Hall, 113; AT VI, 46: CSM I, 134; *Principles* IV, 92).

Bodies are composed of a single sort of matter. 'The chemists' salt, sulfur, and mercury are no more different from each other than the four elements of the philosophers . . . All these bodies are made of the same matter' (AT IV, 570: CSMK, 302). Bodies differ only by shape or arrangement of their parts, and their parts differ 'only by the diversity of their shapes' (AT III, 131). So the human body is constructed 'without being composed of any other matter' than pure extension (AT VI, 46: CSM I, 134); and 'but a single stuff' makes up blood, animal spirits, vapours, sweat, and tears (*Passions* 129).

The unity of physical nature is nevertheless modulated and muted by the suggestion of endless diversity in causal regularities occasioned by endless diversity in configurations of matter. Defending his account of heart movement, Descartes argues that 'various sorts of rarefaction are to be distinguished', and that 'the heat of fire differs in certain respects from the heat of the heart' (AT I, 528: CSMK, 82; AT I, 530: Lindeboom, *Descartes and Medicine*, 115).

Particles of matter are found in the form of three elements, distinguished not qualitatively, but in respect of the modes mentioned above. First-element particles are characterized by extreme agitation and tininess and changeable shape; second-element particles by sphericity and tininess; third-element particles by bulk and resistance (in virtue of position and shape) to movement (AT XI, 24–7; *Principles* III, 49–52).

---

[15] Compare AT IXB, 17 and 20: CSM I, 188 and 189–90.

Descartes explains the diversity among the four traditional elements by their relationship to his own three elements. In particular, terrestrial (mainly third-element) particles take on the form of fire whenever they individually follow the agitated movements of first-element particles (*Principles* IV, 80–108). Many causes can generate such motion; a salient one is the mingling of a liquid either with a solid, as in the combustion of wet hay, or with a different liquid, as in fermentation, in such a way as to drive away fire-extinguishing second-element matter (*Principles* IV, 88–93).

Attributes like colour and heat—the qualities that Boyle and Locke would soon label 'secondary'—are nothing but forms, often dispositional, of the above-mentioned modes of extension (*Principles* IV, 198). In spite of oft-told stories, these qualities are not mere sensations. Descartes' thermodynamic conception of life would be incoherent if heat were only in the mind.[16] Heat is identified with velocity or agitation of component particles (AT XI, 7–10: CSM I, 83–4; AT VI, 236: Olscamp, 266; AT II, 485: CSMK, 133; *Principles* IV, 29).

Certain supposed attributes of bodies do not pass Descartes' test of clear and distinct conceivability. We are prone to believe in them from childhood, when the soul–body union is most influential and our worldview is shaped by practical concerns (AT VII, 441–2: CSM II, 297–8). Such are the substantial forms and real qualities that populate scholastic bodies, and the vegetative and sensitive souls, faculties, and virtues that populate scholastic living things.

Weight (*gravitas*), for example, is sometimes conceived of, not as a mode, but as a 'real quality'—that is, a quasi-substantial quality separable from the heavy body. Descartes interprets substantial forms and real qualities as essences or accidents that are also *res*, or substances, capable of existing separately from what they qualify, on the model of Cartesian souls; and condemns them as unintelligible, useless in scientific explanation, and non-existent.[17]

Descartes' examinations of this conception of weight show that he conceives exactly two ways in which one thing can bring about motion in another—by 'a real contact between two surfaces' and by 'knowledge' (AT III, 667: CSMK, 219; AT VII, 442: CSM II, 298). Conceived as a real quality, a body's weight does not cause its motion by contact between

---

[16] I learned this from Stephen Menn, 'The Greatest Stumbling-block', in Roger Ariew and Marjorie Grene (eds.), *Descartes and his Contemporaries* (Chicago, 1995), 182–207. It rescues Descartes from Dreyfus-Le Foyer's criticism in 'Conceptions', 307–8.

[17] For his interpretation see AT VII, 434: CSM II, 293; AT III, 502, 648: CSMK, 207, 216; AT V, 222–3: CSMK, 358. For his criticism see AT VII, 434–5: CSM II, 293; AT III, 506, 648: CSMK, 208–9, 216; *Principles* IV, 201; AT V, 222: CSMK, 358.

surfaces. But, given the real distinction between soul and body, it cannot do so by knowledge; therefore it must be expunged.

In this way the doctrine of the real distinction is the key to exorcizing illicit principles (AT III, 420–1: CSMK, 188). Employing this doctrine and his extremely short list of explanations of motion, Descartes ruthlessly roots out of his physics an entire panoply of principles for explaining motion.

Descartes understands human anatomy and physiology as applications of physics to the human body. He seeks a detailed account of the human body first experimentally, by dissection; then theoretically, by elaborating an embryology. In *The World*, completed in 1633, he attempts to discover the nature of various physical systems developmentally: learning their genesis, he hopes to learn their structure and mode of operation. The one exception is the anatomy and physiology of the human body. Still, in 1639 he expresses the hope to treat the body in the same way (AT II, 525: CSMK, 134–5). Descartes' hope bears fruit only in 1648, in the embryology of the *Description of the Human Body*. In notes written between 1631 and 1648 (collected in AT XI), which appear to amount to compilations of other people's views and tentative thoughts of his own, he describes how the heart might develop in the human embryo, given the presence of the lungs and liver (AT XI, 508–11, 599). But in the *Description* the heart develops first, and the primary task is to account for its structure and functioning (AT XI, 252–4); for 'it is so important to know the true cause of the heart's movement that without such knowledge it is impossible to know anything which relates to the theory of medicine' (AT XI, 245: CSM I, 319).

The embryology features a systematic account of the heat-generated condensation of the body's organs. The mingling of male and female seminal fluids produces heat, which then induces coagulation of the left ventricle, through which the first blood begins to circulate. Descartes attempts mechanical explanations of the heartbeat, the colour of the blood, the formation of arteries and veins, and the successive construction of the other organs (parts IV and V). The omni-nutritive blood does the work. Unfortunately for Descartes' systematic hopes, this developmental story yields no new information about the nature of the body and its parts. What it does yield is a mechanistic embryology that owes nothing to the soul.

Descartes suggests that heat explains life everywhere (AT III, 122); and he identifies life, in animals with hearts, with the heat in their heart: 'I do not deny life to animals, since I regard it as consisting simply in the heat of the heart' (AT V, 278: CSMK, 366). In 1633 he identifies 'the principle of movement and life' in the machine of the human body with the blood and spirits, agitated by 'the heat of the fire in its heart'. In 1649 he identifies 'the bodily principle of all the movements of our members' with the 'continual heat in our heart, which is a species of fire'.[18] The principle of life and movement, in a human being whose blood and organs are arranged for causing bodily movement, is the heat in the heart. So the heat and movement of human life are due to a corporeal principle, and not to the soul: 'it is an error to believe that the soul imparts motion and heat to the body', and 'death never occurs through the fault of the soul, but only because one of the principal parts of the body disintegrates' (*Passions* 5, 6).

Descartes' informal model for the machine of the body is the thermically run hydraulic automaton (AT XI, 124–5: Hall, 13–15; AT VI, 46–55: CSM I, 134–9; AT XI, 228–45). If his intent had been technological rather than medical, he might have invented the internal combustion engine: the Cartesian heart is a two-stroke combustion engine fitted with eleven valves and four cylinders, which drives the circulatory system.

The heart beats because new blood falls into its ventricles, encounters remains of blood different in character in the heart's tissue, and ignites with a 'fire without light', which Descartes variously likens to fermentation and mixtures of nitric acid and iron powder, or quicklime and water, to make plausible its mechanical nature (AT XI, 123: Hall, 9–10; AT I, 530–1: CSMK, 83–4; AT IV, 189; AT VI, 46: CSM I, 134). Expanding, the heated blood closes the valves to the auricles and opens those to the arteries, and circulates through the body. Descartes never speaks of the traditional, but inexplicable, 'innate heat' of the heart; both the heart and the rest of the body are heated by ignited blood.[19]

The finest and most agitated blood particles leaving the left ventricle go straight to the brain. These are the animal spirits. They are entirely corporeal and unspiritual (AT XI, 130: Hall, 21; *Passions* 10, 15). It would be 'absurd' to think that the spirits could serve as the seat of the soul (AT III, 264: CSMK, 162). Descartes in 1643 retains the traditional panoply of natural, vital, and animal spirits, but he regards each as a blood fraction distinguished only by size and agitation. Only animal spirits exist separately from blood, and only they retain a physiological role (AT III, 687–9: CSMK, 225–6; AT IV, 191).

---

[18] AT XI, 202: Hall, 113; *Passions* 8. Supporting passages: AT XI, 123–6: Hall, 9–15; AT VI, 45–55: CSM I, 134–9; AT XI, 280–2; *Passions* 6–9. See Ann W. MacKenzie, 'A Word about Descartes' Mechanistic Conception of Life', *Journal of the History of Biology*, 8 (1975), 1–13.

[19] AT IV, 189; AT XI, 280–2. Here I disagree with Mirko D. Grmek, 'Réflexions sur des interprétations mécanistes de la vie dans la physiologie du xviie siècle', *Episteme*, 1 (1967), 18–30, at 22.

The pineal gland is the seat of the soul: here 'the soul exercises its functions in a more particular way than in the other parts' (*Passions* 31). Thanks to its extreme mobility, its inclination can be altered by the pattern of animal spirits striking it. Given a particular inclination of the gland and pattern of openness in the brain's pores, animal spirits rebounding from the gland are diverted into particular nerves, with sufficient force to open valves which Descartes supposes serve the muscles. Animal spirits already present then flow out of one muscle into the opposed muscle, causing involuntary movement by lengthening one and contracting the other.

The mutually supporting heat in the heart and circulation of the blood unleash the flow of animal spirits. These three functions account for all the body's activities. Descartes attributes an amazing number of the latter to the body alone. Here is his own list of the functions treated mechanically in the *Treatise of Man*: digestion (without the aid of a vegetative soul or digestive faculty), beat of heart, and arteries (without the aid of a sensitive soul or pulsific faculty), nourishment and growth of members, respiration, waking and sleeping, reception of sensory qualities, imprinting of corporeal ideas on the brain, internal movements of appetites and passions, and instinctive and reflex movements.[20] Thomas Hall rightly concludes that 'in certain ways, the heart of Descartes's endeavor, after he had split reality into material and mental components, was to ascribe as much as possible . . . to the former' (Hall, 92 n. 140).

Descartes is willing to speak—apparently teleologically—of the functions of the parts and processes of the human body. Thus he can speak of the 'true function (*vrai usage*)' of respiration and of the 'part (*office*)' the stomach plays, and evaluate the structure of a particular human body as more or less 'perfect (*accomplie*)' (AT VI, 53: CSM I, 138; *Passions* 98; AT XI, 143–4: Hall, 37).

Perhaps his comparison of the body to a machine encourages such talk: 'Just as when those who are accustomed to considering automata know the use of some machine and see some of its parts, they easily conjecture from this how the other parts which they do not see are made: so, from the perceptible effects and parts of natural bodies, I have attempted to investigate the nature of their causes and of their imperceptible parts' (*Principles* IV, 203). But the comparison only defers the question of how to license talk of the function of a physical thing or process.

Even if we regard the human body as a machine, we cannot discern

[20] AT XI, 202: Hall, 113. Descartes virtually repeats the list in 1641, even adding 'walking, singing and the like, when these occur without the mind attending to them' (AT VII, 229–30: CSM II, 161).

the function of its parts or operations by discovering a purpose internal to it or in the mind of its creator. Descartes forbids the framework of final causation in study of the body's nature, for there is always a 'mechanical' explanation why a bodily part or process has the effect it has (AT VI, 53–5: CSM I, 138–9; *Description, passim*), and the real distinction entails that physical things have no 'natural appetites or inclinations' (AT III, 213: CSMK, 155). But although we cannot discern God's purposes in creating the parts of plants or animals, we can still discern the functions of those parts (AT VII, 374–5: CSM II, 258).

The question remains how. The true function of imbibing water is not to weaken a dropsy patient, though it often does that, and the office of the heart is not to help warm the ambient air, though it always does that. The question cannot be answered within Descartes' physics. Only in the larger context of the union of soul and body does Descartes consider whether the comparison of the body to a machine can ground his attribution of functions to the parts and operations of the human body.

IV. THE METAPHYSICS OF THE UNION: FOUNDATIONS OF PATHOGENESIS AND THERAPY

A close union joins soul and body. Though really distinct, soul and body remain intimately linked until the death of the body. This relation makes possible a range of perceptions in the soul—sensations, appetites, and passions—and a range of movements in the body—voluntary movements and the cerebral movements involved in memory and imagination. Such perceptions are not modes that angels would have, since they 'arise . . . from the close and intimate union of our mind with the body'.[21] The institution of nature is God's creation of the laws of soul–body interaction, specific primitive causal laws ensuring that certain movements of the pineal gland cause certain thoughts (AT VII, 86: CSM II, 59–60; *Passions* 36, 50, 94), and certain thoughts, certain movements (AT V, 65: CSMK, 237; *Passions* 44).

Descartes ordinarily forbids teleological reasoning about the extended universe. But he licenses it with respect to the union between body and soul. The institution of nature marks God's solution—'the best that can be devised'—of a problem in metaphysical geometry: how to create connections between soul and body that are 'as much as possible and as often as possible conducive to the preservation of the healthy human being' who is their composite. True, we do not discover this truth by reasoning in a priori fashion from God's nature or purposes; 'expe-

---

[21] *Principles* I, 48. Cf. AT VII, 81: CSM II, 56.

rience shows' that it is so.[22] Perhaps we can infer that one of God's purposes is to benefit human beings, but Descartes attacks from several
directions the proposition that God made all things for our sake: (i) we
are entitled to say only that human beings can make some use of everything God has created; (ii) it is presumptuous to think God has no other
purpose in creation than to benefit us or gain our praise; and (iii) it is
said that God alone is the universe's final cause.[23] Still, the myriad causal
laws whereby bodily occurrences normally generate sensations,
appetites, and passions serve optimally to benefit human beings.[24] But
Descartes can discover that the institution of nature is optimal for preserving healthy human beings only if he has a way to characterize
health. That problem is equivalent to the problem of characterizing true
function within the human body. His remark, cited four paragraphs
back, about those who consider automata might seem to suggest
extrapolating from our knowledge of the functions of machines to
discern function in nature generally and the human body in particular.
But this suggestion rests on a misunderstanding, exposed in section III,
of Descartes' comparison of the body to a machine. For two reasons the
suggestion goes nowhere. We have ways of learning the purposes that
animate human artificers, but we cannot discover God's purposes in
creating human bodies. Moreover, the human body—unlike most
machines, but like the automata created for the French court which so
entranced Descartes—seems not to serve any definite purpose whatever, except, perhaps, to remain in existence, Rube Goldberg style. The
machines that fascinate Descartes do nothing useful; they simply amuse
the king and amaze his subjects. So, perhaps, with the human body. Our
problem might be closer to a solution if Descartes exhibited the con-
tempt for the body common in dualists, and insisted that it is meant to
minister to the soul. But he does not.

The fundamental text for Descartes' solution to the problem of
ascribing functions to the human body's parts and processes is found in
the Sixth Meditation.[25] It completes the annihilation of the abortive

[22] AT VII, 87: CSM II, 60. Similarly, the function of the parts of organisms 'makes it
appropriate to look with wonder on God as their efficient cause' (AT VII, 374: CSM II,
258).

[23] (i) *Principles* III, 3; AT V, 53–4: CSMK, 321. (ii) *Principles* III, 2; AT III, 431: CSMK,
195; AT IV, 292: CSMK, 266; AT V, 168: CSMK, 349. (iii) AT V, 53–4: CSMK, 321.

[24] AT VII, 83: CSM II, 57 and *Principles* II, 3: the proper purpose of sense perception
is to inform us of what can benefit or harm the soul–body composite. AT VII, 84–5: CSM
II, 58–9: sensations, including what *Principles* IV, 190 calls the 'natural appetites', are
arranged for the benefit of the composite human being. *Passions* 52, 74, 211: the passions
are all by nature good and of utility to us; ibid. 137: they are instituted by nature for the
benefit of the body; ibid. 139: they are equally of benefit to the soul.

[25] In the next two paragraphs I discuss AT VII, 84–5: CSM II, 58–9.

project of inferring function from the nature of the body. Even when a clock is badly made and tells the wrong time, it 'observes all the laws of its nature'. So if we say that a clock that tells the wrong time is 'departing from its nature', we use the term 'nature' in another sense, as a label extraneous (*denominatio extrinseca*) to the clock, since it depends on our thought of 'the wishes of the clockmaker'. In the same way, says Descartes, when we restrict the term 'nature' to what is 'really to be found in the things themselves', a human body affected by dropsy acts consistently with its nature when its throat is dry, even when that disposes the body to drink and aggravate the disease. If we say 'with respect to the body' that such a body 'is deviating from its nature' or 'has a disordered nature', we are again using the term 'nature' extraneously. In short, no physical thing has a function intrinsic to its nature. That includes the human body and its parts.

But one striking fact marks off the human body from every other physical thing. 'The composite, that is, the mind united with this body', does have a nature that is disordered in the case imagined. 'With respect to the composite' there is 'a true error of nature, namely that [the composite] is thirsty at a time when drink is going to cause it harm.' It is the nature of the composite human being, not that of the body, that determines which bodily processes are its true functions and which are malfunctions or accidental concomitants, which bodily conditions are healthy and which are pathological. What is intrinsically good for a human being provides the touchstone of what is good or bad for a human body.

It is, I think, very doubtful, given his other theoretical commitments, that Descartes can characterize bodily function and bodily health in terms of the good of the human being. He tells Elisabeth and Christina that the supreme good is a firm resolution to do what we judge to be best, together with the consequent contentment (AT IV, 271–8: CSMK, 259–62; AT V, 81–6: CSMK, 324–6). But health's link with virtuous resolve is surely so tenuous as to discourage any characterization of health in terms of such resolve. True, disease can take away reason and even freedom (AT IV, 282: CSMK, 262–3), but such cases are exceptional and often remediable; and Descartes' persistent theme is that virtuous resolution and the contentment it brings depend on nothing external to our will.[26]

There are other goods, which merit esteem rather than praise (AT V, 84: CSMK, 325), but the closest Descartes comes to an account of health

---

[26] See e.g. AT IV, 266, 281–7: CSMK, 258, 262–5; AT V, 81–5: CSMK, 324–6; *Passions* 147–61.

in terms of human good is the programmatic statement from the *Discourse* with which this essay begins, and his similar comment to Elisabeth that 'the health of the body and the presence of pleasant objects very much aid the mind to rid itself of all the passions that are involved in sadness and make way for those that are involved in joy' (AT IV, 529: CSMK, 296). Might he characterize health as that condition of the body that is most conducive to a human being's wisdom, joy, and resolve to do what is best? He never tries; it is an interesting open question whether he could.[27]

We must further note a tension with one of Descartes' fundamental commitments: the principle that human phenomena are all analysable as modes of the body or modes of the soul, or relations between body and soul.[28] To define the body's health in terms of the human being's welfare is to go against that grain. And the evidence is that Descartes abandons the attempt. In 1649 he speaks of 'things harmful to the body' and 'useful to it' without offering the theoretical underpinnings he had in the *Meditations* (*Passions* 138). He tips his hand two years earlier, with a subtle shift in his Sixth Meditation discussion of God's problem in metaphysical geometry: in 1641, the problem had been how best to preserve 'the healthy human being (*hominis sani*)'; in the French translation he approved in 1647, it is how best to preserve 'the completely healthy human body (*le corps humain*)' (AT IX, 70).

And here a deeper metaphysical problem emerges. Early on, the union between soul and body is said to be intimate enough to constitute a composite thing—a human being (AT VI, 59: CSM I, 141; AT VII, 81: CSM II, 56). But it is exceedingly difficult to determine which properties are predicable of human beings, consistently with such theses as that of the real distinction. Still more seriously, it is difficult to understand what such predications might signify: it seems that 'The human being is joyful' could record nothing but joy in the soul. The content of common predications of human beings has been stolen by Descartes' new theoretical predications of souls and bodies; and the theory in which those predications are embedded creates massive difficulties in erecting a theory of composite human beings atop it. Descartes' apparent response, present throughout his writings after 1642, is not to try to solve the difficulties, but to end his metaphysical commitment to human

---

[27] I cannot agree with Gueroult's view that Descartes holds 'the health of the body [to be] the condition for the joy of the soul' (Martial Gueroult, *Descartes selon l'ordre des raisons* (2 vols., Paris, 1953), trans. Roger Ariew as *Descartes' Philosophy Interpreted According to the Order of Reasons* (2 vols., Minneapolis, 1985), 2. 199). References are to the English translation of the second volume.

[28] Central texts are listed in n. 3 above.

beings.[29] But that leaves the question of function in the human body swinging in the wind.

The fact that laws governing soul–body interaction are intended for the benefit of human beings does not imply any relaxation in Descartes' mechanistic anatomy and physiology. Those laws govern only the body's generation of sensations, appetites, and passions in the soul and the soul's alteration of existing operations in the brain.

On the other hand, the interaction laws ensure that pathogenesis and therapy cannot be exclusively mechanical. What happens in the soul can harm the body or help heal it. Illnesses like dropsy can give rise to appetites harmful to the body, and defects in the 'temperament of the body or the strength of the soul' can do the same for passions (*Passions* 36). But the interaction laws continue to provide stable and reliable connections between soul and body, and constitute the nomological foundations for psychosomatic therapy.

One form of interaction with particular relevance to medicine is a type of *imagination*: 'our body is so constructed that certain movements in it follow naturally upon certain thoughts'.[30] Such thoughts affect the course of the animal spirits: they might, for example, 'enter the muscles whose function it is to close the opening of the heart, which retards the circulation of the blood'. So they may lead to stasis, the cardinal threat to health.[31] But such thoughts might equally make for health, by the same mechanism. Descartes advises Elisabeth that this is how he banished his own constitutional frailness (AT IV, 220–1: CSMK, 250–1). In this way imagination directly yields a non-mechanical species of pathogenesis and therapy.

But certain soul–body feedback loops make possible both conditioning to alter passions and an enriched arena for psychosomatic medicine. Descartes writes that 'the principle on which everything I have written about [the passions] is based' is 'that there is such a connection between our soul and our body that when we have once joined some bodily action with some thought, one of the two is never present to us afterwards without the other also being present to us'.[32] This principle, which we may label the Principle of Habituation, rests on two theoretical supports. One is the form of imagination just alluded to. The other is *bodily*

---

[29] I argue for this position in 'Descartes: The End of Anthropology', in John Cottingham (ed.), *Reason, Will, and Sensation* (Oxford, 1994), 273–306; 'Le grand Arnauld', in Jean Marie Beyssade and Jean Luc Marion (eds.), *Descartes—objecter et répondre* (Paris, 1994), 385–401; and 'A Spectator at the Theater of the World', in R. J. Gennaro and C. Huenemann (eds.), *New Essays on the Rationalists* (Oxford, 1999), 265–84.

[30] AT V, 65: CSMK, 237. See also *Principles* IV, 190 and *Passions* 91.

[31] AT IV, 313: CSMK, 271. See AT III, 219: CSMK, 250; AT III, 457–8.

[32] *Passions* 136. See also ibid. 44, 50, 107, and 211; AT IV, 407–9, 603–6: CSMK, 285–6, 307–8.

imprinting, the fact that once two states of the human body are con-joined, then when one recurs, the other will tend to recur also (AT V, 65: CSMK, 237; AT IV, 605, 615: CSMK, 307–8, 312–13; *Passions* 107). Thanks to imprinting, accidental or artificial conjoining of bodily states will produce novel 'laws' of physics specific to individual human bodies.

Bodily imprinting helps explain new patterns of causation from body to soul: once a physical stimulus has become associated with a certain passion, it generates that passion from then on, by generating the passion's naturally instituted bodily cause (*Passions* 45–50, 211). It also helps explain new causal paths from soul to body. Thanks to imagina-tion, the passions each have bodily effects. Therefore conditioning that alters passions can in turn alter the functioning of the body. The Princi-ple of Habituation builds on the institution of nature: leaving the insti-tuted causal paths between soul and body inviolate (AT V, 163–4: CSMK, 346), it allows the creation of new 'laws' of interaction specific to habituated individuals. In isolation, bodily imprinting is valuable moral lore in Descartes' neo-Stoic programme to show how to correct the patterns of the passions. Conjoined with imagination, it is valuable medical lore. The physician can manipulate passions by manipulating stimuli, Pavlov-style, and rely on the patient's imagination to alter bodily conditions.

Bodily imprinting may link occurrences in a pregnant woman's body with occurrences in the foetus, for 'it is certain that there is a relation between all the movements of a mother and those of the child in her womb' (*Passions* 136). Descartes thus accepts a principle of *foetal imprinting*. He explains this extended principle mechanically, and not by the discredited avenues of sympathy and the like.[33] He is early scepti-cal of the principle (AT I, 153: CSMK, 26), but assents through the 1630s precisely in so far as a mechanical explanation strikes him as plausible.

The possibilities of soul–body connection, and even connection between one person's body and another's, might seem nearly as exten-sive for Descartes as for a Paracelsus. What counts for Descartes, though, is the explicability of each connection by his distinctive lights.

Descartes regards every operation in the human body as a function of the circulatory system. It follows, he believes, that illness must always be a circulatory malfunction. Such a malfunction might be caused

---

[33] AT XI, 177: Hall, 87; AT VI, 129: Olscamp, 100; AT III, 120–1: CSMK, 148–9. In the last passage Descartes suggests a medical application of this principle, remarking that the same cause encourages us to seek the same remedy. See *Principles* IV, 187. AT XI, 515–16 attempts to explain the sex of the foetus 'propter sympathiam motus cum matre', but such language should not mislead: the explanation is meant to fall within what Jacques Roger, citing AT XI, 277, calls a 'mathematical embryology': *Les Sciences de la vie dans la pensée française du XVIIIe siècle*, 1st edn. (Paris, 1963), 144.

entirely mechanically or partly psychologically (AT III, 457–8; AT IV, 190). He offers three kinds of therapy, which we may label mechanical, psychosomatic, and naturopathic.[34]

First, the physician can seek to repair the body mechanically, for Descartes early pursues a rigorously mechanistic medicine: 'Please look after yourself,' he advises Mersenne in 1630, 'at least until I know whether it is possible to discover a system of medicine which is founded on infallible demonstrations, which is what I am investigating at present' (AT I, 105: CSMK, 17). Secondly, in the 1640s he begins to suggest that it is possible to treat illness psychosomatically, altering the soul's pattern of thoughts to alleviate the body's circulatory disorders (AT IV, 201; AT IV, 218–21: CSMK, 249–51; AT V, 65–6: CSMK, 237). Thirdly, late in the 1640s he begins to offer naturopathic advice, agreeing with Tiberius Caesar that anyone over 30 has enough experience to live by nature's own teachings, guided by sensations, appetites, and passions (AT IV, 329–30: CSMK, 275–6; AT V, 65, 179: CSMK, 237, 354). In the last two cases Descartes calls on the patient to heal herself.

How are we to understand the shifts in Descartes' therapeutic advice? Various authors have wondered whether they reflect developments in the underlying theory.[35] Descartes derives his original and preferred advice from a mechanical understanding of the body and its malfunctioning. The theoretical basis of his subsequent psychosomatic advice is the doctrine of the soul–body union. The theoretical basis of his naturopathic advice is the doctrine that a perfect creator has instituted the union in the best way possible, providing us the means to gather sufficient knowledge to sustain health.[36] Evidently this doctrine explains how Descartes can vacillate with Burman in 1648 over what he could not contemplate in 1641: that even sick people would do well to trust their appetites in the light of their experience.[37] Both doctrines, concerning the soul–body union and God's perfection, are securely in place while Descartes is counselling mechanistic therapy; later, when he is dispensing psychosomatic and naturopathic advice, he continues to accept the doctrines that ground mechanistic advice, and indeed to give it out (AT IXB, 14: CSM I, 186; AT IV, 220: CSMK, 250; AT XI, 223–7: CSM I, 314–16).

[34] Gueroult, *Descartes' Philosophy*, ch. 20.

[35] See Pierre Mesnard, *Essai sur la morale de Descartes* (Paris, 1936); Gueroult, *Descartes' Philosophy*; and Dreyfus-Le Foyer, 'Conceptions'.

[36] See Gueroult, *Descartes' Philosophy*, 199–201.

[37] For 1641 see AT VII, 84: CSM II, 58. For the vacillation in 1648, if we can credit Burman, see AT V, 163–4: CSMK, 346, defending the earlier claim, and AT V, 178–9: CSMK, 353–4, suggesting that 'nature herself works to effect her own recovery' even on behalf of the unhealthy (the teleological excess is no doubt to be cashed in the terms provided by AT XI, 34–5: CSM I, 91).

As with his physics, so with his medicine: Descartes can exult that his many dissections reveal 'nothing whose formation seems inexplicable by natural causes', and indeed that he 'can explain it all in detail . . .'; yet lament, two sentences later, 'for all that, I do not yet know enough to be able to heal even a fever'.[38] Optimistic, he prescribes mechanistic medical techniques; pessimistic, he falls back on other advice that his foundations equally sanction. Heart and soul continue to ground medical theory and practice.

V. CONCLUSIONS

These foundations generate a conception of medicine as science and as art which can be usefully compared with the dominant conceptions of present-day medicine. I will say something about each aspect.

Explanation in medicine   Descartes derives from his metaphysics and physics a general principle: that all bodily occurrences can be explained as the effects of thoughts or mechanical causes. In part I of the *Description of the Human Body*, he offers three arguments for the principle that all bodily occurrences are either the effects of thoughts or functions of the body (AT XI, 224–6: CSM I, 314–15).

First, we find that we know our soul through one function alone—thinking. Other functions sometimes attributed to the soul, like digestion and the beating of heart and arteries, are simply motions in the body. But it is more common for a motion to be caused by a body than by a soul. So these other functions are probably due to the body, not the soul.

Again, the body must be rightly disposed for the soul to produce motion in it. And when the body is perfectly disposed, motion results with no help from the soul. Therefore all motions that we do not *experience to depend on thought* must be caused, not by the soul, but solely by the dispositions of the organs.

Finally, it is possible to 'prove' the principle by thorough explanations of the body's functions, and Descartes sets out to do so in the rest of the *Description*. Consider two key cases, the motion of heart and blood (part II) and nutrition (part III).

The heart's motion is not due to a faculty of the soul, because (i) this is to explain the clear by the obscure, and (ii) still further faculties will be needed for changing the blood in the heart, like Harvey's 'faculty of

---

[38] See the juxtaposition cited in n. 15 above. AT II, 525–6: CSMK, 134–5. Similar laments, from 1645 and 1646: AT IV, 329, 441–2: CSMK, 275, 289.

mutation' for heating it. Explanation by expansion due to heating is better on both counts.[39]

Nourishment cannot be explained by faculties in bodily parts for selecting the blood that will nourish them, 'for to suppose in each part of the body faculties that choose and attract the particles of the food proper to them is to feign incomprehensible chimeras, and to attribute more intelligence to these chimeras than our soul itself has, seeing that it has no knowledge of what they would have to know' (AT XI, 250–1). Instead, Descartes sketches a mechanical explanation.

By contrast, medicine in Descartes' time called imaginatively on an extensive list of explanatory principles: non-mechanical *vitalistic corporeal* principles, like faculties and virtues of bodies and their parts, and non-thinking *animistic spiritual* principles. Descartes rejects both options: everything that happens in the human body can be explained either (a) mechanically, if corporeally, or (b) cognitively, if spiritually. Here is his cleanest statement, in 1649: 'There are two different principles causing our movements. The first is purely mechanical and corporeal, and depends solely on the force of the spirits and the structure of our organs, and can be called the corporeal soul. The other, an incorporeal principle, is the mind or that soul which I have defined as a thinking substance' (AT V, 276: CSMK, 365). The conjunction of these two conditionals is, in its historical setting, extraordinary.

(a) Descartes' own knowledge of mechanical causes is of course limited. He knows nothing of modern chemistry (since it had yet to be created), and static electricity and magnetism reduce to simple mechanics.[40] But it is easy to see that he would agree to the mechanical nature of electromagnetic force and chemical bonding, rather than dismissing them as occult, for his criterion of the mechanical is mathematical clarity and distinctness. It is absolutely true that his own mechanical explanations can look crude, even on standards available in the seventeenth-century. (Look closely at the mechanical embryology!) But his confidence in mechanical explanations, *precisely in the face of the evident shortcomings of those available to him*, makes him look amazingly prescient. (Now look at twentieth-century embryology!)

(b) Minds or souls, or spiritual principles, can affect human bodies only in virtue of their *thoughts*. A spiritual principle can induce heart motion or breathing, or muscle contraction, only in so far as a thought has such causal powers.

There follows something quite extraordinary. Very many twentieth-century medical scientists would endorse Descartes' principle that all the

---

[39] AT XI, 243–4: CSM I, 318–19. See Dreyfus-Le Foyer, 'Conceptions', 289.
[40] Chemistry: AT I, 216–17: CSMK, 33; AT V, 327: CSMK, 370. Electricity: *Principles* IV, 184–6. Magnetism: AT III, 816–18: CSMK, 220; *Principles* III, 87–91, 105–9; IV, 133–83.

functions of the human body are explicable either cognitively (by thought) or mechanically (mathematically). By contrast, what twentieth-century physicists count as explanation diverges radically from what Descartes counts. Descartes is perhaps the earliest figure to anticipate in a principled way what is really a twentieth-century conception of explanation in medicine. His own theory of heart and soul is recognizably reincarnated in the contemporary theory of the mathematical and the cognitive.

The purpose of medicine Descartes' conception of the aim of medicine is captured in his phrase 'the preservation of the healthy human being'.[41] But this aim conjoins two distinct goods: preservation and health. Like Mill's famous description of the aim of morals as the greatest happiness of the greatest number, it includes no instructions for comparing the two goods it mentions. In so far as it provides no grounds for adjudication, it provides no help in resolving triage questions like those that notoriously arise in our own time, when it is possible to keep radically unhealthy people alive for long stretches of time and when measures that make for health may limit longevity.

Health often makes for longevity. But it is not definable simply as the bodily condition that makes for long life. Some cases of ill health, like acne, do not shorten life. And some bodily conditions, like the reduction to atomic particles resulting from a direct nuclear hit, end life, but are in no way medical conditions or health problems.

If health and longevity are human goods, they somehow fall into place with other goods that Descartes values, like knowledge and virtue and the goods of the afterlife. Such things seem incommensurable. But it is the lot of human beings to choose among them. In 1646 Descartes writes to his friend Chanut:

I must say in confidence that what little knowledge of physics I have tried to acquire has been a great help to me in establishing sure foundations in moral philosophy. Indeed I have found it easier to reach satisfactory conclusions on this topic than on many others concerning medicine, on which I have spent much more time. So instead of finding ways to preserve life, I have found another, much easier and surer way, which is not to fear death (AT IV, 441–2: CSMK, 289).

A few months later he writes to him again. What would his critics not say, he wonders, 'if I undertook to examine the right value of all the things we can desire or fear, the state of the soul after death, how far we ought to love life, and how we ought to live in order to have no

---

[41] AT VII, 87: CSM II, 60. For other statements relevant to the aim(s) of medicine see AT I, 649: CSMK, 76; AT VI, 62: CSM I, 143; AT IV, 329–30: CSMK, 275–6; AT XI, 223–4: CSM I, 314.

reason to fear losing our life? . . . And so the best thing I can do hence-forth is to abstain from writing books' (AT IV, 536–7: CSMK, 299–300). In fact he writes much more, about both morals and medicine; but he provides no theory of value sufficient to answer the questions which his own conception of medicine raises.

The domain that encompasses Descartes' medicine demands a conception of human good for at least three reasons: to define true bodily function, and thus health; to adjudicate the claims of longevity and health, and thus define the purpose of medicine; and to adjudicate among these and other human goods, and thus locate medicine as one art among others. But he never stakes out what is good for a human being. This lacuna foreshadows our own century's irresolution about the goods of medicine, with its insufficiently grounded comparisons between quality and quantity of life, its territorial disputes between patient as somehow endowed with worth and dignity and physician as expert mechanic, and the loss we are at about how value attaches to a being who possesses features both cognitive and mathematical.

There are theories of mind and body, or heart and soul, that do not bifurcate medical explanation into the mental and the mathematical, and do not allow the most basic questions about the purposes of the physician's art to go unanswered. How radically would we have to transform Descartes' conception of heart and soul in order to fill the lacunae he bequeaths to the physicians who are his heirs?[42]

[42] My thanks to John P. Wright, François Duchesneau, Gareth Matthews, Fred Michael, Emily Michael, Murat Aydede, Güven Güzeldere, Gürol Irzik, Alan Gabbey, Gary Hatfield, Jonathan Bennett, Vincent Aucante, and Daniel Garber, who questioned doggedly and shared bountifully. I would be astounded if they agreed completely with the results.

9

Bayle and Late Seventeenth-Century Thought

THOMAS M. LENNON

The collective task of the essays in this volume is to provide a diachronic map of the division between mind and body. Pierre Bayle (1647–1706) is of particular interest in charting this philosophical terrain. Like Descartes, for example, he engages the issue and takes a position on it. But, unlike Descartes, he engages, or at least reports, practically everyone else's engagement of the issue. In particular, he testifies to the seventeenth-century dialectic among three views that will serve as sub-headings here: (1) materialism, (2) Cartesian dualism, and (3) the Leibnizean alternative to materialism and dualism. Because Bayle read and discussed just about everyone, and because he was read so widely himself, it is not surprising that Bayle's treatment of this material opens the way to much of the eighteenth century's treatment of the topic.[1]

The first two of these views, materialism and Cartesian dualism, represent the principal positions held on the division between mind and body in the latter half of the seventeenth century: most major philosophers at that time explicitly held, or were regarded as holding, or were committed to holding, one or the other. The third view, monadology and the pre-established harmony based on it, was held by Leibniz. While subscribed to by only a few other thinkers, this view deserves attention, both because of Leibniz's arguments for it and also for the light it sheds on its two competitors and on Bayle's treatment of the whole seventeenth-century scene with respect to the mind–body division.

Materialism is, at least theoretically, the most straightforward response to the mind–body division. On this view, since everything is

[1] Perhaps most notably, Bayle anticipates Berkeley's view in the second of the *Dialogues* between Hylas and Philonous that the body exists only in the mind, and he is the source for Hume's reasoning that 'the immateriality, simplicity, and indivisibility of a thinking substance is a true atheism' (*A Treatise of Human Nature*, ed. L. A. Selby-Bigge (Oxford, 1888), 240). For more on the Bayle–Berkeley connection generally, see G. Bryckman, 'Berkeley: Sa lecture de Malebranche à travers Le Dictionnaire de Bayle', *Revue internationale de philosophie*, 29 (1975), 496–514. For more on the Bayle–Hume connection, see Norman Kemp Smith, *The Philosophy of David Hume* (London, 1966), 506–16.

material, the connection between mind and body is the same as that between any two material things. Atomism was already a materialist option at the outset of the seventeenth century, and was given increasing impetus by the new science of mechanism. Here, minds and bodies would be systems of atoms, all of whose changes are explicable in terms of change of motion upon impact. The names of Galileo, Boyle, and Newton come to mind when thinking of those on a road going in this direction. But very few proceeded along it very far—certainly not those just named—for politico-theological reasons.

Atomism had long been read, as Lucretius intended it to be read, as entailing a denial of Divine Providence and of the immortality of the soul. As a result, the materialistic aspect of atomism was modified in various ways. To allow for something like final causes, and thus to accommodate Providence, Gassendi, for example, introduced a non-mechanistic soul that he metaphorically called the 'efflorescence of matter'; and to allow for immortality, he posited two souls, or parts of soul, in humans, only one of which is material and mechanistic. A different approach was provided by John Locke, whose views on the soul were to become important in the eighteenth century: he took an agnostic stand on the problematic implications of his atomism. Change of motion upon impact was the only kind of change that was intelligible, he said; but there are other kinds of change, which we cannot understand, such as gravity or the production of thought. Moreover, the soul, or whatever it is that thinks, is something whose essence is beyond our understanding. I shall consider an important implication of Locke's view of the soul in the conclusion to this chapter.

Cartesian dualism was the most glamorous of the seventeenth-century views on the mind–body division, approaching something of an enthusiasm, and claiming adherents all along the intellectual spectrum from the *salons* to the most sophisticated mathematical circles. The Cartesians held that minds and bodies are essentially different substances. The essence of mind is thought, and that of body is spatial extension, and nothing that is one can be the other. It has often been thought that because the Cartesians also held that a cause and its effect must be essentially alike, interaction between mind and body posed a problem for them, which they sought to solve, *ad hoc*, with their doctrine of occasionalism. According to this doctrine, only God is a real cause; finite events, such as the collision of billiard-balls, provide only the occasion for God's operation on the balls, whose collisions are thus no more than occasional causes of motion. Applied to the mind–body connection, occasionalism construes God as acting on the mind upon the occasion of a change in the body, and conversely. While it is true that in the latter half of the seventeenth century Cartesians did espouse occasionalism, they were doing so not in *ad hoc* response to a perceived mind–body problem, but for independent, metaphysical reasons transcending this connection. (Indeed, the mind–body connection was held up by their opponents to show that finite things could be real causes.) Whatever the logic of their position, however, Cartesians such as Malebranche, LaForge, Cordemoy, and others did view the mind–body connection in these occasionalist terms.

The third view on this topic is due entirely to Leibniz. One way to understand this view is to note that he began with a conception of truth such that, for every true statement, the concept of the subject contained the concept of its predicate. This 'principle of sufficient reason', as he called it, negated interaction between substances; the reason why a billiard-ball moves at a given time is that its concept includes motion at that time, not because it was struck previously by another billiard-ball. The other billiard-ball, however, is conceptually programmed to move so as to strike it at the time it begins to move, and so, what we take to be causal interaction is in fact a pre-established harmony between parallel changing states. Strictly speaking, for Leibniz, bodies, including the human body, are not substances to which these principles apply directly, but rather phenomena somehow grounded in such substances, which he calls 'monads'. The mind, however, is such a monad. The upshot, then, is that minds and bodies are very different kinds of things (the one real, the other phenomenal), and what we take to be interaction between them is a pre-established harmony on the billiard-ball model. The mind is programmed to harmonize with certain changes in the body, and conversely.[2]

Bayle's treatment of these views—materialism, Cartesian dualism, and the pre-established harmony—is invaluable in the context of the present volume. First of all, Bayle's attitude was that of the good journal editor he was, ensuring that views got accurately represented. Such was certainly the case in his *Historical and Critical Dictionary*,[3] the principal source to be investigated here, but also in all his other work, too—

---

[2] For more on Gassendi, see O. R. Bloch, *La Philosophie de Gassendi: Nominalisme, matérialisme et métaphysique* (The Hague, 1971), 268; M. J. Osler, *Divine Will and the Mechanical Philosophy: Gassendi and Descartes on Contingency and Necessity in the Created World* (Cambridge, 1994), 67–70. For more on occasionalism, see T. M. Lennon, 'Occasionalism and the Cartesian Metaphysic of Motion', *Canadian Journal of Philosophy*, suppl. vol. 1 (1974), 29–40; repr. in V. C. Chappell (ed.), *Cartesian Philosophers* (vol. iii of *Essays in Early Modern Philosophy*) (New York, 1992), 71–92. For more on Leibniz, see B. Mates, *The Philosophy of Leibniz: Metaphysics and Language* (New York, 1986), chs. 5, 9, and 11.

[3] Pierre Bayle, *Dictionnaire historique et critique*, 1st edn. (Rotterdam, 1697); 4th edn. (Amsterdam, 1730). See the article 'Dicéarque'. Cross-referencing the various editions is easy enough by reference to articles and remarks. Particularly useful is the colourful Desmaizeaux translation of 1737.

to the point that it is often hard to distinguish Bayle's own views from those he is reporting.[4]

There is another dimension to the journalistic aspect of Bayle's work that makes him of particular interest to our collective undertaking. Not only does Bayle examine the views of his contemporaries, but often enough he also provides exhaustive historical accounts—sometimes genealogies, sometimes just anticipations—of those views. A good example, relevant to the mind–body question, is the issue whether non-human animals have souls.[5] Bayle is not content with reporting Descartes' suggestion that they do not, or those of his successors and their opponents. Nor is he content even with the question that he debated with du Rondel, Baillet, and Pardies: namely whether the concept of the beast-machine was invented by Descartes, the sixteenth-century Spanish physician Pereira, or by someone much earlier, such as one of the Stoics, or the Cynics, or even Aristotle.[6] Rather, he provides a catalogue of views, detailed with references and quotations, to show that practically all ancient philosophers, and many since them, took the souls of beasts to be rational.[7] This example will become important below.

I. MATERIALISM

Another example of Bayle's exhaustive approach is to be found in the *Historical and Critical Dictionary* article 'Dicaearchus', where the materialist views of this student of Aristotle may well have been intended as

[4] The problem raised by practically everyone from his own time to the present who has written about Bayle as to which of his texts express his 'real' views has come to be canonized as the 'Bayle enigma'. See e.g. Michael Heyd, 'A Disguised Atheist or a Sincere Christian? The Enigma of Pierre Bayle', *Bibliothèque d'humanisme et de renaissance*, 39 (1977), and Jean Pierre Jossua, *Pierre Bayle, ou l'obsession du mal* (Paris, 1977).

[5] The issue is relevant because, for Bayle, Cartesian mind–body dualism entailed the unwelcome consequence that animals are insentient automata. Baillet convinced Bayle that Descartes did not embrace this view, as seemed to be the case, only in order to save his dualism from objections, but that he held it as early as 1619 and no later than 1625, thus no later than twelve years before the *Discourse* and sixteen years before the *Meditations* (*Dictionary*, article 'Pereira', remark D). As will be seen below, however, for Bayle the logical connection remained in place.

[6] Ibid., remarks C, D, H. In the end, Bayle concluded that while the view is indeed first found only in Pereira, its first philosophical defence is to be found in Descartes.

[7] Ibid., remark E. He continues the catalogue in the article 'Rorarius', remark D, including medieval thinkers such as Maimonides and William of Paris, up to 'moderns' such as Valla, Montaigne, and Cureau de La Chambre. The catalogue is supplemented in remark K. See also the article 'Sennert', remarks D, E. It would be difficult to find a better place than Bayle to start research on the topic.

a surrogate for those of Bayle's contemporaries.[8] Bayle is not as precise as we might like in characterizing Dicaearchus's materialism. He variously attributes to him the views that the soul is the harmony of the four elements, that the soul is a virtue found in all living things, that the soul is not distinct from the body, and that the soul and the body are a 'single, simple being'.[9] Perhaps the reason for this lack of precision is that, from Bayle's own perspective, they all come to the same thing, because, as he puts it, 'what is not distinct from the body is essentially the body'. He uses this principle to draw the conclusion that feeling could never cease to belong to a body if a body could once feel. He probably gets his general claim, which we might call the distinctness principle, from his nominalism, which he invokes in many contexts throughout his work. Nominalism here is the view that only individuals are real or capable of independent existence, and in particular that properties are not real. On the assumption that distinctness is *real* distinctness—that is, assuming that what is distinct is capable of existing apart[10]—the drift of his thinking might be reconstructed as follows: only substances can exist apart from each other; properties cannot exist apart from the substance of which they are properties; properties are thus *really* not distinct from that substance; but what is really not distinct is necessarily connected—that is, essential. The distinctness principle may thus be expressed by saying that all properties, *a fortiori* those of a body, are essential to those substances they belong to. A property of a thing, as the Cartesians put it, just is that thing existing in a certain way—a *façon d'être*. If a property of a thing could cease to belong to a thing, then we *ipso facto* have a distinct thing. That is, all properties are essential.

There are two versions of this view. The stronger version is that the *numerical* identity of a thing requires the retention of all its properties. The weaker version is that the *qualitative* identity of a thing requires all its properties—that is, without all its properties, it would not be the same *kind* of thing. It is the weaker version that will become relevant below.

[8] Certainly for Locke, on whom Bayle produces a remark at the end of the article, and Spinoza, whose views are never far from Bayle's consciousness. The case of Hobbes is less straightforward. The issue of the mind–body connection is raised by Bayle obliquely in relation to the question of whether Hobbes was, as some claimed, afraid of ghosts and demons. His biographer Sorbière argued that his philosophy relieved him of such fears, and that Hobbes feared being alone only because of potential murderers. But even someone who believes that there are no substances distinct from matter can have such fears, according to Bayle, for an evil-doing material substance can cause in us visions of demons. See article 'Hobbes', remark N.

[9] 'Dicéarque', remark L, n. 53; remark C. Dicaearchus is, quite apart from Bayle's treatment of him, an elusive figure. See the sources cited above by Heinrich von Staden, n. 69.

[10] This is the scholastic notion that Descartes recognizes at *Principles*, I, 51.

The deep background to the distinctness principle and to Bayle's nominalism is his opposition to the Catholic doctrine of the Real Presence, which for him is the real difference between Rome and Geneva. Understood in terms of transubstantiation, this doctrine requires properties that are distinct and can exist apart, specifically the properties of bread and wine which become really distinct from the substance of which they are the properties. Now there is a connection between this issue and the mind–body issue. Ruth Whelan has convincingly shown that Bayle saw a close analogy between the Incarnation, the Eucharist— which parallels the Incarnation in so far as it involves the material presence of an immaterial body—and the human mind–body relation. All three involve a relation between an immaterial substance and a material substance. Bayle defended Cartesianism because it upset the Aristotelian doctrine of real properties on which the Catholic view of the Eucharist was based;[11] he was thus able to defend both Nestorius's heretical position on the Incarnation, which challenged the hypostatic union, and Calvin's view on the Eucharist, both of which emphasized the real difference of Christ from anything material. Bayle was not content with this result, however, and in the end argued that the relation in all three cases was incomprehensible.[12] Of the ultimate incomprehensibility of the mind–body connection for Bayle, more below.

More immediately, the distinctness principle is crucial to Bayle's refutation of the materialism of Dicaearchus. His argument might be expressed as follows:

(1) What is not distinct from a thing is essential to that thing.
(2) Matter is a kind of thing.
(3) What is not distinct from matter is essentially matter.
(4) Suppose that thought were not distinct from matter.
(5) Then thought would be essential to matter, and all material things would think.
(6) But this is shown by experience to be false: there are unthinking things.
(7) Therefore, thought is distinct from matter, and there must be non-material things which think.[13]

The ontology that most straightforwardly comports with the distinctness principle would seem to be phenomenalism, the thesis that a thing

---

[11] This is the thrust of Bayle's anthology, *Recueil de quelques pièces curieuses concernant la philosophie de Monsieur Descartes* (Amsterdam, 1684).

[12] Ruth Whelan, *The Anatomy of Superstition: A Study of the Historical Theory and Practice of Pierre Bayle* (Oxford, 1989), 35–7.

[13] I am very grateful to J. P. Wright, G. Matthews, F. Michael, and D. Conter for discussion with me of this argument.

is nothing more than its properties. On this view, shagginess is essential to the dog Melampus, because Melampus just is shagginess, brownness, four-leggedness, and the rest of his properties. This Berkeleian class-inclusion model of predication makes the distinctness principle fairly trivial, yielding an essentialism without essences, as it were. With respect to the mind–body relation, the drift is toward neutral monism, with minds and bodies distinguished only contextually in the way that some think Hume distinguished them. In response to an objection to his argument, Bayle in fact employs the count-noun model, and introduces a far from trivial notion of essence.[14]

The objection is that sensation might be a modification of matter occurring when, but only when, it is part of the organized machine that is a living body. Bayle regards this objection as 'absurd', because a 'modality' ceases only when replaced by a modality 'of the same sort'. A thing loses its shape or place, for instance, only by assuming another shape or place. The order of nature is such, he says, that being is never converted into non-being—there is no annihilation. Thus, whatever thinks always thinks. Here Bayle takes shape and thought—the essential properties that cannot be annihilated—as determinables; the determinates are individual shapes and thoughts, which do come into and pass out of existence.[15]

This line of argument not only supports his argument against materialism by rebutting the objection, it also generates another argument, which Bayle in fact does not give at this point. Consider how colour, or attunement, is a determinable, and specific colours, or pitches, are its determinates. If a thing has a single essence and that essence is determinable, then nothing is both a thinking thing and an extended thing; for determinates exclude other determinates, not only of the same, but of different determinables, as red excludes not just blue but a certain attunement. Nothing is both red and C-sharp. But with respect to all statements about essence, the question of how things are divided is begged, for intuitively we can say that what has a certain determinate colour can also have a certain determinate shape.[16]

[14] That minds and bodies should be *essentially* different is crucial to the most important version of the mind–body problem facing the Cartesians. See R. A. Watson, *The Downfall of Cartesianism* (The Hague, 1968).

[15] How to account for this behaviour of determinates, given Bayle's denial of annihilation? Bayle does not give an answer, but the historical background would be to construe the determinable as a substance and its determinates as properties only conceptually distinct from it. In this sense, only substances are real, while their properties are mere appearances. Determinates are not annihilated, then; they just disappear.

[16] Bayle later used something like this argument against Locke's hypothesis that matter might think (*Réponse aux questions d'un provincial*, in *Oeuvres diverses* (hereafter OD, with volume and page number) (The Hague, 1737), III, 942). Roughly, the idea is that an ontological kind can perform only one ontological job. See my 'Bayle, Locke

One of the most important roles Bayle played was to set out views that he might never have held with, none the less, very cogent arguments on their behalf. This journalistic aspect of Bayle's work, noted above, not only makes it difficult to discuss his own views, but has also raised for some the question of Bayle's sincerity. For on such topics as scepticism, atheism, and even Manicheanism, Bayle served as a source-book for later thinkers holding very different views from the ones he professed. Materialism, in particular, was a topic in which Bayle proved to be, in this sense, the 'Arsenal of the Enlightenment'. For he continues the above objection by saying that what Dicaearchus held about the human soul is what Descartes held about the animal soul. A dog differs from a stone, according to Descartes, only in the complexity of the arrangement of its parts. Thus Dicaearchus 'reduced man to the condition of a machine, whence it follows that the human race is not distinct from the body, but is only a construction, a mechanical disposition of several parts of matter'. Bayle's reply is that we can understand how the impenetrable extension of the parts of a watch can account for its behaviour, and in this an animal is like a watch. But we cannot explain how from the impenetrable parts of a body, its shape, or its motion, we can get a man's thoughts. The latter, as we might say, are emergent properties, and as such they are inexplicable. This may beg the question that thought cannot be explained mechanistically; but from Bayle's point of view, the materialist gratuitously invokes two essentially different kinds of material properties: shape and shape that thinks. For Bayle, it is absurd to maintain 'that there are two kinds of roundness, one that consists simply in the fact that the parts of the circumference of a body are equally distant from the centre, the other in that it in addition is an act by which the round body perceives that it exists and sees several bodies in its vicinity'.[17]

II. THE LEIBNIZIAN ALTERNATIVE

Another possibility, one that overcomes at least some of the obstacles raised thus far to materialism, is that all matter essentially thinks. Bayle thus considers this possibility both in the article 'Epicurus', remark F, where, following Augustine, he attributes the view to Democritus that all atoms are animate, and, at greater length, in the article 'Leucippus',

and the Metaphysics of Toleration', in M. A. Stewart (ed.), *Studies in Seventeenth-Century Philosophy* (Oxford, 1997), 181.

[17] 'Dicéarque', remark L. Again, the ontological principle of one kind, one job, would be violated.

remark E, where he is less certain about what Democritus held.[18] In particular, this view obviously answered the objections attributed to Plutarch and Galen, that no assemblage of atoms could be animate and conscious if its constituent atoms were inanimate and unconscious. This is the view, in other words, that thought cannot be an emergent property. Here Plutarch and Galen may be surrogates for Locke, who raised the same objection to materialism.[19]

Bayle presents the hypothesis that the soul consists of indivisible thinking atoms as a solution to the problem he has raised about deriving thought from unthinking matter. But he immediately introduces an objection to this new hypothesis. The objection is based on what we might call the 'synthetic unity of perception'. The fact is that we can perceive the whole of something, an object like a horse or a geographical area, as a whole, and not just as a series of parts or even an assemblage of them. But no ordinary physical thing could represent such a whole—a thinking globe, for example, would be such that at best its parts would map but a part of the world. Now, Bayle's argument here is very crude; for, after all, the individual parts (points, really) map nothing at all—it is the whole globe that maps the whole area. But the problem is a real one: how else but in a unitary mind could a multiplicity of objects be represented? The mapping relation between parts of the globe and parts of the area must be perceived by the mind, just as the different, perceived parts of a horse must be brought together by it.[20]

The feature of thinking atoms that may be thought to overcome these difficulties and ground the synthetic unity of perception is their indivisibility. But at least within the tradition of physicalist atomism, which is Bayle's context, the indivisibility of atoms does not preclude their having distinguishable physical parts; so the same difficulties in

---

[18] The issue gets some discussion in the article 'Démocrite', remark P, where Bayle likens Democritus's theory of perception, viz. that our images of things are emanations from the gods, to Malebranche's theory of the vision of all things in God. Given Democritus's panpsychism, Leibniz would have been a better comparison, but Bayle may not have understood Leibniz's view at this point.

[19] John Locke, *An Essay Concerning Human Understanding*, 4, 10, 10, ed. P. H. Nidditch (Oxford, 1975), 623–4. Beyond Locke, the views of a number of philosophers from Gassendi leading up to Hume are of relevance. The (irregular) progression is from inert, unconscious atoms to intrinsically active and, ultimately, conscious atoms.

[20] Later in this remark Bayle produces a defence, presumably of the physicalist position of a divisible soul, that a soul perceives the parts of a horse in such rapid succession that the perceptions of them blur into each other to form the impression of a single object—just as 'the soul believes it sees a circle of fire when a piece of burning wood is spun around'. His explanation is that an impression can last longer than the object's action on the soul; but this does not explain how we might see a fixed object such as a wall whose parts would act on the soul simultaneously.

representing multiplicities arise again. Only *non-physical* atoms will do, which is what Bayle wants anyhow, given his overriding concern with the immortality of the soul. These non-physical atoms are, of course, what Leibniz called 'monads', the concept of which is remarkably approximated by Bayle, despite his restriction of the discussion to a physicalist model.[21] The argument here deserves close attention.

As he typically does, Bayle pursues the issue in *sic et non* fashion, via objection and response, followed by rebuttals, further objections, etc. The objection, or question, that Bayle raises for materialism is the following: how is it that the whole soul, or sensitive being, which on the materialist hypothesis is supposedly composed of an infinity of parts, is able to feel a pain when only some few of these parts receive the direct blow of a stick? One response is that the sensation is communicated from these few parts to all the others. To this response Bayle offers a number of rebuttals, each of which, as it happens, illustrates an important feature of the Leibnizian monads. That is, features or consequences of physical atoms that prevent them from solving the problem at hand turn out to be welcome features or consequences of non-physical atoms or monads. For example, the sensation that is supposedly communicated from one part to another cannot be numerically the same, according to Bayle; otherwise there would be a violation of the maxim that 'accidents do not pass from one subject to another'. The maxim is another instance of the nominalism expressed in the distinctness principle. A body's accidents, such as its motion, are not really distinct from that body, hence are essentially that body, and cannot pass from it to another body. Here the maxim is invoked by Bayle to argue that individual substances such as atoms are supposed to be cannot communicate, that they are, as Leibniz would put it, windowless. Moreover, even if they could communicate, one atom would convey motion or sensation to another only to the extent that it lost its own motion or sensation. The upshot would be a dispersal of sensation beyond the threshold of sensibility. For Bayle, this shows that the soul cannot be made up of thinking material atoms. But the resulting *petites perceptions* play an important role in Leibniz's theory of perception. The sound of an individual drop of water striking the beach is imperceptible, but is none the less registered by a percipient who hears the whole wave. Finally, according to Bayle, there would be in a sentient being such as a starving dog an infinity of sentient beings

---

[21] Leibniz made these points in a text of 1695, 'A New System of the Nature and Communication of Substances and the Union of Body and Soul'. Atoms of *matter* do not yield real unities, which instead are had only by *metaphysical* points (G. W. Leibniz, *Philosophical Essays*, ed. and trans. R. Ariew and D. Garber (Indianapolis, 1989), 142). The way was perhaps shown to Leibniz by the arguments for atomism of the Cartesian Cordemoy. See Leibniz's 1686 paper, 'Primary Truths', in ibid. 34.

that feel hunger—a 'monstrous' view. But this is close to Leibniz's view that all monads perceive—indeed, perceive from their perspective—the rest of the world.[22]

There are differences between Bayle's hypothetical thinking atoms and Leibnizian monads; for example, Bayle suggests that every one of the infinite substances in a man who is reading not only reads but knows that it is reading—an apperceptive feature that Leibniz reserves for the chief monad. But the physicalist model serves Bayle so well that the question is why he did not embrace monadism. Indeed, he concludes the long remark E of 'Leucippus' with the observation that it is no more difficult to conceive of atoms as endowed with thought than as uncreated and endowed with a motor force. (Nor is this connection itself irrelevant, for Bayle notes that the power of self-motion is for such philosophers as Aristotle the basis of the principal properties of the soul.) Why, then, did Bayle not become a Leibnizian?

III. OCCASIONALISM

Elsewhere I have detailed the extensive debate between Bayle and Leibniz over the nature of the causal relation between minds and bodies.[23] Bayle defended the Cartesian doctrine of occasionalism against Leibniz's solution in terms of his doctrine of the pre-established harmony.[24] Bayle's individual arguments are not very cogent. Sometimes, as he had done in the arguments against Democritean thinking atoms, Bayle produces *reductio ad absurdum* arguments, the conclusion of which Leibniz would happily accept. For example, Bayle failed to see the full implications of Leibniz's doctrine of the pre-established harmony when he argued that the spontaneity of the substances composing the body would have to be constrained by that of surrounding bodies. Sometimes Bayle just failed to understand important principles at play in Leibniz's arguments. For example, the dog's being struck by

[22] Bayle's position is that 'each of us knows by experience that there is only one thing that makes that thing read, be hungry, feel pain, or joy, etc.'. This is Leibniz's view as well, compatible with a multiplicity of non-physical atoms. What Bayle does in effect is to give reasons why these atoms cannot be physical.

[23] Thomas M. Lennon, 'Mechanism as a Silly Mouse', in Steven Nadler (ed.), *Causation in Early Modern Philosophy* (University Park, Pa., 1993), 179–95.

[24] Both Bayle and Leibniz regarded occasionalism narrowly as an attempt to solve the problems of the influence of mind on body and body on mind, even though it had its origins in a much more general problem of causation. For an indication that they had this restricted view of occasionalism, see Bayle, *Réponse aux questions d'un provincial*, OD, III, 1064, and Leibniz, 'The Nature and Communication of Substances', in *Philosophical Essays*, 142–3.

a stick, although not irrelevant to the pain it feels, is not the sufficient reason for that pain as Bayle, commonsensically, thinks it is.

The speculation that I advanced is that Bayle's distaste for the pre-established harmony derived from an analogy that Leibniz's immaterial atoms shared with physical atoms: namely that their behaviour is *mechanical*.[25] The states of a monad are determined by its individual concept in a way that precludes dialogue, and hence any narratological account of human history. Most notably, the sort of negotiation that takes place between God and his people, where the responses of one party have no sense outside the context of the responses of the other, cannot be accounted for by the pre-established harmony, which has the parties, not negotiating, but reciting pre-written lines. This religious problem is a much more significant one for Bayle than the ones he actually invokes against Leibniz—for example, the a priori implausibility of Caesar's body spontaneously entering the Senate and producing 'the sounds we associate with his ambitious plans'.

The requirements of narratological explanation may also explain why it is occasionalism that Bayle defends against the Leibnizian account.[26] God as the only real cause acts by *creating* what serves as the occasional cause of his action. This *sui generis* relation between God and the world provides the vertical dimension of causation that even an infinite series of horizontal causes, mechanical or otherwise, can never supply. Moreover, the God of the occasionalists is immanent, a God in whom we live and move and have our being. He is present everywhere to his creation. The personal presence of God, however, does not upset his transcendence. God must be different from his creation in order to enter into a dialogue with his people.[27] He acts, not mechanically, but as a character in a story. The conceptions of God as both immanent and transcendent come together in Bayle's support for Arnauld's conception of Providence as involving *particular* volitions against Malebranche's more mechanistic conception in terms of a *general* volition.[28] God is apart from creation, but has a constantly renewed interest in it.

Quite apart from this speculation, Bayle defends occasionalism because all other views of causation pose a threat to religion. Now, in

---

[25] In a text of 1698, Leibniz actually refers to his monads as immaterial automata: 'Clarification of the difficulties which Mr. Bayle has found in the new system of the union of soul and body', in G. W. Leibniz, *Philosophical Letters and Papers*, ed. and trans. Leroy F. Loemker, 2nd edn. (Dordrecht, 1976), 492–7, at 496.

[26] Once again, the direct arguments that Bayle gives on behalf of the view seem insufficiently cogent to explain his adherence: Lennon, 'Mechanism as a Silly Mouse', 182–4.

[27] Hence Bayle's hostility everywhere to Spinozism. See E. Labrousse, *Pierre Bayle* (The Hague, 1964), ii. 198–204. Double aspect theories as a solution to the mind–body problem would thus be beyond the pale for him.

[28] Lennon, 'Mechanism as a Silly Mouse', 189–93.

his earliest, pedagogical works, Bayle adopted the *novantique* strategy of employing at least Aristotelian language to advance essentially neo-Aristotelian views. For example, he calls extended substance 'primary matter', and the motion, size, shape, and situation of a body its 'form'.[29] But later Bayle directly attacks the neo-Aristotelian view of substantial forms really distinct from matter. One very important reason for the attack, already noted above, is the use to which the view was put in expli-cating the Catholic doctrine of transubstantiation. Another reason emerges in the *Historical and Critical Dictionary*, where Bayle attacks the view as having very 'dangerous' consequences and as 'leading insen-sibly to atheism'. Here is how the argument goes. Aristotle, like most ancient philosophers, linked the soul to motion; on his view, the soul is a kind of prime mover. It is not just the human soul, but also the animal soul, and indeed every substantial form, that is a prime mover. A heavy body moves toward the centre of the universe, a light body away from it, and the heavens in their circles, without the need for a universal prime mover. An advantage of Cartesianism from Bayle's perspective is that it recognizes God as the sole motor force in the universe, without any division of it between him and his creatures.[30]

Bayle explicitly links this view of the soul as a prime mover with certain Eastern thinkers, with the Socinians, and with the atomists,[31] but he does not mention Leibniz. He might well have done so, because Leibniz, invoking even the language of substantial forms, placed himself in this expanded Aristotelian tradition by construing his monads as prime movers.

Later, Bayle took an even stronger position when Lady Masham, Damaris Cudworth, wrote to the *Bibliothèque choisie*, taking exception to Bayle's claim that her father's principles favoured atheism. Bayle replied that all views on causation except that of the Cartesian occa-sionalists favour atheism, since they all fail to restrict causation to the operation of a conscious cause.[32] This conception of a real cause, which is associated with Malebranche and especially with Geulincx, also weighs against intrinsically active atoms, certainly of the Democritean

[29] Bayle, *Systema*, OD, IV, 278, 287–9, and *passim*.

[30] Article '[Jacques] Zabarella', remark G. Recall my earlier suggestion that, in reac-tion to the mechanical relation of God with his creatures implied by Leibniz's pre-established harmony, Bayle supported occasionalism in order to secure a dialogical rela-tion. The question whether a view that makes God the sole real cause allows for dia-logue is too large to be treated here. I will only mention that, according to Bakhtin, Dostoevsky enters into a dialogue with the characters he creates. I expand on this theme in my *Reading Bayle* (Toronto, 1999).

[31] See also the article 'Spinoza', remark X.

[32] See Labrousse, *Pierre Bayle*, ii. 215 n. 114. See also my 'Mechanism', 193, for other texts in which Bayle restricts real causation to conscious operation.

material sort, but also against the Leibnizian immaterial monads, most of which are not conscious. Perhaps Bayle was inclined to follow Geulincx, in allowing finite minds as real causes, rather than his principal source, Malebranche, who had additional arguments to show that only the infinite mind could have real causal efficacy. As it happens, this difference is of limited interest, because Bayle came eventually to reject occasionalism and to entertain doubts even about Cartesian dualism.

IV. FROM CARTESIAN DUALISM TO FIDEISM

An indication of Bayle's most characteristic view on these issues can be had by returning to the doctrine that non-human animals have no soul. Recall that for Bayle the Cartesians quite properly argue that, given their mind–body dualism, animals must be automata. Not only is their reasoning valid, but their conclusion supports religion, on at least two counts. First, by preserving dualism, the doctrine of the bestial automaton preserves the argument for the immortality of the human soul based on the claim that it alone is immaterial and hence indivisible. This argument is repeated by Bayle at many places in his work. But there is another reason, set out in the article 'Rorarius', which is of particular interest because of Bayle's influence on subsequent discussion of the mind–body relation.[33] The doctrine that animals have no souls removes the objection to divine justice that animals, innocent of sin, which is the only justification for suffering, none the less suffer. (Pain or suffering in children, for example, is attributable to original sin, which does not apply to animals.) On the Cartesian view, of course, animals do not suffer, because they are not conscious.[34]

The Scholastic view that attributes a sensitive soul to animals is considered by Bayle to be particularly dangerous to religion. This view is that animals are sentient, but incapable of abstract thought, inference, or self-reflection, which are reserved for the rational souls of men. According to Bayle, however, these incapacities are attributable to differences in organs between animals and men, just as are the same differences between a child and a mature man. His view is that one has the

---

[33] Ordinarily, there is very little connection between the body and the remarks of the *Dictionary* articles, especially the philosophically interesting ones. The article 'Rorarius' is unusual in that the philosophical content of the remarks actually bears some illustrative relation to the body of the article. Rorarius was papal nuncio under Clement VII to the court of Ferdinand of Hungary. In conversation he once heard a 'learned man' say that Charles V was not the equal of the Ottos, or of Frederick Barbarossa. This opinion led him to conclude that animals are more reasonable than men, a view which he defended in a treatise published *c*.1547. Of Bayle's ten remarks, eight are very long discussions of various aspects of the bestial soul issue.   [34] Ibid., remark C.

full nature of a soul, in principle capable of all thought, or not at all. The Scholastics are therefore faced with the dilemma of either immortal animals, if they have this immaterial soul, or mortal men, if they do not.[35]

In setting out this dilemma, of course, Bayle appears to support the Cartesian view as a way of avoiding the dilemma. But so strongly does he express the dichotomy, that the way is shown to later thinkers, who embrace the latter horn in responding materialistically to mind–body issues. That way is paved by the next remark of the article 'Rorarius', where Bayle sets out the Scholastics' attempt to refute the Cartesians by detailing actions of animals that cannot be explained merely by mechanical principles. While he observes that they go too far, nevertheless Bayle makes it clear that the scholastics themselves attribute to a purely material form powers sophisticated enough to explain the actions of men.[36] A purely material account of the higher cognitive functions was, of course, the aim of many of Bayle's successors in the eighteenth century.

Although the Scholastics receive the heaviest blows, no view on the animal soul, not even the Cartesian, is in the end defensible, according to Bayle, who wistfully observes, 'it is too bad that Descartes's view is so difficult to maintain and so remote from likelihood, for it is otherwise very useful to religion'.[37] Nor should this outcome be surprising, says Bayle in the article 'Pereira'. 'Of all physical objects, none is more abstruse or embarrassing than the bestial soul. The extreme views on this topic are either absurd or dangerous, the mean that is sought between them is indefensible.'[38] In the article 'Rorarius' he continues this thought by saying that God distributes knowledge in such a way that no sect is ever able definitively to overcome its opponents; the tide washes back and forth rather like the battle between the Greeks and Trojans before the fall of Troy.[39] The objections to Cartesianism that he relates are obvious ones based on common sense, but also on theory. For example, he thinks that the Jesuit Gabriel Daniel in his *Voyage du monde de Descartes* (1690) raised objections that destroy the Cartesian view. One is that, according to the Cartesians, the omnipotent deity can create a triangle without three angles, or make two and two not equal four; he should, therefore, be able to make a soul capable only of sensation (or at least only having sensations as a matter of fact), but without rational capacities.[40]

---

[35] Ibid., remark E.   [36] Ibid., remark F.   [37] Ibid.

[38] Article 'Pereira'. 'Object' must be used in the sense of *object of study*: i.e. in the sense, more or less, of Descartes' *esse objectivum*.   [39] 'Rorarius', remark G.

[40] Ibid. Daniel's own view, the mean referred to in the Pereira article, fares no better than any other. His hypothesis of a being intermediary between Cartesian thought and extension fails to satisfy the constraints on any acceptable view of the bestial soul: (1) being without extension, it would not be divisible, hence not mortal; (2) no specific

What is to be made of this remarkable turn-about, especially in view of Bayle's endorsement of the validity of the Cartesians' reasoning? There are two observations to be made. First, the validity of the Cartesians' argument stands for Bayle. Given their dualism, they must hold that animals are automata. But, given the indefensibility of the bestial automaton, dualism is thereby undermined. In the article 'Jupiter', Bayle confesses that 'nothing seems to me founded on clearer or more distinct ideas than the immateriality of everything that thinks'.[41] Yet he observes that there are intelligent, Christian philosophers who think that extension is capable of thought. These cases, presumably Locke's in particular, lead Bayle to raise a pair of questions. (Despite appearances, they are not the same question, and they are not rhetorical questions.) 'Can the clarity of ideas be trusted thereafter?' The answer for the sceptic Bayle is in the negative, with the result that we are ultimately left in the dark about dualism and all other such questions. 'Don't these philosophers see that on such a foundation the ancient pagans erred to the point of saying that all intelligent substances had a beginning (i.e. there is no God, properly speaking), and that only matter is eternal?' This question indicates the status that Bayle assigns to the Cartesians' view, which is the second observation to be made about his endorsement of their reasoning.

Dualism is of interest to Bayle because of its support for immortality. But in the article 'Charron', Bayle argues that Charron is not to be criticized for admitting that philosophical arguments fail to establish the immortality of the soul, which is based instead on revelation. For, on the one hand, Aristotle's principles make all souls out to be material, hence mortal, and on the other, the new philosophy—that is, Cartesianism—leads to one of two 'abysses', either that the bestial soul is immortal, or that animals are automata. In the article 'Pomponace',[42] Bayle defends Jurieu's fideism against Elie Saurin's rationalist attempts to prove the immortality of the soul. According to Jurieu, we have no clear idea on the issues—that is, no proofs. Saurin thinks that the soul is an individual, hence indivisible, hence immortal substance. But, asks Bayle, how do we know that matter might not think? Moreover, even clarity is useless, since there is no difference as far as we are concerned between true and apparent clarity, as Gassendi had insisted. In fact, Arnauld is quoted by Bayle to show that, with respect to this very issue, Gassendi's objections show that what Descartes took to be clear proofs are anything but clear; for in Naples, according to Arnauld, some people were

difference would be established between men and animals if the intermediary entity were capable of all thought; (3) sensation by itself cannot account for the 'remarkable industry of bees, dogs, monkeys and elephants'.

[41] 'Jupiter', remark G.   [42] 'Charron', remarks F, G.

led by Gassendi's arguments to embrace Epicurus's view on the mortality of the soul.[43]

In the article '[Nicolas] Perrot', Bayle argues the general case that philosophical arguments are, at best, somewhat of a support for doctrines which are accepted on entirely independent grounds.[44] 'Belief based on natural light must be considered in a Christian like eloquence in a philosopher, or stylistics in histories, or beauty in an athlete. They are things the privation of which is no great ill, although it is no disadvantage to possess them.'[45] Specifically with respect to immortality, the efforts of philosophical reason are not only inefficacious, but irrelevant.

Must not a Christian, if he wishes to act as a Christian, believe in the immortality of the soul because God promises us eternal happiness? If he believes in the immortality of the soul for philosophical reasons, he will not be performing an act of faith; and yet this is what he must do if he is to fulfill the duties of religion and be pleasing to God.

These are Perrot's views as well as Locke's, as expressed in the *Third Reply to Stillingfleet*, which Bayle here approvingly quotes in Leclerc's excerpt.

V. SOME CONCLUDING RUMINATIONS

It may well be that the mind–body connection has received the attention it has only because it has been assumed that the mind is in some sense the person or self. Thus, in the most obvious case of Cartesian dualism, a mind that is separable from the body is of interest to me only if it is I who survive that separation. If this rumination is at all plausible, then Locke's raising of the issue of personal identity, and the terms in which he discusses it, may have great significance for the mind–body problem, especially from Bayle's perspective.

Against the widely held doctrine that identity of person consists in identity of substance, Locke argues that personal identity is a matter of unity of consciousness.[46] This conception of personal identity is of interest here for at least two reasons. First, it invites us to regard the person as a construct, not as a given; it tends to obviate reification, dualism, and ontology generally. Such a conception should sit well with Bayle's belief

---

[43] See also the article 'Zabarella', remark F, where Bayle carefully distinguishes, on Zabarella's behalf, between holding that the soul is immortal and holding that its immortality can be defended. No worries for the Protestant Bayle of the sort that Emily Michael has detailed above in relationship to the Fifth Lateran Council.

[44] Hence his support for Cartesian dualism, which if true, he thinks, upsets the Catholic doctrine of transubstantiation.   [45] 'Perrot', remark L.

[46] Locke, *Essay Concerning Human Understanding*, 2, 27.

in the bearer of immortality that is accepted independently of philosophical argument. Second, Locke characterizes the person in forensic terms, as the object of reward and punishment. Indeed, he might have gone further and characterized it as the bearer of the rights and responsibilities that are so crucial to his theorizing elsewhere. One might well ruminate on the significance for the mind–body problem of adopting a legal framework in which the relevant relation is that of possession: I *have* a body and I *have* a mind. Of more immediate relevance is the suitability of this framework to the sort of narrative explanation indicated above as so important to Bayle. In addition, a narratological approach invests much of what else Locke says about personal identity with more interest. For example, to say that the same person is the same consciousness seems hopelessly psychologistic (I am what seems to be me when I look into myself). But perhaps we can think of identifying persons as we do characters in a novel; to take Locke's own examples, what would it be like to have been the same person as Nestor at the siege of Troy, or to have been the same person as someone who witnessed the great flood?

There is an inkling in the *Historical and Critical Dictionary* that Bayle was prepared to draw Locke's distinction between substance and self. In the article 'Leucippus', he says that the hypothesis of thinking atoms joins thought to an indivisible *subject*.[47] The suggestion is that, distinct from a substantial self, is a logical or perhaps moral self. But handicapped by his lack of English and perhaps by the late appearance of the chapter on identity, Bayle seems not to have known of Locke's views; so he did not explore the actual path opened up by Locke. His own, independent account is disappointing.

Bayle effectively raises the issue of identity in the article on Lucretius, where he criticizes Lucretius's efforts to allay fears about death.[48] Lucretius's view is that sensation ceases with the dissolution of the body, thus with death, but that even if sensation continued in the dissolved parts, we individually have no ground for concern. His argument, as reported by Bayle, is based on a conception of identity which in fact is very much like Locke's conception of the identity of a man. Each of us is a compound of body and soul, and what concerns us does so only in so far as each of us is this compound. The soul separated from the body of a man—for example, Scipio—is not a man, and thus any pain it felt would not be felt by Scipio. Moreover, even if at some point the same body should be reconstituted by the exact same atoms and be reunited to the soul of the former man, the resulting organism would be of no

[47] 'Leucippus', remark E.   [48] 'Lucretius', remark Q.

interest to him because of 'the interruption of life'. In Lockean terms, it would not be the same organic unity.

Bayle's response is to offer an analogy that appeals to a more primitive conception of identity. If a watch which we assume to be capable of perception were dismantled, with its perception continuing, the watch should be concerned about these future perceptions, not as a watch, but as a percipient *substance*. Bayle thus appeals to precisely the Cartesian dualism that he elsewhere renounces as a philosophical dead-end. One would have hoped for something of greater interest from Bayle, especially in this context, where the ultimate issue is immortality. Instead, immortality is given a very literal reading: transition from this life to the next seems to be like the transition from one room to another. He concludes his long remark with the observation that the only way to calm fears of an afterlife is the promise of the happiness of heaven (a state which in these terms is not a part of our consciousness), or the assumption of a total extinction of perception. Bayle accepts the former, of course, but on non-philosophical grounds as an act of faith. The best-informed witness to the late seventeenth-century dialectics of mind and body thus ends by concluding that none of the theories proposed is philosophically acceptable.

10

Stahl, Leibniz, and the Territories of Soul and Body

FRANÇOIS DUCHESNEAU

As a medical theorist, Georg Ernst Stahl (1659–1734) is known for the particular kind of anti-mechanist theory of physiology and pathology he proposed, animism. In a celebrated controversy, Gottfried Wilhelm Leibniz (1646–1716) attacked the main theses developed in Stahl's *Theoria medica vera* of 1708;[1] shortly after the work's appearance, Leibniz drafted *Animadversiones in G. E. Stahlii Theoriam medicam veram*, which was forwarded to Stahl through the intermediary Karl Hildebrandt von Canstein in July 1709.[2] To the thirty-one *Dubia* of Leibniz, Stahl replied with an identical number of *Enodationes*, accompanied by a summary of the points of discussion (*Conspectus*). A second round succeeded with the exchange of thirty-one *Exceptiones* by Leibniz, followed by as many *Replicationes* by Stahl. After Leibniz's death, Stahl published the whole exchange in a volume entitled *Negotium otiosum* (1720).[3] The controversy was in part motivated by what Leibniz refers to as metaphysical 'paradoxes' about the nature and destiny of the human soul that follow from Stahl's doctrine. Leibniz is

---

[1] G. E. Stahl, *Theoria medica vera, physiologiam et pathologiam, tanquam doctrinae medicae partes vere contemplativas, e naturae et artis veris fundamentis . . . sistens* (Halle, 1708). My references are to the 2nd edn. (Halle, 1737) (hereafter *Theoria*). Where the translation is not too inaccurate, I refer also to *Oeuvres médico-philosophiques et pratiques*, trans. T. Blondin, vols. II, III, IV, and VI (Paris, 1859–64) (hereafter *Oeuvres*).

[2] Cf. Leibniz's note in the manuscript *LH* III, 1, 5b, fo. 1: 'Fortgeschikt an Herrn von Canstein 29 Jul. 1709', in *Die Leibniz-Handschriften*, ed. E. Bodemann (Hildesheim, 1966), 43.

[3] G. E. Stahl, *Negotium otiosum, seu Σκιαμαχία, adversus positiones aliquas fundamentales Theoriae medicae verae a viro quodam celeberrimo intentata* (Halle, 1720). For an analytical summary of the controversy, cf. L. J. Rather and J. B. Frerichs, 'The Leibniz–Stahl Controversy—I. Leibniz's Opening Objections to the *Theoria medica vera*', *Clio Medica*, 3 (1968), 21–40 (hereafter Rather); 'The Leibniz–Stahl Controversy—II. Stahl's Survey of the Principal Points of Doubt', *Clio Medica*, 5 (1970), 53–67; P. Hoffmann, 'La controverse entre Leibniz et Stahl sur la nature de l'âme', *Studies on Voltaire and the Eighteenth Century*, 199 (1981), 237–49.

particularly concerned that natural theology will be undermined by a conception of the soul that makes it divisible and mortal, within a system of nature governed by quasi-miraculous determinations.[4] However, the core of the polemic is methodological and epistemological: how the body–soul relationship is to be analysed, and what are the most appropriate theoretical models in physiology and medicine. Leibniz's criticism is directed primarily against Stahl's conception of organism—more precisely, against the organismic connection he assumes to exist between the soul and body in actual living beings. In opposition to Stahl's theory, Leibniz proposes an intricate system of physiological mechanisms capable of explaining the laws of organic life according to the then current axiom, *omnia fieri mechanice in natura*. I shall examine in turn the organismic geography of the body–soul relationship in Stahl, and then Leibniz's criticism: in this way I hope to work out in detail the different concepts of organism represented in the two men's theories.

I. THE THEORY OF GEORG ERNST STAHL

Stahl portrays the organism as a whole as a heterogeneous aggregate made up of many homogeneous organic aggregates corresponding to the structures in which specific functions are exercised. The integration of these diverse functions is carried out by a governing agent capable of assuring the creation and maintenance of the heterogeneous aggregate by a dynamic co-ordination of its various homogeneous instruments.

In developing this theory, Stahl establishes a radical distinction between organism and mechanism, making it the subject of one of the treatises leading up to the *Theoria medica vera*, the *Disquisitio de mechanismi et organismi diversitate* (1706). By mechanism, Stahl understands a kind of physical reality which is completely explicable by geometrical and mechanical principles describing a moving force acting without purpose, even in those cases where the force is immanent and acts autonomously.[5] A mechanism is a more or less complex structure capable of being moved as if by an external force. The components of such a mechanism are incapable of spontaneously adjusting themselves in order to produce an integrated harmonious activity of the whole. Stahl rejects any move to endow such mechanical structures with tendencies or functional dispositions suggestive of immanent dynamic purposes: specific appetites, attractions, sympathies, etc.[6]

---

[4] Leibniz expresses his metaphysical concerns in the undated draft of a letter to Canstein commenting on Stahl's first set of replies (*Enodationes*). This manuscript is to be found in *Lbr* 142 at the Leibniz-Archiv in Hannover.

[5] Cf. *Disquisitio*, §29, in *Theoria*, 12–13; *Oeuvres*, II, 197.

[6] Cf. *Disquisitio*, §30, in *Theoria*, 13; *Oeuvres*, II, 197–8.

By contrast, Stahl regards a true organism as the site of an autonomous instrumental relationship; that is, the characteristic functions of the organism reflect the operation of an efficient cause which is acting in and by means of the body in such a way as to accomplish its own purposes. In an *organism*, this efficient cause operates rationally, using the body as an instrument.[7] Stahl raises questions about artificial machines and the theory of the living automaton. He refers in particular to the metaphor of the clock. If this artificially constructed mechanism adequately fulfils its purpose of marking time with the required accuracy, it is truly an organ or an instrument: in this case its directed action represents exactly the conscious intention that prevailed over its construction. If, on the other hand, some failure of fabrication or operation prevents it from fulfilling its ultimate purpose as instrument, it falls back into the category of simple mechanism: the movements that are taking place in it fulfil the laws of external necessity, but not the teleological requirement of possessing the power of acting through an efficient cause adequate for the accomplishment of the predetermined end.[8] Beyond the solid structures of the biological 'clock', there must also be a rational power which integrates the innumerable internal micro-operations to establish a harmony between them. From this point of view, the organism is not an instrument under the power of an external efficient causality; it cannot be reduced to a mechanism animated by some sort of purpose from the outside; it cannot be conceived of as *anatome animata*. The organism must retain the power of engendering its own organization by means of subtle and complex movements which take place in the heterogeneous aggregate—that is, at the heart of a chemical automaton whose structure is both unstable and complex. The treatise *De vera diversitate corporis mixti et vivi* (1707), another precursor to *Theoria medica vera*, aims to establish in precisely this way that the living organism, in particular the human being, is, as a complex aggregate, constantly subject to forces of corruption, but that an opposing motor disposition never ceases to act in a continual and suitable manner, at least in the normal state, when free of disturbances connected with disease.[9] It is the recognition of this formal and instrumental reason, resisting corruption and acting as efficient cause of the integrated physiological processes, that leads Stahl to animism. It is at just this juncture in his account that Stahl introduces a soul with these specific characteristics, and grants it hegemony over the vast territory of physiological phenomena.

The ontological status of the soul hardly interests Stahl, who is quite

---

[7] Cf. *Disquisitio*, §36, in *Theoria*, 14: 'Talem instrumentalis rationis tanquam supremo loco exquisitam indolem vere κυρίως Organismum appellandum esse nemo dubitaverit' (*Oeuvres*, II, 261–7).　　[8] Cf. *Disquisitio*, §41, in *Theoria*, 17; *Oeuvres*, II, 205–6.

[9] Cf. esp. *De vera diversitate*, §10, in *Theoria*, 70–3; *Oeuvres*, II, 261–7.

willing to abandon metaphysical conceptions: in his eyes, these represent mere abstractions bereft of any foundation in physical reality, the
object of experience. In general, he is content to treat the soul as a
modern analogue to the nature (*physis*) of antiquity: the soul is an
active, immaterial substance, efficient and final cause of the vital and
organic motions, as well as the conscious affections of the human
subject. Stahl also emphasizes several times that the soul does not exist
except in and for the body, which is its true instrument in the strict sense
in which he understands a complex structure adapted and adaptable to
its functions. For example:

> [T]he life of man or of the *human soul* consists not simply and *generally* in
> *action*, but more particularly in action exercised and carried out *in a body*, *by
> means of* a body, *on* and *affecting* bodily activities, and even on the soul's *own
> body* itself. This is all we are able to conceive clearly and truly with regard to
> the soul, as a simple, physical notion.[10]

In my monograph *La Physiologie des Lumières*,[11] I argue, on the one
hand, that animism must be taken as the necessary consequence of
Stahl's theory of organ instrumentalism, and, on the other, that he
attempts to avoid *sui generis* vital principles of an intermediate kind,
such as the *archaeus* of van Helmont, specific attractions, or even the
animal spirits of the physiologists, which could elicit phenomena not
reducible to the strict causal relationships of instrumentalism.[12] Because
he adheres to a form of corpuscular, teleological mechanism, Stahl must
retain an immaterial psychic entity as the agent of the intentionality of
organic processes. He rejects Cartesianism, which makes an epistemological and methodological distinction between the bodily elements and
the psychological functions.[13] Stahl bases his integrated concept of the
relationship of soul and body on a series of arguments: thought can only
exercise its action freely and effectively within the limits of the imaginative representation of the geometrical and mechanical properties of
bodies; the fact that the soul can intervene in physiological processes
implies that it knows their function as well as the complex structures of
the body itself; the system of the organic constitution, being highly susceptible to corruption, requires recourse to a principle of life of the spiritual type.[14] These arguments lead Stahl to conceive of the soul as a
non-material formal cause of vital movements of the organism—that is,

---

[10] *De vera diversitate*, §51, in *Theoria*, 88; *Oeuvres*, II, 298.
[11] Cf. F. Duchesneau, *La Physiologie des Lumières: Empirisme, modèles et théories*
(The Hague, 1982), 1–31.
[12] Cf. *De vera diversitate*, §62, in *Theoria*, 92; *Oeuvres*, II, 307.
[13] Cf. *Disquisitio*, §42, in *Theoria*, 21.
[14] Cf. *Disquisitio*, §68, in *Theoria*, 28–9; *Oeuvres*, II, 224–5.

of the organismic structure in action. But it is not simply a being of reason, symbolizing the organic phenomena and referring back to some truly inaccessible metaphysical entity. The purpose of Stahl's analysis is, rather, to explain the soul's governance of corporeal movements. For effects that are concrete and empirically assignable, an efficient cause as well as a formal cause is necessary.

For Stahl, vital motions cannot be reduced to purely material phenomena—that is, to the properties of bodies understood solely according to geometrical and mechanical categories. These motions must be considered as immaterial in their very nature. Although they take place in and for the body, they actually possess properties that are incorporeal, such as persistence through time, a degree of energy, and a harmony relating the structure of the organ to the set purpose of the process.

In the same way that an effect always testifies to the nature of its particular cause, similarly an action, in so far as it is an immaterial thing, testifies to the nature of its *cause*, which is of its own nature [i.e. *immaterial*].[15]

The incorporeal properties of motion lead back to what may be defined as 'rational intentions'. Stahl's project consists in rationalizing and intellectualizing the formal cause of vital motions according to a psychological analogy. He employs as a model of the relationship of organ instrumentalism the one that the human soul entertains with various organic states. Thus he attributes the phenomenon of birth defects to the imagination of the mother, who impresses various traumatic or teratologic characteristics on the structures of the foetus. More generally, he examines in detail cases where affective states—emotions and passions—alter physiological processes, especially blood flow and secretory functions. He also examines phenomena of sensation and the relationships which exist between states of representational perception and the sensory apparatus. But, ultimately, he explains organic functions by reference to rational intentions. His main principle is that

the soul has a particular knowledge of the organs that belong to it, and ... by this means it is aware of the proportionate relationship they have with various purposes; ... the soul also knows fully the proportion and the aptitude of these organs to be subject to an action, which, to be sure, may be singularly and positively modified according to the arbitrary intentions of the soul itself.[16]

Stahl holds that knowledge of organic functions is accompanied by a kind of volition like that which is observed reflectively in voluntary motions. But he also points out that functional motions are often

---

[15] *Disquisitio*, §86, in *Theoria*, 36.
[16] *Disquisitio*, §90, in *Theoria*, 38; *Oeuvres*, II, 243.

interfered with by emotions, and that such a pathology of the will provides an explanation for dysfunctional organic changes.[17]

This whole analogical construct might be invalidated by the objection that 'the soul *has no consciousness* whatsoever of its own co-operation and involvement in [most of] these cases',[18] and that it cannot exert the least control over the infinitely detailed series of vital actions which lie completely outside conscious perception. Stahl's response consists in drawing a strategic distinction between intellectual function that is subject to the process of sensible perception and representational imagination and intellectual function that is spontaneous and without representation, a kind of rational instinct. The part of the intellectual process that is accompanied by consciousness is determined by what may be represented—that is, by the empirical limits of sensibility and imagination. As rational instinct, intellectual function without representation exercises a blind mental control, which is nevertheless subject to the particular modalities of the soul–body relationship. This explains the fact that while, on the whole, this intellectual function adequately maintains the conditions of life and health in a non-conscious and non-reflective way, it is by no means infallible, and its occasional deficiencies permit disease and death. Thus there is a double form of organic knowledge in one and the same dynamic substrate, which shares its activity between instinctive reason on the one hand and representational consciousness on the other. This opposition of psychic functions is, according to Stahl, 'between reason and reasoning, between λόγος and λογισμός, between simple intelligence and a collective idea of a multitude of details conceived in some manner, between a simple notion and judgement or reflexion, whether this be distinct or even confused'.[19] Among the functions of the soul assignable to the *logos* and analysed at great length in *Theoria medica vera*, I might point out the central role assigned to nutrition, to the circulation of the blood, to secretion and excretion (assimilation/disassimilation), to reproduction attached to a specific appetite,[20] and to regeneration within the limits prescribed for the particular kind

---

[17] On this subject, cf. P. Hoffmann, 'L'âme et les passions dans la philosophie médicale de Georg-Ernst Stahl', *Dix-huitième siècle*, 23 (1991), 31–43.

[18] *Disquisitio*, §90, in *Theoria*, 38; *Oeuvres*, II, 243–4.

[19] *Disquisitio*, §90, in *Theoria*, 38; *Oeuvres*, II, 245.

[20] On the notion of appetite, cf. *Disquisitio*, §83, in *Theoria*, 35: 'accedit libera illa activitas, quam anima habet, non solum in organa sensuum secundum suam voluntatem instruenda, sed etiam in praecipua organa vitalia, imo totos complexus actionum vitalium, per ita dicta *animi pathemata*. Quibus rebus colophonis loco accedunt appetituum, uti vulgo vocamus, tam jucunditatis quam adversitatis arbitrorum, si penitius aestimentur, non obscurae relationes atque proportiones, ad melius atque commodius conservandum, defendendum, fovendum corpus, et nocumenta ab ipso arcendum inservientes, et ultimo sui effectu etiam ad hoc habiles; aut ultimo sui effectu ad speciei conservationem tendentes, vel etiam speciali convenientia typi, structurae atque motuum, similitudinem inquam corporis atque morum nitentes.'

of organic structure concerned. To the *logismos* are attributed specifically the voluntary movements, sensory activity, and affective sensibility, imagination, and thought.

In these circumstances, the soul, in combining the functions attributed respectively to the *logos* and the *logismos*, may seem to integrate a causal determining power which comprises all the functions included among the activities of a living organism. And thus it is even possible to go so far as to say that Stahl is proposing a 'holistic' conception of the organism.[21] If one is willing to call a physiological doctrine promulgated at the beginning of the Enlightenment 'holistic', it seems that Stahl is attaching to a plurality of psychological and psycho-physiological properties the various functions of the living being. But, in fact, the analytical distinction between the *logos* and the *logismos* suggests that, far from possessing an actual principle of determination which is global and integrated, the organism is endowed with a precarious functional unity: it is the function of a plurality of acts of the soul, whose substantial foundation we cannot grasp once we go beyond the range of the psychosomatic phenomena.

II. LEIBNIZ'S THEORY

Leibniz's criticism of Stahl's theoretical and methodological positions constitutes an important testimony to the possibility of accounting for organic life in terms of a reformed mechanistic theory. The result is a new conception of the organism and of the soul–body relationship, representing a view apparently antinomic to the one Stahl offers.

Leibniz's theory of the organism did not originate with his critical reading of *Theoria medica vera*. In fact, a fragment edited by Louis Couturat, clearly datable to the beginning of the eighteenth century,[22] gives a full account of the principal theses of Leibniz's theory, in which the principle of sufficient reason is conceived as the foundation of possible models for explaining bodily phenomena. No reference to occult faculties, to sympathies and antipathies, to *archaei*, to operative ideas, to a plastic force, to souls, or to other incorporeal entities is justifiable, since such concepts fail to provide any determinable connection with the phenomena to be explained. The principle of sufficient reason compels us to explain bodily phenomena step by step—that is, by links that are continuous and gradual. Such an explanation rests on the intelligible

---

[21] Cf. e.g. J. Geyer-Kordesch, 'Georg Ernst Stahl's Radical Pietist Medicine and its Influence on the German Enlightenment', in A. Cunningham and R. French (eds.), *The Medical Enlightenment of the Eighteenth Century* (Cambridge, 1990), 67–87, esp. 68–9.

[22] Cf. G. W. Leibniz, *Opuscules et fragments inédits*, ed. L. Couturat (Hildesheim, 1988) (hereafter C), 11–16.

qualities of bodies—size, shape, and motion—except that we need to
presuppose underlying forces as the cause of such geometrical and
mechanical properties. Leibniz connects his methodology with the
axiom *omnia in corporibus fieri mechanice*. At the same time, however,
everything within souls can be explained *vitaliter* by intelligible qualities of the psychic order—that is, perceptions and appetitions. The phenomena belonging to the 'animated body' which we observe in the
biological sphere reveal a double jurisdiction from the epistemological
and methodological points of view: their analysis must be conceived in
terms of the idea of a governing harmony between vitality and mechanism.[23] Thus, what takes place mechanically in the body is the object
of a vital representation in the soul; what is conceived in the soul as
representation requires its analogue in a mechanical process of the
body. By virtue of the relationship of fixed expression, the affections of
the soul can serve to inform us about bodily processes, and vice versa.
In fact, the correspondence goes far beyond the strict field of distinct
perceptions and conscious appetitions that seem to govern voluntary
movements. As organic phenomena correspond to vital phenomena, so
final causes double the link of the efficient causes, and make it possible
in certain cases to anticipate physical explanations. Leibniz's examples
have to do with the laws of dioptrics and catoptrics, and with the
anatomicophysiological analysis of the uses of the parts.

One important point of Leibniz's theory concerns the substantial
status of the animated body. He distinguishes first what is substantial
from what is accidental; and in the category of the substantial he distinguishes again between what is substance and what is substantiated
(*substantiatum*): this latter concept refers to any aggregate of substances,
and is the status of each phenomenal body as such. Among substances
must be counted simple substances and compound substances: animals
are of this second kind, since they consist of a soul and an organic body.
Every organic body is, as such, an aggregate of more elementary living
components; correlatively, it must be noted that a simple substance is
always endowed with a certain organic body.

Just as a simple substance which comprises an infinite variety of representations can concentrate distinctly on a determined part of its phe-
nomenological horizon, so too the complex of soul and organic body
that permanently constitutes the animal can know successive phases of
development and envelopment: seminal organism, growth and decay,
return as a subtle organism following death. As the nature of the animal
is the result of the infinite artifice of God, there is an organic structure
in its internal parts as far back as the analytical regression can be fol-

[23] Cf. G. W. Leibniz, §3, C, 12.

lowed. By contrast with mechanisms constructed by humans, organisms are mechanisms so subtly integrated that they are self-sufficient and develop their states following an infinite series of functional processes: 'And the organism of living beings is nothing but a more divine mechanism advanced to an infinite degree in its subtlety.'[24] Since the animal is a corporeal substance composed of a soul and an organic body, the latter must itself be conceived as an aggregate of more elementary living things, which are unspecifiable. The soul of the composite substance corresponds to a dominant monad, the organic body to a machine of nature as opposed to some machine made by humans: 'the animal [is this] corporeal substance that the monad, exercising its power over the machine, makes one'.[25] The character of this natural machine is always to be an 'organism':

I hold not only that these souls or entelechies all have a manner of organic body with them in proportion to their perceptions, but even that [they] will always have it and have always had it as long as they have existed: so that not only the soul, but even the animal itself (or that which is analogous to the soul and animal, to avoid arguing over names) remains, and so generation and death can be nothing but developments and envelopments of which nature shows us visibly certain examples, according to her custom, to help us divine what she is hiding. And consequently neither iron nor fire, nor all the other violent forces of nature, no matter what destruction they commit in the body of an animal, would be able to prevent the soul from retaining a certain organic body (in so far as the *organism*, that is to say the order and the construction, is something essential to the material produced and arranged by the Sovereign Wisdom), the production always retaining the traces of its author.[26]

Leibniz begins his controversy with Stahl in his *Animadversiones circa assertiones aliquas Theoriae medicae verae* (1707) with a brief account of the principal theses underlying his theory of the organism. The central claim is that there are two independent series which act in parallel:

In the organic body of the living being, where the soul resides as a proper ruler, nothing that is contrary to the laws of the body takes place, even though every source of action is in the soul, and in turn nothing arises in the soul except through her own laws even though the source of her affections arises from matter. Therefore when the soul wills something with success the machine is inclined and ready to do this spontaneously out of its own natural motions; and on the other hand, when the soul perceives changes in the body she draws new

---

[24] Ibid., §13, C, 16: 'Et nihil aliud organismus viventium est quam divinior mechanismus in infinitum subtilitate procedens.'

[25] Letter to De Volder, 20 June 1703, in G. W. Leibniz, *Die philosophischen Schriften*, ed. C. I. Gerhardt (Hildesheim, 1965) (hereafter GP), II, 252: 'Animal seu substantiam corpoream, quam Unam facit Monas dominans in Machinam.'

[26] Letter to Lady Masham, beginning of May 1704: GP, III, 340.

perceptions from her own series of earlier (but confused) perceptions rather than from the fact that the body is disturbing the laws of the soul.[27]

This specific relationship between the soul and the organic body that is consubstantial with it consists in the fact that the soul represents the causal sequences of the particular organic functions of the parts and micro-parts. Similarly, the successive states and motions of the body itself and its integral parts translate the formal and teleological requirements of an active and integrating principle underlying the animated machine. To support this representative system of the organic structure, Leibniz extends analogically our reflective experience of the integration of soul and body. He postulates the existence of unconscious modalities of the perceptive-appetitive apparatus which symbolize purposes corresponding to most organic actions. Volitions and conscious perceptions themselves signify the way in which organic dispositions produce functionally ordered sequences of motions in the sensory-motor apparatus.

What becomes of the epistemological division between the territories of the soul and the body on Leibniz's theory? Though he postulates a parallelism and pre-established harmony between the formal and material realms, he stresses the independence of each of their epistemological principles. The formal realm furnishes the metaphysical framework of sufficient reasons underlying organic functions; but it cannot provide an explanation of material structures and mechanical processes. Inversely, the material realm and the geometrical and mechanical concepts and laws which express it cannot account for the functions of physiological processes and their integration in 'harmonic' systems. *A fortiori*, it is impossible on the basis of such concepts and laws to account for psychological phenomena and their apparently intentional causality.

In spite of the epistemological divide that this independence of principles seems to create, Leibniz envisages certain analogical trade-offs between the formal and the material realms which have the effect of opening up original methodological perspectives. The phenomena of conscious perception and appetition supply material for an empirical investigation of the sensory-motor systems and processes correlative to the representations of the soul. And, by virtue of his architectonic principles of continuity and of the identity of indiscernibles, Leibniz can extend empirical investigation by forming analogous hypotheses correlating physiological mechanisms and unconscious representations— what he calls 'small perceptions' and 'appetites transforming themselves into instincts'.

[27] Rather, 26: *Animadversiones*, Introduction, §3, in G. W. Leibniz, *Opera omnia*, ed. L. Dutens (Geneva, 1768) (hereafter Dutens), II-2, 133; *Negotium*, 4–5.

Another methodological gain results from the convergence in organisms of the series of efficient and final causes. In cases where it seems impossible to analyse the complex mechanical dispositions which result in a series of mechanical states, Leibniz relies on teleology. The classic case which he draws on is the discovery of the laws of dioptrics and catoptrics by means of a teleological argument derived by the calculus of optimal forms: the easiest and most determined path of the light ray in the various possible cases of reflection and refraction was ascertained without any analysis of the material nature of light. He transfers this procedure to the phenomena of the living being:

With this same procedure there is hope that much about the animal economy and medical practice will be discovered by studying the uses of the parts, and the goals of Nature. For even if effects arise from the internal movements and the structure of the machine, still, because the interior parts of the latter are unknown, the former can be divined more easily from the goals than from the mechanism.[28]

Thus Leibniz is proposing an analysis whereby functional characteristics which are empirically observed establish a hypothetical explanation of the phenomena, while at the same time the underlying mechanisms remain unknown. These functional characteristics are under the jurisdiction of the dominant entelechy, and provide interpretations of a psychological kind, following the analogy of perceptions and volitions. But these psychological interpretations of the organic phenomena must be subordinated to *teleological laws of nature*—that is, to the architectonic principles that underlie the *mechanical* linkage of the phenomena. Like Leibnizian physics, which is dominated by the theory of force and by a set of principles derived from the principle of sufficient reason, Leibnizian physiology rests firmly on teleological models.[29]

III. LEIBNIZ'S CONTROVERSY WITH STAHL

At the same time, Leibniz discards the theoretical entities put forward by the proponents of 'vitalistic medicine'. He considers Stahl to be one of the heirs to this tradition, whose forerunners include Paracelsus, van Helmont, and the Cambridge Platonists Henry More and Ralph Cudworth, who set forth the theory of 'plastic natures'. Just before entering upon his criticism of Stahl, Leibniz had completed an extensive critical analysis of the concept of plastic natures in reply to Jean Le

---

[28] Rather, 28: *Animadversiones*, Introduction, §3, Dutens, II-2, 135; *Negotium*, 6–7.

[29] On Leibniz's physiological model, cf. Duchesneau, *La Physiologie des Lumières*, esp. 65–102.

Clerc.[30] Le Clerc had published excerpts from Cudworth's major work, *The True Intellectual System of the Universe* (1678), in the *Bibliothèque choisie* (1703–6), in order to counter theorists who sought to give a mechanical account of living beings. Pierre Bayle, fearing that atheists could draw advantage from the theory of plastic natures, which allowed that living beings were formed and animated on their own, engaged in a polemical exchange with Le Clerc (1704–6), to which he recruited Leibniz. Le Clerc, too, solicited Leibniz's opinion on the opposing theses, asking him specifically to clarify his theoretical position. In response, Leibniz set to work to differentiate his own theory of the organism from the revived doctrine of plastic natures; and in 1705, he published *Considérations sur les principes de vie et sur les natures plastiques* in the *Histoire des ouvrages des savants* of Basnage de Beauval. Leibniz objected to the fact that the theory postulated autonomous agents with psychological characteristics capable of producing effects in matter that are not mechanical: for example, reproduction, the formation of organisms, regeneration of their parts, and functional operations (both vegetative and animal) characteristic of the living being. He opposed the thesis that psychic agents intervene directly in the course of bodily processes, on the margin of the laws of mechanism.[31]

In arguing against the tradition of plastic natures, Leibniz intends to furnish a counterweight to the Stahlian theory of the soul as an agent struggling against the ineluctable and imminent corruption of the corporeal aggregate. In so doing, he reaffirms the thesis of the soul as an entelechy, as a simple substance which is incorporeal and immaterial, and endowed solely with the powers of perception and appetition, making these latter powers the essential characteristics of life.[32] The organism itself is conceived as an infinitely complex mechanism, endowed only with material characteristics, which none the less include

---

[30] For Leibniz's texts relating to plastic natures, cf. GP, VI, 539–55. On the controversy over plastic natures, cf. J. Roger, *Les Sciences de la vie dans la pensée française du XVIIIe siècle*, 2nd edn. (Paris, 1971), 418–27; Roger also provides a valuable comparative evaluation of Stahl's medical doctrine and the conceptions of Cudworth and Grew (ibid. 427–31).

[31] Cf. the unfinished letter to Ralph Cudworth's daughter, Lady Masham, GP, III, 374: 'je ne voudrais pas employer dans les choses naturelles cette direction particulière de Dieu qui ne peut être que miraculeuse, ni recourir à des natures plastiques incorporelles qui n'auront aucun avantage sur la machine. Je dirai donc que les corps ont en eux des natures plastiques, mais que ces natures ne sont autre chose que leur machine même, laquelle produit des ouvrages excellents sans avoir connaissance de ce qu'elle fait, parce que ces machines ont été inventées par un Maître encore plus excellent. La force plastique est dans la Machine, mais l'idée de ce qu'elle fait est en Dieu. Ainsi je n'accorde point de pouvoir aux créatures dont on ne conçoive clairement la possibilité.'

[32] *Animadversiones*, §8, Dutens, II-2, 137; *Negotium*, 11: 'Vitam ego collocare solebam in perceptione et adpetitu.' Cf. also *Exceptiones*, §8, Dutens, II-2, 146; *Negotium*, 247.

dynamic properties resulting from integrated structural dispositions. The spontaneity of the organism cannot be reduced to mere passive matter.[33] Leibniz emphasizes that integrated structural dispositions form the basis of the plurality of functions possible in a chemical mechanism.[34] If he uses the metaphor of a hydraulic-pneumatic machine to represent the living body,[35] he adds to it the possession of built-in microsystems able to store and redeploy motive force in a functional way. This is how he interprets the theory of animal spirits: they represent the sole material agents required to animate the organic machine and give it autonomous mechanical powers corresponding to the powers of representation of the dominant entelechy.[36] In arguing against plastic natures in the introductory remarks to his *Animadversiones*, he affirms that

[t]here is no need to conceive of anything in the body other than containers, contents, and movers, or to call upon appetites other than those of the soul. In like manner the *archaeus* ought not to be sought for except in the soul and in the corporeal spirits according with it.[37]

And similarly, in the conclusion to his remarks, he writes:

It surprises me that . . . [Stahl] rejects vital and animal spirits, i.e. an imperceptible, swiftly flowing fluid in the body. For a correct understanding of the matter does not allow that there be no motive force in the body other than the soul. Furthermore it is established that motive forces exist even in things devoid of life. . . . Therefore, since the actions of bodies suffice, why should we fly to the influence of incorporeals, or indeed, more than this, to something supernatural or incapable of being explained from the natures of things.[38]

Explanation in the physical order—and physiology belongs to this category—requires strict limitation to the geometrical-mechanistic models corresponding to the observable connection of causes that link the

---

[33] *Animadversiones*, §30, Dutens, II-2, 143; *Negotium*, 19: 'Nam ut nihil aliud sit in Corpore impetum faciens, quam Anima, ratio non fert. Praeterea impetum facientia etiam in rebus Vitae expertibus esse constat, et saepe cor animali evulsum pulsare notum est.'

[34] Cf. *Animadversiones*, §13, Dutens, II-2, 139; *Negotium*, 13: this may possibly be influenced by T. Willis.

[35] *Animadversiones*, §13, Dutens, II-2, 139; *Negotium*, 13: 'Et dici potest, corpus nostrum non tantum machinam hydraulico-pneumaticam, sed et pyriam esse.'

[36] Cf. *Exceptiones* §§9 and 15, Dutens, II-2, 146-7, 149-50; *Negotium*, 153, 164.

[37] Rather, 29: *Animadversiones*, Introduction, §3, Dutens, II-2, 136; *Negotium*, 22. Cf. *Exceptiones*, §13, Dutens, II-2, 149; *Negotium*, 265: 'Corpus animale esse machinam Hydraulico-Pneumatico-pyriam, et impetus in eo oriri ab explosionibus, quae sint pyriis similes, vix quisquam amplius dubitat, nisi chimaericis principiis animum occupatum habeat, veluti animabus divisibilibus, naturis plasticis, speciebus intentionalibus, ideis operatricibus, principiis hylarchicis, archaeis aliisque, quae nihil significant, nisi in mechanica resolvantur.'

[38] Rather, 36: *Animadversiones*, §31, Dutens, II-2, 143; *Negotium*, 19.

phenomena to one another. As Leibniz emphatically affirms in his
Exceptiones, 'there is certainly in nature no other motive principle than
a body that is already in motion, and that mechanically produces new
motions'.[39]

But beyond the physical is the metaphysical order, which is analysed
in terms of relationships of perceptive-appetitive representations linked
according to relations of final causation. As we have seen, Leibniz, who
is unwilling to permit a confusion of these orders, nevertheless author-
izes certain strategies of hypothetical interpretation of the phenomena
which rest on their harmonic convergence. The complex integration of
organisms as machines of nature, being susceptible to an apparently infinite analysis, opens the door to a correlative and holistic interpretation
of the series and to the attribution of vital and functional dispositions
to the micro-systems of the organism. This strategy is re-enforced by the
assumption of a dynamic foundation underlying the mechanical properties and interactions. Thus, in preparatory notes to his *Éclaircissement
sur les natures plastiques et les principes de vie et de mouvement*, Leibniz
develops a close analogy between *dynamic* and *plastic laws* of nature.
The former depend on some organic feature in the material order
underlying such properties as elasticity—namely the interlocking of
corporeal systems interacting according to dynamic principles. Correlatively, organisms considered as plastic natures imply an integrated
system of organs, whose operations obey specific laws expressing the
functions of the organism.[40]

The greatest problem in explaining Leibniz's theory remains that of
determining how the soul and the body interact, or seem to interact, and
within what limits. Certainly, Leibniz attacks Stahl's view that the imag-
inings, emotions, and volitions of the soul provoke, suspend, and modify
organic movements outside of any physical regularity which can be
experimentally determined or rationally deduced. For Leibniz, to invest
the soul with such a power would be to hide the infinity of possible
physical actions somewhere outside all jurisdiction of the laws of nature.
Why, if the hypothesis of Stahl were true, could the soul not command
the body to jump to any height at all?

If the soul had the power over the machine to command it to do something
beyond what it could do spontaneously, there would then be no reason why she
could not command whatever she wished, since there is no proportion between

---

[39] *Exceptiones*, §15, Dutens, II-2, 149; *Negotium*, 163.
[40] Cf. the Hannover manuscript *LH* IV, 1, 2a, fo. 15: *Die Leibniz-Handschriften*, ed.
Bodemann, 51–2: 'Duplices naturae leges dynamicae et plasticae seu organicae. Est
tamen et in dynamicis hoc velut organicum, quod obtineri non possint nisi materia ubique
elastica esset, neque elasticum ubique in materia, nisi systemata in systematibus collo-
carentur. In quo dynamica respondent plasticis, quae semper organa in organis habent.'

the soul and body, nor can any reason be found why the power of the soul should be restrained within a limited range of force. Thus if we were to jump by means of the force of the soul rather than by the power of a fluid undergoing expansion there would be no reason why we could not leap to any height whatsoever. Nor could the soul be offered any hindrance at all by the body, and nature (that is the soul, according to [Stahl]) would then be the most effective healer of all ills and never miss her aim.[41]

Rejecting such a position as absurd, Leibniz emphasizes its incompatibility both with the data of experience and with the requirements of the principle of sufficient reason. From this he draws the conclusion that no change in the soul can exert an effect on the body; or, at least, it cannot do so unless movements of the subtle parts induce this effect in the organism through innate or acquired dispositions.[42] The soul cannot command and execute what the body cannot accomplish spontaneously:

It seems a wonder to [Stahl] that the movements of the vital domain, the healthy as well as the diseased, are not under the control of the soul. I believe that there will be many on the other hand to whom it will seem a wonder for the power of the soul to extend thus far. There is much truth on both sides: the vital movements precisely correspond to the appetites of the soul—confused and remote from our awareness as these for the greater part are—just as if they were obeying them. But in turn the machine would not subserve the appetite unless it were to tend of itself where the appetite is born.[43]

The truth of Stahl's position, according to Leibniz, is reducible to the fact that, within the limits of conscious experience, the soul seems to exert its power of determination over certain bodily actions. The deeper truth, according to Leibniz, derives from the fact that the organism possesses the necessary physical-chemical resources to carry out actions conforming to the representations of the soul, which extend well beyond the limits of conscious perception.[44]

---

[41] Rather, 34: *Animadversiones*, §21, Dutens, II-2, 141; *Negotium*, 16.

[42] Cf. *Animadversiones*, §15, Dutens, II-2, 139; *Negotium*, 13–14, esp. §28, Dutens, II-1, 142; *Negotium*, 18: 'Quod habetur . . . magis aut minus, fortius aut segnius, continue aut interrupte moveri, rem esse, quae non dependeat a Corporis organici dispositione, sed ab Anima; id quidem dici valde miror. Ita consequetur . . . quantamvis vim ab Anima imprimi in Corpus posse. Certum utique est, explosiones, fermentationes aliosque motus intestinos, gradu variari: pro fluidorum et vasorum, tum etiam pro impetum facientium, ratione. Etiam in crassiore mechanismo fontes habemus inaequaliter et per intervalla fluentes. Consuetudo, quae hic allegatur, non minus Corpus quam Animam ad agendum aptat.'   [43] Rather, 34: *Animadversiones*, §20, Dutens, II-2, 141; *Negotium*, 16.

[44] Cf. e.g. *Exceptiones*, §16, Dutens, II-2, 150; *Negotium*, 164: 'Uti nuper perceptionem, ita hic appetitum accipio, ut nempe etiam minutiores et obscuriores animae conatus ad aliquid conveniens obtinendum, aut inconveniens repellendum, ex perceptionibus non minus confusis ortos, sub *appetitus* nomine comprehendam. Itaque non magis omnem nostrum appetitum, quam omnem nostram perceptionem animadvertimus, et hoc sensu statuo, corporis motus etiam nobis animadversos appetitibus animae respondere.'

From the viewpoint of medical practice, in cases where stable correlations can be established empirically, Leibniz considers it acceptable to
assume that states of the soul can directly regulate or disturb organic
motions. Not, of course, that such correlations are made by a proper
deduction according to the order of physical efficient causes:[45] from a
theoretical point of view, such action of the soul on the body must be
considered as a hypothesis without substance or justification:

> To all the perceptions and intentions of the soul there are corresponding cor-
> poreal figures and movements whence derive, in the machine, effects which are
> consequently not necessarily to be attributed to the action of the soul exercis-
> ing its influence by a means more than mechanical. Furthermore, it is evident
> that the soul can in no way achieve such effects unless we take it itself to be a
> subtle body.[46]

Thus, according to Leibniz, Stahl's doctrine logically implies a materialist conception of the soul. In fact, Stahl speaks of a proportionality
between the actions of the soul and the physiological movements which
take place in the body, conceived as its instrument. He does not hesi-
tate to assign to the psychical principle the continued movements made
by the heart when it is excised from the body. However, for Leibniz,
these are to be explained as the residual effect of forces inherent in the
structures of that organ.[47]

Leibniz's theoretical position on the question of the relationship of
the soul and the body in the organism becomes particularly clear in the
argument he develops in the *Exceptiones*. On the one hand, the soul
(or dominant monad, to use the technical term henceforth in effect
in Leibniz's system) of the organism is a simple immaterial substance
to which perceptions and appetitions are assigned, some of which are
confused and instinctive, others of which manifest intelligence and a
rational power. These latter permit a more or less limited access to the
knowledge of the laws of nature and to the *ratio essendi* of realities. On
the other hand, the sufficient cause of physical movements resides in
active and passive forces which in turn are based in the formal disposi-

---

[45] Cf. *Exceptiones*, §19, Dutens, II-2, 152; *Negotium*, 171: 'Utilis interim haec animae
pathematum consideratio est, quia ex iis cognoscere possumus multa, quae in corpore
fiunt, cum anima nobis sit corpore notior; et efficere etiam multa, quae in corporibus pro-
ducere volumus. Nam effectibus excitatis aut sopitis per causas morales in anima, effec-
tus physicos per causas physicas respondentes in corpore obtinere licet. Itaque non raro
praxis *assertionis* stare potest, etsi theoria vacillet. Quod etiam de multis aliorum Medicorum doctrinis dici potest. Nam praxis phaenomenis inaedificari debet, theoriae non raro
hypothesibus et conjecturis constant.'

[46] *Exceptiones*, §19, Dutens, II-2, 152; *Negotium*, 170–1.

[47] Cf. *Exceptiones*, §21.17, Dutens, II-2, 147; *Negotium*, 181: 'Sed non quaevis pars corporis organici corpus organicum est: ideo, etsi motum aliquandiu retineat cor ex corpore
evulsum, non ideo hinc probatur, cor esse corpus animatum, sufficit enim nudus mechanismus ad hunc motum nonnihil continuandum, etsi perceptio et appetitus absint.'

tions of the corresponding monads.[48] Leibniz emphasizes the necessity of postulating that the system of mechanical laws governing the phenomenal universe develops in parallel with the system of monadic determinations.

Governed by a pre-established harmony, the parallel physical and psychological series give rise to an infinite number of organisms, each ruled by one monad and comprising an integrated system of states and mechanical processes. Only in living organisms is this system empirically recognizable, especially when organisms acquire a reflective apprehension, as in the case of conscious subjects representing their own bodies. Indeed, it is then through an inference that such a soul–body structure is projected on to animal organisms being observed from the outside. But, according to the deductive requirements of Leibniz's system, these organisms themselves are composed of an infinite multitude of 'microorganisms'. One might say that each macroscopic body, including the bodies of non-living things, which appear as undifferentiated aggregates, is in fact composed of a variety of organic bodies. As far as the 'microorganisms' enveloped in the material of living bodies are concerned, one cannot arrive at a reflective apprehension of their function, or of the limits of their possible analytic investigation, through sensible experience.[49] But, without these teleological structures and without the 'microbodies' that are organically connected to them, the structural-functional mechanisms of organisms which are their integrated emergent expression would lack a foundation.

On this basis, Leibniz turns a significant critical argument to account against Stahl. The soul's power to directly intervene in the body can never be established in any regular way, because there is a fundamental heterogeneity between the essential characteristics on the two sides when rational volition and bodily movement are to be related to one another.[50] In considering the states of the soul, it will be impossible to assign any specific degrees of *impetus* to movements which are supposed to derive directly from them:

[If one takes into account the degrees of velocity that fix the proportion of movements in relationships to one another,] it will not follow that one can determine the degree of speed, within the body, according to the perceptions

---

[48] Cf. *Exceptiones*, §21.4, Dutens, II-2, 154; *Negotium*, 177: 'Distinguo ergo Entelechiam primitivam seu animam, quae perstat, ab Entelechia derivata seu impetu, qui varie mutatur. Impetum autem rursus distinguo a motu: est enim impetus seu vis derivata res revera existens, at motus nunquam existit, cum nunquam habeat partes simul, sed consistit in successione ut tempus.'

[49] Cf. *Exceptiones*, §21.5, Dutens, II-2, 155; *Negotium*, 177–8: 'quia enim [omnia corpora] continent in se corpora organica, etsi non semper perceptibilia.'

[50] Cf. e.g. *Exceptiones*, §21.10, Dutens, II-2, 156; *Negotium*, 179–80: 'Interim nulla est proportio inter rationem et motum, quia ratio pro objecto essentiali habet consequentias veritatum, quae in unoquoque motus gradu aeque locum habet.'

of the soul. In the same way, one cannot determine the exact size of a palace from its representation on a small scale in a convex mirror, unless other circumstances are also in play, such as the form . . . of the mirror and its distance from the palace. Such circumstances are not available in the case of the soul.[51]

For Leibniz, this argument illustrates that any change in the organism must presuppose sufficient reasons in the material dispositions of the body and in the antecedent movements that affect them. Without these there is no way of unravelling the difficulties which vitiate Stahl's physiological theory from the point of view both of the powers of the soul and of those of the body itself. Leibniz writes that:

One can well conceive perception and appetite in the soul, but not how from these the motion is produced in the body by which the appetite is satisfied, unless by invoking the medium of mechanical laws.[52]

But reciprocally:

I am not putting forth the principle that the body conforms in this way to the appetite because it perceives it—for in my judgement no perception at all may be attributed to the body—but rather that it conforms in this way because it is already determined by mechanical laws to conform.[53]

Leibniz never tires of denouncing the errors which Stahl has committed in assigning causes in the cases of both physiological and psychological phenomena. Stahl confuses movement with action—that is, an event taking place in the order of extended phenomena with a formal cause of movement requiring analysis in terms of perceptive and appetitive representations. As we have seen, Leibniz also argues that the author of the *Theoria medica vera* may be seen as effectively materializing the soul, by attributing properties to it which actually derive from organic micro-systems and from powers of subtle spirits. At the same time, Stahl unduly psychologizes organic function by postulating the radical inadequacy of any physical-chemical model intended to explain the phenomena of the healing power of nature. Stahl substitutes the powers of the *logos*—its powers of construction, actualization, and regulation of the corruptible organic body—for a geometrical and mechanical analysis. And nothing, according to Leibniz, justifies Stahl's view that such a *logos* acts at one time in a correct way, and at other times is subject to errors and perversions, just as if it were operating as a voluntary agent in the moral sphere.

---

[51] *Exceptiones* §21.13, Dutens, II-2, 156; *Negotium*, 180.
[52] *Exceptiones*, §21.14, Dutens, II-2, 156; *Negotium*, 180-1.
[53] *Exceptiones*, §21.27, Dutens, II-2, 159; *Negotium*, 183.

IV. CONCLUSION

As the *Theoria medica vera* (1708) shows, Stahl radically opposes the mechanism of the moderns and the absolute distinction of soul and body that underlies every theory of the living being constructed from a Cartesian perspective. He proposes a new concept of organism, according to which all bodily structures are formed, preserved, repaired, and functionally adapted by the action of an immaterial principle, the soul. This soul possesses perceptive and appetitive powers extending from the conscious to the unconscious; it assures the integral maintenance of the organism in opposition to natural tendencies toward dissolution resulting from the material composition of the body itself. It causes and orders in a direct way the vital and animal operations attributed to the organism in both natural and pathological states. The *logos* exercised by this soul would appear, then, to be an integral determining principle of all the functions of the living being. When faced with the difficulties of this theory, Stahl flees willingly to empirical justifications which can furnish him with a practical medicine centred around the phenomena of psychosomatic interaction. He further rejects any obligation to reconcile his theory of the organism with the interpretation of physiological effects according to mechanist models. For him, comprehension of the living being could never be achieved merely by meeting the methodological requirements of the physical-chemical sciences. The soul of Stahl corresponds to the postulate of a psychosomatic intelligibility prevailing integrally over the whole territory of the living organism, a territory unanalysable in the framework of a mechanistic physics. Leibniz's theory of the organism aims to overcome the problems engendered by such a system, by proposing a parallelism between psychological states governed by the laws of teleology and physiological states analysable in a geometrical-mechanical grid and subject to the laws of efficient cause. At the same time, however, Leibniz attempts to discover the formal foundation of the organism, which he locates in the capacity of perception-appetition proper to the dominant monad. He then extends this capacity analogically to account for the structures and integrated dispositions of the corresponding phenomenal body which is apprehended through our senses.

Substance versus Function Dualism in Eighteenth-Century Medicine

JOHN P. WRIGHT

My aim here is to distinguish and discuss two quite different types of soul–body dualism found in the writings of eighteenth-century medical theorists. These dualisms I shall call 'substance dualism' and 'function dualism'. The first, substance dualism, was considered by many thinkers, in particular those concerned with the requirements of religious ortho-doxy, to be absolute: they maintained that soul and body were sub-stances of entirely different and incompatible natures. The issues surrounding this dualism affected primarily what David Hume's friend, the renowned Edinburgh medical professor William Cullen, called 'the business of religion';[1] its opposite was materialism. The second type of soul–body dualism was, by contrast, of great importance in medicine itself, and of particular significance for what is commonly discussed in the twentieth century under the rubric of 'psychosomatic medicine'.[2] Rejecting the traditional conception of the soul as that which gives life to the body, proponents of function dualism followed Descartes in dis-tinguishing two basic kinds of functions of the human being: thought functions (assigned to the soul or mind) and life functions (assigned to the body). They then proceeded to discuss the possibility of interaction between these two realms. From the beginning of the eighteenth century onwards, the function dualists were the object of attacks by animists such as G. Stahl, who denied that life functions could take place without the direct action of the soul.

In the first section of this chapter I shall examine discussions of sub-stance dualism in early modern medical thought, beginning with two

---

[1] William Cullen, 'The Institutes of Medicine by Dr Cullen Oct. 28, 1772' (5 vols.), National Library of Medicine, Bethesda, Md., MS B4 (henceforth NLM), II, fol. 25.

[2] The term 'psychosomatic' is generally used to refer to somatic diseases which are thought to have as a major component causes which can be identified only psychologi-cally. See the discussion by Franz Alexander, *Pychosomatic Medicine* (New York, 1950), 50 ff.

predecessors of Descartes—Francis Bacon and Timothy Bright. I argue that while Descartes changed the way of identifying substance dualism—by stipulating that the soul is a thinking substance and the body an extended substance—he did not significantly change the theological role that this dualism played in medical discussions of the soul and body. And while, after Descartes, substance dualism was widely held to imply an essential distinction between thinking states (soul), on the one hand, and purely mechanical states of the brain (body), on the other, several major eighteenth-century medical writers argued that the mental states were, none the less, entirely dependent on brain states.

All this, as William Cullen pointed out, left an entirely different soul–body problem to be discussed by medicine—namely the problem of how thinking states, irrespective of whether they are assigned to the soul or to the brain, affect those organs of the body upon which life more directly depends. This soul–body problem presupposed function dualism—the fundamental distinction between thought functions and life functions. I argue that this dualism played a significant role in eighteenth-century medical thought, by providing the conceptual context for current discoveries in physiology, as well as for clinical practice. It left open the possibility of the influence of the soul on the life functions of the body, a possibility which was discussed extensively by such thinkers as Haller, Gaub, Cullen, and La Mettrie. In my conclusion, as a support for my thesis that these two kinds of dualism which underlay eighteenth-century medical discussions of the relationship of soul and body truly are distinguishable, I present the cases of two writers— La Mettrie and Robert Whytt—each of whom accepted one kind, while rejecting the other.

I. SUBSTANCE DUALISM

By 'substance dualism' I mean that dualism between a material body substance and a non-material soul substance which is commonly invoked by both philosophical and medical writers in the seventeenth and eighteenth centuries. The basic distinction between soul and body is described as a distinction between two different things with two entirely different natures or essences. This dualism is often said to have originated with Descartes, but, while Descartes' particular way of dividing mind and body had great importance for eighteenth-century medical writers, substance dualism in fact goes back to antiquity (e.g. Plato).

Francis Bacon, writing some years before Descartes, argued that the study of the substance of the soul had to do with theology and not philosophy (i.e. science). Since God directly created 'the substance of the soul' and did not extract it out of the material creation, it is not '(otherwise than by accident) subject to the laws of heaven and earth, which are the subject of philosophy'.[3] When Bacon says here that the body can affect the mind only *accidentally*, he is thinking of cases where the mind becomes deranged by the 'humours and affects of the body'. He complains of men of 'weak judgment' who 'conceive that this suffering of the mind from the body doth either question the immortality, or derogate from the sovereignty of the soul', and offers two analogies—that of the 'infant in the mother's womb' and that of 'a monarch and his servants'—to show that one thing may be strongly affected by another, yet still remain completely sovereign and independent (108). Bacon divides the substance of the soul from that of the human body by using the criterion of simplicity: 'the Body of man of all other things is of the most compounded mass. The Soul on the other side is the simplest of substances' (110).

Similar discussions are to be found in the writings of late Renaissance physicians. In 1586, for example, in *A Treatise of Melancholie*, Timothy Bright asserts that whatever the effects of the body on the soul may be, these can never result in any 'alteration of substance, or nature'. He maintains that the body cannot affect the 'facultie' or 'qualities' which 'are essentiall unto the soule'.[4] The chief faculty which Bright had in mind is the power of giving life to the body, for he wrote that life lies neither in the body itself, nor in the spirits which are intermediate between the body and the soul, but 'rather in the essence, or substance of the soule, giving it to a fit organed body' (63). Without the soul, even natural actions of the body such as nourishment cannot take place. This is evident from the fact that a part of the body decays if the mind transports the spirits elsewhere through 'sudden conceit, study, or passion'. This can even result in death, though the soul itself, being 'of stocke divine, of immortall perpetuity' is 'exempt from all corruption'. While Bright held that a soul is required to give life to the body, he considered it to be substantially distinct from the body, and so able to exist after the body's destruction.

The central role which theological concerns regarding the immortality of the soul play in these discussions of substance dualism is obvious. This is equally true for Descartes. The *locus classicus* in which he distinguishes between the soul and the body as distinct substances— namely his *Meditations on First Philosophy*—appeared in 1641 with a

---

[3] Francis Bacon, *The Advancement of Learning*, 1st edn. (London, 1605), ed. G. W. Kitchin (London, 1973), 118.

[4] Timothy Bright, *A Treatise of Melancholie* (London, 1586), 39.

dedication to 'the Dean and Doctors of the Sacred Faculty of Theology in Paris'.[5] In the subtitle of the first edition of this work, Descartes claimed not only to demonstrate 'the existence of God' but also 'the immortality of the soul' (CSM II, 1: AT VII, xix). While this claim was omitted from the subtitle of the second edition of 1642, Descartes added a Synopsis in which he still claimed to have shown that 'the decay of the body does not imply the destruction of the mind' (CSM II, 10: AT VII, 13).

The novel feature of Descartes' distinction of the substance of the soul from that of the body was his claim that the soul is a thinking or a conscious substance, while the body is an extended substance (CSM II, 54: AT VII, 78). We shall see that the claim that thought characterizes the soul was also central for his discussion of function dualism. However, it is interesting to note that, when two of the first critics of the *Meditations* pointed out to Descartes that his identification of the soul as a thinking substance is not sufficient to establish the continuance of the soul after death (CSM II, 91, 143–4: AT VII, 128, 204), he fell back on to a traditional method of distinguishing the two substances.

These critics had argued that there is nothing to guarantee that thinking, however distinct from the body, continues to exist when the body is destroyed. Descartes' response was to appeal to the essential property of the soul which Bacon had employed, namely its simplicity. In his Synopsis, Descartes replied that:

we cannot understand a body except as being divisible, while by contrast we cannot understand a mind except as being indivisible. For we cannot conceive of half a mind, while we can conceive of half of a body, however small; and this leads us to recognize that the natures of mind and body are not only different, but in some way opposite (CSM II, 9–10: AT VII, 13–14).

He went on to argue that the human body can cease to exist 'merely as a result of the change in the shape of some of its parts'. On the other hand, because of its simplicity, the mind does not change when its accidents (i.e. its thoughts) change: it is 'immortal by its very nature'. Thus, by stipulating that the soul is simple and indivisible, Descartes sought to guarantee its indestructibility.[6]

Major eighteenth-century medical writers, such as Hermann Boer-

---

[5] *The Philosophical Works of Descartes*, trans. John Cottingham, Robert Stoothoff, and Dugald Murdoch (2 vols., Cambridge, 1985–6) (henceforth CSM), II, 3–4: *Oeuvres de Descartes*, ed. Charles Adam and Paul Tannery (11 vols., Paris 1964–74) (henceforth AT), VII, 1–3. Descartes claims in his dedication to be following the Lateran Council held under Pope Leo X which enjoined Christian philosophers to prove the immortality of the soul. See Emily Michael's discussion in Ch. 7 above, esp. pp. 156–7.

[6] I am here following the convincing account presented by Ben Mijuskovic in *The Achilles of Rationalist Arguments* (The Hague, 1974), 27–32.

haave, employed the basic Cartesian distinction between a thinking substance and an extended substance in establishing substance dualism. Yet they too sometimes reverted to the criterion of simplicity in order to distinguish the soul from the body. Boerhaave received his doctorate in philosophy at the University of Leiden in 1690 for a thesis entitled *De distinctione mentis a corpore*. In this thesis, he argues that a thing which thinks cannot have distinct parts (i.e. be extended), since it could not then form unified thoughts. He also appeals to an argument of one of his teachers, Gerard de Vries, to support the claim that thinking, since it involves consciousness or reflective thought, cannot exist in an impenetrable body.[7]

Later, in his popular *Academical Lectures on the Institutes of Medicine*,[8] Boerhaave came to characterize mind primarily by the criterion of consciousness: 'the essential Nature of Mind', he writes, 'is to be conscious, or to think (*esse conscium sive cogitare*)'.[9] In contrast, 'the essential nature of Body is Extension and Resistance'. Boerhaave stresses that 'these Attributes have nothing in common to each other'. Elsewhere in his *Academical Lectures* Boerhaave employs the idea that the essential nature of the mind is thought or consciousness, in order to clear himself of any suspicion of Spinozism. In discussing sensory perception, he stresses that 'changes in the Sensitive Organ are . . . different from the Ideas they excite', and that sensation 'is nothing either in the Object or the Nerve affected; but a certain Idea which God has determined or assigned to each particular Change in the corporeal Sensory' in the brain. He took issue with Spinoza's definition of sensation as 'a Motion of the Mind generated from the Motion of a Body', on the ground that there is no such property as motion in a thinking thing (§570.7). Boerhaave's concern to distance himself from any form of materialism is clear from the beginning of the *Academical Lectures*, where he claims that abstract thinking, independent of any sensory ideas, gives evidence that the mind 'may live hereafter without any Commerce with its Body' (§27.4). He gives as evidence the experience of the mathematician Vieta,

[7] Hermann Boerhaave, *Disputatio philosophica inauguralis de distinctione mentis a corpore* (Leiden, 1690), ch. 3. It is interesting to note that de Vries himself had opposed orthodox Cartesians by claiming that a belief in innate ideas is irreconcilable with the principle that all thought must be conscious. See G. Lewis, *Le Problème de l'inconscient et le Cartésianisme* (Paris, 1950), 70, 140–8.

[8] Hermann Boerhaave, *Praelectiones academicae in proprias institutiones rei medicae*, ed. Albrecht von Haller, 2nd edn. (6 vols., Venice, 1743–5). Here I quote from an anonymous English translation: *Dr. Boerhaave's Academical Lectures on the Theory of Physic, being a Translation of his Institutes and Explanatory Comment* (5 vols., London, 1752–8) (henceforth *Academical Lectures*); reference is to Boerhaave's numbered propositions (§) and to his numbered notes on each of these.

[9] *Academical Lectures*, §27.4. Like Descartes, Boerhaave makes no distinction between mind and soul. See n. 18 below.

who was once so preoccupied with an intellectual problem that he became insensible of everything else for 'three whole days and nights'. Boerhaave claims that 'the mind [can] perform some actions by mere thought, without any effect upon the body' (§27).

However, this substantial distinction between mind and body played no medical or physiological role for Boerhaave. He insisted that mind and body are united, and that 'there is such a reciprocal connection and consent between the particular thought and affections of the mind and the body, that a change in one also produces a change in the other, and the reverse' (§27). He held that there was no way of explaining 'the manner in which the body and mind reciprocally act upon each other', and, after considering three current hypotheses concerning their connection—'physical influx', 'occasional Causes', and 'a Harmony established by God'—said he favoured the last (§27.7). More importantly, he argued that physicians need only attend to the condition of the body. Even in mental diseases, they do not need to pay any attention to the mind itself, since when the body 'is set to rights', the mind 'will quickly return to its Office' (§27.8).

Albrecht von Haller followed his teacher Boerhaave in insisting that while mental events have corresponding processes in the brain upon which they depend, the mental events are themselves entirely 'distinct' from the brain processes. In his *First Lines of Physiology*, first published in 1747,[10] Haller presents three arguments to show the distinctness of mental events. In the first place, he argues that the motions in my nerves and brain when I hear a sound, perceive light, or feel pain are not perceived (§556). Secondly, there are thoughts of the mind which do not correspond to any sensory input; he mentions in particular 'abstract ideas and affections of the mind': pride has no colour, nor envy any magnitude. Finally, Haller points out that there are some actions of the mind which are impossible in a body—in particular, reasoning and voluntary action. How could a body compare distinct ideas without combining them, and determine their similarities and differences? And how could it pass from rest to motion or motion to rest without the influence of any external cause? Or how could a body change the direction of its own motion? These are actions which can only be 'the attribute of the mind alone' (§569).

Yet it is important to recognize that for Haller each mental event requires a physical event in the brain. Of the relation between sensory input in the body and the changes which take place in the mind, Haller writes that 'it is established as a perpetual law by the Creator, that

---

[10] I quote from the English translation, *First Lines of Physiology*, ed. William Cullen (Edinburgh, 1786) (henceforth *First Lines*); references are to Haller's section numbers.

certain changes, first made in the nerve, and then in the common sensory, shall produce certain new corresponding thoughts in the mind, which have an indissoluble connection with each other' (§556; cf. §571). He notes that the affections of the mind are directly connected with certain changes both in the will and in the involuntary operations of the body (§565). And finally, he stresses that the use of reason and the ability to judge correctly depend 'upon a perfect and healthy constitution of the brain'. He describes how physical changes in the brain cause hallucinations, or break 'the connection of the ideas, so that mind cannot compare them together . . . and is consequently unable to judge of, or foresee, their proportions, differences, or consequences' (§563).

From Boerhaave and Haller's insistence that all medical explanations and treatments be mechanical, it is a very small step to the materialism espoused by Julien Offray de La Mettrie. La Mettrie had studied with Boerhaave at the University of Leiden in 1733 and 1734, and published a French translation with commentary of Boerhaave's *Academical Lectures* in 1739–40. In 1747, he mischievously dedicated his notorious *L'Homme-machine* to Haller, claiming in the dedication to be his friend and disciple. In the work itself La Mettrie wrote of solving 'the riddle of substances'.[11] According to him, this riddle is solved by the 'most incontestable observation' which shows that 'organized matter is endowed with a motive principle and . . . that everything in an animal depends on the diversity of this organization'. While La Mettrie accepts the Cartesian use of the term 'soul' for 'the part in us which thinks' (180), he insists in addition that it is 'a material and sensible part of the brain, which one can, without fear of error, consider as the principle spring of the whole machine' (186). For La Mettrie, the fact that thought influences other parts of the body is a clear indication that thought itself is performed by a part of the body. Apparently responding to Boerhaave's argument about the mathematician Vieta, La Mettrie asked rhetorically:

If that which thinks in my brain, were not a part of this organ and consequently of the whole body, why is it that [my] blood boils when I am lying calmly in my bed and forming a plan for a book, or when I follow an abstract bit of reasoning? (184)

La Mettrie is arguing, against Boerhaave, that there are no actions of the mind, including the most abstract acts of thought, which take place independently of the body. In rejecting substance dualism and arguing for 'the material unity of man', La Mettrie is arguing that that which thinks and wills in us is the brain itself.

[11] Julien Offray de La Mettrie, *L'Homme-machine*, ed. Aram Vartanian (Princeton, 1960), 189–90.

However, substance dualism continued to be espoused by later eighteenth-century medical writers who, unlike La Mettrie, were concerned for their religious orthodoxy. In what appears to be a private note appended to the physiology lectures he presented to Edinburgh medical students in the mid-1760s, William Cullen wrote that the reason why mental states such as 'thought, Intellect, & will' are ascribed to 'a Substance very different from our bodies' is that the mechanism by which they are produced 'is not [at] all obvious'. Yet, like his predecessors Boerhaave and Haller, he believed that these states are clearly 'inseparable from some conditions in the body'. Indeed, if one maintains that the mind can act 'independent[ly] of the state of the body', as do Stahl and his followers, this 'will render all reasoning on the animal oeconomy precarious'. Nevertheless, Cullen wrote, he will adopt the substance dualism of Boerhaave and Haller who had never been 'Suspected of irreligion'.[12] In adopting the doctrine of two distinct substances, even though he insisted on a one-to-one correspondence between their states, Cullen distanced himself clearly from La Mettrie's materialism.

In his lectures, Cullen denied that he had any understanding of the connection between mental states and the brain states with which they are correlated. He considered the same alternative hypotheses concerning the connection of mind and body as were mentioned by Boerhaave—physical influx, occasional causes, and Leibniz's 'Doctrine of the pre-established harmonies'—claiming that there are difficulties connected with each of them.[13] Thus, Cullen argued, the dualism of the two substances cannot be bridged. And he asserted that this problem of the connection of mind and body lies entirely outside the purview of medicine.

Yet, in the private note of 1766, Cullen had gone on to point out that there is still a genuine problem of the relation of mind and body which needs to be addressed by physicians:

It reduces the problem of the action of the mind upon the body to this—how one State of the body or of one part can affect another part of it. This is a problem the solution of which we may hope to attain.[14]

In his subsequent lectures Cullen discusses at length the problem of how certain states of the brain—namely mental ones—can affect the states of other organs of the body—especially the lungs, the organs of digestion, and the heart, those organs on which life primarily depends.

---

[12] William Cullen, 'Lectures on Physiology', Royal College of Physicians of Edinburgh, MS Cullen 16(I) (henceforth RCPE), preliminary fols.
[13] William Cullen, 'Lectures on the Institutes of Medicine by Dr Cullen, 1770–71', National Library of Scotland, Edinburgh, MS 3535 (henceforth NLS), fols. 78–9.
[14] RCPE, preliminary fols.

II. FUNCTION DUALISM AND MEDICAL THOUGHT

In the passage discussed in the last paragraph, Cullen identifies a dualism which is very different from substance dualism. The problem of substance dualism, especially after Descartes, was essentially a problem of how states of an immaterial substance—the soul or mind—relate to states of a bodily organ, the brain. The medical problem identified by Cullen is how mental states—states ascribed to the soul or mind *and* to the brain—affect those of other organs of the body. The dualism which allows us to formulate this problem is a dualism between two basic kinds of *functions* of human beings: the thinking functions and the life functions. This *function dualism* can be bridged: we can empirically investigate the influence of mental (i.e. brain) states on the vital organs of the body. Moreover, according to Cullen, such an investigation 'may be useful & necessary in explaining the causes & cure of diseases' (RCPE, preliminary fols.).

In order to understand the medical problem of mind and body focused on by Cullen, it is useful to retrace its history from the writings of Descartes. For it was Descartes who first clearly distinguished the life functions of the body from the thought functions of the soul. In his *Description of the Human Body*, for example, he took issue with those who had attributed functions 'such as moving the heart and arteries, digesting food in the stomach' to the soul. For, according to him, these 'do not involve any thought, and are simply bodily movements'. He identified the thought functions as understanding, willing, imagining, and sensing, and argued that only these are to be ascribed to the soul. Against those who considered the soul to be the source of the life functions in the body, Descartes argued that 'the heat in the heart is like the great spring or principle responsible for all the movements' of the body. In so doing, he claimed to be giving a purely mechanical description of the basic motive force of the body.[15]

One should not assume, however, that because Descartes stressed the mechanical nature of the life force of the body, he rejected the idea that there are mechanical changes corresponding to the functions he ascribes to the soul. It is true that he sometimes suggested that pure understanding does not require any brain activity;[16] but he more characteristically argued that 'the soul has its principal seat in the small [pineal] gland located in the middle of the brain' (*Passions of the Soul*, art. 34;

---

[15] CSM I, 314–15: AT XI, 223–6. Compare Stephen Voss's discussion in Ch. 8 above, pp. 183–4.

[16] CSM II, 248: AT VII, 358. See the discussion in Margaret Wilson, *Descartes* (London, 1978), 177–85. Compare, however, John Cottingham, 'Cartesian Dualism', in *idem* (ed.), *The Cambridge Companion to Descartes* (Cambridge, 1992), 236–57, esp. 241–5.

CSM I, 341: AT IX, 354), and that it is in the brain 'alone that the soul not only understands and imagines, but also has sensory awareness' (*Principles of Philosophy*, §IV, 189; CSM I, 279–80: AT VIIIA, 315). In his *Treatise of Man* he gave mechanical descriptions of the changes in the brain which accompany psychological processes such as sensation, memory, imagination, appetite, and the passions. Thus, just as he located the life functions in the heart and blood, so he located the thought functions of the soul in the brain, in particular in the pineal gland (CSM I, 108: AT XI, 201–2).

While he argued that the life functions could take place entirely independently of the soul, Descartes was still interested in the influences of mental states on these functions. For although the soul exercises its functions in the centre of the brain, it also 'radiates through the rest of the body by means of the animal spirits, nerves, and even the blood' (*Passions of the Soul*, art. 34; CSM I, 341: AT XI, 354). The chief physiological link between the brain and the heart, then, is via the animal spirits, the finest and most agitated particles of the blood, which initially enter the pineal gland after being rarefied by the heat of the heart (art. 10; CSM I, 332: AT XI, 334–5). In the brain the animal spirits take on particular 'impressions', which depend on the stimuli received by the brain from external objects (art. 34; CSM I, 341: AT XI, 354–5). These changes in the structure and motion of the particles of the animal spirits cause certain pores to open in the brain which make the spirits move not only to certain muscles of the body which move the external limbs, but also 'to nerves which serve to expand or constrict the orifices of the heart, or else to nerves which agitate other parts of the body from which blood is sent to the heart, so that the blood is rarefied in a different manner from usual' (art. 36; CSM I, 342: AT XI, 356–7). This, in turn, causes a change in the nature of the animal spirits which enter the pineal gland.

The animal spirits are also the physiological cause of those thoughts which Descartes calls 'the passions of the soul'. These are defined as 'perceptions, sensations, or emotions' which are 'caused, maintained, and strengthened by some movement of the [animal] spirits' (*Passions of the Soul*, art. 27). Thus the account given in the last paragraph accurately illustrates Descartes' belief about how impressions of the senses excite changes in the vital organs of the body through the physiological medium of the passions. However, in Descartes' account, these changes do not involve any actions of the soul on the body, since both sensations and passions are experienced as being passively received by the soul (cf. art. 17; CSM I, 335: AT XI, 342). Indeed, he maintained that most human behaviour, such as that which occurs when we breathe, walk, or eat without any explicit act of will, takes place automatically, without any act of the mind (art. 16; CSM I, 334–5: AT XI, 341–2).

For Descartes, the action of the soul on the body involves the indirect, but voluntary control of the animal spirits by thoughts which are directly under the control of the soul. These thoughts are images of the imagination (*Passions of the Soul*, arts. 20, 43; CSM I, 336 and 344: AT XI, 344 and 361), which have natural links to certain passions: for example, the image of a frightening object is originally or habitually linked to the passion of fear, or the image of a joyful object is linked to the passion of joy. Descartes argues that, in order to control the passions, we need to represent to ourselves objects 'which are usually joined with the passions we wish to have and opposed to the passions we wish to reject' (art. 45; CSM I, 345: AT XI, 362–3). Thus, in order to overcome fear, we need to imagine things which will make us feel pride and joy in acts of self-defence.

Descartes held that through this indirect control of the passions, the soul can affect the life processes of the body. In his correspondence with Princess Elisabeth of Bohemia, he argued that through the imagination one can actually overcome disease. He first describes the way in which prolonged grief can cause a constriction of the heart, and a subsequent illness of the lungs. Then he argues that this process can be reversed by concentrating one's imagination on 'objects which could furnish contentment and joy'. Indeed, he claims, 'this by itself would be capable of restoring [a person] to health, even if his spleen and lungs were already in a poor condition because of the bad condition of the blood caused by sadness'.[17] Descartes thereby clearly expressed the belief that the thoughts which are under the direct control of the soul can affect the vital organs of the body via the passions.

Boerhaave, no less than Descartes, was concerned to deny that the fundamental motions on which life depends derive from the soul. He took issue with those in his day who had postulated the need for an 'animating Principle' in medicine—the *archaeus* of van Helmont, or the 'cogitative Principle' of Stahl (*Academical Lectures*, §697.7). He wrote that the soul or 'psyche' is that part of us which thinks,[18] and which acts on the body only through voluntary motion (§695.13). Like Descartes, Boerhaave argued that the source of the life functions is to be found in the automatic processes of the body itself (§4.1). However, unlike Descartes, he considered the heart to be a muscle, and argued that it keeps beating only because it is constantly supplied with new animal spirits through the nerves (§409). According to Boerhaave, the 'moving

---

[17] *The Philosophical Writings of Descartes: The Correspondence*, trans. John Cottingham, Robert Stoothoff, Dugald Murdoch, and Anthony Kenny (Cambridge, 1991), 249–50: AT IV, 218–20; cf. CSMK 237: AT I, 63.

[18] Boerhaave, *Praelectiones*, VI, 5: '*psyche*' is here translated as 'Mind' in the English *Academical Lectures*, §695.11.

powers' of all the involuntary muscles, including those of the heart, stomach, intestines, and lungs, derive not from the brain itself, the cerebrum, but from the cerebellum (§401.7). On the other hand, he located thought functions—including voluntary motion, sensation, and memory—in the cerebrum. He cited evidence to show that although these thought functions cease when the cerebrum is compressed, the life functions continue as long as the cerebellum is intact.

In spite of the fact that he locates the source of both thought functions and life functions in the central nervous system, Boerhaave denies that there is any interaction between them. He rejects the claim that the 'vital actions . . . are dependent on, or determined by, the Mind' (§695.11). In a passage later criticized by Cullen, he argues that the physician does not need to 'take notice of the Mind' in defining *disease*, because 'the same State of the Body inseparably accompanies the determinate State of the Mind' (§696). While he briefly mentions the passions as an 'accessory to the remote Cause' of disease (§§743, 744, and 744.3), Boerhaave never explains their influence, or considers how this is physiologically possible. And far from considering the manner in which voluntary action can affect the vital organs, as Descartes did, Boerhaave stressed the inability of the mind to control the automatic motions of the body (§4.1). In general, there is good reason to conclude that, in the hands of this extremely influential eighteenth-century medical figure, function dualism precluded a belief in the power of the mind over the visceral organs of the body.

Haller also argued against those who, like Stahl, maintained that the soul is responsible for all motions of the body, including those involved in the life functions (*First Lines*, §§572 ff.). His definitive argument against this view was based on his own discovery that muscles, especially the muscles of the heart, can retain their power of movement even after they have been separated from the rest of the body for some time. In a note appended to his important commentaries on Boerhaave's *Academical Lectures* (1739), Haller first took issue with Boerhaave's claim that the movement of the heart is caused by a force which is derived from the central nervous system; Haller ascribed it, rather, to 'an unknown cause' which lies 'concealed in the very structure of the heart itself'.[19] He later called this mechanical life force, which exists to a greater or lesser degree in all the muscles of the body, a *vis insita*. He argued that 'Irritability of the muscle fibres', especially when they are entirely

---

[19] Haller records the history of his own discovery of 'irritability' in *De partibus corporis humani sensibilibus et irritabilibus* (Göttingen, 1753). I cite from Owsei Temkin, 'Albrecht von Haller, "A Dissertation on the Sensible and Irritable Parts of Animals"', *Bulletin of the History of Medicine*, 4 (1936), 651–99, esp. 694.

removed from the body, shows that their basic action is totally 'independent of the nerves'. These operate on the muscles in a secondary way through *sensibility*. Thus Haller, more than any of the physiologists we have discussed thus far, separated the life functions of the body from mental functions. He concludes a piece of reasoning in his *First Lines of Physiology* with the statement that, while 'the will excites and removes the nervous power, ... it has no power over the *vis insita*' (§404).

It is therefore somewhat surprising to find that Haller, unlike Boerhaave, discusses in detail the effect of the passions on disease. As we shall see in a moment, this may be because, at the time he was writing, the question of the influence of the mind on the body had become a central focus of interest for Boerhaave's successor in the chair of medicine at Leiden, Jerome Gaub. Haller himself stressed that, by way of the passions, the mind 'exercises ... dominion over the pulse, respiration, appetite, strength, affections of the heart, nerves, and stomach'. He went on to discuss the different effects of anger, grief, fear, terror, and shame on disease. Anger, he thought, has a beneficial effect, since, by exciting 'a violent motion of the spirits ... it frequently removes obstructions, or eases chronical diseases'. Grief, on the other hand, 'retards the motion of the pulse', and causes a number of 'slow diseases' which arise 'from a stagnation of the humours' (*First Lines*, §565). Haller went on to propose a theory to explain the extensive influence of the passions: according to this theory, there are nerves which cover the arteries and can constrict or relax them in order to send a greater or lesser amount of blood to a certain organ. However, he noted that since 'it is shown by our experiments, that the nerves are at rest during the action of the muscles ... we must abandon this elegant theory' (§566). Clearly, Haller thought that his own physiological discoveries were in conflict with what was shown to him by clinical experience.

Boerhaave's successor, Jerome Gaub, appears to be the first medical writer of the eighteenth century to explore in detail the full range of medical issues surrounding the mutual interaction of the mind and body. In contrast to Haller, he put clinical experience in the forefront of his discussions. In his essay *De regimine mentis* of 1747, Gaub explained to his readers that the division between mental functions and life functions is absolute so long as the body is in a tranquil state:

There are two orders of function in man. Part of these are such that they clearly relate to both mind and body, as when something is accomplished in the body at the behest of the mind or arises in the mind as the result of changes in the bodily state. Others, however, and these of greater importance if number and need be taken into account, are purely corporeal. They are separated from the mind by so great a distance, as it were, that they take place not only in the absence of volition and sentience but without its awareness at all and even against the will.[20]

Like Descartes, Boerhaave, and Haller, Gaub stresses that the life functions take place automatically and without any effect from the soul or mind. He specifically lists the beating of the heart and arteries and the digestion of food as being of this latter kind. Gaub claimed that normally these activities do not 'permit of increase, decrease, or interruption, even though the strongest will be brought into play'. Moreover, Gaub argued that even functions that involve both mind and body are not totally under the control of the mind, since the mind is passive and influenced by the body in both external and internal sensation (§23). He argues that, on the whole, the mind is controlled by the body 'to even a greater extent than body is by mind' (§24).

However, Gaub went on to discuss the different kind of mind–body interaction which takes place when either the mind or the body is greatly disturbed. He argues that when the mind is overcome by some passion, it extends its dominion over the whole body (Rather, *Mind and Body*, 53–4; §27). Under such conditions, 'the heart and pulse beat unnaturally, the digestion and distribution of the nutriment, the circulation of the humours, the secretions and excretions . . . are deranged'. Gaub considers the mind as operating under such circumstances in a completely irrational way: it 'simultaneously desires and rejects, doing what it does now not wish to do, and desiring what it cannot obtain' (§28). It is particularly interesting to note that Gaub, in accord with much medical tradition, but in opposition to both Descartes and Boerhaave, considers the desires which arise from such violent passions to be actions of the mind.[21] Thus, according to Gaub, a mind operating under the influence of the passions is affecting the body.

It is clear from a brief look at Cullen's lectures on the institutions of medicine that he had studied the views of his predecessors, including Gaub, with some care. Like Gaub, Cullen considers the operations of the passions on the vital organs of the body as a case of the mind acting on the body. However, before considering his analysis of the passions and the control of the mind over the vital organs, let us reconsider his stand on the basic issue of function dualism.

Like Gaub, Cullen held that the vital processes of the body normally

---

[20] Trans. in L. J. Rather, *Mind and Body in Eighteenth-Century Medicine: A Study Based on Jerome Gaub's De regimine mentis* (Berkeley, 1965) (henceforth Rather, *Mind and Body*), §22: I refer to this work by section numbers.

[21] This is stressed by Rather (ibid. 14–15, 63–4). Descartes held that everything which opposes our reason is to be attributed to the body. See *Passions of the Soul*, §47; CSM I, 345–7: AT XI, 364–6.

take place purely automatically—that is, without being influenced by any mental state. At the same time, he rejected Haller's view that they take place without any nervous power; he stressed that in a living body these motions require a constant energy from the brain. According to Cullen, 'the motions of the heart and arteries of the organs of respiration, of the stomach, intestines, and perhaps other parts' are caused by 'certain internal impressions . . . which produce no sensation, nor motions of which we are conscious except when exercised in an unusual manner'.[22] For Cullen, the impressions of the brain that are the motive power of life functions are unaccompanied by any mental states.

Yet Cullen, from the very beginning of his lectures, expressed a strong interest in the question of the effect of the mind on the body—in particular, on the vital organs. He began his lectures on physiology by defining his subject as one 'which explains the conditions of the body *and of the mind* necessary to life and health' (*Institutions*, §4, my italics). He took issue with his predecessors who left the mind out of their accounts. For, 'it is not less certain that the Conditions of the Mind . . . affect the Body' than that 'the Conditions of the Body do affect the Mind' (NLS, fols. 25–6). Later on in his lectures, he specifically objected to Boerhaave, who (as we have seen) denied that the state of the mind needs to be taken into account in thinking about disease, and claimed that the vital functions operate automatically (fol. 76).

Cullen lists a number of states of mind which, by means of changes in the brain, move various parts of the body. These states of mind include voluntary actions, emotions and passions, imitation, appetites caused by external objects, and propensities to remove an 'uneasy sensation' in the body. He writes that in each of these 'some Volition is concerned' (*Institutions*, §119.5). He notes that the motions of the heart and lungs are particularly affected by the passions, which he called 'more general and vehement volitions' (§119.2). There is 'nothing more evident than that the passions of the mind affect the motion of the heart'—for example, that anger will produce violent beating of the heart, and grief will slow it (NLM, II, fol. 274).

But Cullen's reflections did not stop here. He distinguished the question of whether the visceral motions of the body are 'affected' by the mind from the question of whether they could be 'directed' by the mind (NLM, II, fol. 287). Consideration of the passions as such convinces us that the vital motions are constantly affected by the mind. But Cullen argues that they can also be voluntarily directed by the mind or soul, though only in one 'limited sense'. He saw himself as correcting the

---

[22] William Cullen, *Institutions of Medicine: Part I, Physiology*, 3rd edn. (Edinburgh, 1785) (henceforth *Institutions*), §119; cf. §§80 and 122.

views of the Stahlian physicians, who maintained that the soul constantly acts voluntarily and unconsciously in controlling the vital motions of the body.[23] According to Cullen, the mind directs or controls the body only through the conscious choice of passions.

Like Descartes, Cullen maintains that, when we are calm, we have some control over our vital functions through our imagination. What we must do is to recall certain thoughts to which our passions are conjoined. In explaining an observation by a contemporary physician of a man who could, simply by the power of his mind, slow the motion of his heartbeat to the point that it was undetectable, Cullen speculated that this could be done simply by thinking thoughts which cause a great deal of grief. He concluded that 'the heart itself is not clearly separated <from> the voluntary motions in a certain view of it' (NLM, II, fols. 273–5).

III. CONCLUSION

My aim in this paper has been to argue that there are two quite distinct dualisms to be found in eighteenth-century discussions of the relation of mind and body. The first, which I have called 'substance dualism', stems from the need to establish the possibility of the immortality of the soul, and thereby to avoid theological censure. After Descartes, many medical thinkers formulated this dualism as an essential difference between psychological states and their physical correlates in the brain. The second dualism, which I call 'function dualism', involves a distinction between mental functions—considered as either soul functions or brain functions—and those unperceived functions on which life immediately depends. It contends that life functions occur in the body completely automatically, and are not maintained by the soul. Nevertheless, as I have shown, even the proponents of function dualism discussed at length the question of whether mental states could in certain instances influence the vital organs.

Generally, the proponents of function dualism were also proponents of substance dualism. In concluding, I wish to propose an experiment to test my hypothesis that these two dualisms underlying eighteenth-century medical thought—at least until the time of Cullen—really are distinct and separable. Can writers of the time be found who espouse one of these forms of dualism, but not the other?

My first example is La Mettrie, who, while clearly rejecting substance dualism (see p. 243 above), nevertheless accepted the function dualism of Haller. In his *L'Homme-machine*, La Mettrie happily adopts Haller's

---

[23] In his lectures Cullen spoke of Stahlian views as very widespread among the medical writers of his time (NLS, fol. 167). On the views of Stahl, see François Duchesneau, Ch. 10 above.

account of the *vis insita*, arguing that this is evidence that all motions in the body, involuntary and voluntary, arise from the unknown structure of the parts. Citing ten pieces of evidence, including the claim that the heart of a frog can continue to beat for an hour and a half after being removed from its body, La Mettrie writes:

Here are many more facts than we need to show in an incontestable way that each small fibre, or part of an organized body moves itself by a principle which belongs to it, and its action does not depend on the nerves, as do voluntary actions (181–2).

This is a clear statement of Haller's view that the life forces are independent of the nervous system, and therefore of all psychic functions. La Mettrie writes of the organization in the fibres of the body as the 'springs of the human machine'. At the same time, he contrasts these many 'springs' of the animal machine with the greater spring centred in the brain, which controls voluntary motion, and is 'the source of all our sentiments, all our pleasures, all our passions, and all our thoughts' (183). In spite of this clear separation of life functions from mental functions, La Mettrie acknowledges that there is interaction between the two. He gives as an example of the influence of the mind on the body the early death of Pierre Bayle, which he attributes to consumption caused by over-stimulation of his mind (184–5)! In general, La Mettrie's view of these matters seems identical to that of Haller. Thus, there is good reason to regard La Mettrie as a proponent of function dualism, in spite of the fact that he is an outspoken substance monist (i.e. a materialist).

Finally, let me mention a medical writer who, while clearly rejecting function dualism, accepted a form of substance dualism. Robert Whytt, Cullen's predecessor in the chair of the theory of medicine at Edinburgh, published one of the most important eighteenth-century books on physiology in 1751, four years after the publication of La Mettrie's *L'Homme-machine*. In his *Essay on the Vital and Other Involuntary Motions of Animals*, Whytt claimed to be proposing a system which would show how 'unjustly the study of Medicine has been accused of leading men into Scepticism and irreligion'.[24] As the motto for his book, Whytt chose a passage from Cicero's *Tusculan Disputations* which, he claimed, showed that some of the ancients attributed all animal motions 'to the energy of a living principle wholly distinct from the body' (*Essay*, 266). Cicero had described the 'essence' of the soul as self-movement,[25] and had claimed that the motive force in an animal is 'not a quality of

---

[24] Robert Whytt, *An essay on the Vital and Other Involuntary Motions of Animals* (Edinburgh, 1751) (henceforth *Essay*), 266.
[25] Cicero, *Tusculan Disputations*, trans. J. E. King (Cambridge, 1945), I. xxiii, pp. 64–5: 'Inanimum est enim omne, quod pulsu agitur externo; quod autem est animal, id motu cietur interiore et suo. Nam haec est propria natura animi atque vis.'

heart, or blood, or brain, or atoms'.[26] Whytt took these passages to support his own view that all motions of a living body must 'be referred to the power of an *immaterial* principle' (*Essay*, 391). In so doing, he was clearly endorsing substance dualism, albeit not in precisely the form that Descartes had.

But while he accepted substance dualism, Whytt rejected the function dualism of all the medical writers examined in the last section. Whytt held that 'the involuntary motions in man are not owing to a principle distinct from the . . . soul' (*Essay*, 148). The cause of the vital motions of the body, including the beating of the heart, is a 'sensible principle' (152)—a feeling principle which operates in the body unconsciously. According to Whytt, this principle is absolutely necessary for all muscular motion, and shows the continuous operation of the soul in the body. Even when a muscle is removed from the body, according to Whytt, its living reactions show the continuing influence of the sensible principle which is retained in the nerves. Whytt later became involved in a prolonged debate with Haller which touched on both metaphysical issues and physiological ones. Citing numerous experiments, Whytt continued to reject the view that the motions of the body can occur purely mechanically, without a vital soul operating by a primitive power of sensation.[27]

In a certain way, Whytt appears as the mirror image of La Mettrie— that is, as a physician who accepts substance dualism while rejecting function dualism. Between the two of them, they bring home the great importance of distinguishing between these two different forms of soul–body dualism in eighteenth-century medical writers.

[26] *Tusculan Disputations*, I. xxv, pp. 70–1. 'Quae sit illa vis et unde sit, intelligendum puto. Non est certe nec cordis nec sanguinis nec cerebri nec atomorum'.

[27] See my 'Metaphysics and Physiology: Mind, Body, and the Animal Economy in Eighteenth-Century Scotland', in M. A. Stewart (ed.), *Studies in the Philosophy of the Scottish Enlightenment* (Oxford, 1990), 251–301, esp. 290–2; F. Duchesneau, *La Physiologie des Lumières: Empirisme, modèles et théories* (The Hague, 1982), ch. 6; and R. K. French, *Robert Whytt, the Soul and Medicine* (London, 1969), ch. 6. Paradoxically, Whytt argued that function dualism leads to the rejection of substance dualism. He expresses surprise that theologians would not have recognized sooner that, once they admitted with Descartes that 'all the actions of the most perfect brutes . . . result from mere mechanism', it would follow as 'a natural and easy consequence' that 'every action in man' would be ascribed to 'no higher a principle' (*Essay*, 153). He almost certainly had in mind the arguments of La Mettrie for materialism. Nevertheless, it is important to note that, before La Mettrie, eighteenth-century physicians had no difficulty admitting that most higher functions of human beings had mechanical correlates, while at the same time adopting substance dualism.

Psyche, Soma, and the Vitalist Philosophy of Medicine

ROSELYNE REY†

I. VITALISM

In order to understand the positions held by vitalist physicians in the second half of the eighteenth century, it is important to be aware of the intellectual milieu in which vitalism developed, and of the specific theories to which its proponents were reacting. Vitalism[1] was a view on the relationship of the body and soul (*âme*) whose main feature may be seen as the rejection of any form of simplistic dualism. In fact, in the course of their simultaneous attacks on both mechanist and animist views, the eighteenth-century vitalists tended to circumscribe the problems they were facing rather than to provide a final, unified response to them. Cartesian dualism had opened up a radical discontinuity between the activity of the rational soul, on the one hand, and the mechanism of the body, on the other, making possible a study of the body alone, as is undertaken in Descartes' *Traité de l'homme*. The vitalists questioned the applicability of this Cartesian dualism, mainly on methodological grounds. But equally, they were led to reject the views of the animists, who, in restoring the soul's power over the body in organic functions such as digestion and the secretions, were guilty in their eyes of having given too much to the soul, and taken too much from the body—and in so doing, of having created a purely passive bodily machine.

[1] I apply this term to the collection of positions which are to be found in France in the school of Montpellier and also elsewhere (J. F. Blumenbach (1752–1840) in Germany, John Hunter (1728–93) in England), and whose main representatives are Ménuret de Chambaud, Bordeu, Fouquet, Barthez, J. C. Grimaud (1750–89), and V. De Sèze (1760–1830); although the word 'vitalist' became current only later, these physicians shared, in spite of their differences, a critical attitude to both iatro-mechanism and to the animism of Stahl, with whom they have often been confused, and a positive position on the power of sensibility. For more details, see Roselyne Rey, *Naissance et développement du vitalisme en France, de la deuxième moitié du XVIIIe siècle à la fin du Premier Empire* (Ph.D. thesis, Paris-I, 1987), published in Studies on Voltaire and the Eighteenth Century (Oxford, 1999).

The vitalists' primary thesis was an affirmation of the unity of man, a being which must always be studied as a whole, and whose *physical* and *moral* aspects are closely conjoined. The belief in this unity, which presupposes a continual interaction between the physical and the moral, is reflected in their conviction that medicine and morality are interconnected, in their conceptualization of mental illness, and in their careful observation of the effects of psychological states on the health of the body (the sign of a nascent psychosomatic medicine). Although the thesis of the unity of the physical and moral aspects of life is often attributed to Pierre Cabanis (1757–1808) and the *idéologues*, it was in fact formulated long before, in the middle of the eighteenth century, by the Parisian physician Louis de Lacaze (1703–65), in his *Specimen novi medicinae conspectus* of 1749, and then in 1755 in his *Idée de l'homme physique et moral*. It is to him that the Montpellier physician Jean Jacques Ménuret de Chambaud (1733–1815) refers constantly in the articles he contributed to the *Encyclopédie*. Indeed, the great number, diversity, and persistence of references to Lacaze[2] throughout the century show his wide influence. Although he was neither the first nor the only physician to confront the problem of the relation between psychic and somatic activities, he was without doubt the first to crystallize a group of previously unconnected ideas concerning the principles of action and reaction among three centres: the centre of phrenic forces located in the epigastric region, the brain, and the general external organ. He conceived of life as a system of forces and oscillations—not necessarily mechanical—among these connected poles of energy. Lacaze's long chapter on the 'affections of the soul' demonstrates his belief in the importance of sensory stimulation in maintaining equilibrium among the three centres. The result of his work is a theory encompassing needs and passions, their modifications in social life, and the role of habit. Lacaze's writings, as characterized by Ménuret in the *Encyclopédie*, deal as much with morality and happiness as with medicine.[3]

However, the idea of a reciprocal movement from the moral to the physical and from the physical to the moral is not, of itself, adequate to define vitalism. The Stahlians too had claimed to demonstrate the influ-

---

[2] He is mentioned and discussed by, among others, Bordeu, Roussel, Barthez, and Buffon. On this subject see Henri Fouquet, 'Sensibilité', in D. Diderot and J. D'Alembert (eds.), *Encyclopédie, ou Dictionnaire raisonné des sciences, des arts et des métiers* (Paris, 1751–65), xv. 41b.

[3] Jean Jacques Ménuret de Chambaud, 'Oeconomie animale', in *Encyclopédie*, xi. 366b. Ménuret writes: 'But one of the main advantages of this new medical approach, and in which it is eminently preferable and truly unique, is the great light it casts on hygiene, or the science of regimen, this branch of medicine so precious and so neglected, and its embracing the regimen of the sensations and passions in such a positive and clear way as to result in a medical treatise of morality and happiness.'

ence of the soul on the body, especially in diseases, and the mechanists on their side emphasized the dependence of the soul on bodily states. (La Mettrie, for example, argued that phenomena such as vertigo, or the effects of indigestion or inebriation, show that the soul is completely subject to the organization of the body, and on this basis he questioned the distinct existence of the soul.) The vitalists, for their part, ridiculed the Stahlian idea that the soul commits errors in fighting off disease, and objected to the very principle of appealing to the soul in normal organic functions:

To refer to the soul for an explanation of life and as a place to discover the laws of the animal economy is to cut the knot rather than to untie it, to beg the question, and to enshroud it in the same obscurity this spiritual being (the soul) itself possesses for us.[4]

Ménuret rejected both the Stahlian and the mechanist positions for the same basic reason: namely, that they gave an inadequate description of the body itself:

The idea that the soul is the efficient cause of inflammation because it is the principle of vital movement is not an incontestable truth. It is true that if our body were an inanimate machine, lacking life, some other agent would have to exist to direct, maintain, and initiate its movements. And in fact the errors of the mechanists, I believe, arise precisely from their not considering animals as complex and organized living bodies.[5]

In their rejection of the two main contemporary medical currents, the vitalists took up a position whose central feature was the requirement that account be taken of the 'sense of the vector' which moves 'from the moral to the physical'. But this did not mean that they thought of such an influence in Stahlian terms, as resulting from a soul operating either consciously and reflectively (Stahl's *logismos*) or simply in some instinctual reasoning capacity (*logos*).

This last point merits particular attention, since it nicely illustrates the difficulties and the special character of the vitalist position. Ménuret de Chambaud, Théophile Bordeu (1722–76), and Henri Fouquet (1727–1806) continue to write of a soul, and even to write of it as a reality incommensurable with the physical, as something immortal and immaterial. But this soul, which turns up on occasion in such common expressions as 'passions of the soul', has literally lost its meaning. Lacking any power over the body, this spiritual entity has ceased to have any relevance to medicine or even to morality. As a referent without a signification, it can cast no shadow over what for the vitalists becomes

---

[4] Ibid. 364b.
[5] Ménuret de Chambaud, 'Inflammation', in *Encyclopédie*, viii. 713a.

the essential property of living matter, *sensibility*. For it is from this property that they seek to reconstruct the whole complex nature of the living being. Vitalists such as Paul Joseph Barthez (1734–1806) refer to the soul, distinguishing it from both the body and the vital principle; but when they come to analyse the functions performed in the living being, these are ascribed to sensibility or to the vital principle. Thus, the vitalist position is expounded independently of the traditional dualist problem of the relation of the soul and body. These writers attempt to describe the nature of a reality capable of accounting for the whole gamut of vital phenomena, from the most complex sensations and perceptions down to the most elementary manifestations of life.

II. SENSIBILITY: A PSYCHO-PHYSIOLOGICAL IDEA

Although Henri Fouquet is not as well known as other physicians of the Montpellier school, such as Barthez or Bordeu, his long article on 'Sensibilité' in the *Encyclopédie* documents well the widening of this concept, and its significance for the question of dualism. While at the beginning of the article he defines sensibility functionally, as 'the property certain parts have of perceiving the impressions of external objects and of then producing movements in proportion to the intensity of this perception',[6] this concept is developed further in the course of his historical discussion of the sensitive soul and the question of its material nature. He traces a succession of theories of the sensitive soul from antiquity to the seventeenth century, arguing that the weight of authority would lead one to conclude that 'sensibility, or the sensitive soul, is substantial', and not merely some sort of intermediate quality between soul and body. Fouquet recalls that the ancients, 'not conceiving that two opposites like soul and body could interact in any other way than by a medium, imagined this medium in several different ways',[7] as spirit in the literal sense, as form, or as '*je ne sais quoi*'. However, after citing the views of the ancient atomists and a number of modern writers who consider the sensitive soul as a substantial reality within the animal, he embraces the view of J. B. van Helmont and T. Willis, who consider it to be a kind of 'vital flame'. (Similarly, Ménuret, in the article on 'Animal Economy', in considering a list of equivalents to sensibility, cites the *archaeus* of van Helmont, the *impetus*, the *enormon*, and the fine atoms and fiery soul of P. Gassendi.) Fouquet favours the theories of the atomists, not only because they consider the sensible soul to be material, but also because they consider it to be decentralized and spread through-

---

[6] Fouquet, 'Sensibilité', 38b.   [7] Ibid. 39a.

out the body. Indeed, for the vitalists, sensibility is a general property of living beings, irrespective of their possessing consciousness. The writers of the *Encyclopédie*, long before Cabanis, affirmed that 'to live is to feel', and held that sensibility is found both in the most complex as well as the simplest animals, such as the polyp or the snail. In his article, Fouquet was not merely postulating a soul which is reasonable and intellectual; sensibility explains all the functions of a living being.

Fouquet postulated elementary sensations which are at the root of all other sensations: the feeling of existence and the feeling of pleasure and pain. These sensations depend upon the number of nerve fibres in each organ, which vary according to an individual's habits, age, sex, etc. Sensibility depends on the states and stages of life from the embryo to adulthood. Following Lacaze, he held that pleasure and pain obey a reciprocal double movement of expansion and contraction which, rather than being limited to the nerve fibres themselves, takes place at the level of the centres of sensitivity, which are also the centres of activity. Sensibility includes both the property of sensing and that of responding to a sensation by some movement or organic change.

Fouquet rejects adding to these sensations 'moral conditions' ascribed to the reasonable soul,[8] arguing that, considered in this way, they add nothing to the understanding of what is happening in the individual. In fact, 'the operations of the soul are no less dependent upon sensibility'[9] than, for example, the functioning of the heart and vessels. The concept of sensibility here goes beyond its strictly physiological meaning to include the realms of aesthetic emotion and sentiment. It resolves a confusion concerning psychic activity and conscious activity by opening up a space for acts, behaviours, and thoughts that are not directly limited to sensation, but grow out of it.

The physicians of Montpellier used the concept of sensibility to provide an explanation not only for mental diseases, but also for a class of normal phenomena collected under the names of habit, sympathy, and antipathy. Bordeu says that in a decentralized conception of sensibility each organ has its region and its field of action, as well as a kind of taste or instinct which impels it to seek certain nutriments, to choose one kind

[8] Ibid. 40a: 'And so it is a condition inseparable from the animal state, this perception or material sensing, or as one says, sensing in the substance. The reasonable soul may, without doubt, add to these sensations through moral circumstances, but once again, these circumstances do not belong to the animal considered as such, and it is even probable do not take place in many.'

[9] Ibid. 40b: 'The operations of the soul are no less dependent upon sensibility, pleasure, and grief, and all the passions seem to be represented in the remarkable centre formed in the epigastric region by the many nervous plexuses. And indeed, there is no difficult calculation, strong concentration, or straining of the memory in which at the outset the stomach and epigastric centre are not as it were contracted.'

of behaviour rather than another,[10] and to feel itself in agreement with one state of affairs rather than with another. Fouquet postulates a non-conscious psychic activity which does not originate in the intellectual functions, but which, while it models itself on secretion,[11] goes beyond what is conventionally recognized as the sphere of action of the organic functions. This expanded concept of sensibility is used to explain the effects of music, the impression that beauty makes, and the secret inclinations we sometimes feel. 'All this is a disposition of the organs, a matter of taste in the sensitive soul which occurs in some manner or other without our having any awareness of it.'[12]

III. A SOUL WITHOUT A USE

The views of Ménuret de Chambaud are perhaps even more precise than those of Fouquet. Like Fouquet, he continues to refer to a spiritual soul, but these references seem to be purely a matter of form, and in certain articles it is clear that he is trying to protect himself from being accused of materialism. In his article on 'Animal Economy', for example, Ménuret distinguishes mental or 'animal functions' from vital and natural functions; he reports that these are commonly thought to result from the union of soul and body:

They are named in this way (i.e. 'animal') because they are thought to result from the interaction of the soul with the body; they are unable to function (in man) without the common operation of these two agents; these are the movements called voluntary, and the external and internal sensations.[13]

But he goes on to attribute psychic functions to the same general cause as other functions, and only adds a reference to the union of the soul and body as an afterthought:

The movement of the fibres of the brain (in concert with the operations of the soul and consequently with the laws governing its union with the body) determines the internal sensations, ideas, imagination, judgement, and memory.[14]

---

[10] The term 'behaviour' applied to an organ may seem surprising: nevertheless, in comparing the 'secretory habits' of one or other organ to the behaviour of a snake which has just been decapitated but still seeks refuge in its habitual hole, or again to the instinct that is roused in the presence of a loved object, Fouquet places in the realm of sensibility a class of spontaneous phenomena, instinctive and involuntary, which could be thought to belong to the domain of non-conscious psychic life.

[11] Fouquet, 'Sécretion', in *Encyclopédie*, xiv. 871–6, which contains a good account of Bordeu's doctrine on the activity of the glands.   [12] Fouquet, 'Sensibilité', 45a.

[13] Ménuret de Chambaud, 'Oeconomie animale', 362a.   [14] Ibid. 361b.

In the article 'Death', Ménuret makes it clear at the outset that there is no rational basis for considering this subject from any metaphysical perspective in terms of the relationship between the soul and the body:

The separation of the soul from the body, a mystery perhaps more comprehensible than its union, is a theological dogma certified by religion and thus incontestable; but it is neither in conformity with any light of reason, nor supported by any observation of medicine.[15]

In spite of the fact that his discussion of psychic functions is spread over several cross-referenced articles of the *Encylopédie*, no doubt as part of a strategy of dissimulation, it all points to the conclusion that animal functions can be analysed entirely in the framework of sensibility and the properties of living fibre. This framework does not deny the difference of viewpoint which may exist between psychic activity and the organic functions, but it fails to imply any difference of nature between body and soul, any opposition between two substances.

Pathological states illustrate well how the gap between psychic and organic functions was bridged by vitalist writers. In his article on 'Somnambulism' in the *Encyclopédie*, Ménuret went beyond the common observation (found, for example, in S. A. Tissot's *Traité des nerfs et de leurs maladies* of 1782) that there is a dissociation between the waking state and the state of the somnambulist, to show that these are not totally opposed. He discusses the story of a clergyman who wrote sermons during the night, even rising to correct hiatuses he had left,[16] and who, believing that he was swimming in icy water to save a child, made all the appropriate movements, completely unaware that he was at the time in his bed. For Ménuret the interest of the story lies in the discovery of a double system of psychic activity and of partial interferences between the two psychic streams. Ménuret asks:

How is it possible that while asleep [the somnambulist] can recall to memory something that had happened to him when he was awake, and also know what he had done during other periods of sleep, but that on waking he retains no memory at all? In fact, in his waking state he was surprised on occasion to be accused of being a somnambulist, and of working, writing, and talking during the night. He could not understand how these accusations could be made against him, a person who slept soundly the whole night through, and who could only be roused with difficulty. This double memory is a remarkable phenomenon.[17]

---

[15] Ménuret, 'Mort', in *Encyclopédie*, x. 718b.

[16] Ménuret, 'Somnambulisme', in *Encyclopédie*, xv. 341a: the ecclesiastic whose story Ménuret recounts had written 'ce divin enfant', then, noticing the hiatus, corrected it to 'cet adorable enfant'. But if one substituted a piece of paper similar to the one he had just written on, he did not notice it.   [17] Ibid. 341b.

This story overthrows a number of received opinions, for one cannot simply say that there are automatic processes taking place in the state of somnambulism which have no relationship with waking life. The somnambulist is able to perceive certain sense impressions, such as hot and cold or the texture of a piece of paper, though he is unable to interpret the whole collection of stimuli he receives the way he could if he were awake. Somnambulism shows that memory, imagination, and sensibility function in a selective and intermittent way. Neither the opposition between waking and sleep, nor that between psychic and somatic states, can be taken as absolute.

IV. VITALIST ACCOUNTS OF MENTAL PATHOLOGY

Ménuret's analyses of the causes and treatment of melancholy and mania also illustrate the way in which mental and physical states are considered as part of the same continuum. Although the most frequently cited explanation of melancholy invokes troubles in the epigastric region, where various nervous plexuses are concentrated, the physician must take account of many possible factors, such as passions of the soul, intense application of the mind, profound meditations, as well as modifications in the excremental fluxes. Mental illness can be approached by using cases where the mind and the body each play a particular role, where the physician acts upon the one in order better to reach the other. Thus the vitalists were already well on the way to developing what later—when it was systematized and amplified by the alienists of the end of the eighteenth century—came to be called the 'moral treatment' of these disorders. Ménuret writes:

It is necessary in the treatment of melancholy, in order that success be more certain, to begin by curing the mind, and then to attack the faults of the body when these become known. For this reason, a prudent physician must know how to win the confidence of his patient, whether by entering into his way of thought, or by accommodating to his ravings, or by appearing to be persuaded that things are such as the patient imagines them to be.[18]

In mania (or 'universal delirium'), on the contrary, therapy is directed first to the body, in which it aims to produce a shock and a deep disturbance. It is striking to see the persistence of traditional physical remedies—sudden immersion in cold water, letting the patient fall, cautery, emetics, violent smelling salts, physical exercise, horseback riding, etc.—

[18] Ménuret, 'Melancholie', in *Encyclopédie*, x. 310a; the article is not signed, but several references and a comparison with the article 'Mania', signed by Ménuret, demonstrate his authorship.

which are, however, given a new interpretation by the vitalists. No longer are these measures justified because they stimulate evacuation or provoke a modification in the movement of the humours, but rather because they produce a general commotion of the body (thereby justifying the name 'perturbative method'). Ménuret writes:

I believe that in order to cure mania one must violently and suddenly disturb the whole body, and thereby bring about a radical change: this is why the violent remedies prescribed by ignorant but fearless empirics sometimes succeed.[19]

The aim is to act roughly on the body in order to provoke a violent reaction of the mind.

The unified approach to psychic and physical states is even more pronounced in the conception of those 'diseases called nervous or vaporous'. Ideas initially presented in Théophile Bordeu's *Recherches sur les maladies chroniques* (1775) were developed in more detail by Paul Joseph Barthez in his *Nouveaux eléments de la science de l'homme* (1806). Independent of any lesion, the vaporous man, or more often woman,[20] suffers feelings of constriction that pass upward from the lower abdomen towards the throat, palpitations, sweating, and syncope. Barthez conceives of the disease as a morbid state of sensibility, revealed not in a lesion of a single fibre or specific organ, but at the level of the entire organism. It is manifested in a response disproportionate to the strength of the stimulus that provokes it; for example, a mild irritation causes a violent reaction, or a strong irritation is only weakly felt. The therapy of Barthez is based on an alternation and combination of remedies which act in opposite directions, sedatives and tonics administered with the aim of 'breaking the habitual tendency' of the disease. In proposing a general alteration of the system of sensitive forces and of their influence on the motor forces, Barthez is drawing from the revival of ancient Methodist ideas of spasm and atony initiated by Friedrich Hoffmann.

Since one cannot point to any specific lesion in one part of the body as the cause of the vapours, Barthez finds it natural to turn, at one and the same time, to both a moral cause and to the vital principle itself:

The principle cause, in my opinion, lies in the fact that contemporary social customs in Europe habitually forbid the demonstration of strong passions, as was possible in earlier and cruder ages; and that today these strong passions are replaced by a large number of weak passions, frustrated in turn by

---

[19] Ménuret, 'Manie', in *Encyclopédie*, x. 33b.

[20] The question of the greater susceptibility of women to the vapours than men was long debated; but Barthez, like Ménuret, explains this predilection not by a greater natural susceptibility, but by the greater number of constraints that social life places upon women.

numerous obstacles of corresponding size. It is through the action of all these minor passions that the moral being of man is continually bruised, checked, and tormented in every way: and the habit of these moral affections perverts in a similar way the physical state of the forces and functions of the vital principle as a result of the wide influence that the soul has on this principle.[21]

The principal cause of the disease lies, then, in the frustration of our stronger passions by the customs of our society. This in turn causes physical changes in the vital principle.

V. BARTHEZ'S ACCOUNT OF THE VITALIST PRINCIPLE

What, then, is the vital principle, according to Barthez? He stresses that his vital principle is not the thinking and reasonable soul; nor is it to be confounded with the body.[22] Unlike Ménuret, he vigorously resists any attempt to make the vital principle a substance distinct from both soul and body, suggesting instead that it could well turn out to be nothing but a mode of matter: 'It is doubtful whether the vital principle exists by itself . . . or whether it only exists as a faculty attached to the combinations of movement and material of which a living body consists.'[23] He also considers it as an abstraction, like a mathematical variable x, y, or z, which is postulated in order to shorten and facilitate the calculation of phenomena. In other places he stresses our lack of knowledge of the nature of the vital principle, although he refuses to ascribe its operations to a purely mechanical activity. More positively, he considers it to be the unity of a living being which is generated through the correspondence of all the parts of the body, and which accounts for the fact that the being maintains itself through the processes of assimilation, destruction, and repair.[24]

While it is definitely not a separate substance, the vital principle is understood by Barthez as lying at the interface of the notions of soul and body. Although he denies that these can act directly on each other, he sketches the hypothesis of a pre-established harmony which unites the vital principle both with the thinking soul and with the body. His effort to give a meaning to the relationship between vital forces and the psychic state reveals itself particularly in his attempts to explain in terms of contemporary medicine several Hippocratic concepts such as 'tem-

[21] Paul Joseph Barthez, *Nouveaux eléments de la science de l'homme* (Paris, 1806), ii. 174.
[22] Ibid. i. ch. 3, 'Sceptic considerations regarding the nature of the vital principle in man', esp. 84 ff.
[23] Ibid. 100.   [24] Ibid. 109–10.

perament' and 'habit'. The idea that ultimately emerges as central is that of 'energy'. Barthez argues that this concept is more general than the concept of 'sensibility', and less subject to confusion.[25] It consists in a parallelism of the two series of facts, psychic and physical, which both have 'a great analogy' and 'very clear relationships'[26] with the vital principle. Energy, then, is the theoretical meeting-point between these two orders of facts, and the analysis of its features will allow the elaboration of the new 'science of man' which Barthez is attempting to found.

VI. CONCLUSION

We can distinguish two basic directions in which the vitalist physicians were working, both of which represent their answer to the apparently simple question of the distinction between psyche and soma. First, it must be emphasized that this distinction, whenever it was once posited, immediately began to shift, since each of the two sides tended to melt away and disappear. In particular, by discarding the identity of sensibility and consciousness, vitalist physiologists and physicians were able to secure access to a collection of phenomena like somnambulism or such dissociative states as catalepsy, which called into question the simplicity and oneness of psychic activity. (It should not be thought, however, that they arrived at the idea of the unconscious, as has sometimes been claimed.) Sensibility, on its side, allowed a progression from confused, undifferentiated, and local sensation to a combination of sensations capable of explaining judgement, memory, and imagination. The contribution of M. F. X. Bichat[27] to this division of sensibility into the two categories 'organic' and 'animal' was decisive, as was his idea that there is a transformation from one to the other according to various thresholds of intensity. In the second place, the vitalists were particularly interested in boundary concepts that are difficult to assign clearly to either the physical or the moral sphere—for example, temperament, the effects of habit, the process of sleep, irregularities of activity or energy. Against a static and localizing view of living functions, the vitalists proposed a more integrated approach, which reflected an awareness of the complexity of the interaction between the different components of the human being.

---

[25] The concept of energy, as opposed to that of sensibility, to which it is nevertheless closely related, is not exclusively attached to an anatomical structure or to the properties of tissue. Its significance, then, goes beyond the problem of the sensibility of nervous tissue. [26] Barthez, *Eléments*, ii. 231.

[27] The main writings of Bichat are: *Traité des membranes en général et diverses membranes en particulier* (Paris, 1800); *Anatomie générale, appliquée à la physiologie et à la médecine* (4 vols., Paris, 1802); *Traité d'anatomie descriptive* (5 vols., Paris 1801–3).

13

Physique and *Moral*

FRANÇOIS AZOUVI

The year 1802 saw the publication, in Paris, of Pierre Jean Georges Cabanis's two-volume *Rapports du physique et du moral de l'homme*. One might speculate that in this work Cabanis, familiar with the ideas that had been developed in the Montpellier school, was making an allusion to the work of Louis de Lacaze published in 1755 under the title *Idée de l'homme physique et moral, pour servir d'introduction à un traité de médecine*. Indeed, the pair *homme physique/homme moral* is present from the earliest pages of Cabanis's book, used to support his contention that 'the moralist and the physician always walk the same path': medicine can never gain a complete knowledge of physical man unless it considers him in the various states into which variations of sensibility bring him; equally, the moralist cannot hope to know moral man unless he examines him under the most varied physical circumstances.[1]

It could also be, however, that Cabanis was not thinking particularly of Lacaze's book, for by 1802 a multitude of French publications included the pair *physique/moral* in their titles. To note some of these: L. B. Castel, *L'Homme moral opposé à l'homme physique de M. Rousseau: Lettres philosophiques où l'on réfute le déisme du jour* (1756); P. H. D. d'Holbach, *Système de la nature ou des lois du monde physique et du monde moral* (1770); Beaux de Maguielles, *Lettre sur la philosophie nouvelle et sur les principes de l'Essai de philosophie élémentaire sur le système de l'univers, ou des lois du monde physique, du monde moral et du monde intelligible* (1775); P. Roussel, *Système physique et moral de la femme* (1775); A. J. Pernety, *La Connaissance de l'homme*

---

[1] Pierre Jean Georges Cabanis, *Rapports du physique et du moral de l'homme*, ed. C. Lehec and J. Cazeneuve (Paris, 1954), I, 110. Among the recent work on Cabanis the most extensive is that of M. S. Staum, *Cabanis: Enlightenment and Medical Philosophy in the French Revolution* (Princeton, 1980); particularly pertinent is ch. 7: 'Sensitivity: Source of Physique and Moral'. Older works include the following: F. Colonna d'Istria, 'Cabanis et les origines de la vie psychologique', *Revue de métaphysique et de morale*, 19 (1911), 177–98; *idem*, 'L'influence du moral sur le physique d'après Cabanis et Maine de Biran', *Revue de métaphysique et de morale*, 21 (1913), 451–561.

moral par celle de l'homme physique (1776); J. A. Borelly, *Introduction à la connaissance et au perfectionnement de l'homme physique et moral* (1796); and, in the same year, *Considérations physiques et morales sur la nature de l'homme* by J. A. Perreau. And this is but a selection from a much vaster literature on the subject. Thus Cabanis was by no means necessarily calling up Lacaze when he chose to give this title to the collection of twelve papers he had read before the National Institute of Sciences and Arts between 1796 and 1801. The pair *physique/moral* had by that date become as commonplace as the pair body/soul a century earlier.

In the years that followed, Cabanis's book was to call forth a series of replies: by M. F. P. Maine de Biran in 1811, under the title of *Rapport du physique et du moral de l'homme*; by F. J. Bérard in 1823 entitled *Doctrine des rapports du physique et du moral, pour servir de fondement à la metaphysique*; then by Maine de Biran again in response to Bérard's work, his *Nouvelles Considérations sur les rapports du physique et du moral de l'homme* (1823).

Looking back, we may ask whether the work of Lacaze was the first to include the pair *physique/moral* in its title? Not at all. In 1749, a French translation of the famous work of F. Hutcheson, *An Inquiry into the Original of our Ideas of Beauty and Virtue* (1725) had appeared; for the second part of the English subtitle '*In two Treatises [. . .] II Concerning Moral Good and Evil*' the translator offers, somewhat freely '*Le second, sur le Bien et le Mal physique et moral*'. Lacaze may also have been inspired by the work of Father André which appeared in 1741 under the title *Essai sur le beau, où l'on examine en quoi consiste précisément le beau dans le physique, dans le moral . . . .* But we can also go back to the seventeenth century: in 1673 F. Poullain de La Barre published his celebrated *De l'égalité des deux sexes*, whose subtitle reads *Discours physique et moral où l'on voit l'importance de se défaire des préjugés*, and this had been preceded by a certain Lazare Meyssonnier, who published in 1657 a *Grand Almanach chrétien-catholique, moral, physique, historique et astronomique*.

Hence, it is clear that long before Cabanis, and even long before Lacaze, the pair *physique/moral* had made its entry into the French language.[2] Dictionaries, too, throw light on the pair. For example, in the 1721 edition of the *Dictionnaire de Trévoux*, *physique* as an adjective

---

[2] The study which follows deals mainly with France. It could well be expanded to include other countries. For Italy see the work of Frediano Elici, *Arca novella di sanità: Trattato fisico morale con alcune regole per conservarsi sano e vivere virtuosamente* (Lucca, 1656). In English see William Winstanley, *The New Help to Discourse, Wit, and Mirth, Intermix'd with most Serious Matters, Consisting of a Pleasant, Philosophical, Historical, Moral, and Political Question and Answer* (London, 1721).

means 'real, existing in nature', whereas *moral* means 'that which concerns morals, conduct of life'. Thus one says 'assurance morale, sûreté morale' for probability, likelihood. But one also says 'preuve, démonstration morale' as opposed to 'démonstration physique ou mathématique'. The *Dictionnaire* here makes reference to P. D. Huet's *Demonstratio evangelica*. But an adverbial usage is also included: 'physiquement' meaning 'd'une manière réelle'. The authors add that 'in most questions, one makes a distinction between *physiquement parlant* and *moralement parlant*'. Let us take note of this formulation, and of the date at which it is made 'in most questions'. By 1721, then, the usage opposing *physique* and *moral* already seems widespread. But it also seems that this usage had its origin in domains—aesthetics and morals—other than the one where it was destined to develop its final form—medicine. Thus, for example, Andrew Ramsay remarks in his *Voyages de Cyrus* (1727) that 'physical evil is necessary to cure moral evil'.[3] And Abbé Dubos writes in 1719 in his *Réflexions critiques sur la poésie et sur la peinture*: 'Why shall we not believe that it is the physical which gives its law to the moral?'[4]

Furthermore, the *Dictionnaire de l'Académie française* includes the pair *physique/moral* from its 1694 edition onward, with examples and the same meaning we noted above in the *Dictionnaire de Trévoux* (1721):

One says *assurance morale, sûreté morale* to signify: probable assurance, apparent confidence; in that case *morale* is set in opposition to *physique*. Thus one says: 'We cannot give you physical confidence on this subject, but moral confidence exists.'

This is not, however, the meaning that N. Malebranche understands in his *Méditations chrétiennes et métaphysiques* (1683), when he introduces the opposition *physique* and *moral* in the framework of a discussion on general laws and the particular acts of volition of the Creator. 'You are much more admirable', he says to God, 'when you cover the earth with fruits and flowers by the general laws of Nature, than when by particular volitions you send fire from heaven to reduce to ashes sinners and their cities.' He continues: 'But if you had combined the physical with the moral, just as the universal flood and other considerable events followed necessarily from natural laws, would there not have been . . . wisdom in your actions?'[5] What does the term *moral* refer to here? It is

[3] Andrew Ramsay, *Les Voyages de Cyrus, avec un discours sur la mythologie* (Paris, 1727), II, 186.
[4] Charles Dubos, *Réflections critiques sur la poésie et sur la peinture*, 2nd edn. (Paris, 1738), II, 310.
[5] Nicolas Malebranche, *Méditations chrétiennes et métaphysiques*, in *Oeuvres complètes*, ed. A. Robinet (Paris, 1959), X, 79. This is cited by Sergio Moravia, the author of the only study devoted to the pair *physique/moral* of which I am aware: *Il pensiero degli*

not easy to say with precision, but, in any case, it cannot refer to likelihood or probability. Is there a contradiction between this usage and that of the dictionary of the *Académie française*? Not really, for in both cases *moral* is that which, taken in a general sense, does not belong to the order of physical reality.

Moral is introduced, it seems, when the necessity is felt to designate a realm of experience which is opposed not only to that of physical nature, but also to that of the soul, in the then accepted sense of the term. Let me put forward a hypothesis which I shall attempt to establish in the rest of the chapter: when, as a result of the Cartesian revolution, soul became synonymous with thought, and body with movement, the need arose for a new term to designate the opposite of material reality, to designate the realm to which we refer today with the word *psychique*—in English, 'psychological'—a term as indispensable as it is vague. *Moral*, then, would be the ancestor of *psychique*, referring to something non-material, which is nevertheless not pure thought.

To verify this hypothesis, I propose that we set out from Cabanis's *Rapports du physique et du moral* and work our way backward through time. Beginning in the preface of his work, Cabanis sets the study of physical and moral man into historical perspective; in so doing, he expresses an idea of which all his contemporaries were also convinced, and which modern historians have taken over from them: 'ever since it has been judged proper to draw a line of separation between the study of physical man and moral man, the principles pertaining to the latter field have found themselves necessarily obscured by the vagueness of metaphysical hypotheses'.[6] Before John Locke—that is, before there was finally a rigorous philosophy to set the intellectual and moral world into relationship with its organic and vital causes—the moral sciences had no fixed basis. Let us translate the point Cabanis is making: the dualism of Descartes dug out a chasm between physical and moral man which subsequent philosophy and medicine have striven to fill up. The discipline called the 'science of man' (*anthropologie*) owes its novelty and its importance to the decision made at its inception to handle together both the science of physical man (or physiology) and the science of moral man (or the study of ideas, or again, of ideology). It is in opposition to Descartes, in opposition to his dualism of soul and body, that the science of man defends and cultivates the study of the relationship between the physical and the moral. What Cabanis means by

---

Idéologues: Scienza e filosofia in Francia (1780–1815) (Florence, 1974), 165–79. Consult also Bernard Baertschi, *Les Rapports de l'âme et du corps: Descartes, Diderot et Maine de Biran* (Paris, 1992).

[6] Cabanis, *Rapports*, 111.

'physical' presents hardly any difficulty. We can form a precise idea merely by reading the table of contents of his work. After the 'General considerations on the study of man' and a 'Physiological account of the sensations' comes a series of *Mémoires*: 'On the influence of the different ages of life upon the ideas and the moral affections', 'On the influence of differences of sex upon the character of the ideas and the moral affections', 'On the influence of temperaments . . .', 'On the influence of climate . . .', etc. The principle on which these explanations rest is relatively simple and well known, having been presented in the first *Mémoire*: sensibility is the ultimate fact at which one arrives in the study of the phenomena of life and, at the same time, the most general fact revealed by an analysis of the moral faculties. In other words, the human being is defined by its sensitive unity. Every event occurring in physical man is capable of 'influencing' moral man through this common sensitivity. In this passage, Cabanis formulates a kind of anti-Cartesian 'cogito' which shows clearly his true philosophical designs: 'From the moment we have sensation, we are.'[7]

The consequence of this 'psycho-physiological unity', to use a phrase from Sergio Moravia, is immediately drawn by Cabanis himself. If physical man and moral man are ruled by the same principle, then 'the *physique* and the *moral* originate from the same common stream, or, more explicitly, the moral is only the physical regarded from certain particular points of view'. This formulation is obviously a little enigmatic: what are these 'points of view' upon whose differences the appellation 'moral man' depends? The expression is taken up again in the sixth *Mémoire*, where it receives its explanation. Cabanis repeats that physical man constitutes, in fact, by himself all the faculties of man: 'for the language of philosophy only distinguishes the modifications *physique* and *moral* because observers, in order not to become confused in their primary analyses, were forced to consider the phenomena of life from two different points of view'.[8] This is explained in more detail a number of pages later, where Cabanis affirms that it is from the way the nervous system functions 'that one must deduce the differences observed in the functions, or in the faculties, which are in turn nothing more than the functions themselves or their general results'.[9] When one considers the nervous system as being capable of receiving excitations in its sensory organs, this 'point of view' gives rise to the idea of physical man; but when one considers it as capable of producing spontaneous acts, either motor or representational, one has to do with moral man. In the language of today, we might perhaps say that physical man is the peripheral nervous system, moral man the central nervous system. Cabanis

---

[7] Ibid. 142.   [8] Ibid. 317.   [9] Ibid. 322.

himself uses a different language, one taken over from Sydenham: 'the other name for moral man is interior man, that is, the cerebral organ'.[10]

In this light, the celebrated assertions of the eleventh *Mémoire*, entitled 'On the influence of the moral on the physical', may be understood without difficulty. Of what does this so-called influence consist? It denotes the action of one particular organ—the brain—on the other organs.[11] In this way, the enigma contained in the title—how could there be any relationship between the physical and the moral?—is resolved. There is only, if you will, a relationship between the physical and the physical.

It is certain that Cabanis, however original his work may be, is here the heir of an intellectual tradition which he could not but recognize. The reduction of the moral to the physical once again—to take up the expression of Maine de Biran[12]—had by 1802 received its letters patent of nobility, if one may use such a metaphor in regard to a doctrine which continued to appear so ignoble. In 1785, C. M. Dupaty had already noted with regret that the philosophers were not making any progress in their study of the nervous system, or physical man: for 'it is there that moral man is hidden'.[13] Is Dupaty taking an idea of Abbé Raynal, who in 1783 wrote in his *Histoire philosophique ... des Deux Indes* that the more one studies the physical and the moral, the more one becomes convinced that only the physical exists, and that it directs everything?[14] In fact, there were many thinkers in those years who thought, like Jacques in D. Diderot's *Jacques le fataliste*, that any distinction between a moral world and a physical world was meaningless.

But in all probability it was of d'Holbach that Cabanis was thinking when he spoke of the moral as *a point of view*. In his *Système de la Nature* published in 1770 d'Holbach wrote:

People have clearly misused the distinction which has so often been made between *physical* man and *moral* man. Man is a purely physical being: moral man is nothing but this physical being considered from a particular point of view, that is, relative to certain types of action which are determined by his specific organization.[15]

[10] Cabanis, *Rapports*, 209. Thomas Sydenham writes: 'Quemadmodum enim homo quidam exterior conspicitur ex partibus sensui obviis compaginatus, ita procul dubio et interior est quidam homo e debita spirituum serie et quasi fabrica constans, solo rationis lumine contemplandus' (*Opera omnia*, ed. W. A. Greenhill (London, 1846), 371).

[11] Ibid. 616.

[12] Marie François Pierre Maine de Biran, *Nouvelles considérations sur les rapports du physique et du moral de l'homme* (Paris, 1823), in *Oeuvres*, ed. B. Baertschi (Paris, 1990), IX, 66.   [13] C. M. Dupaty, *Lettres sur l'Italie, écrites en 1785* (Paris, 1825), I, 123.

[14] Abbé Raynal, *Histoire philosophique et politique des établissements et du commerce des Européens dans les Deux Indes* (Geneva, 1783), X, 14.

[15] Paul Henri Dietrich d'Holbach, *Système de la nature ou des lois du monde physique et du monde moral* (London, 1770), I, 66. The study of A. C. Kors, *D'Holbach's Coterie: An Enlightenment in Paris* (Princeton, 1972), is full of useful information.

For d'Holbach, then, as incidentally for C. A. Helvetius before him, 'moral' is the more or less useful designation of the ways which physical man has of acting: as a sensing, reasoning, imagining, or remembering being. According to these writers, it is a matter of some particular function or other becoming privileged, and taking for itself alone, or almost alone, the role of moral man. Moreover, it is understood that we are dealing here with a condensed form of expression that focuses on this function as such, and not on its origin. In 1748 J. O. de La Mettrie had given this way of seeing things considerable publicity when he said in his *L'Homme-machine* that the word 'soul' (*âme*) is a hollow word which should be used only to signify 'the part in us that thinks'. He added that 'the principle of movement' is completely adequate to explain how the animated body senses, thinks, and repents—in short, how it conducts itself 'in the physical sense, and in the moral sense that depends upon this'.[16]

The best and most consistent model for this conception of the relationship between the physical and the moral that Cabanis propounds at the end of the century was probably Louis de Lacaze's *Idée de l'homme physique et moral* (1755). Not that Lacaze forbids the use of the term 'soul' (*âme*): in fact, on first reading him, one might even think that he had a quite traditional view of the relationship of the soul to the body. For example, he writes that 'when the soul wishes to enter a state of reflection, it produces in the brain an increase of activity so that the brain will be able to maintain for as long ... as is necessary the images that the soul wishes to perceive clearly and distinctly.'[17] In reality, however, all the analyses which the book contains, as well as all its principles, reject the traditional position that these lines seem to suggest. The tone of the work is set in its very first pages, where Lacaze explains that the essential properties of the living body are movement and sensibility, and that these two properties are 'linked by a most intimate correspondence, whether this connection results from the union of their different organs with one another, or whether these organs, having at bottom the same nature, differ only in some particular modification that constitutes their properties'.[18] Of course, one could always say that these considerations do not absolutely prejudge the question of the existence of the soul; they certainly do, however, strongly suggest leaving the soul

---

[16] Julien Offray de La Mettrie, *L'Homme-machine* (Leiden, 1748), in *Oeuvres philosophiques* (Hildesheim, 1970), II, 331. For a critical edition of this text see Aram Vartanian, *La Mettrie's L'Homme-machine: A Study in the Origins of an Idea* (Princeton, 1960). Compare also the useful study of Ann Thomson, *Materialism and Society in the Mid-Eighteenth Century: La Mettrie's Discours préliminaire* (Geneva, 1981).

[17] Louis de Lacaze, *Idée de l'homme physique et moral* (Paris, 1755), 380. Jacques Roger was the first to draw attention to this long-forgotten physician: *Les Sciences de la vie dans la pensée française au XVIIIᵉ siècle*, 2nd edn. (Paris, 1971).

[18] Lacaze, *Idée*, 12–13.

to the side, and treating all aspects of moral man on the same plane as physical man. The main new insight of Lacaze was to see an interdependence of actions and reactions occurring in the body between three poles—brain, external organ (musculature), and 'centre phrénique' (diaphragm). Thus, one may conclude that the two problems of the influence of the physical on the moral and of the moral on the physical are to be treated in the same way as any other problem in physiology, and within the same conceptual framework. They are to be treated as an interplay of reciprocal actions and reactions between the three organ systems of the body.

Let us take as an example the role of sensations on the actions of organs, or, in other words, the influence of the moral on the physical. Lacaze is aware that this influence is well recognized: he certainly knew La Mettrie's *L'Homme-machine*, and probably also *De regimine mentis* by J. Gaub (1747), both of which gave very full information on the subject. But had actual progress been made in understanding these phenomena? Quite correctly, Lacaze notes that the question had never been raised whether, and to what degree, the 'effects' of the sensations on 'the action of the organs' are 'essential to that action', in what way they are 'determining causes of the activity of the animal economy'. If the head had only one 'relative action'—that is to say, if one considers only the influence it has on the rest of the body—then our existence would quickly become vegetative, and doubtless be of only short duration. Such a 'relative action' of the head assumes that the diaphragm comes into play, and becomes in turn a 'relative cause' of cerebral action; but then again that this action of the diaphragm demands an action of the external organ, which itself becomes in turn a relative cause of the actions of the diaphragm and the head.[19]

This highly speculative physiology is certainly less important for the detailed explanations it gives than for the idea it promotes of a reciprocity of functions. The relationship between the physical and the moral ceases to be that of two clearly differentiated phenomena like the soul and the body, and becomes two ways of seeing relationships that are in essence always circular. In short, they are two 'points of view'. It is here, in my opinion, that Lacaze prepares the way for Cabanis.

There can be no doubt that some of Cabanis's predecessors already used the terms *physique* and *moral* in the way he did. However, it does not follow that this intellectual current was the only one, or that its import was simply anti-dualist. For even if one reduces, as d'Holbach and Cabanis do, the moral to a 'point of view', this point of view still

---

[19] Lacaze, *Idée*, 380–1.

has a legitimacy. Otherwise, Cabanis would not have felt the need to entitle his book *Rapports du physique et du moral*; it would have been enough to explain the effects of the physical on the physical. If dualism now seems to have been eliminated from the realm of causes, or of origins, it has reappeared—perhaps necessarily—at the level of the functions.

The need to reassess the significance of the pair *physique/moral* in light of this simple consideration is greatly re-enforced by the fact that others writing at the same time employ the terms without giving either the moral, or its relationship with the physical, the same meaning as Lacaze, d'Holbach, La Mettrie, and Cabanis. My concern is not so much to point out exceptions to a dominant tendency towards 'materialism', as to show that hitherto one line of thought has been unduly emphasized, and the arguments advanced by these particular authors taken incorrectly for the general significance of the pair *physique/moral*.

The most instructive counter-example is undoubtedly that of J. J. Rousseau. His *Discours sur l'origine et les fondements de l'inégalité parmi les hommes* opens with those well-known observations which we must now reread in the light of our own investigation—to see what the difference is between the two pairs *physique/moral* and soul/body.

I conceive of two kinds of inequality in the human species, one of which I call natural or physical (*physique*), because it is established by nature, and consists of differences in age, health, bodily strength, qualities of mind or soul. The other, which may be called moral or political inequality, because it depends upon a sort of convention, and is established, or at least authorized, by the consent of men.[20]

No one will have missed seeing that here *physique* includes both bodily *and* mental qualities, while *moral* denotes the fact of being more or less rich, honoured, or powerful; the pair *physique/moral* is equivalent to the pair natural/political. Also, after describing man 'such as he issues from the hand of nature' and before he is cast into history, Rousseau interrupts himself and adds: 'So far I have only considered physical man: let us now try to observe him from the metaphysical and moral side.'[21]

Physical man is man in the state of nature, or again, what remains of this in social man. Accordingly, for example, one can 'distinguish the moral from the physical in the sentiment of love'.[22] Rousseau provides

[20] Jean Jacques Rousseau, *Discours sur l'origine de l'inégalité* (Amsterdam, 1755), in *Oeuvres complètes* (Paris, 1964), III, 131. Cf. also J. Starobinski, *J. J. Rousseau: La transparence et l'obstacle* (Paris, 1971); H. Gouhier, *Les Méditations métaphysiques de Jean Jacques Rousseau* (Paris, 1970); P. Burgelin, *La Philosophie de l'existence de J. J. Rousseau* (Paris, 1952); M. Rang, *Rousseaus Lehre vom Menschen* (Göttingen, 1959).
[21] Rousseau, *Discours*, 141.   [22] Ibid. 157.

every detail that could be desired in order to render the content of these two concepts precise. 'The physical is this general desire directed towards joining oneself to another.' This is what is *natural* in love. 'The moral is what orients this desire and fixes it exclusively on one object.' One would say, in the language of contemporary psychology, that the moral consists in the *object choice*; and that, consequently, it pertains to the part of love which is variable, impetuous, or 'invented'. Rousseau has a word for what he is talking about, 'imagination'. This must be noted for the light it sheds on the genesis of the terms *physique* and *moral*: it is clear from Rousseau's example that the term *moral* is being used to designate an aspect of man which, without being bodily, is at the same time not reducible to thought (*pensée*).

As surprising as it might at first sight seem, a comparison of the terminology of Rousseau and Cabanis reveals a certain degree of lexical continuity. No doubt, between Rousseau and Cabanis the term *physique* loses part of its signification: the 'qualities of the soul' leave the sphere of the physical, which is henceforth identified with the order of the body. However, like Rousseau, Cabanis continues to use the term *moral* to signify something which, although it has its origin and causes among the determinations of physical sensibility, is irreducible to thought (*pensée*) or volition. Thus the famous hypotheses of the tenth *Mémoire* of the *Rapports du physique et du moral* which advance the idea that there may be 'a sort of *true self*' in every nervous centre, and that, in any case, the *self* that resides in the brain (the 'common centre') 'shares the condition of all the other organs: among its affections and operations some are perceived by the individual, others are not'.[23] There is *moral*, then, that is not conscious: this is the great lesson of the tenth *Mémoire*, a lesson which clarifies retrospectively the history of the term itself, and which necessitates a revision of the interpretation generally given to it. It is not from any anti-metaphysical—that is, anti-dualist—intention that the pair *physique/moral* appears; nor is it introduced to replace the pair soul/body with terms that are more empirical and phenomenalist. One sees this clearly in the case of Cabanis, whose *Rapports du physique et du moral* is no less speculative, whatever might be said, than the *Passions de l'âme* of Descartes. The distinction *physique/moral* emerged because it was needed to conceptualize something different from what was understood by the Cartesian pair, body and soul. *Physique* served to designate something bodily which cannot be reduced to the merely mechanical, *moral* something mental which cannot be reduced to simple consciousness. It is not a

---

[23] Cabanis, *Rapports*, 538.

question, then, of suppressing the dualism of soul/body with the pair *physique/moral*, but of replacing it with another much less stable, much more problematical dualism.

This point is demonstrated, for example, by the case of Maine de Biran. Undeniably, this writer appears to show a commitment to an earlier conception, in fact to the one which the invention of the pair *physique/moral* was destined to replace: for he makes *moral* and *conscious* completely identical in restricting the field of the moral to that which is *compos et conscius sui*. Maine de Biran reinstates a definition of the moral which is anachronistic compared to that of Cabanis. On the other hand, Maine de Biran's definition of the word *physique* is so greatly expanded that, in the end, he is very close to agreeing with Cabanis in saying that, in most of the cases considered, the so-called influence of the physical on the moral reduces itself to the influence of the physical on the physical. As an example, let us take the case of a man driven by sexual appetite. Biran is returning to the example used earlier by Rousseau and G. L. Buffon, and, as it were, like them, asks, 'In what does the *physique* of love consist?' His answer is clear: it is 'the affection' felt by the man, and the 'inclinations' he is impelled to satisfy. That is, the 'affective sentiments', on the one hand, and the 'co-ordinated movements', on the other, are both in the realm of the physical and, considered thus far, no influence of the physical on the moral exists. Where, then, does the moral begin? With the 'judgements' and 'ideas of duty' through which the *self* suspends the action of the organic force which previously ruled alone.[24] Everything Maine de Biran has removed from the moral—determinations which are obscure and unconscious—he transfers to the physical. If his definition of the moral is as narrow as Descartes' definition of the soul, it is because his definition of the physical is so very wide. In his own way, Biran too gives evidence of the general change that took place after Descartes, leading to a complete redistribution of the functions and faculties of man. The *homo duplex* so dear to Boerhaave, Buffon, and Maine de Biran,[25] is, if one looks closely, physical and moral man—a man just as *double* as Descartes', but divided in a different way.

Among those who take up the formula *homo duplex* again in the nineteenth century and make use of it on their own account is J. E. D. Esquirol, who followed P. Pinel in the utilization of what the earliest

[24] Maine de Biran, *Notes psychologiques* (1811), in *Oeuvres*, XI-2, 113–14.
[25] Hermann Boerhaave, *Praelectiones de morbis nervorum* (Leiden, 1761), II, 497; Georges Louis Leclerc de Buffon, *Histoire naturelle de l'homme* (Paris, 1749), in *Oeuvres complètes* (Paris, 1828), XI, 399; Maine de Biran, *Considérations sur les principes d'une division des faits psychologiques et physiologiques* (1823), in *Oeuvres*, IX, 153–4.

alienists called the 'moral treatment' of mental diseases. Of course, this is not treatment by morality, an idea which Pinel rejected at the outset.[26] It is treatment *of* the moral *by* the moral, 'of some lesion or other in the intellectual and affective faculties'[27] which, while leaving the patient prey to his impulses, does not deprive him totally of his reason, thus making his recovery in principle possible. If in the patient there is a separation of two entities, one of which overwhelms the other, while the other witnesses its own confusion, this is certainly not a matter of soul versus body. Here the term *moral* has taken on a meaning that the term *soul* did not easily accommodate, and from which the expression 'moral treatment' acquires its justification. In the article 'Manie' in the *Dictionnaire des sciences médicales* Esquirol wrote: 'the person loses the faculty of directing his actions because he has lost the unity of the *self*; he has become the *homo duplex* of Saint Paul and of Buffon, driven to evil by one impulse, held back by another'.[28] Certainly neither Pinel nor Esquirol is imagining anything like a moral phenomenon unconnected with the physical, or madness without an organic basis or organic repercussions. Just as the *moral* cannot be reduced to pure thought, so it cannot be isolated from the physical. Once again, the pair *physique/moral* is being used not with the intent of ultimately forcing the surrender of one of its terms, but rather to designate a division at the core of the matter under consideration, a division different from the classic psyche/soma division. This new division's particular character is to lack stability, exactness, and clarity, as something from the soma moves over into the psyche, something of the psyche cleaves to the soma: but no one can say exactly what, or how the passage from the one to the other occurs.

Hence, the significance of the pair *physique* and *moral*, as distinct from body and soul, becomes clear. Contrary to what is so often asserted, a study of man based on the first pair is no less dualist than one based on the second pair. Modern anthropology—I mean here the field that establishes itself at the beginning of the nineteenth century—does not give up dualism, however differently it conceives it than did Descartes, the Cartesians, and the classical thinkers. In fact, it is this same new kind of dualism which reappears with Sigmund Freud, and through him plays such a large role in twentieth-century psychology, in the concepts of drive (*Trieb*) and its various manifestations, conversion, and somatic compliance. What we term 'psychosomatic', far from reflect-

---

[26] Philippe Pinel, *Traité médico-philosophique sur l'aliénation mentale ou la manie* (1st edn. Paris, 1801), (Geneva, 1980), p. xxii.   [27] Ibid. p. L.

[28] Quoted by Gladys Swain, *Dialogue avec l'insensé: Essais d'histoire de la psychiatrie* (Paris, 1994), 42. See also Marcel Gauchet and Gladys Swain, *La Pratique de l'esprit humain: L'institution asilaire et la révolution démocratique* (Paris, 1980).

ing a monist or holist view of the human being, instead reaffirms a physical/psychological dualism in the very moment that it attempts to elucidate its components' interactions: viewed in this light, it is nothing but a late product of the new dualism whose genesis in the eighteenth century I have attempted in this chapter to trace.

SELECT BIBLIOGRAPHY

PRIMARY SOURCES AND MODERN EDITIONS AND TRANSLATIONS

ACHILLINI, ALESSANDRO, *De elementis* (Venice, 1505).

ALEXANDER, ALEXANDER, *Philosophemata libera* (Aberdeen, 1669).

ARISTOTLE, *De anima*, ed. and trans. R. D. Hicks (Cambridge, 1907).

—— *The Works . . . translated into English*, ed. W. D. Ross (12 vols., Oxford, 1928–52).

AUGUSTINE, *The Literal Meaning of Genesis*, trans. J. H. Taylor (New York, 1982).

—— *The Trinity*, trans. Stephen McKenna (Washington, 1963).

BACON, FRANCIS, *The Advancement of Learning*, 1st edn. (London, 1605), ed. G. W. Kitchin (London, 1973).

BARTHEZ, PAUL JOSEPH, *Nouveaux eléments de la science de l'homme*, 2nd edn. (Paris, 1806).

BAXTER, R., *The Reasons of the Christian Religion . . .* (London, 1667).

BAYLE, PIERRE, *Dictionnaire historique et critique*, 1st edn. (Rotterdam, 1697), 4th edn. (Amsterdam, 1730).

—— *Recueil de quelques pièces curieuses concernant la philosophie de Monsieur Descartes* (Amsterdam, 1684).

—— *Oeuvres diverses* (The Hague, 1727–31).

BOERHAAVE, HERMANN, *Praelectiones academicae in proprias institutiones rei medicae*, ed. Albrecht von Haller, 2nd edn. (6 vols., Venice, 1743–5).

—— *Dr. Boerhaave's Academical Lectures on the Theory of Physic, being a Translation of his Institutes and Explanatory Comment* (5 vols., London, 1752–8).

BRIGHT, TIMOTHY, *A Treatise of Melancholie* (London, 1586).

BUFFON, GEORGES LOUIS LECLERC DE, *Histoire naturelle de l'homme* (Paris, 1749), in *Oeuvres complètes*, XI (Paris, 1828).

CABANIS, PIERRE JEAN GEORGES, *Rapports du physique et du moral de l'homme*, 1st edn. (Paris, 1802), ed. C. Lehec and J. Cazeneuve (Paris, 1954).

CAMPANELLA, TOMMASO, *Prodromus philosophiae instaurandae*, ed. T. Adami (Frankfurt, 1617).

—— *Universalis philosophiae, seu metaphysicarum rerum iuxta propria dogmata, partes tres . . .* (Paris, 1638).

CASTELLANI, P. N., *Opus de immortalitate animorum . . .* (Faenza, 1525).

CHAMPAIGNAC, JEAN DE, *Traicté de l'immortalité de l'âme* (Bordeaux, 1595).

CHARLETON, WALTER, *The Immortality of the Human Soul* (London, 1657).

—— *Natural History of the Passions* (London, 1674).

[Collegium Conimbricense] *Commentarii Collegii Conimbricensis Societatis Iesu, in tres libros De anima Aristotelis* (Coimbra, 1649).

CONTARINI, GASPAR, *De immortalitate animae . . .* (Paris, 1571).

CULLEN, WILLIAM, 'Lectures on the Institutes of Medicine by Dr Cullen, 1770–71', National Library of Scotland, Edinburgh, MS 3535.

—— 'The Institutes of Medicine by Dr Cullen Oct. 28, 1772' (5 vols.), National Library of Medicine, Bethesda, Md., MS B4.

—— 'Lectures on Physiology', Royal College of Physicians of Edinburgh, MS Cullen 16(I).

—— *Institutions of Medicine: Part I, Physiology*, 3rd edn. (Edinburgh, 1785).

DESCARTES, RENÉ, *Oeuvres de Descartes*, ed. Charles Adam and Paul Tannery (11 vols., Paris, 1964–74).

—— *Oeuvres philosophiques 1638–42*, ed. F. Alquié (Paris, 1967).

—— *The Philosophical Writings of Descartes*, trans. John Cottingham, Robert Stoothoff, and Dugald Murdoch (2 vols., Cambridge, 1985–6).

—— *The Philosophical Writings of Descartes: The Correspondence*, trans. John Cottingham, Robert Stoothoff, Dugald Murdoch, and Anthony Kenny (Cambridge, 1991).

—— *Discourse on Method, Optics, Geometry, and Meteorology*, trans. Paul J. Olscamp (Indianapolis, 1965).

—— *Passions of the Soul*, trans. Stephan Voss (Indianapolis, 1989).

—— *Philosophical Letters*, trans. A. Kenny (Minneapolis, 1970).

—— *Principles of Philosophy*, trans. V. R. Miller and R. P. Miller (Dordrecht, 1983).

—— *Treatise of Man*, trans. Thomas Steele Hall (Cambridge, Mass., 1972).

DIDEROT, D., and D'ALEMBERT, J., *Encyclopédie, ou Dictionnaire raisonné des sciences, des arts et des métiers* (Paris, 1751–65).

DIGBY, KENELM, *Demonstratio immortalitatis animae rationalis . . .* (Paris, 1651).

—— *Two Treatises: In the One of which the Nature of Bodies; in the Other the Nature of Mans Soule is Looked into in the way of Discovery of the Immortality of Reasonable Soules* (London, 1665).

ELICI, FREDIANO, *Arca novella di sanità: Trattato fisico morale con alcune regole per conservarsi sano e vivere virtuosamente* (Lucca, 1656).

EPICURUS, *The Extant Remains*, ed. and trans. Cyril Bailey (Oxford, 1926).

——. See Usener.

EUSTACHIUS A SANCTO PAULO, *Summa philosophiae quadripartita: de rebus dialecticis, moralibus, physicis, et metaphysicis* (Paris, 1609).

FLANDINUS, A., *De animorum immortalitate . . . liber contra assertorem mortalitatis* (Mantua, 1519).

GALEN, *Claudii Galeni opera omnia*, ed. C. G. Kühn (20 vols., Leipzig, 1821–33).

—— *Galenus, Scripta minora*, ed. J. Marquardt, I. von Müller, and G. Helmreich (3 vols., Leipzig, 1884–93).

GASSENDI P., *Syntagma philosophicum*, in *Opera omnia*, i–ii (Lyon, 1658).

GAUB, JEROME, *De regimine mentis* (Leiden, 1747).

——. See Rather.

GLANVILL, J., *Essays on Several Important Subjects in Philosophy and Religion* (London, 1676).

HALLER, ALBRECHT VON, *De partibus corporis humani sensibilibus et irritabilibus* (Göttingen, 1753).

——*First Lines of Physiology*, ed. William Cullen (Edinburgh, 1786).

HEROPHILUS. See Staden.

HIEROCLES, *Elementa ethica*, ed. Hans von Arnim, Berliner Klassiker Texte, 4 (Berlin, 1906).

HIERONYMUS LUCENSIS, *Apologia pro animae immortalitate in Petrum Pomponatium Mantuanum philosophicum . . .* (Bologna, 1518).

HIPPOCRATES, *Oeuvres complètes d'Hippocrate*, ed. É. Littré (10 vols., Paris, 1839–61).

——*On Regimen*, in *Hippocrates*, IV, Loeb Classical Library, trans. W. H. S. Jones (London, 1931).

——*On the Sacred Disease*, in *Hippocrates*, II, Loeb Classical Library, trans. W. H. S. Jones (London, 1923).

HOLBACH, PAUL HENRI DIETRICH D', *Système de la nature ou des lois du monde physique et du monde moral* (London, 1770).

HUME, DAVID, *A Treatise of Human Nature*, 1st edn. (London, 1739–40), ed. L. A. Selby-Bigge (Oxford, 1888).

JAVELLI, CRISOSTOMO, *Solutiones rationum animi mortalitatem probantium quae in defensorio contra Niphum . . . a P. Pomponatio formantur* (n.p., 1523).

LACAZE, LOUIS DE, *Specimen novi medicinae conspectus* (Paris, 1749).

——*Idée de l'homme physique et moral, pour servir d'introduction à un traité de médecine* (Paris, 1755).

LAGALLA, J. C., *De immortalitate animorum* (Rome, 1622).

LAMBERTUS DE MONTE, *Copulata super libros De anima Aristotelis* (Cologne, 1485, 1492).

——*Expositio . . . circa tres libros De anima Aristotelis* (Cologne, 1496).

LA METTRIE, JULIEN OFFRAY DE, *L'Homme-machine*, 1st edn. (Leiden, 1748), in *Oeuvres philosophiques* (Hildesheim, 1970).

——. See Vartanian.

LAMY, GUILLAUME, *De principiis rerum libri tres* (Paris, 1669).

LEIBNIZ, G. W., *Opera omnia*, ed. L. Dutens (Geneva, 1768).

——*Die philosophischen Schriften*, ed. C. I. Gerhardt (Hildesheim, 1965).

——*Die Leibniz-Handschriften*, ed. E. Bodemann (Hildesheim, 1966).

——*Opuscules et fragments inédits*, ed. L. Couturat (Hildesheim, 1988).

——*Philosophical Essays*, ed. and trans. R. Ariew and D. Garber (Indianapolis, 1989).

——*Philosophical Letters and Papers*, ed. and trans. Leroy F. Loemker, 2nd edn. (Dordrecht, 1976).

LICETI, FORTUNIUS, *De animarum rationalium immortalitate . . .* (Padua, 1629).

——*De ortu animae humanae* (Genoa, 1602).

——*De rationalis animae varia propensione ad corpus libri duo* (Padua, 1634).

LOCKE, JOHN, *An Essay Concerning Human Understanding*, 1st edn. (London, 1690), ed. P. H. Nidditch (Oxford, 1975).

LUTHER, MARTIN, *Studienausgabe*, ed. H.-U. Delius (Berlin, 1992).

MAINE DE BIRAN, MARIE FRANÇOIS PIERRE, *Nouvelles Considérations sur les rapports du physique et du moral de l'homme* (Paris, 1834), in *Oeuvres*, ed. B. Baertschi (Paris, 1990).

——*Rapport du physique et du moral de l'homme* (Paris, 1811).

MALEBRANCHE, NICOLAS, *Méditations chrétiennes et métaphysiques*, 1st edn. (Cologne, 1683), in *Oeuvres complètes*, ed. A. Robinet (Paris, 1959), x.

MARTINEZ, P., *In tres libros Aristotelis De anima . . . animae nostrae immortalitas asseritur et probatur* (Siguenza, 1575).

MELANCHTHON, PHILIPP, *Commentarius de anima* (Wittenberg, 1548).

——*Opera quae supersunt omnia*, ed. C. G. Bretschneider (28 vols., Halle 1834–60).

MERSENNE, M., *L'Impiété des déistes, athées . . .* (Paris, 1624).

MORE, H., *The Immortality of the Soul* (London, 1662).

NANCEL, N., *De immortalitate animae, velitatio adversus Galenum* (Paris, 1587).

NIFO, AGOSTINO, *De immortalitate animae libellus . . .* (Venice, 1518).

OCKHAM, WILLIAM OF, *Quodlibetal Questions*, trans. A. J. Freddoso and F. E. Kelley (New Haven, 1991).

ODONI, R., *Disputatio de animo . . . utrum Aristoteli mortalis sit, an immortalis* (Paris, 1558).

OREGIUS, A., *Aristotelis vera de rationalis animae immortalitate sententia . . .* (Rome, 1632).

PALEARIO, A., *De animorum immortalitate* (Lyons, 1536).

PERREAU, J. A., *Considérations physiques et morales sur la nature de l'homme* (Paris, 1796).

PICCOLOMINI, F., *De rerum definitionibus* (Venice, 1600).

——*Librorum ad scientiam de natura attinentium* (Frankfurt, 1597).

PLATO, *The Collected Dialogues of Plato*, ed. E. Hamilton and H. Cairns (New York, 1963).

POMPONAZZI, PIETRO, *Tractatus de immortalitate animae* (Bologna, 1516).

——'On Immortality', ed. and trans. William H. Hay, in E. Cassirer (ed.), *The Renaissance Philosophy of Man* (Chicago, 1956).

PONTANUS, H., *De immortalitate animae ex sententia Aristotelis* (Rome, 1597).

RICHEOME, L., *L'Immortalité de l'âme* (Paris, 1621).

RIOLAN, J., *De immortalitate* (c.1580; published by his son in the collected works (Paris, 1610)).

ROCCUS, A., *Animae rationalis immortalitas . . .* (Frankfurt, 1644).

ROUSSEAU, JEAN JACQUES, *Discours sur l'origine de l'inégalité* (Amsterdam, 1755), in *Oeuvres complètes*, III (Paris, 1964).

ROUSSEL, P., *Système physique et moral de la femme* (Paris, 1775).

RUDIUS, E., *Liber de anima, in quo . . . rationalis animae immortalitas efficacissimis rationibus probatur* (Padua, 1611).

SILHON, JEAN DE, *De l'immortalité de l'âme* (Paris, 1634).

SPINA, BARTOLOMEO, *Tutela veritatis de immortalitate animae . . .* (Venice, 1519).

STAHL, GEORG ERNST, *Oeuvres médico-philosophiques et pratiques*, trans. T. Blondin (Paris, 1859–64).

——*Negotium otiosum, seu Σκιαμαχία, adversus positiones aliquas fundamentales Theoriae medicae verae a viro quodam celeberrimo intentata* (Halle, 1720).

——*Theoria medica vera, physiologiam et pathologiam, tanquam doctrinae medicae partes vere contemplativas, e naturae et artis veris fundamentis . . . sistens*, 2nd edn. (Halle, 1737).

STILLINGFLEET, EDWARD, *Origines sacrae*, 3rd edn. (London, 1666).

TERTULLIAN, *De anima*, ed. J. H. Waszink (Amsterdam, 1947).

TROMBETTA, ANTONIO, *Tractatus singularis contra Averroystas de humanarum animarum plurificatione ad catholice fidei obsequium Patavii editus* (Padua, 1498).

VIO, THOMAS DE, *Commentaria de anima* (Florence, 1509).

WHYTT, ROBERT, *An essay on the Vital and Other Involuntary Motions of Animals* (Edinburgh, 1751).

WILLIS, THOMAS, *Two Discourses Concerning the Soul of Brutes, which is that of the Vital and Sensitive of Man*, trans. S. Pordage (London, 1683).

WYSS, CASPAR, *Cursus philosophici* (Geneva, 1669).

ZABARELLA, IACOPO, *Commentarii... in tres Aristotelis libros De anima...* (Frankfurt, 1606).

—— *De rebus naturalibus libri XXX...* (Venice and Cologne, 1590).

SECONDARY SOURCES

ADAMS, M. M., *William Ockham* (Notre Dame, Ind., 1987).

ANNAS, JULIA, *Hellenistic Philosophy of Mind* (Berkeley, 1992).

AUCANTE, VINCENT, 'L'horizon métaphysique de la médecine de Descartes' (Ph.D. thesis, Paris-IV, 1998).

BAERTSCHI, BERNARD, *Les Rapports de l'âme et du corps: Descartes, Diderot et Maine de Biran* (Paris, 1992).

BARNES, J., SCHOFIELD, M., and SORABJI, R. (eds.), *Articles on Aristotle*, iv: *Psychology and Aesthetics* (London, 1979).

BERNARD, W., *Rezeptivität und Spontaneität der Wahrnehmung bei Aristoteles* (Baden-Baden, 1988).

BLOCH, O. R., *La Philosophie de Gassendi: Nominalisme, matérialisme et métaphysique* (The Hague, 1971).

BLOCK, I., 'Aristotle on the Common Sense: a Reply to Kahn and Others', *Ancient Philosophy*, 8 (1988), 235–50.

—— 'The Order of Aristotle's Psychological Writings', *American Journal of Philology*, 82 (1961), 50–77.

BRYCKMAN, G., 'Berkeley: Sa lecture de Malebranche à travers Le Dictionnaire de Bayle', *Revue internationale de philosophie* 29 (1975), 496–514.

BULTMANN, RUDOLF, *Theologie des Neuen Testaments*, 9th edn., ed. O. Merk (Tübingen, 1984).

BURKERT, WALTER, *Weisheit und Wissenschaft* (Nuremberg, 1962); trans. Edwin L. Minar jr., as *Lore and Science in Ancient Pythagoreanism* (Cambridge, Mass., 1972).

BURNET, JOHN, 'The Socratic Doctrine of the Soul', *Proceedings of the British Academy*, 7 (1916), 235–59.

BURNYEAT, M., 'Is an Aristotelian Philosophy of Mind still Credible? A Draft', in Nussbaum and Oksenberg Rorty, 15–26.

CAMBIANO, GIUSEPPE, 'Une intérpretation "matérialiste" des rêves, du Régime IV', in M. D. Grmek (ed.), *Hippocratica* (Paris, 1980), 87–96.

CLAUS, DAVID B., *Toward the Soul* (New Haven, 1981).

COLONNA D'ISTRIA, F., 'Cabanis et les origines de la vie psychologique', *Revue de métaphysique et de morale*, 19 (1911), 177–98.

——'L'influence du moral sur le physique d'après Cabanis et Maine de Biran', *Revue de métaphysique et de morale*, 21 (1913), 451–561.

COTTINGHAM, JOHN, 'Cartesian Dualism', in *idem* (ed.), *The Cambridge Companion to Descartes* (Cambridge, 1992), 236–57.

DAUTZENBERG, GERHARD, 'Seele . . . im biblischen Denken sowie das Verhältnis von Unsterblichkeit und Auferstehung', in K. Kremer (ed.), *Seele* (Leiden, 1984), 186–203.

DI BENEDETTO, VINCENZO, *Il medico e la malattia* (Turin, 1986).

DODDS, E. R., *The Greeks and the Irrational* (Berkeley, 1951).

DRABKIN, I. E., 'Remarks on Ancient Psychopathology', *Isis*, 46 (1955), 223–34.

DREYFUS-LE FOYER, H., 'Les conceptions médicales de Descartes', *Revue métaphysique et morale*, 44 (1937), 237–86; repr. in Geneviève Rodis-Lewis (ed.), *La Science chez Descartes* (New York, 1987), 281–330.

DUCHESNEAU, F., *La Physiologie des Lumières: Empirisme, modèles et théories* (The Hague, 1982).

ECCLES, J., and POPPER, K., *The Self and the Brain* (Berlin, 1977).

EDWARDS, WILLIAM F., 'The Logic of Iacopo Zabarella (1533–1589)' (Columbia Ph.D. thesis, 1960).

FORTENBAUGH, W. W., *Aristotle on Emotion* (London, 1975).

——'Recent Scholarship on the Psychology of Aristotle', *Classical World*, 60 (1967), 316–27.

FRENCH, R. K., *Robert Whytt, the Soul and Medicine* (London, 1969).

FREUDENTHAL, G., *Aristotle's Theory of Material Substance: Heat and Pneuma, Form and Soul* (Oxford, 1995).

GABBEY, ALAN, 'Between *Ars* and *Philosophia Naturalis*', in J. V. Field and Frank A. J. L. James (eds.), *Renaissance and Revolution* (Cambridge, 1993), 133–46.

——'Descartes's Physics and Descartes's Mechanics: Chicken and Egg?', in Stephen Voss (ed.), *Essays on the Philosophy and Science of René Descartes* (New York, 1993), 311–23.

GARCIA BALLESTER, LUIS, 'La "Psique" en el somaticismo medico de la antiguedad: la actitud de Galeno', *Episteme*, 3 (1969), 195–209.

GAUCHET, MARCEL, and SWAIN, GLADYS, *La Pratique de l'esprit humain: L'institution asilaire et la révolution démocratique* (Paris, 1980).

GRENSEMANN, H., *Die hippokratische Schrift 'Über die heilige Krankheit'* (Berlin, 1968).

GRMEK, M. D., 'Réflexions sur des interprétations mécanistes de la vie dans la physiologie du xviiᵉ siècle', *Episteme*, 1 (1967), 18–30.

GUEROULT, MARTIAL, *Descartes selon l'ordre des raisons* (2 vols., Paris, 1953), trans. Roger Ariew as *Descartes' Philosophy Interpreted According to the Order of Reasons* (2 vols., Minneapolis, 1985).

GUTBROD, WALTER, *Die Paulinische Anthropologie* (Stuttgart, 1934).

GUTHRIE, W. K. C., *The Greeks and their Gods* (Boston, 1955).

HANKINSON, R. J., 'Galen's Anatomy of the Soul', *Phronesis*, 36 (1991), 197–233.

HARDIE, W. F. R., 'Aristotle's Treatment of the Relation between the Soul and the Body', *Philosophical Quarterly*, 14 (1964), 53–72.

HARRIS, C. R. S., *The Heart and the Vascular System in Ancient Greek Medicine from Alcmeon to Galen* (Oxford, 1973).

HARTMAN, E., *Substance, Body and Soul: Aristotelian Investigations* (Princeton, 1977).

HATFIELD, GARY, 'Remaking the Science of Mind', in C. Fox, R. Porter, and R. Wokler (eds.), *Inventing Human Science: Eighteenth-Century Domains* (Berkeley, 1995), 184–231.

HECKEL, THEO K., *Der Innere Mensch* (Tübingen, 1993).

HEYD, MICHAEL, 'A Disguised Atheist or a Sincere Christian? The Enigma of Pierre Bayle', *Bibliothèque d'humanisme et de renaissance*, 39 (1977).

HOFFMANN, P., 'La controverse entre Leibniz et Stahl sur la nature de l'âme', *Studies on Voltaire and the Eighteenth Century*, 199 (1981), 237–49.

——'L'âme et les passions dans la philosophie médicale de Georg-Ernst Stahl', *Dix-huitième siècle*, 23 (1991), 31–43.

HÜFFMEIER, F., 'Phronesis in den Schriften des Corpus Hippocraticum', *Hermes*, 89 (1961), 51–84.

JACOB, EDMOND, ' "Psyche" B: Die Anthropologie des Alten Testaments', in *Theologisches Wörterbuch zum Neuen Testament* (Stuttgart, 1973), ix. 614–29.

JAHN, THOMAS, *Zum Wortfeld 'Seele-Geist' in der Sprache Homers* (Munich, 1987).

JOHANSEN, T. K., *Aristotle on the Sense-Organs* (Cambridge, 1997).

JOLY, ROBERT, *Recherches sur le traité pseudo-hippocratique Du Régime* (Paris, 1960).

JOSSUA, JEAN PIERRE, *Pierre Bayle, ou l'obsession du mal* (Paris, 1977).

JOUANNA, J., 'La théorie de l'intelligence et de l'âme dans le traité hippocratique du Régime; ses rapports avec Empédocle et le Timée de Plato', *Revue des études grecques*, 79 (1966), pp. xv–xviii.

——'L'interprétation des rêves et la théorie micro-macrocosmique dans le traité Hippocratique du Régime: sémiotique et mimesis', in K. D. Fischer, D. Nickel, and P. Potter (eds.), *Text and Tradition: Studies on Ancient Medicine and its Transmission* (Leiden, 1998), 161–74.

KAHN, C., 'Sensation and Consciousness in Aristotle's Psychology', repr. in Barnes, Schofield, and Sorabji, 1–31.

KÄSEMANN, ERNST, *Paulinische Perspektiven* (Tübingen, 1969).

KERFERD, G. B., 'Epicurus' Doctrine of the Soul', *Phronesis*, 16 (1971), 80–96.

KREMER, KLAUS, *Seele: Ihre Wirklichkeit, ihr Verhältnis zum Leib und zur menschlichen Person* (Leiden, 1984).

KRISTELLER, P. O., 'The Immortality of the Soul', in *Renaissance Concepts of Man and Other Essays* (New York, 1972), 22–42.

——'Paduan Averroism and Alexandrism in the Light of Recent Studies', in *Renaissance Thought II: Papers on Humanism and the Arts* (New York, 1965), 111–18.

LAPORTE, JEAN, *Le Rationalisme de Descartes*, 2nd edn. (Paris, 1950).

LEFÈVRE, C., *Sur l'évolution d'Aristote en psychologie* (Louvain, 1972).

——'Sur le statut de l'âme dans le De Anima et les Parva Naturalia', in Lloyd and Owen, 21–67.

LEWIS, G., *Le Problème de l'inconscient et le Cartésianisme* (Paris, 1950).

LINDEBOOM, G. A., *Descartes and Medicine* (Amsterdam, 1978).

LINDEMANN, ANDREAS, 'Die Kirche als Leib', *Zeitschrift für Theologie und Kirche*, 92 (1995), 140–65.

LLOYD, G. E. R., *Science, Folklore and Ideology* (Cambridge, 1983).

——, and Owen, G. E. L. (eds.), *Aristotle on Mind and the Senses* (Cambridge, 1978).

LONG, A. A., 'Soul and Body in Stoicism', *Phronesis*, 27 (1982), 34–57.

LONG, A. A., and Sedley, D. N., *The Hellenistic Philosophers* (2 vols., Cambridge, 1987).

MACKENZIE, ANN W., 'A Word about Descartes' Mechanistic Conception of Life', *Journal of the History of Biology*, 8 (1975), 1–13.

MANULI, PAOLA, and VEGETTI, MARIO, *Cuore, sangue e cervello* (Milan, 1977).

——(eds.), *Le opere psicologiche di Galeno* (Naples, 1988).

MATSEN, HERBERT, *Alessandro Achillini (1463–1512) and his Doctrine of 'Universals' and 'Transcendentals'* (Lewisburg, Pa., 1974).

MATTHEWS, GARETH, 'Descartes and the Problem of Other Minds', in Amelie O. Rorty (ed.), *Essays on Descartes' Meditations*, (Berkeley, 1986), 141–51.

——*Thought's Ego in Augustine and Descartes* (Ithaca, NY, 1992).

MICHAEL, E., and MICHAEL, F., 'Two Early Modern Concepts of Mind: Reflecting Substance vs. Thinking Substance', *Journal of the History of Philosophy*, 27 (1989), 29–47.

MIJUSKOVIC, BEN, *The Achilles of Rationalist Arguments* (The Hague, 1974).

MILLER, H. W., 'A Medical Theory of Cognition', *Transactions of the American Philological Association*, 79 (1948), 168–83.

MODRAK, D. K. W., *Aristotle: The Power of Perception* (Chicago, 1987).

MORAVIA, SERGIO, *Il pensiero degli Idéologues: Scienza e filosofia in Francia (1780–1815)* (Florence, 1974).

MÜRI, WALTER, 'Bemerkungen zur hippokratischen Psychologie', in *Festschrift Edouard Tièche* (Bern, 1947), 71–85.

NUSSBAUM, M. C., and OKSENBERG RORTY, A. (eds.), *Essays on Aristotle's De Anima* (Oxford, 1992).

NUYENS, F., *L'Évolution de la psychologie d'Aristote* (Louvain, 1948).

ONIANS, R. B., *The Origins of European Thought about the Body, the Mind, the Soul, the World, Time, and Fate*, 2nd edn. (Cambridge, 1954).

OSER-GROTE, C., *Aristoteles und das Corpus Hippocraticum* (forthcoming).

OSLER, M. J., *Divine Will and the Mechanical Philosophy: Gassendi and Descartes on Contingency and Necessity in the Created World* (Cambridge, 1994).

PIGEAUD, JACKIE, *Folie et cures de la folie chez les médecins de l'antiquité Gréco-Romaine* (Paris, 1987).

——*La Maladie de l'âme* (Paris, 1981).

POPPI, A., 'L'antiverroismo della scolastica padovana alla fine del secolo XV', *Studia patavina*, 11 (1964), 102–24.

——*La dottrina della scienza in Giacomo Zabarella* (Padua, 1972).

——*Introduzione all' aristotelismo padovano* (Padua, 1970).

——'Lo scotista patavino Antonio Trombetta (1436–1517)', *Il Santo*, 2 (1962), 349–67.

PREUSS, HORST, *Theologie des Alten Testaments* (Stuttgart, 1992).

RANG, M., *Rousseaus Lehre vom Menschen* (Göttingen, 1959).

RATHER, L. J., *Mind and Body in Eighteenth-Century Medicine: A Study Based on Jerome Gaub's De regimine mentis* (Berkeley, 1965).

——, and FRERICHS, J. B., 'The Leibniz–Stahl Controversy—I. Leibniz's Opening Objections to the *Theoria medica vera*', *Clio Medica*, 3 (1968), 21–40.

———— 'The Leibniz–Stahl Controversy—II. Stahl's Survey of the Principal Points of Doubt', *Clio Medica*, 5 (1970), 53–67.

RENAN, E., *Averroës et l'averroisme* (Paris, 1852).

REY, ROSELYNE, *Naissance et développement du vitalisme en France, de la deuxième moitié du XVIIIe siècle à la fin du Premier Empire* (Oxford, 1999).

ROBINSON, T. M., *Plato's Psychology*, 2nd edn. (Toronto, 1995).

RODIS-LEWIS, GENEVIÈVE, 'Descartes' Life and the Development of his Philosophy', in John Cottingham (ed.), *The Cambridge Companion to Descartes* (Cambridge, 1992), 21–57.

—— 'Limitations of the Mechanical Model in the Cartesian Conception of the Organism', in Michael Hooker (ed.), *Descartes* (Baltimore, 1978), 152–70.

ROENSCH, FREDERICK J., *Early Thomistic School* (Dubuque, Ia., 1964).

ROGER, JACQUES, *Les Sciences de la vie dans la pensée française du XVIIIe siècle*, 1st edn. 1963, 2nd edn. (Paris, 1971).

ROHDE, E., *Psyche: Seelencult und Unsterblichkeitsglaube der Griechen*, 7th and 8th edn. (2 vols., Tübingen, 1921); trans. W. B. Hillis as *Psyche: The Cult of Souls and Belief in Immortality among the Greeks* (London, 1925).

ROLOFF, JÜRGEN, *Die Kirche im Neuen Testament* (Göttingen, 1993).

RÜSCHE, F., *Blut, Leben, Seele* (Paderborn, 1930).

SCHOFIELD, MALCOLM, 'The Syllogisms of Zeno of Citium', *Phronesis*, 28 (1983), 31–58.

SCHWEIZER, EDUARD, 'Soma', in *Theologisches Wörterbuch zum Neuen Testament* (Stuttgart, 1964), vii. 1024–91.

SELLIN, GERHARD, *Der Streit um die Auferstehung der Toten* (Göttingen, 1986).

SHINER, R. A., 'Soul in *Rep.* X, 611', *Apeiron*, 6 (1972), 23–30.

SIMON, B., *Mind and Madness in Ancient Greece: The Classical Roots of Modern Psychiatry* (Ithaca, NY, 1978).

SINGER, P. N., 'Some Hippocratic Mind–Body Problems', in J. A. López Férez (ed.), *Tratados Hipocráticos* (Madrid, 1992), 131–43.

SISKO, J., 'Material Alteration and Cognitive Activity in Aristotle's De Anima', *Phronesis*, 41 (1996), 138–57.

SMITH, NORMAN KEMP, *The Philosophy of David Hume* (London, 1966).

SOLER, JORGE L., 'The Psychology of Iacopo Zabarella (1533–1589)' (Ph.D. thesis, Buffalo, 1971).

SOLMSEN, FRIEDRICH, 'Greek Philosophy and the Discovery of the Nerves', *Museum Helveticum*, 18 (1961); repr. in *idem*, *Kleine Schriften* (3 vols., Hildesheim, 1968–82), i. 536–82.

SORABJI, R., 'Intentionality and Physiological Processes: Aristotle's Theory of Sense-Perception', in Nussbaum and Oksenberg Rorty, 195–226.

—— *Matter, Space, and Motion* (Ithaca, NY, 1988).

—— *Necessity, Cause and Blame* (London, 1980).

STADEN, H. VON, 'Affinities and Elisions: Helen and Hellenocentrism', *Isis*, 83 (1992), 578–95.

—— 'Cardiovascular Puzzles in Erasistratus and Herophilus', in *XXXI Congresso Internazionale di Storia della Medicina* (Bologna, 1988), 681–7.

STADEN, H. VON, 'Experiment and Experience in Hellenistic Medicine', *Bulletin of the Institute of Classical Studies*, 22 (1975), 178–99.

—— *Herophilus: The Art of Medicine in Early Alexandria* (Cambridge, 1989).

—— 'Teleology and Mechanism: Aristotelian Biology and Early Hellenistic Medicine', in W. Kullmann and S. Föllinger (eds.), *Aristotelische Biologie: Intentionen, Methoden, Ergebnisse* (Stuttgart, 1997), 183–208.

STAUM, M. S., *Cabanis: Enlightenment and Medical Philosophy in the French Revolution* (Princeton, 1980).

SULLIVAN, SHIRLEY DARCUS, *Psychological and Ethical Ideas: What Early Greeks Say* (Leiden, 1995).

TEMKIN, OWSEI, 'Albrecht von Haller, "A Dissertation on the Sensible and Irritable Parts of Animals" ', *Bulletin of the History of Medicine*, 4 (1936), 651–99.

—— 'On Galen's Pneumatology', *Gesnerus*, 8 (1951), 180–9.

THOMSON, ANN, *Materialism and Society in the Mid-Eighteenth Century: La Mettrie's Discours préliminaire* (Geneva, 1981).

TIELEMAN, TEUN, *Galen and Chrysippus on the Soul: Argument and Refutation in the De Placitis Books II–III* (Leiden, 1996).

TODD, ROBERT B., *Alexander of Aphrodisias on Stoic Physics* (Leiden, 1976).

TRACY, T. J., 'Heart and Soul in Aristotle', in J. Anton and A. Preus (eds.), *Essays in Ancient Greek Philosophy*, ii (Albany, NY, 1983), 321–39.

—— *Physiological Theory and the Doctrine of the Mean in Plato and Aristotle* (The Hague and Paris, 1969).

TREVISANI, FRANCESCO, 'Descartes et la médecine', Bulletin cartésien, 9, 1–22, in *Archives de philosophie*, 44 (1981).

USENER, HERMANN, *Epicurea* (Leipzig, 1887).

VAN DER EIJK, P. J., *Aristoteles: De insomniis, De divinatione per somnum* (Berlin, 1994).

—— 'Aristotle on "Distinguished Physicians" and the Medical Significance of Dreams', in P. J. van der Eijk, H. F. J. Horstmanshoff, and P. H. Schrijvers (eds.), *Ancient Medicine in its Socio-cultural Context* (Amsterdam and Atlanta, 1995), ii, 447–59.

—— 'Aristoteles über die Melancholie', *Mnemosyne*, 43 (1990), 33–72.

—— 'Hart en hersenen, bloed en pneuma: Hippocrates, Aristoteles en Diocles over de lokalisering van cognitieve functies', *Gewina*, 18 (1995), 214–29.

—— 'The Matter of Mind: Aristotle on the Biology of "Psychic" Processes and the Bodily Aspects of Thinking', in W. Kullmann and S. Föllinger (eds.), *Aristotelische Biologie: Intentionen, Methoden, Ergebnisse* (Stuttgart, 1997), 231–58.

VAN STEENBERGHEN, F., *Maitre Siger de Brabant* (Louvain, 1977).

—— *Thomas Aquinas and Radical Aristotelianism* (Washington, 1980).

VARTANIAN, ARAM, *La Mettrie's L'Homme-machine: A Study in the Origins of an Idea* (Princeton, 1960).

VEGETTI, MARIO, 'Anima e corpo', in *idem* (ed.), Il sapere degli antichi (Turin, 1985), 201–28.

——'I nervi dell' anima', in J. Kollesch and D. Nickel (eds.), *Galen und das hellenistische Erbe* (Stuttgart, 1993), 63–77.

VOLLENWEIDER, SAMUEL, 'Der Geist Gottes als Selbst der Glaubenden', *Zeitschrift für Theologie und Kirche*, 93 (1996), 163–92.

VOSS, STEPHEN, 'Descartes: The End of Anthropology', in John Cottingham (ed.), *Reason, Will, and Sensation* (Oxford, 1994), 273–306.

——'Le grand Arnauld', in Jean Marie Beyssade and Jean Luc Marion (eds.), *Descartes—objecter et répondre* (Paris, 1994), 385–401.

——'A Spectator at the Theater of the World', in R. J. Gennaro and C. Huenemann (eds.), *New Essays on the Rationalists* (Oxford, 1999), 265–84.

WATSON, G., '*Phantasia* in Aristotle's De anima 3.3', *Classical Quarterly*, 32 (1982), 100–13.

WEBB, P., 'Bodily Structure and Psychic Faculties in Aristotle's Theory of Perception', *Hermes*, 110 (1982), 25–50.

WEDIN, M., *Mind and Imagination in Aristotle* (London, 1988).

WEISHEIPL, JAMES A., *The Development of Physical Theory in the Middle Ages* (Ann Arbor, 1959).

WELSCH, W., *Aisthesis: Grundzüge und Perspektiven der Aristotelischen Sinneslehre* (Stuttgart, 1987).

WHELAN, RUTH, *The Anatomy of Superstition: A Study of the Historical Theory and Practice of Pierre Bayle* (Oxford, 1989).

WIESNER, J., 'The Unity of De somno and the Physiological Explanation of Sleep', in Lloyd and Owen, 241–80.

WIJSENBEEK-WIJLER, H., *Aristotle's Concept of Soul, Sleep, and Dreams* (Amsterdam, 1976).

WOLFF, HANS, *Anthropologie des Alten Testaments*, 6th edn. (Munich, 1994).

WRIGHT, JOHN P., 'Metaphysics and Physiology: Mind, Body, and the Animal Economy in Eighteenth-Century Scotland', in M. A. Stewart (ed.), *Studies in the Philosophy of the Scottish Enlightenment* (Oxford, 1990), 251–301.

ZAVALLONI, ROBERTO, *Richard de Mediavilla et la controverse sur la pluralité des formes* (Louvain, 1951).

INDEX